TERRORISM FINANCING
AND STATE RESPONSES

EDITED BY JEANNE K. GIRALDO
AND HAROLD A. TRINKUNAS

Terrorism Financing
and State Responses

A Comparative Perspective

STANFORD UNIVERSITY PRESS

STANFORD, CALIFORNIA 2007

Stanford University Press
Stanford, California

Printed in the United States of America on acid-free,
archival-quality paper

Library of Congress Cataloging-in-Publication Data

Terrorism financing and state responses :
a comparative perspective / edited by Jeanne K.
Giraldo and Harold A. Trinkunas.
    p. cm.
   Includes bibliographical references and index.
   ISBN 978-0-8047-5565-8 (cloth : alk. paper) —
   ISBN 978-0-8047-5566-5 (pbk. : alk. paper)
   1. Terrorism — Finance. 2. Terrorism —
Finance — Prevention — Case studies.
3. Terrorism — Prevention — Cross-cultural
studies. I. Giraldo, Jeanne K. II. Trinkunas,
Harold A.
HV6431.T4654   2007
363.325'17 — dc22   2006035059

Typeset by BookMatters in 10/14 Janson.

CONTENTS

To our families.

ACKNOWLEDGMENTS

This volume is the product of a project that came to fruition with the conference Terrorism Financing and State Responses in Comparative Perspective, held in November 2004 at the Naval Postgraduate School in Monterey, California, with support from the school's Center for Homeland Defense and Security. We thank all of our contributing authors for their hard work and their patience with our questions and requests for clarification. We would also like to thank the conference discussants who helped the authors reformulate their arguments: David Mares, Feroz Khan, Maria Rasmussen, and Anne Marie Baylouny. Our conference coordinator, Surinder Rana, and our managing editor for this project, Jeffrey Larsen, made invaluable contributions by ensuring that the project, the contributors, and the editors stayed on track. We also thank the Center for Civil-Military Relations at the Naval Postgraduate School for providing support for the completion of this volume. Finally, we would also like to underline that the views expressed in this volume are those of the authors, and do not represent those of their employers, the Department of Defense, or the U.S. government.

ABOUT THE EDITORS AND CONTRIBUTORS

EDITORS

JEANNE K. GIRALDO teaches in the National Security Affairs Department at the Naval Postgraduate School, where she has headed the Program for Drug Control Strategy and Policy of the Center for Civil-Military Relations. Her recent publications include two chapters in *Who Guards the Guardians and How: Democratic Civil-Military Relations* (Thomas Bruneau and Scott Tollefson, eds.) and a chapter on transnational crime (co-authored with Harold Trinkunas) in *Contemporary Security Studies* (Alan Collins, ed.). She is co-organizer of the project Terrorism Financing and State Responses in a Comparative Perspective, sponsored by the Center for Homeland Defense and Security at the Naval Postgraduate School. She received a National Science Foundation fellowship for her doctoral work in the Department of Government at Harvard University.

HAROLD A. TRINKUNAS is an Associate Professor in the Department of National Security Affairs at the Naval Postgraduate School in Monterey, California. He most recently authored *Crafting Civilian Control of the Military in Venezuela: A Comparative Perspective* (University of North Carolina Press, 2005). He is also co-organizer of the project Terrorism Financing and State Responses in a Comparative Perspective, sponsored by the Center for Homeland Defense and Security at the Naval Postgraduate School. He received his PhD in Political Science from Stanford University in 1999.

CONTRIBUTORS

DANIEL BARLOW is research associate at the Center for Nonproliferation Studies Terrorism Research Project and at the Department for National Security Affairs at the Naval Postgraduate School. He received his MA in international studies from the Monterey Institute for International Studies.

ANNE L. CLUNAN is an Assistant Professor in the Department of National Security Affairs at the Naval Postgraduate School. She received her PhD in political science from the University of California at Berkeley in December 2001. Her book manuscript, "Constructing National Interests: Russian Identity and the Sources of Security Policy," in which she investigates how and why states, in particular post-Soviet Russia, develop national security interests in times of dramatic change, is under review by Cornell University Press. Anne Clunan is the author of "Constructing Concepts of Identity: Prospects and Pitfalls of a Sociological Approach to World Politics," in Rudra Sil and Eileen Doherty, eds., *Beyond Boundaries? Disciplines, Paradigms, and Theoretical Integration in International Studies* (Albany: SUNY Press, 2000).

VICTOR COMRAS served in the U.S. foreign service, reaching the rank of ambassador, and most recently served as one of five international monitors charged with overseeing the implementation of U.N. Security Council measures against al Qaeda and the Taliban. He is an expert in regulatory matters related to homeland and national security, including immigration, trade, investment, and financial and money laundering controls. Mr. Comras is a graduate of Georgetown University and the University of Florida Law School. He also has a master of laws in international trade law from Harvard Law School.

AUREL CROISSANT is a Professor at the University of Heidelberg in Germany. Dr. Croissant has published more than 50 articles and book chapters on politics in Southeast and East Asia, political theory, political institutions, civil society, and democratization. His most recent books are *Southeast Asian Election Year 2004* (Münster and New York: Lit Verlag) and *The Politics of Death. Political Violence, Democracy and Power in Southeast Asia* (Münster: Lit Verlag), both published in 2005.

THOMAS H. JOHNSON is a Research Professor at the Naval Postgraduate School's National Security Affairs Department. He has conducted research on Afghanistan, Central Asia, and terrorism. His most recent publications include "A Hard Day's Night? The United States and the Global War on Terror," with James Russell, *Comparative Strategy* 24, no. 2, 2005. His earlier work has appeared in such journals as the *American Political Science Review*, the *Journal of Politics*, the *Brown Journal of World Affairs*, and in numerous edited volumes and scholarly texts. Professor Johnson has taught at the University of Southern California, George Mason University, and the Foreign Service Institute. He is a past recipient of the Charles E. Merriam Award for Outstanding Public Policy Research, from the University of Illinois.

MATTHEW LEVITT was Director of Terrorism Studies and Senior Fellow at the Washington Institute for Near East Policy at the time of his contribution to this volume. In November 2005, Dr. Levitt became the Deputy Assistant Secretary for Intelligence and Analysis at the Department of the Treasury. Levitt previously served as an FBI analyst providing tactical and strategic analysis in support of counter-terrorism operations. His special focus has been on fundraising and logistical support networks for Middle East terrorist groups. In addition, he has participated as a team member in a number of crisis situations, including the terrorist threat surrounding the turn of the millennium and the September 11 attacks. Levitt holds an MA and PhD in law and diplomacy from Tufts University's Fletcher School of Law and Diplomacy.

JOHN L. LOMBARDI is a senior U.S. government analyst, formerly at the United States Southern Command and now assigned to the Pentagon. He has extensive experience with, and knowledge of, Latin American security and intelligence issues.

LORETTA NAPOLEONI is an Italian economist and journalist. She is the author of *Modern Jihad*, which traces the money behind global terrorism. She regularly lectures on the economics of terrorism. She has an MPhil in terrorism from the London School of Economics, a PhD in economics from University of Rome, and a master in international relations from Johns Hopkins University.

NIKOS PASSAS is Professor of Criminal Justice at Northeastern University. His law degree is from the University of Athens (LLB), his Master's from the University of Paris-Paris II (D.E.A.) and his PhD from the University of Edinburgh Faculty of Law. He is a member of the Athens (Greece) Bar. He specializes in the study of terrorism, white-collar crime, corruption, organized crime, and international and transnational crimes. He is the author of *Legislative Guide for the Implementation of the UN Convention against Transnational Organized Crime* (2003), *Informal Value Transfer Systems and Criminal Organizations: A Study into So-called Underground Banking Networks* (1999) and the editor of *International Crimes* (2003), *Upperworld and Underworld in Cross-Border Crime* (2002), and *Transnational Crime* (1999).

RAPHAEL PERL is the Senior Analyst for Terrorism Policy with the Congressional Research Service of the Library of Congress. A graduate of Georgetown University's Foreign Service and Law schools, he is the author of numerous congressional and academic publications, including *Terrorism and National Security* (Congressional Research Service, 2004), and *Terrorism—Looking Ahead: Issues and Options for Congress* (a report prepared for the Permanent Select Committee on Intelligence, 1996).

JOHN T. PICARELLI is an expert in transnational threats and their impact on national and homeland security. He is currently a Fellow at TraCCC at American University. Some of his recent publications include "Corruption and the Trafficking in Persons: The Ties That Bind" and "Global Crime Inc.," co-authored with Louise Shelley and Chris Corpora, in Marianne Cusimano Love (ed.), *Beyond Sovereignty* (2nd Edition) and "Information Technologies and Transnational Organized Crime," co-authored with Phil Williams, in *Information Age Anthology, Vol. II.*, Dan Papp (ed.). Picarelli completed his doctoral studies at the School of International Service at American University in 2006.

JESSICA PIOMBO is an Assistant Professor and Regional Coordinator for Sub-Saharan Africa in the Department of National Security Affairs at the Naval Postgraduate School, where she teaches courses on African politics, comparative politics, and ethnic politics and conflicts. Piombo is also a research associate at Stanford's Center for African Studies. Her research specializes in democratization and electoral politics, transitional governance, and ethnic politics and conflict management. She is the editor of *Electoral Politics in South Africa: Assessing the First Democratic Decade* (with Lia Nijzink, Palgrave Macmillan, 2005), and *Interim Governments: Institutional Bridges to Peace and Democracy?* (with Karen Guttieri, U.S. Institute of Peace Press, forthcoming). She is also the author of "Political Institutions, Social Demographics and the Decline of Ethnic Mobilization in South Africa, 1994–1999" (*Party Politics*, July 2005) and "Opposition Parties and the Voters in South Africa's 1999 Election" (with Robert Mattes, *Democratization*, Autumn 2001). She received her PhD from the Massachusetts Institute of Technology in 2003.

MOYARA DE MORAES RUEHSEN is an Associate Professor of International Policy Studies at the Monterey Institute of International Studies in Monterey, California. She received her MHS, MA, and PhD from Johns Hopkins University. Professor Ruehsen has published in a variety of academic journals and other periodicals and is currently serving on the editorial advisory board of *Money Laundering Alert*.

DAVID J. SANCHEZ is a United States Navy officer formerly assigned to United States Southern Command, where he has worked on issues related to terrorism and the Tri-Border region. Lieutenant Sanchez graduated from the Naval Postgraduate School, earning an MA in National Security Affairs, with distinction.

JACOB N. SHAPIRO is an Organizational Learning Fellow at the Center for International Security and Cooperation at Stanford University. His research focuses on the role of economic motivations in terrorist organizations. He is a Naval Reserve officer with tours at the Office of Naval Intelligence and the Naval Warfare Development Command.

LOUISE I. SHELLEY is a Professor in the School of International Service and the School of Public Affairs at American University. She is the founder and director of the Transnational Crime and Corruption Center. She is the author of many books, articles, and book chapters focusing on transnational crime, the links between crime and terrorism, and the crime patterns of formerly socialist countries. She is the recipient of Guggenheim, Fulbright, NEH, IREX, and Kennan Institute fellowships.

PHIL WILLIAMS is Professor of International Security in the Graduate School of Public and International Affairs at the University of Pittsburgh. Professor Williams has published extensively in the field of international affairs. He has edited or co-edited books on the Carter, Reagan, and Bush presidencies, as well as on classic readings in international relations. During the last ten years his research has focused primarily on transnational organized crime, and he has written articles on various aspects of this subject in *Survival, Washington Quarterly, The Bulletin on Narcotics, Temps Strategique, Scientific American, Criminal Organizations,* and *Cross Border Control.*

TERRORISM FINANCING
AND STATE RESPONSES

Introduction

JEANNE K. GIRALDO AND HAROLD A. TRINKUNAS

Financial and material resources are correctly perceived as the lifeblood of terrorist operations, and governments have determined that fighting the financial infrastructure of terrorist organizations is the key to their defeat. Since the attacks of September 11, 2001, a good deal has been learned about sources and mechanisms used to finance the "new terrorism," which is religiously motivated and exponentially more deadly than previous generations of terrorist organizations. New policies have been devised to combat the threat, and existing policies have been enacted with greater vigor than ever before. Five years into the battle against terrorist financing, it is time to take stock of the emerging literature on terrorist financing, cut through a number of myths that have developed around the issue, and assess the current policy debates.

Through a series of thematic chapters and organizational and regional case studies, this volume provides a comprehensive assessment of the state of our knowledge about the nature of terrorism financing, the evolution of terrorist strategies and government responses, and the effectiveness of both. It develops a political economy framework that sheds new light on the problem, focused on the preferences of major actors within terrorist networks and government agencies and the domestic and international contexts in which they make decisions and execute their strategies. It argues that both terrorism financing and government responses face problems of coordination, oversight, and information asymmetries that render them vulnerable to disruption.

The first choice we make in this volume is to focus on the interests and preferences of individuals within terrorist groups and how they organize to raise, transfer, and spend their funds. This provides an explanation for some of the inexplicable shortcomings we see in terrorist operations, such as the repeated failure of terrorist plots due to lack of financing. It also leads us to challenge the conventional wisdom that emphasizes the efficiency of network-based terrorist organizations. The theoretically informed approach underpinning this volume is particularly important in studying terrorist financing since even the classified data on the topic is fragmentary, and theory allows us to fill in the frequent gaps in the data with informed analysis.

This approach also provides new insights on the policies states select to combat transnational Islamic terrorism and why the global effort to coordinate counter-terrorism finance policy is meeting resistance despite the frequent reminders of the threat provided by terrorist attacks in Bali in 2003, Madrid in 2004, and London in 2005. A key premise of the volume is that it is difficult to assess the effectiveness of policies without having a clear understanding of how the policies have actually been implemented in practice and the factors that shape this. Although it has become commonplace to assert that many governments lack the resources and "political will" to counter-terrorist financing, the reasons behind this lack of political will have not been clearly articulated—arguably a necessary first step in devising strategies to secure cooperation among U.S. government agencies as well as with their counterparts abroad. Understanding the interests of governments and other affected actors (e.g., the private sector) provides an explanation for policy success and failure that complements the traditional focus on the technical soundness of policies.

The second choice we have made in this volume is to take a comparative approach to terrorism financing. The comparison of different terrorist organizations and different state responses across time allows us to identify the sources of variation in both phenomena. We can disaggregate the nature of the terrorist threat and explain why the emerging global jihadi movement is more deadly than previous generations of terrorists. A comparative approach also leads us to better understand how structural factors at the international level explain commonalities in government policies on terrorist financing and how domestic factors explain variation in the ability and willingness of states to respond. The successes and failures of counter-terrorism operations, the noisy debates about the appropriate policies to pursue in response to the threat, and the extensive coverage of the issue in academic, journalistic, and policy circles have generated a great deal of new comparative data. There is considerably more open-source material available on a much broader scale than ever before with which to analyze terrorist and counter-terrorist successes and failures.

The book is organized in two sections. The first section provides a thematic and theoretical overview of the nature of the threat, surveying our knowledge of terrorist financing sources and applying political economy and rational choice approaches to understanding the internal dynamic of funding networks within terrorist organizations. It also provides a critical analysis of the fund-raising activities and mechanisms of fund transfer employed by terrorists, and the distinctions and commonalities that exist between terrorist and other illegal financial structures, such as those used by organized crime. Finally, it previews the key debates surrounding existing counter-terrorism policy and recommends greater attention to intelligence-based strategies.

The second section of the book compares three different types of terrorist organizations: insurgent and state-sponsored terrorist movements in Afghanistan, socially and territorially based terrorist organizations in the case of Hezbollah, and the new terrorist movements exemplified by al Qaeda and its associated organizations. It also conducts a comparative survey of terrorist financing and government responses to the problem in the regions most targeted by global jihadi organizations, which include East Africa, Europe, Latin America, the Middle East, and Southeast Asia. Here, we explain the obstacles faced even by highly motivated states in successfully countering terrorist finances, particularly in the form of a lack of consensus over appropriate policy responses, the mismatch between policy and outcomes, and the constraints imposed by the international order and domestic political and social actors. Two chapters focus on the response of U.S. and international actors to terrorism financing, highlighting policy debates and attempting to explain shortcomings in the response. The volume concludes with a comparative chapter that assesses similarities and variations in individual government policies.

PART I

The Nature of the Problem and the Response

CHAPTER ONE

The Political Economy of Terrorism Financing

JEANNE K. GIRALDO AND HAROLD A. TRINKUNAS

A rash of terrorist attacks in the 1990s, all designed to cause mass casualties—
the February 1993 bombing of the World Trade Center, the March 1995
sarin gas attack in the Tokyo subway, the April 1995 bombing of the federal
building in Oklahoma City—seemed to signal the arrival on the scene of a
new and more deadly kind of terrorism. Observers often cited the religious
fundamentalism of the "new terrorists," who exhibited a degree of fanaticism
apparently beyond reason or mercy, to explain their willingness to engage in
attacks of unprecedented lethality.[1] In this chapter we argue that the growing
deadliness of the "new terrorism," however merciless, is actually the product
of terrorists' reasoned response to loosening constraints on their behavior
caused by changes in funding sources. In fact, what is new about terrorism
writ large by the end of the twentieth century—and not just for the religiously motivated groups identified as part of the "new terrorism"—is the
diversification of the sources of funding upon which they rely and the declining importance of state and popular support within their funding portfolios.

This chapter sketches key trends in terrorism financing over the past few
decades, arguing that the acceleration of globalization and an apparent increase

in the incidence of poor governance, state failure, and ungoverned areas explain the dominance of a "new" financial model in which terrorists rely increasingly upon their own licit and illicit enterprises for their funding. The chapter also develops a political economy framework, which analyzes the interests of actors within terrorist organizations and those external to the group who form part of the terrorist financial support network, to shed light on the way in which funding sources can shape the behavior of terrorist groups. A political economy framework also leads us to explore key vulnerabilities within the terrorist organization created by potentially conflicting preferences among terrorist leaders, financial middlemen, and operatives. This approach calls into question standard accounts of the efficiency and robustness of network-based terrorist organizations and the new financing model.

While terrorist organizations that depend on state sponsorship or societal support have historically faced limits on what activities are acceptable, "new terrorist" organizations such as al Qaeda and a wide variety of other self-sufficient groups find themselves increasingly able to operate free from such constraints. This approach thus provides an alternative to conventional religion-centered explanations for the increased lethality of Islamist terrorism. It also helps explain the increasing brutality of many non-religious terrorist groups as well. Using the political economy framework to understand the challenges of driving a wedge between terrorists and their funding sources under the new financing model helps us explain why counter-terrorism financing (CTF) policies have assumed a higher profile within broader counter-terrorism efforts since the turn of the century.

Trends in Terrorism Financing

The fund-raising methods of a wide range of groups are most often lumped together under the general rubric of "terrorism financing."[2] These include the urban, Marxist-Leninist-inspired terrorist groups of the 1960s and 1970s; the religiously motivated terrorist groups that assumed increasing importance in the 1980s and 1990s; and insurgent groups, variously motivated by religion, ideology, or ethnicity. To the extent that these groups all use violence against non-combatants to achieve a political goal, they are rightly understood as terrorists. However, this delineation glosses over some important differences between the groups that are relevant to understanding

how funding sources influence behavior. Insurgencies are typically territorially based organizations that field an army in an effort to create an alternative
system of government. The need to sustain thousands of fighters, buy
weaponry, and potentially provide social services to the population whose
support the organization may be trying to win creates great financial
demands on insurgent groups. By contrast, terrorists spend much less on
operations, and their budget for training camps and personnel is likely to be
less than that of insurgent groups. In addition, insurgent control of territory
creates opportunities for taxing the population and activities under the
group's control, mechanisms less likely to be available to terrorists.

Notwithstanding these differences, scholars and policy makers over-
whelmingly agree that the end of the Cold War marked a watershed moment
in the nature of terrorist finances. During the Cold War, terrorists were said
to be heavily dependent on state sponsors for their funding, but they became
increasingly self-sufficient during the 1990s, relying instead on crime and
other self-financing methods.[3] Two factors related to the Cold War are usually cited to explain this shift in funding sources. First, the end of the superpower rivalry reduced the incentives for Washington and Moscow to fund
proxies in pursuing their ideological and geopolitical goals. Second, other
state sponsors of terrorism (like Libya and Syria) faced a less polarized international environment, in which countries were more willing and able to take
concerted action against terrorism and its sponsors. While there is a great
deal of truth to this standard interpretation, it understates the importance of
non-state sources of funds for terrorists prior to the end of the Cold War and
exaggerates the importance of the end of the Cold War in accounting for the
changes that were apparent in terrorism financing by the 1990s.

The overall flow of hard cash to terrorists was undoubtedly greater during the Cold War than after it, especially if insurgent groups engaged in so-
called superpower proxy wars (such as those in Afghanistan, El Salvador, and
Nicaragua) are included in the tally. In addition to the funding provided by
the superpowers, oil-rich regimes began pumping large sums of money into
the terrorist financial system; the regimes included most notably Libya, led
by Colonel Muammar al Gaddafi, beginning in the 1970s, and Iran under
Ayatollah Khomeini, beginning in the 1980s. States also sometimes supported terrorists (most often insurgents) operating in neighboring countries
to generate geopolitical pressure, both before and after the Cold War. The
reduction in U.S., Soviet, and Libyan support for terrorism by the 1990s is

in and of itself enough to explain a sharp decline in the role of states in providing financial support for terrorism.[4]

More questionable, however, is the accompanying claim that the terrorist shift to self-financing was driven by a drying up of funds associated with the end of the Cold War. Many of the urban, Marxist-Leninist groups of the 1960s and 1970s relied on various criminal activities—particularly kidnapping, robbery, and extortion—to supplement their state funding. Some organizations, like the Fuerzas Armadas Revolucionarias de Colombia (FARC) in Colombia or Shining Path in Peru, never received significant amounts of funds from state sponsors and relied instead on drug trafficking for their revenues. Others, like the Irish Republican Army (IRA) or the Liberation Tigers of Tamil Eelam (LTTE), received infusions of cash from state sponsors at critical periods in their development but experienced the withdrawal of these funds prior to the end of the Cold War. This loss was not crippling for the IRA and LTTE because they could draw on already well-developed alternative revenue streams from organized crime and donations from the Irish and Tamil diasporas. Still others, like the Palestine Liberation Organization (PLO), diversified their funding sources long before the end of the Cold War in order to reduce their dependence on fickle state sponsors. Even Hezbollah, which receives approximately $100 million a year in support from Iran, has cultivated the Lebanese diaspora as a means of support and relied on extortion and crime in the Tri-Border Area of South America to supplement their state funding. Therefore, terrorist organizations— either out of a desire to maximize their revenue or an understanding that state sponsors are often fickle (or both)—cultivate multiple sources of income if at all possible, regardless of levels of state funding. Terrorism financing is driven more by the availability of opportunities than by a shortfall in revenues from state sponsors.[5]

More importantly, the end of the Cold War was a significant turning point in the history of terrorist finance because it simultaneously eliminated the last barriers to globalization and it led to a proliferation of failed states and ungoverned regions. Globalization allowed terrorist organizations to take full advantage of a highly integrated international financial system, ever greater options for moving personnel, and ever greater ease of communication through the internet and cellular and satellite telephony. Globalization made it easier to mount terrorist operations as well as to conduct terrorist financial affairs. While illicit revenue sources for terrorists were somewhat limited in the 1960s and 1970s, increasing levels of globalization by the 1980s created new opportunities to derive funding from crime as well as to draw on sympathetic diaspora communities for support. The breakdown of states in the Horn of Africa, the Balkans, Central Asia, and the emergence of ungoverned regions in many parts of the world proved another boon to terrorists. Failed states and misgoverned regions provided cover for terrorist infrastructure, easier access to lucrative criminal enterprises such as arms and drug smuggling and trafficking in persons, and zones where government responses and countermeasures became more difficult.

Analysts took greater note of the trend towards alternative funding mechanisms with the emergence of al Qaeda and related groups in the 1990s. For the most part, these religiously motivated, transnational terrorists did not serve a specific geopolitical interest, and hence were unlikely to receive state sponsorship. Although al Qaeda might cooperate with groups that had a specific national goal (e.g., the liberation of Afghanistan), self-sufficiency and independence were seen as the defining characteristics of the "new terrorism."[6] Lacking a national or ethnic constituency, they did not rely on a particular domestic or diaspora community for financial support.

The portrait of terrorism financing that has emerged since the September 2001 attacks on the United States is of a formal and informal global financial system that terrorists can manipulate with ease. Diverse and dispersed sources of funding and methods of transferring funds are exploited by equally decentralized and flexible terrorist networks that can easily shift from one means to another in response to efforts to thwart their activities. Not only al Qaeda and al Qaeda–inspired groups but also most contemporary terrorist organizations increasingly exploit sources of funds that do not require the ideological sympathy or consent of the provider. Instead, terrorists rely on a variety of more impersonal and self-contained mechanisms such as independent criminal ventures, diversion of funds from charities, and licit businesses. The implications of this increased self-sufficiency are explored in the following section.

The Political Economy of Funding Sources: Lessening of Constraints?

A political economy approach to terrorism financing focuses on how the potentially divergent interests of the key actors engaged in the raising, distribution, and spending of funds—and the institutional settings in which decisions about financing are made—might affect outcomes. Insights into the divergent interests involved in the fund-raising process crop up periodically in the terrorism literature; here they are further developed to shed new light on the evolution of terrorist fund-raising practices and the constraints that particular funding sources might impose on terrorist behavior.

Often the source of funds for a terrorist network—whether it be a state, a population, or an allied criminal organization—does not have interests that coincide neatly with those of the terrorists. Sometimes, these divergent interests present an opportunity for government policy makers to drive a wedge between the terrorists and their funding sources, or, as has more often been the case, circumstances may create a breach that limits the availability of funds. Even if the diverging preferences do not lead to a falling out, terrorists may find that the sensibilities of their sponsors constrain their behavior. In the past, policy makers had been able to take some comfort in the notion that state and popular sources of funding for terrorists were often more moderate than the organizations themselves and had a broader range of interests that encouraged them to set limits on the lethality of terrorism. Today, the diversity of terrorist funding sources increases their independence of action, which is of particular concern to policy makers.

States have long had geopolitical (and other) motives to provide financial support to terrorist groups operating within the territories of their rivals.[7] Despite their shared interest in destabilizing certain regimes, terrorists and states may part ways on the particulars of how this should be done. Often, states view terrorists as loose cannons whose actions may be counterproductive for the state sponsor.[8] Terrorist pursuit of a diversified funding portfolio is therefore a rational course of action since state sponsors are often willing to sacrifice the terrorists' non-negotiable goal of destabilization if it begins to undermine the pursuit of other national interests.[9] States seem to be particularly unreliable sponsors if there are multiple terrorist groups in a particular area whom they might choose to support, as Thomas Johnson points out in chapter 6 on Afghanistan. By contrast, if financial patronage of a group is public knowledge and important domestic constituencies of the state sponsor support a terrorist organization, the state will find it much harder to withdraw its support in response to changing circumstances. If it is too costly to withdraw its sponsorship, a state may seek to modify the agenda of the receiving organization so that its behavior does not reflect negatively on the state in international circles.

Historically, terrorists (particularly insurgents) have also relied on popular support for their funding needs. These payments may take the form of voluntary contributions, taxes rendered in return for services provided by the insurgency, or extortion. When there is a limited convergence of interests between the terrorists and the targeted party, extortion must be used to secure payment. Terrorists run a protection racket, threatening violence against individuals or their property unless a sum is paid. While many victims of extortion have little choice but to pay, others will resist if they have the means. This imposes a certain ceiling on fund-raising efforts, and excessive taxation can potentially create a backlash against the terrorist group. For example, large companies in Northern Ireland seem to be in a better position than small, local businesses in resisting extortion attempts from Protestant paramilitaries.[10] In Colombia, landowners faced with FARC extortion attempts had the choice of paying the insurgents, leaving their land, or forming self-defense groups in an effort to thwart the FARC. Over time, the capacity of landowners to resist these efforts increased, not only as a result of military collusion with paramilitaries but also because well-armed and well-financed drug traffickers bought up most of the land in rural areas where FARC had a presence. In this case, extortion efforts backfired on a massive scale, as paramilitaries launched offensives against the FARC, not only to cleanse their own local areas but to rid the entire country of a guerrilla presence.

In other cases where there is a greater convergence of interests between terrorists and their domestic or diaspora constituency, payments take on more of a voluntary character. In drug-producing areas, for example, insurgents may defend peasant growers from government eradication efforts and secure better prices for their raw product from drug traffickers; in return the peasants are willing to pay a tax on their crop.[11] The Tamil Tigers have been able to raise a great deal of money from diaspora populations in countries like Britain and Canada by monopolizing the Tamil community's cultural and social organizations and media outlets. In this way, the LTTE cultivates a certain level of legitimacy (and hence contributions) by providing basic social services and promoting their views in the Tamil language media.[12] Nevertheless, the commitment of the donor to the terrorist cause can be somewhat unreliable and fluctuate over time. In the case of the Tamil Tigers, for example, peace talks in 1990 and 1994 reduced diaspora giving, leading the LTTE to shift more of its funds into legitimate investments as a relatively more stable source of revenue.[13]

Terrorist dependence on a domestic or external population base for support is often viewed as a factor that will moderate the behavior of otherwise radical terrorist groups. Socially embedded groups have usually proved to be less likely to engage in behavior that their support group finds unacceptable—or if they do engage in such behavior, they risk extinction. In contrast, groups with independent sources of financing, such as that provided by natural resources, need not take popular opinion into account. This argument is commonly made about rebel groups in Africa, such as the Revolutionary United Front (RUF) in Sierra Leone and various rebel groups in the Democratic Republic of the Congo,[14] and there is some evidence that the FARC may have increased its levels of indiscriminate violence against civilians as it became increasingly reliant on the drug trade in the late 1990s.[15]

Of course, the notion that a popular support base exerts a moderating influence depends on the assumption that the civilian population is less radical than the terrorist group. This may not always be the case. For example, there is evidence that Palestinian terrorist groups increased their suicide bombings during the second Intifadah in an effort to compete with one another for support from a population radicalized by heavy-handed Israeli tactics.[16] Similarly, Paul Collier and Anke Hoeffler find that large U.S.-residing diasporas are correlated with higher chances of renewed conflict in a country after five years of peace. They attribute this to the financial support provided by diasporas, arguing that wealthy diasporas are more willing and able to fund conflict than domestic populations, since they do not suffer any of the costs of conflict.[17]

Although crime has long been a staple of terrorism financing, it was only in the 1980s that analysts and policy makers began expressing a real concern over the crime-terror nexus. In part this may be because, historically, crime as a source of financing seemed to be self-limiting. Terrorists could only rob so many banks or extort a limited number of individuals. This view began to change in the 1980s and 1990s as connections between terrorist groups and the drug trade, as well as evidence of insurgent exploitation of other natural resources like diamonds and oil, became more prominent. Interestingly enough, however, much of the debate prior to 9/11 was not over how much money the terrorists were making but over the extent to which criminals and terrorists had convergent interests: was the nexus a strategic alliance or a mere marriage of convenience? Advocates of the former perspective believed that terrorists and criminals would work hand in glove in pursuit of their shared interest in profit making and destabilizing the state; the multiplier effect of such cooperation would be potentially devastating. Critics of this view stressed the different motives possessed by the two groups (profit versus ideology) and argued that criminal groups would most likely eschew collaboration in order to stay off the government's radar screen. Cooperation would be tactical and short-term, and thus of little significance. In short, many observers took comfort in the presumably self-limiting nature of terrorist involvement in crime.

Today, analysts are less likely to stress these limits.[18] Although criminals still jealously guard their control over illicit enterprises, thus creating barriers to entry for terrorists interested in crime, the increase in weak states and the spread of globalization since the end of the Cold War have vastly expanded criminal opportunities, and terrorists have taken advantage (as Picarelli and Shelley point out in their contribution to this volume). In addition, there is evidence that criminals and terrorists who share jail cells also develop shared interests in joint criminal and terrorist ventures upon their release. This has been documented not only in South Asia but also in the Madrid bombings, in which a radicalized drug dealing organization played an instrumental role.[19]

In the past, CTF policies did not play a significant role in counterterrorism efforts. In part, this is because the targeting of finances was largely subsumed under broader counter-terrorism efforts such as the targeting of state sponsors of terrorism or efforts to win the hearts and minds of domestic populations. In both instances, the funds that states or the people provided to terrorists would presumably be reduced by these campaigns, but other forms of support were usually singled out as more significant targets of policy. In contrast, by the mid to late 1990s, there was increasing recognition that the diverse sources of terrorist fund-raising and transfer needed to be identified and combated individually. Much of the focus has been on developing a comprehensive view of both the sources of funds and the mechanisms that can be used by terrorists for the transfer and storage of their funds. Diplomats, intelligence agencies, law enforcement, and the financial sector would all need to be enlisted in the efforts to devise more diverse policy tools and to apply more widely existing sanctions. The goal was to increase the costs associated with providing assistance to terrorists, thus creating divergent interests between the two groups.

Potential Inefficiencies of the New Financing Model

The preceding discussion would seem to support the prevailing notion that terrorist fund-raising is relatively easy. Terrorists simply need to engage in readily mastered licit or illicit activities to fund their operations, and the lack of attached strings provides groups with a terrifying freedom of action. Indeed, most analysts highlight the efficiency with which terrorist groups, and al Qaeda in particular, organize themselves to raise funds. In part, this is thought to be a product of the nature of the task—the sources and methods of terrorism financing are decentralized and diverse, thus requiring a similarly organized financial apparatus. The efficiency is seen as a product of intentional design because a decentralized, networked al Qaeda composed of self-funded cells is more flexible and less vulnerable to attack. The financial network is also thought to be characterized by a great deal of redundancy: attack one source of income or one means of transferring funds, and terrorists can readily shift to another.[20]

The problem with these interpretations of terrorist financial networks is that they tend to be driven as much by existing theories about organizations—for example, network theory or complexity theory—as by the evidence.[21] This is inevitable, given the fragmentary nature of the evidence available. Some kind of theory is necessary to help make sense of the fragments and fill in the gaps. There is certainly a good deal of evidence that supports these interpretations of terrorist financial networks—and they may ultimately end up being accurate. The problem, however, is that these theories fail to explain all the fragments of evidence, and in particular, they tend to ignore or discount the examples of inefficiencies in the system. As the federal commission investigating the September 11th terrorist attacks noted:

> Given the catastrophic results of the 9/11 attacks, it is tempting to
> depict the plot as a set plan executed to near perfection. This would be
> a mistake. . . . The 9/11 conspirators confronted operational difficulties,
> internal disagreements and even dissenting opinions within the leadership
> of al Qaeda. In the end, the plot proved sufficiently flexible to adapt and
> evolve as challenges arose.[22]

While it is possible that terrorist organizations will also be flexible enough to overcome the internal disagreements and tensions caused by the fund-raising and distribution process, this is a possibility that needs to be examined rather than assumed.

A sometimes noted but quickly dismissed, inefficiency in the terrorism financing process is the frequency with which terrorist operations have been underfunded. This has often resulted in the failure of the mission—either directly through a lack of funds or indirectly through the capture of the operatives while they are engaging in crime to raise money. The most commonly cited example is the World Trade Center bombing of 1993, which failed in part because the plotters did not have enough money to create a larger bomb. Incredibly, the terrorists were caught because they attempted to claim their deposit on the rental van used in the operation. Similarly, al Qaeda leader Zawahiri acknowledged that his inability to provide adequate funds to a cell in Pakistan prevented the targeting of the U.S. embassy and resulted instead in the selection of the third-choice target, the Egyptian embassy in Islamabad, which was bombed in November of 1995.[23] This puzzling pattern of underfunded operations persisted throughout the 1990s and continues to characterize terrorist fund distributions in the post-9/11 period.[24]

How can this phenomenon be explained if terrorist operations are inexpensive to carry out and al Qaeda has nearly unlimited resources at its disposal and multiple channels for transferring the funds to operational cells? If this underfunding is the result of successful government counter-terrorism policies, then the conventional wisdom about the breadth and depth of the terrorist financial network needs to be revised.[25] However, another plausible hypothesis suggests that terrorists face a number of organizational dilemmas that impede the raising, transfer, and spending of their resources, despite a structurally favorable international environment. In essence, terrorist leaders and their followers in financial and operational elements are likely to have different preferences over how funds should be employed, and this divergence may become so great that it impedes operational success. In chapter 4, Jacob Shapiro develops a rational choice approach to understanding when the preferences and interests of terrorist leaders and the individuals charged with distributing funds diverge, and the conditions under which this might lead to inefficient outcomes.

Counter to conventional views of terrorist effectiveness, Shapiro argues that terrorist leaders face substantial challenges to maintaining control and oversight of far-flung operational, support, and financial cells. The secrecy that characterizes these organizations provides terror cells, especially those focused on financing, with both the incentive and the cover to divert funding to personal ends rather than to support the aims of the terrorist leadership. Shapiro details the circumstances under which this organizational dynamic may lead to sub-optimal policies and performance. Shapiro's argument applies primarily to hierarchical terrorist organizations, such as al Qaeda in its pre-9/11 incarnation.

However, since September 11, 2001, groups inspired by al Qaeda have been responsible for four times as many terrorist attacks per year as al Qaeda proper.[26] Most accounts note that these affiliated groups finance themselves through criminal activities, and they stress the efficiency of this form of financing, since it presumably falls outside the purview of government CTF efforts. Nonetheless, a notable number of al Qaeda operatives have been arrested as they engage in criminal activities. For example, Ahmed Ressam and his associates were arrested in the United States and Canada in December 1999 for credit card fraud and petty theft. The chief logistician for the 2002 Bali bombing was arrested as a result of his participation in a bank robbery. This suggests that this decentralized approach to fund-raising exposes terrorist organization to a new set of risks, raises the chances of detection by local law enforcement agencies, and consequently increases the risk of failure.

An increasing number of analysts argue that use of criminal activities for fund-raising creates another vulnerability for terrorist organizations: the temptation of corruption and a loss of focus among members.[27] Attracted by "easy money" and the lure of the criminal lifestyle, terrorists are thought to abandon their ideological goals in favor of pecuniary rewards. For the most part, however, speculation about "fighters turned felons" remains just that. The Islamic Movement of Uzbekistan (IMU), for example, was widely cited as an organization that had lost its direction as a result of heavy involvement in the Central Asian heroin trade. Nonetheless, many key members of this supposedly criminal group fought to the death in defense of the Taliban regime in 2001 and 2002. There is some risk that sub-groups within a terrorist organization may begin to identify more closely with illicit fund-raising activities than with the group's political goals. The risk seems to be greatest in hierarchical groups where specialized units are tasked with fund-raising, and it most often manifests itself in divergent interests about the desirability of peace, as analysts of the Provisional Irish Republican Army

(PIRA) have stressed.[28] Nonetheless, decentralized groups or cells that engage in both fund-raising and operations (the increasingly common modus operandi for al Qaeda–inspired groups) seem relatively immune from this kind of factionalism.

Conclusion

The conventional wisdom about terrorists and their finances has tended to exaggerate the efficiency and effectiveness of terrorists and their funding networks. It is true that the end of the Cold War and globalization have accelerated and facilitated the diversification of the terrorist funding portfolio. The consequence has been a loosening of constraints on such organizations and a subsequent increase in the lethality of attacks. Globalization has also made it easier for terrorist organizations to communicate, plan, and organize funding on truly global scale. As the chapters that follow will show, few governments have been able to prepare adequately to deal with the shifting nature of the terrorist threat. The fragmented and networked nature of contemporary transnational jihadi terrorism is difficult for governments to attack effectively, particularly if we take into account more recent trends, such as the self-organizing al Qaeda–inspired cells we have begun to see in Europe and Iraq.

However, this brave new world also holds considerable risks for these groups. The lack of a state sponsor or a sympathetic popular base means that terrorists have less access to secure rear areas in which to rest and reorganize. The growing lethality of attacks is a double-edged sword, since the savagery makes it easier for states to achieve international (and domestic) consensus on the need to root out such organizations. Globalization makes it possible to organize world-spanning networks, but it makes it ever more difficult for terrorist leaders to control, oversee, and account for the activities of their followers. Self-funding not only exposes terrorists to the risk of detection and capture by law enforcement but may also make them potential targets for criminal enterprises intent on relieving them of their financial assets. An ungoverned region, such as Somalia, can be both a source of cover for terrorists and a threat to their operations, because terrorists run greater risks to their personal security from local warlords and criminals. In other words, even terrorists run the risk of being mugged in the highly globalized underworld in which they operate.

In short, the changing international environment brings opportunity, but it also creates new sources of inefficiency and vulnerability for terrorist organizations that can be exploited by governments. Subsequent chapters in this volume illustrate terrorists' successes and failures. They also underline the difficult challenges facing governments as they try to formulate a response. However, at the very least, the task facing counter-terrorism financing agencies becomes easier if they develop a realistic assessment of the threat, identify the flaws and shortcomings that characterize all terrorist enterprises, and, most importantly, avoid overestimating the power, flexibility, and capabilities of the groups.

CHAPTER TWO

Terrorism Financing Mechanisms and Policy Dilemmas

NIKOS PASSAS

We will direct every resource at our command to win the war against terrorists, every means of diplomacy, every tool of intelligence, every instrument of law enforcement, every financial influence. We will starve the terrorists of funding, turn them against each other, rout them out of their safe hiding places, and bring them to justice.

— PRESIDENT GEORGE W. BUSH, SEPTEMBER 24, 2001

We operate every day with the knowledge that our enemies are changing based on how we change.

— SECRETARY OF HOMELAND SECURITY TOM RIDGE,
MARCH 31, 2004

If there's one concern I have about intelligence, it is that often there are state-ments made about an uncorroborated source with indirect access. And then there is a stating of a particular fact. . . . I think there has to be a balance between the information we get and the foundation of that information.

— FBI DIRECTOR ROBERT S. MUELLER, APRIL 14, 2004

Financial controls are an essential and indispensable counter-terrorism tool, although this view was not fully adopted by key states until after the 9/11 attacks. The United Nations 1999 Convention for the Suppression of the Financing of Terrorism did not come into force until April 10, 2002. The United States ratified it on June 26 of that year, after adopting an official policy aimed at choking off al Qaeda's and other terrorists' money. A series of measures at the national, regional, and international levels were introduced and enforced in an effort to deprive militants of the means to inflict serious damage by attacking their sources of support.[1]

The question is what the impact of this arsenal of policy weapons has been and whether the assumptions and understandings underlying these controls are accurate. The short answer is that, unfortunately, we still have incomplete knowledge in this regard, and there are debates over some of the knowledge we do possess. One set of debates revolves around the nature of terrorist financing. Disagreements are not so much about whether this or that type of funding or method of transfer has been used by extremists. As will be seen, there is such a diversity of sources and transfer methods that one can hardly find a single way in which funds have not been raised or transferred by some militant group. The debates are rather about such things as the relative extent and significance of different fund-raising and transfer methods for specific groups; the overall importance of informal value transfer systems (such as *hawala*); the trade in various commodities (including precious stones, metals, and tobacco); and the role of charitable organizations.[2] This uncertainty about which means of fund-raising and fund transfers are preferred by terrorist organizations has serious consequences when it comes to constructing policy, developing enforcement mechanisms, and allocating resources to countering such activities.

There is also a good deal of debate over the ways in which national authorities and the international community can effectively respond to terrorism financing and the foreseeable consequences of current and proposed courses of action. In part, this is due to uncertainty about how much can actually be achieved in the overall war on terror by targeting finance. I argue that the specific functions of financial controls are to (1) prevent terror acts, (2) reduce the harm of terror acts, (3) monitor activities and anticipate moves, (4) force militants to talk to each other and change financial methods (thus generating more opportunities for intelligence gathering on them), and (5) offer clues on the modus operandi of militants, thereby enabling the disruption and control of terrorism. Beliefs that financial measures can achieve more than this are unrealistic and risky.[3]

The underlying theme of this chapter is that lofty or misguided expectations and misapplication of financial controls may be not only ineffective but also deeply counter-productive, ultimately hurting U.S. national interests. It is thus imperative that we understand well the limits and risks of such controls. We also require solid data regarding the social organization of terrorist groups we deem as top priorities so as to fine tune the application of counter-terrorism financing (CTF) policies. The financial aspects of terrorist organizations are embedded in a social context, and therefore governments must constantly monitor the evolution of terrorist groups so as to track their shifting preferences in regard to finances. This chapter seeks to provide a sound basis on which to move this debate forward towards consensus building and a commonly accepted empirical ground. The first part of the chapter outlines a number of issues relative to the nature of terrorist financing, while the second part discusses the challenges of addressing this problem.

The Nature of Terrorist Financing

Terrorist financing was far from a priority for intelligence collection or academic research before the attacks of 9/11, and thus information on the topic was thin and relied mostly on a few secondary or superficial sources. Given the general propensity to create and believe in "facts by repetition," we must treat the secondary literature and data with caution and a critical spirit, especially in the age of the internet, or else run the risk of making misguided policy decisions on the basis of rumor.[4] The challenge faced by scholarly and public policy efforts to establish the facts around terrorist finance is exemplified by the public debate over the sources of al Qaeda monies, a debate that was characterized by a number of baseless but persistent media reports and speculation. For example, the report of the 9/11 Commission dispelled the popular myth that al Qaeda was drawing on bin Laden's personal fortune from inheritance or businesses he had in Sudan. It is now clear that, particularly after his move from Sudan to Afghanistan, he did not have much personal wealth or a network of businesses to rely on.[5]

Although the 9/11 Commission has been able to debunk some common misperceptions, devising a more complete picture of terrorist financing is difficult. As the 9/11 Commission frankly admitted,

> The nature and extent of al Qaeda fund-raising and money movement make intelligence collection exceedingly difficult, and gaps appear to remain in

the intelligence community's understanding of the issue. Because of the complexity and variety of ways to collect and move small amounts of money in a vast worldwide financial system, gathering intelligence on al Qaeda financial flows will remain a hard target for the foreseeable future.[6]

Based on the findings of the 9/11 Commission and the research of leading scholars in the field of terrorist financing, this section attempts to provide a "myth-free" description of our collective wisdom on the main elements of terrorist fund-raising and fund transfers and identifies the most pressing areas in which our knowledge is lacking

FUND-RAISING METHODS

Terrorist fund-raising methods and sources are rarely innovative, since most of them rely on common legal and illegal financial transactions, although some techniques are most commonly associated with particular groups. In the past, funding sources often included sovereign states, but this has changed in recent years. Nowadays, some of the funding sources, such as ordinary businesses, investments, charitable organizations, and cultural activities, are legitimate. Other sources, including petty crime, kidnapping, and criminal enterprises of various types, are illegitimate.

The nature of terrorist fund-raising changed substantially at the end of the Cold War with the marked decline in state sponsorship of terrorist organizations. During the Cold War the major powers funded and supported militant groups and death squads in various parts of the globe under the guise of "counter-insurgency" or "international solidarity." Apart from widely discussed past examples of politics and "diplomacy by other means" engaged in by France, the United States, or the Soviet Union, several smaller states made their own contributions to bloody conflicts and support for terrorist organizations. Afghanistan, Cuba, Iran, Iraq, Libya, North Korea, Pakistan, Saudi Arabia, Syria, and Turkey have been among the usual suspects at different times.[7] Even though there is consensus today that state sponsorship is in decline, the phenomenon has not disappeared. A long list of groups regarded by many as terrorist or subversive are currently supported by states; these include Hamas, Hezbollah, Hizbul Mujahidin, the Islamic Militant Union (IMU), Islamic Jihad, Lashkar e Taiba (LeT), Jaish-e-Mohammad (JeM), and Sipah-e-Sahiba (SSP).

Decline in state sponsorship required terrorists to find operational funding through other means. To some extent, ethnic diasporas and wealthy individuals could be counted on to fill the gap, which meant that terrorists could receive contributions from originally legal sources. In virtually every conflict, ethnic communities, members, outside supporters, and wealthy sympathizers at home and abroad have contributed to their respective causes.[8] This may occur through informal revolutionary taxes levied on businesses or entire communities or through direct voluntary contributions and the holding of fund-raising events. Inter-group exchanges have also been reported (for example, Jemaah Islamiyah with al Qaeda or Kashmir militants receiving funds from other radical Islamic groups).

The use of charities, mosques, and non-governmental organizations as terrorist fund-raising mechanisms has drawn a great deal of attention, but we should remember that they fall into two categories: those that have had their funds unknowingly diverted and those that have been corrupted and act as fronts.[9] Media and other reports have recently cited the Global Relief Foundation (associated with al Qaeda); the Holy Land Foundation for Relief and Development and the Quranic Literacy Institute (Hamas); and the Islamic Concern Project, World and Islam Studies Enterprises, and the Islamic Academy of Florida (Palestinian Islamic Jihad). Mosques and non-governmental organizations mentioned in the African embassy bombing trial included the Farouq mosque in Brooklyn, the non-governmental organization Help Africa People, and the relief agency Mercy International.[10] When it comes to al Qaeda, the 9/11 Commission reported that prior to the 9/11 attacks al Qaeda relied on diversions from Islamic charities and financial facilitators who gathered money from witting and unwitting donors, primarily from the Arabian Gulf region.

Finally, but quite importantly for the most resilient and well-organized groups, a diversification into legal businesses has been noted. The Abu Nidal Organization, LeT, Liberation Tigers of Tamil Eelam (LTTE), Fuerzas Armadas Revolucionarias de Colombia (FARC), Hezbollah, the Irish Republican Army (IRA), and Jemaah Islamiyah (JI) are among a cluster of organizations that make money through legitimate investments and business activities. This does not begin to address the much larger issue of the use of legal businesses by sympathizers of groups such as al Qaeda to raise money that is then donated to the cause.

The crackdown on charities sympathetic to terrorist causes since 9/11 seems to have reduced the amount of money available through legal sources and may have forced terrorists to rely increasingly on "ordinary" crime to raise funds. Facilitators and local crime are reported to be the main fundraising options for al Qaeda now, according to the UN Monitoring Team.[11] Officials acknowledge that petty and ordinary crime is a primary source of funds for militancy throughout Europe.[12] The increased reliance on crime may also be explained by the supposed decentralization of the al Qaeda movement and by the radicalization of criminal offenders inside prisons or in their communities.

There are few criminal activities that terrorists have not engaged in to raise funds. Contemporary terrorist groups have employed extortion, kidnapping, hijacking, blackmail, and fraud with differing degrees of scope and complexity. This includes credit card, insurance, ATM, and tax fraud; document forgery schemes; and counterfeiting of currency and goods. About a quarter of 38 countries surveyed observed the link between terrorism and the smuggling of illegal migrants.[13]

The two most controversial aspects of the link between crime and terrorist financing are drug trafficking and diamond smuggling. Although some nexus between terrorism and the illegal drug trade is clear—according to a survey of 38 countries, about half of them noticed some link between the two—the exact nature of this relationship has often been misunderstood.[14] Often associated in the media with left-wing insurgents such as the Colombian FARC, the drug trade has attracted militant groups of all races, colors, creeds, and ideological orientations, and some of the heaviest involvement in this trade has been by right-wing paramilitaries and terrorists.[15]

Finally, the nature of the relationship between terrorists and drug traffickers is most often viewed, erroneously, as a strategic alliance instead of the more common marriages of convenience or even antagonism that characterizes such ties.[16] A number of symbiotic or parasitic relationships are possible. First, one of the most publicized is the levying of taxes on growers or traffickers of drugs in areas that guerrillas control, as has occurred in Colombia with the FARC and in Peru with Sendero Luminoso. Second, ideology may be simply camouflage for a criminal enterprise, and some suggestions in that direction have surfaced regarding Northern Alliance groups in Afghanistan and the Kosovo Liberation Army. Third, a militant group may be involved in the trade itself, such as may be the case with the Islamic Movement of Uzbekistan or Abu Sayyaf. Fourth, militants and traffickers may be partners in the trade, or it can be that individual members of a group occasionally get involved in the trade, as is the case with the IRA and the LTTE. Finally, some traffickers may sympathize with a particular cause and make a contribution in the same way that a legitimate businessman might. A similar range of arrangements, albeit by no means as frequent as with drugs, have been reported with tobacco smuggling, particularly for Hamas, Hezbollah, and the IRA, and with the trade in natural resources, such as oil and timber. The involvement of al Qaeda in the drug trade, both before and after the 9/11 attacks, has been the subject of some controversy, but no evidence of significant links has ever been produced.

CONFLICT DIAMONDS

Persistent reports of al Qaeda's involvement in the rough diamond trade in West Africa have also caused a good deal of alarm even though they have been contradicted by intelligence and law enforcement agencies, as well as The 9/11 Commission Report.[17] Media reports indicate that al Qaeda associates have been involved in the conflict diamonds trade, particularly rough diamonds from Sierra Leone mined by the Revolutionary United Front (RUF). At first, it was reported that al Qaeda wished to raise funds, but then simply sought to convert cash into portable, valuable, and easily convertible commodities such as diamonds and gold.

While there is cause for concern that the diamond industry can be used to support terrorist activity, the argument that al Qaeda has had a significant involvement in West African conflict diamonds is very weak. The al Qaeda–diamonds nexus theory emanates from five main authors.[18] Despite their own characterization as "independent findings," they routinely refer to each other and rely on the same or similar sources. None of these sources can substantiate the allegation that precious stones have been or are a significant fund-raising or value storage method of al Qaeda.

My own review of the cited sources, interviews with those directly involved in such investigations, and other primary data disconfirm these links. Some of these sources (e.g., the FBI and Belgian federal police) strongly disagree with the media reports and have failed to find unusual transactions and prices at critical times or to corroborate the important components of the media theory.[19] The 9/11 Commission, which has taken into account additional non-public data (e.g., from al Qaeda detainees), has also pointed out that there is "no persuasive evidence that al Qaeda funded itself by trading in African conflict diamonds."[20] A Belgian Parliament inquiry and Canadian intelligence sources came to the same conclusion.[21] A review of the 1998 African U.S. Embassy bombing trial shows that the same people who reportedly raised funds from diamonds also turned to the trade in animal hides, asphalt, assembly watches, bananas, bicycles, butcher equipment, calculators, camels, canned food, cars and tires, cement, fava beans, fish, gold, hibiscus, honey, gemstones, insecticides, iron, lathing machines, leather, lemons, ostrich eyes, palm oil, peanuts, salt, seeds, sesame, shower pipes, soap, sugar, sunflower, tanzanite, textiles, tractors and tractor parts, wheat, white corn, and wood.[22] One has to wonder why al Qaeda associates would stretch themselves so thin, if they could raise the reported millions of dollars through diamonds.

If al Qaeda operatives sought to store substantial assets in rough diamonds, they would have lost about half of their value, as they supposedly bought at a 15–20 percent premium and then saw the price fall another 30 percent after 9/11.[23] In addition, such voluminous activities by newcomers would not have gone unnoticed by the Lebanese, Jewish, and Indian participants in this market or, indeed, the whole industry. In short, the conclusion is that some terrorist groups or persons associated with them may have engaged in diamond transactions, although the amounts involved do not appear to be substantial. However, the sector is vulnerable to future use by militants. The vulnerability seems to be particularly acute with polished stones (as opposed to the rough diamonds on which most reports have focused so far). Where the value is certain, as with polished stones, one does not have to be an insider to participate and one can much more easily store and hide value or transfer it across borders.

It is important to note that the identified vulnerabilities are not specific to diamonds, but apply equally to trade in general. Trade is currently not transparent and represents a significant threat to all efforts countering money laundering, terrorist finance, or other financial crime. One need only break up financial and commercial transactions into a series of discrete operations in order to obscure the investigative trail controllers may wish to follow. The creation of such "black holes" is easy since financial and trade transactions are not matched. As a result, irregularities, suspicious transactions, and blatant abuses go largely unnoticed. The heated debate on the role of conflict diamonds in the financing of al Qaeda has diverted attention from other parts of the precious stones pipeline and other commercial sectors. The possibility of substantial amounts raised or transferred undetected or without the authorities' ability to identify the contracting parties is a cause for serious concern and a matter that requires urgent attention.

FUND TRANSFER METHODS

One can hardly find a method that has not been used by one group or another to make payments or transfer funds. Terrorists have been able to exploit relatively well-regulated financial systems (as was the case with the 9/11 hijackers), poorly regulated formal banking and wire transfer systems, and largely unregulated informal value transfer systems (IVTS). IVTS refers to ways in which value can be transferred either without leaving easily identifiable traces or entirely outside the formal financial system.[24] These include *hawala* and similar ethnic networks,[25] physical couriers, invoice manipulation, trade-facilitated hidden transactions, the use of transnational charities and non-governmental organizations, as well as the illegal use of correspondent accounts (intended for bank-to-bank transactions) to hide transfers for individual clients.[26]

Hawala has drawn intense attention and regulatory concern after 9/11 on the assumption that this was one of the main methods of fund transfer for the hijackers. This is a trust-based, efficient, convenient, and inexpensive informal funds transfer method extremely popular in South Asia, the Middle East, and parts of Africa. All it takes is a series of agents who take the remitters' money, consolidate it, and fax payment instructions to counterparts overseas for delivery in minutes or hours. Agents settle up through formal and informal channels, sometimes directly and sometimes through a series of third parties.[27] Kashmiri, Hamas, JI, LTTE, and other Asian groups have indeed resorted to *hawala*, as have many other organizations, both legal and criminal. Al Qaeda has relied on it when it operated in places where no formal infrastructure or other options were available, such as Afghanistan. The 9/11 operations, however, involved no *hawala* or similar transfers.[28] In fact, there is still no case in the United States, Canada, or Europe where terrorists have used *hawala* for their operations, even though this is an important channel for militants operating in South Asia and Africa.

Nevertheless, IVTS are hardly the preferred mechanism for terrorist funding transfers, and the formal banking system has often been exploited as well. The State Department has argued that terrorist organizations "have exploited poorly regulated banking systems and their built-in impediments to international regulatory and law enforcement cooperation, and have made use of their financial services to originate wire transfers and establish accounts that require minimal or no identification or disclosure of ownership."[29] However, the problems go well beyond some ill-managed institutions or countries.

Pointing to the challenges financial controllers must face, The 9/11 Commission Report made clear that al Qaeda funded the hijackers in the United States by three main "unexceptional" means: (1) wire or bank-to-bank transfers from overseas to the United States; (2) hand carrying cash or traveler's checks into the United States; and (3) debit or credit cards to access funds held in foreign financial institutions. Instead of going through ostensibly weak spots, tax havens, secrecy jurisdictions, or "underground" channels, all of the hijackers used the U.S. banking system to store their funds and facilitate their transactions. Contrary to media and popular belief, The 9/11 Commission Report noted that "there is no evidence the hijackers ever used false Social Security numbers to open any bank accounts" and "no financial institution filed a Suspicious Activity Report . . . with respect to any transaction of any of the 19 hijackers before 9/11."[30]

There is a growing consensus among experts that militants are now moving more towards informal value transfer methods as a result of increased international attention paid by regulatory and law enforcement agencies to formal banking sectors after the September 11 attacks. Such methods are preferred because of their reliability and assumed lower detectability.[31] Hand deliveries through trusted individuals, in particular, are presumably on the rise and have indeed been used by al Qaeda and many other groups.[32]

INTERNATIONAL TRADE

An even greater problem lies in the nearly unregulated international trading system, where it is almost impossible to disentangle truthful from deceptive international trade and invoicing practices. This is an area in which tremendous wealth crosses borders without leaving traces and without raising suspicions, as the paperwork and shipments may look perfectly legitimate to outside inspection. Under- and over-invoicing practices are very frequent even for "ordinary" purposes, such as corruption, tax evasion, fraud, and capital flight.[33] They amount to billions of dollars in transactions each year and can evidently provide cover for terrorist finance.[34] For example, by creating a $350,000 invoice for computer or medical equipment actually valued at $300,000 and using otherwise perfectly legitimate-looking and proper paperwork, it is possible to transfer $50,000 without raising red flags even for customs officials checking the shipment. One would have to have specific information on market prices and check on the specifications of the equipment in order to discover such invoice manipulation, an occurrence that is highly unlikely due to the enormous volume of international trade.

The improper invoicing in the honey trade by al Qaeda supporters, even if it has not been confirmed in any court of law, is but a hint of what militants may have been doing and, more importantly, what they may do next.[35] By simply understating the value of a commodity, the seller can easily provide funds to the buyer, who sells it at a higher price and keeps the difference for any legal or criminal purpose, including finance of terrorist operations. The volume of trade and glaring control inefficiencies render this an area in need of urgent attention. Interviews with U.S. Customs officials and analysis of U.S. import data demonstrate that there are serious gaps in the way the United States and other governments deal with trade transactions. Incomplete, erroneous, or illegal documentation can be found through routine review of forms filed with customs authorities.

SCOPE AND ORGANIZATION OF TERRORIST FINANCING

Little is known about the amount of money involved in terrorist financing and how this is distributed within terrorist organizations. As a result, it is difficult to know whether financial controls targeting large transactions or smaller sums may be more useful and where these controls should be targeted.

It is widely agreed that individual terrorist operations are surprisingly inexpensive. The first World Trade Center attack is estimated to have cost less than $19,000; the Bali bombings less then $20,000; the Madrid train bombing about $10,000;[36] and a reported attempt at chemical attack in Amman, Jordan, that might have caused large numbers of fatalities would have cost about $180,000. The 9/11 operation cost an estimated $350,000– 500,000 over many months. The truth is that such small amounts cannot be stopped.

After noting the low cost of terrorist attacks, most analysts are usually quick to point out that it is expensive to maintain a terrorist organization. This affirmation, however, must be viewed critically. Depending on the anticipated longevity, size, and objectives of a group, large infrastructures may or may not be necessary to support its activities. Many insurgent and militant organizations have extensive recruitment, arming, training, command and control, welfare, education and social work, intelligence, and other functions to perform, especially when they succeed in bringing geographic areas under their direct control, as was the case with the FARC, Hezbollah, and the LTTE. Al Qaeda has operated in this fashion in the past, when it was based in Sudan and later in Afghanistan. According to CIA estimates accepted by the 9/11 Commission, al Qaeda had a $30 million budget for the overall organization. For this amount of funding—most of which needed to be raised internationally and thus required fund transfers—the type of financial controls introduced in the aftermath of 9/11 are not unreasonable. It is not clear, however, whether al Qaeda in its current form requires (or possesses) such large amounts of funding or whether the raising and distribution of funds continues to be organized in the same manner as before.

The amount of money available to al Qaeda (or to other terrorist organizations) is a matter of some debate. Current estimates of terrorist revenues, with the notable exception of The 9/11 Commission Report, are often out of touch with the empirical reality as it emerges from trial evidence and investigations. If we put together all the theories available to explain al Qaeda financing, the group would have to be awash with millions of dollars from rough diamonds, gold, charitable donations, legitimate businesses, and criminal enterprises, including drug trafficking. Yet operatives have been found to be under-resourced or required to raise their own funds for operations. For example, as al Qaeda departed the Sudan for Afghanistan, many operatives were left behind because leaders could not afford to pay their agents' modest salaries. And the militants behind the first World Trade Center attack regretted not having a few thousand dollars more to pack additional explosives and increase their impact.[37]

Different assumptions of what is, or what has become of, al Qaeda lead to radically different policy approaches and measures.[38] To the extent that al Qaeda now operates more as an idea or worldview that inspires locally operating individuals and groups, the amount of funds we would be seeking to control would be much smaller, the means used to raise them would vary widely and depend on the local conditions, ordinary crime might be used frequently, there would be much less need for fund transfers, and the communications among groups (or other intelligence we may seek to extract by monitoring such operations) would be minimal. By contrast, if we believe al Qaeda is a relatively stable network or even possesses some elements of a hierarchical organization, then we would expect more predictable flows of information and monies that could be targeted with the policies in place against the financing of terrorism, based on models used in anti-money laundering (AML) and counter-drug efforts. Interestingly, to the extent that U.S.-led efforts degrade the more stable organizational patterns and network nodes of al Qaeda, such as those that existed in Afghanistan under the Taliban, we may yet complete this movement's transformation into a loose coalition of small cells held together by a worldview rather than a network— an unintended consequence that would make them very difficult to identify and attack.

Policy Challenges

In the aftermath of 9/11, a number of policies and measures were implemented in order to track and stop money flows to terrorists, their groups, and their supporters by identifying and freezing their assets. The United States led the way with aggressive laws, joint task forces, a new emphasis on terrorist finance in law enforcement, and international efforts.[39] In addition to the speedy entry into force of the UN Convention for the Suppression of the Financing of Terrorism, the Financial Action Task Force (FATF) published new recommendations specially designed to fight terrorist finance, and countries had to report regularly to the UN on their progress toward implementation of a variety of measures. In general, new controls enabled government authorities to trace the source and destination of various funds and assets,[40] task forces were set up to investigate and prosecute terrorist financing,[41] international cooperation between countries and agencies was encouraged,[42] new laws criminalized the financing of terrorism, know-your-customer and suspicious activity reporting requirements contributed to promoting greater financial transparency,[43] and name-and-shame policies sought to induce compliance.

The success of these controls has been measured most often by the amount of money and number of bank accounts that have been frozen, or the number of suspicious activity reports filed by financial institutions. By these standards, controls over formal financial institutions may be considered successful. Even though it is difficult to determine how many terrorist attacks have actually been thwarted by these actions, it is possible that amounts that could have been used to support militant infrastructures or operations have been taken away.

However, we do not know yet to what extent state responses have been ineffective, counterproductive, or have produced collateral damage. We need to identify priorities and critical intermediate goals of maximizing compliance and increasing the transparency and traceability of both financial and trade transactions. Priorities can only be set properly on the basis of solid evidence and careful analysis. If we do no systematic and careful studies, if we have little analytic capacity, priorities and policies in general are more likely to be misguided.

ACHIEVING TRANSPARENCY AND TRACEABILITY IN FINANCIAL AND TRADE TRANSACTIONS

We need to recognize that countering terrorist finance is not the same as anti-money laundering. Money laundering occurs when dirty funds are intended for legitimate use and need to show a legally acceptable origin. If funds, dirty or clean, are to be used for criminal or terrorist purposes, there is simply no need for laundering them. Gun runners and nuclear proliferators do not ask for receipts or explanations on the provenance of funds. In addition, the amounts involved in terrorist transactions pale by comparison to the volume of criminal proceeds laundered, suggesting that alternatives to the AML mechanisms should be developed to target this area.

This is not to say that AML mechanisms are useless in controlling terrorist financing. The data provided by AML measures is necessary to understand terrorist activities, even if only ex post facto. Otherwise there is little irregular or uncommon about the transactions before the identification of terrorist actors. The data provided are useful to both prosecutors and intelligence agencies. Also, to the extent that we go on designating supporters of terrorist groups and freezing or seizing their assets, sympathizers willing to offer financial support will wish to cover their name and the origin of their funds. In such scenarios, it is plausible to assume that money laundering infrastructures may also be used for this purpose. A chief aim of financial controls is to achieve transparency and traceability of transactions, thereby enabling the identification of suspicious transactions and gaining the ability to monitor activities, prevent or stop serious crimes, and facilitate the investigation and punishment of those involved. A partnership with the private sector is indispensable to achieve this.[44] However, the best way to earn this cooperation is by implementing rules and procedures that do not produce unmanageable burdens for private entities or the government agencies that regulate them. Otherwise, the all too likely result is evasion and non-compliance.

Some recent regulatory requirements miss their target. Both bank compliance officers and government officials have confirmed what the 9/11 Commission reported: the 9/11 hijackers' financial activities were not unusual, did not trigger reports by financial institutions, and should not have done so, either. The point, reiterated in both the United States and overseas, is that even if the rules we have now were in place before 9/11, including the FATF's nine special recommendations, the terrorists' activities would not have been red-flagged.

Another example where regulation is missing its target in the United States is the informal money transfer sector, or *hawala*-type networks. This is because of federal requirements to register, keep records, and file suspicious activities reports. At the state level, most jurisdictions require licensing and impose rules, such as ones demanding hundreds of thousands of dollars worth of bond or capitalization, that are hardly realistic and affordable. No corner store helping immigrants send their small remittances back home can afford this. So, they either stop offering the service or do not comply. Media articles and reports of crackdowns on unlicensed remitters since 9/11 point to a de facto "criminalization" of informal remitters and constitute indicators of increased underground activity rather than successful controls.[45] An alternative worth considering in addressing this form of IVTS is the British approach to *hawala* regulation, one that is intelligence-led and risk-based. In addition, the requirements on informal and other remitters (not just *hawala*) are affordable and more reasonable than in the United States. As a result, authorities in the United Kingdom can target problematic operators or businesses without driving everyone underground.

We need to transcend the notion that one set of standards can be equally productive, useful, or applicable throughout the world. Instead, we should take into account the context of each region, properly prioritize sectors to be regulated by vulnerability and risk, and, most importantly, stop employing formal and legalistic criteria of compliance and begin judging the effect and efficiency of measures on the substance of the problem.

When it comes to funds for specific operations, we are indeed searching for a needle in a gigantic haystack. Over-zealousness and too-strict enforcement of new rules and regulations to achieve unrealistic policy objectives may backfire. The more effort required to meet these new requirements, the more tempted people will be to see them as unnecessary, particularly if the rules are not considered legitimate and the benefits are not immediate and obvious.

AVOIDING COUNTERPRODUCTIVE POLICIES

Some of the measures may be not just ineffective in increasing transparency, traceability, and prevention of terrorist finance but also counter-productive. As the 9/11 Commission and others have pointed out, in several cases, asset freezing and designations turned out to be premature and problematic.[46] Most of the funds and assets that have been frozen are of "suspected" or "alleged" terrorists and supporters.[47] In many cases, there has been no evidence at all to support the arrests, freezing of assets, and statements that government officials have made, leaving innocent people to pick up their lives where they left off after being uprooted based on suspicions and weak evidence, through processes that afford them no opportunity to challenge their designation, and without formal charges leveled against them.[48] This lack of due process undermines the legitimacy of the U.S. counter-terrorist financing efforts and the willingness of others to cooperate in said efforts.

In seeking to control militant fund-raising, we also need to understand and appreciate the consequences of financial controls for the larger communities that they operate within. Unrealistic and aggressive practices against ethnic money remitters may not produce any results and may alienate communities that would otherwise be inclined to join in coalitions against terrorism. Similar points can be made with respect to charities. At the very least, we should not be creating new motives for sympathizers and outsiders to support or turn a blind eye to terrorist actions. In general, there has been little effort to calculate the *costs* of CTF methods in general. When collateral damage is foreseeable, our preference should be monitoring and intelligence gathering approaches rather than a focus solely on ending the practice.

RESPECTING FUNDAMENTAL DEMOCRATIC LEGAL PRINCIPLES

For some, legitimacy is a goal in itself; for others, it is a pre-condition for success in the long term. Either way it is a *conditio sine qua non* for effective policies and long-term success. We cannot defend democracy, human rights, and due process by undermining them at home or internationally. Legitimacy can be strengthened and preserved as we make clear and visible efforts to

- act on the basis of solid evidence and sound analysis;
- minimize negative consequences of CTF policies for innocent actors;
- protect our Constitution, strengthen the rule of law, and abide by international principles we have long promoted;
- promote effective and efficient policies and measures in collaboration with other countries and international bodies, thus speeding up the exchange of information and reducing unnecessary and avoidable administrative or legal asymmetries; and
- address root causes of terrorism beyond military and law enforcement actions.

Conclusion

We may have been successful in neutralizing the organizational infrastructure of al Qaeda in Afghanistan, but many mechanisms of financial control to counter terrorism need re-thinking and re-adjustment. This not an appeal for reform only on legal, ethical, or moral grounds but also to improve the effectiveness of CTF policies in the United States and the international community. In some respects, we have been fighting terror with error, causing collateral damage to ourselves.

In many ways, terrorism is cheap, and small amounts of financing will always be available to any militant cause. We have to clearly identify our priorities, collect and analyze critically the evidence on their financing and support, and then focus on consistently applied policies that minimize the externalities and adverse effects.

We must keep working to facilitate monitoring and to enable investigations, as well as to enhance cooperation within and across national borders.

We must not lose sight of our critical intermediate goals: to maximize compliance, to increase transparency and traceability in economic transactions (both financial and trade), and to control financial crime. An important but as yet unaddressed vulnerability is that of trade transparency; dealing with that problem is imperative and urgent. These goals can be attained through consensus building efforts with the private sector, our own communities, and allies so as to maximize the legitimacy of CTF policies.

CHAPTER THREE

Organized Crime and Terrorism

JOHN T. PICARELLI AND LOUISE I. SHELLEY

Although recent discussions of terrorism have tended to focus on either state sponsorship, popular support, or legitimate businesses as sources of funding, organized crime has increasingly become an important avenue for terrorist financing. Unlike other sources of terrorist financing, crime provides both pecuniary and logistical assistance to terrorist groups. In addition, the evolution of a more sophisticated and globally interconnected illicit political economy offers an increasing number and breadth of opportunities for terrorists to engage in criminal activities.

In this chapter, we examine four major questions at the intersection of crime and terrorist financing. First, why do terrorists turn to crime? Second, what kinds of criminal activities are most attractive to terrorist groups? Third, what ramifications might knowing how terrorists engage in crime hold for our understanding of terrorist and organized crime groups? And, finally, what practical measures can we suggest based on an increased understanding of the terrorist-criminal synthesis?

To answer these questions, we draw on the initial findings of our year-long investigation into the convergences and divergences among transnational criminal organizations and international terrorist groups. Using case studies, official reports, and interviews with key stakeholders, as well as empirical data on transactions among different actors, we hope to identify areas of cooperation and convergence between organized crime and terrorism.

Our research suggests at least two realities. First, the range of interactions between terrorists and criminals is much more diverse than is commonly assumed. Second, these interactions encompass a wider range of illegal financing sources than law enforcement or intelligence communities tend to consider. Although the terrorist-criminal synthesis is of the greatest intensity and duration in the major conflict regions, including such areas as Northern Ireland, Colombia, West Africa, Asia, and parts of the former Soviet Union, the patterns of interaction that we discuss are not geographically confined or limited to one form of terrorist organization. They are also highly prevalent in urban areas in developed countries in North America, Western Europe, and Australia.

Motives and Benefits for Terrorists to Engage in Criminal Activities

Terrorist groups are turning to crime and to criminals for assistance for several reasons. In the past, the predominant source of terrorist financing was state sponsorship. The close of the Cold War and the international community's increasing emphasis and agreement on counter-terrorism led to a decline in the number of potential state sponsors of terrorism as well as the overall amount of sponsorship. New forms of financing have arisen to supplant these lost funds. Crime, specifically forms of organized crime (defined as crime that involves repeated activity involving more than two people), rose in prominence as a source of terrorist financing. Networks of terrorist cells cooperate among themselves and with criminals to engage in crime.

As a method of financing, crime provides cash on a rapid and repeatable basis for terrorist groups. If one thinks of terrorist financing as a portfolio, legitimate businesses and charities certainly provide some income. Proceeds from criminal enterprises, however, allow terrorists to diversify financial sources and to diffuse risk across multiple sources of financing. Terrorist groups seek to avoid leaving evidence of their operations in the legitimate business world, where law enforcement and security forces can easily obtain business and transaction records. Money obtained through crime, however, allows terrorist groups to operate in shadow or gray markets—away from the eyes of regulators or of detailed record keepers.

Funds earned from crime do not always require laundering since they are often used to purchase items or services in these same black or gray economies. The monies earned in criminal enterprises can remain stored in the same illicit political economy, available for purchasing fraudulent documents, arms, or for funding the movement of operatives via smuggling groups. However, such money need not be used for such nefarious activities. The payment of apartment rental fees "off the books" in cash or the purchase of automobiles directly from a private citizen can be made without raising suspicion. Such "off the books" practices can reduce the risk of detection by state authorities or other monitoring agencies.

Criminal activities can directly enhance the operational capabilities of terrorist groups through the provision of goods and services that mimic the services offered in the legitimate business world while bypassing regulatory structures designed to frustrate terrorist groups. Document fraud, for example, provides terrorists the ability to move within and across national borders with reduced risk of discovery. Smuggling moves supplies and personnel quietly into place for operations without risking exposure during customs exams or accidental discoveries by private sector hauling companies. Corruption also provides terrorist groups safe haven and protection from prosecution. Terrorist groups often engage in other forms of organized crime, such as operating protection rackets or brothels in regions under their control or using smuggling networks to move narcotics. Often this is done in conjunction with the criminals. Each of these forms of crime putatively provides terrorist groups additional security and increased operational proficiency, while helping generate the revenue needed.

In sum, terrorists turn to crime and criminals to obtain needed funds and services to run their operations. As the following sections will demonstrate, terrorist involvement in crime for financial gain is shaped by the different criminal opportunities available in their environment, their contact with criminal groups, their own organizational capabilities, and the entry costs (i.e., the funds and equipment required to start up a venture as well as the levels of competition from criminal groups). In contrast, terrorist reliance on crime to fulfill their operational and logistical goals is driven by need.

TERRORIST RELIANCE ON CRIME AS A SOURCE OF
FINANCIAL SUPPORT

Terrorist groups continue to engage in a wide range of criminal activities. The nexus between drugs and terrorist funding has been widely discussed. Increasingly, however, terrorists are turning from drugs to other areas of illicit activity—where the competition is not so high and the risks of being apprehended are much lower. Although we need to briefly address the familiar linkages between terrorism financing and drugs, we will concentrate on exploring the growing diversity of crime connections.

Narcotics still remain the most significant money generator in the illicit political economy, and analyses often link terrorist groups with this criminal activity. Ties between the drug trade and terrorism have been well documented, from Colombia to Thailand to Afghanistan. Having re-emerged on a massive scale in northern Afghanistan, the drug trade in Afghanistan owes part of its resurgence to groups in Pakistan connected with, or sympathetic to, the remnants of the Taliban.[1] Numerous reports continue to link al Qaeda and its sub-organizations to the drug trade as one of their vehicles for generating funds for operations.[2] In addition, the bizarre and dangerous Aum Shinrikyo cult has used its knowledge of chemistry and its profound production capabilities to produce and sell major amounts of methamphetamine—the drug of choice in Japan.

Terrorists, particularly those operating in Africa, have been linked to illicit trade in natural resources. Experts tracing an elaborate international trade linking weapons dealers to illegally harvested diamonds from Africa have uncovered connections to terrorist groups, particularly al Qaeda.[3] Likewise, reports of similar patterns found in the tanzanite market led to a U.S. State Department investigation in 2002, which resulted in the Tucson protocols—an international agreement that increases the safeguards and transparency of the tanzanite market. Terrorists have reportedly tapped into other international extractive markets that include oil, precious metals, and even timber. Douglas Farah's testimony before the U.S. House of Representatives cited evidence of terrorist involvement in the illicit trade in diamonds, gold, tanzanite, and other gemstones.[4]

Other forms of smuggling also provide important sources of capital for terrorist groups. Cigarette smuggling has proved to be a lucrative outlet for terrorists. One cigarette smuggling ring in North Carolina helped fund

Hezbollah.[5] The research of our money laundering team also found that a cigarette firm in the country of Georgia that was heavily engaged in cigarette smuggling had questionable Iraqi investors.[6] The Royal Canadian Mounted Police (RCMP) has reported that Hezbollah leaders tapped into the trade of automobiles and vehicles stolen and smuggled from North America by criminal groups. Ten percent of the profits of this illegal trade were contributed to the cause.[7] This smuggling can be done by the terrorists alone or in conjunction with crime groups.

Terrorists also participate in the illicit movement of human beings, which often links them to crime groups working in this arena. Such movement comes in two predominant forms. To support their own operations, terrorist groups have paid alien smugglers to deliver one or more persons to a specified country. Terrorists also garner profits from the lucrative transnational criminal enterprise in human smuggling. Evidence suggests that the Liberation Tigers of Tamil Eelam (LTTE) are involved in smuggling of Sri Lankans.[8] Likewise, experts have also tied the Partiya Karkaren Kurdistan (PKK) to alien smuggling. Finally, numerous incidents have tied Islamic fundamentalist terrorist groups to migrants smuggled from North Africa into Italy.

The other, more pernicious, form of illicit movement of people involves the recruitment and movement of men, women, and children into slavery and labor exploitation. While such trafficking is not often associated with terrorist groups, some examples indicate their involvement. For example, Maoist insurgents in Nepal have financed their activities by exploiting the long-standing trade of young girls taken from Nepal and placed in the brothels of India.[9]

Adopting another form of organized crime, terrorists have long used extortion for the purpose of raising funds. In 1971, the United Nations adopted a Convention to Prevent and Punish Acts of Terrorism Taking the Form of Crimes against Persons and Related Extortion. Noted examples include payments made by Middle Eastern businesspeople to al Qaeda to prevent attacks on their interests and the collection of "revolutionary taxes" from Filipino residents and businesses by the Abu Sayyaf Group.[10] Likewise, terrorist groups often exploit overseas émigré communities through protection rackets and extortion. Such schemes are used not only by ethnonationalist groups like the LTTE and the PKK but also by Islamic fundamentalist groups in northern Italy. Finally, Hezbollah is known to collect payments from Arab-owned illicit and licit businesses in the Tri-Border region of Argentina, Brazil, and Paraguay, often collecting up to 20 percent of the income of Lebanese store owners.[11] In territories it controls, the FARC practices this type of extortion against large-scale cattle ranchers and other businesses.

Related to extortion, terrorists have turned to kidnapping, not only as an operational tactic, as in Iraq, but also as a traditional form of obtaining money. For example, the Abu Sayyaf Group repeatedly kidnapped foreign tourists and aid workers—in one case receiving ransom payments of several million dollars. Kidnapping has also been used in Russia and Colombia to fund terrorist activity.[12] In another example, in 2003, the Salafist Group for Prayer and Combat (SGPC) in Algeria tried to collect $2.2 million from the Algerian government for the release of Western tourists they had kidnapped.[13]

Counterfeiting of both goods and fiscal instruments is a tried and true source of terrorist funding. Recent advances in technology have made this even easier and cheaper. The production of counterfeit goods in the Tri-Border Area of Argentina, Brazil, and Paraguay remains an important source of terrorist funding.[14] Counterfeiters focus on all types of intellectual property, including technology and commercial goods like compact discs, digital video discs, shampoos, perfume, shoes, and computers. Interpol has identified numerous cases of intellectual property theft, citing examples from Russia, Serbia, Lebanon, and other countries.[15] The counterfeiting and sale of airline tickets has also proved to be a lucrative money generator for terrorist groups. This activity is sometimes perpetrated in conjunction with criminals who are in the document fraud business. A terrorism expert in the United Kingdom's Home Office noted that while enterprises like the ones described here are often smaller in scope than other criminal enterprises, the average profits measure in the tens to hundreds of thousands—sums significant enough to mount localized terror campaigns.[16] Finally, one cannot overlook that terrorists make money the old-fashioned way: they print it. Reports have noted that Hezbollah uses sophisticated Itaglio presses for the manufacture of U.S. currency.[17]

Terrorists have adopted three other staples of the illicit political economy. Fraud and scams remain popular choices with terrorist groups such as al Qaeda, Hezbollah, and Hamas. In one example, a Middle Eastern man sponsored a retail coupon scam (where retailers submit unused coupons for payment from manufacturers) in a series of stores he owned and used the profits to support one of the 1993 World Trade Center bombers. Credit card theft and fraud continue to be used by terrorists. Canadian authorities have linked forms of credit card fraud to Ahmed Ressam, the Millennium plot leader, as well as to operatives of the SGPC.[18] Finally, armed robbery remains a standard method for groups to raise funds.

In table 3.1, we present a basic comparison of the criminal enterprises discussed in this section and the reasons why terrorist groups might select them. Our analysis focuses on the three elements driving participation in particular crimes for fund-raising purposes: capabilities, opportunities, and entry costs. We have also found examples where criminal and terrorist groups have collaborated to profit from these criminal enterprises. A recent study by the Transnational Crime and Corruption Center discovered that the depth and breadth of crime-terror interaction is far more complex than most experts believe.[19]

Most criminal enterprises require little or no expertise, and terrorists will tend to gravitate initially to those areas that do not require special capabilities. For example, kidnapping, extortion, and armed robbery are often chosen because they require force but limited skill. In areas with ineffective law enforcement, terrorists have a chance to refine their capabilities at the beginning of their criminal careers with limited chance of arrest. In areas that require the most expertise such as identity theft, counterfeiting, and trafficking in persons and smuggling of goods, terrorists often use the services or the support structures of the crime groups. Therefore, they are able to easily obtain access to specialists.

Similarly, most terrorists find that there are abundant opportunities for illicit enrichment. Many of the crimes listed present an almost unlimited market for criminal entrepreneurs. For example, an increasing demand for the services of human smugglers, coupled with the enormous demand for cheap or enslaved labor, suggests that there are substantial possibilities for profit. Terrorists' choice of criminal activities seem to be most often shaped by the degree (or lack of) law enforcement in their environment, the availability of targets of opportunity to be exploited, and the possibility of observing and learning from other criminals.

In contrast, about half of the criminal enterprises present at least moderate entry costs—through required start-up capital outlays or barriers to entry created by the existence of competition from criminal groups. The franchising system that al Qaeda established to provide initial funding for a

TABLE 3.1 *Comparison of Possible Terrorist-Related Criminal Enterprises*

CRIMES	CAPABILITIES	ENTRY COSTS	OPPORTUNITIES
Narcotics smuggling	Expertise required for production, but little to no expertise required for transport or distribution.	Moderate financial outlays. Likely barriers due to high competition.	Limited for production of agriculturally based drugs. Open for transportation and distribution assuming demand is present.
Commodity smuggling	Little expertise required.	Moderate to acquire commodities. Barriers include access to commodities or linkages to those with access.	Limited markets and opportunities to access resources.
Goods smuggling	Little expertise required.	Low, though some types of goods might require some financial outlays or present competition barriers.	Nearly unlimited.
Migrant smuggling	Some knowledge of border controls required.	Low, though some borders might require access to fraudulent documents or payments to border guards.	Somewhat limited due to the nature of global migratory flows.
Trafficking in persons	Expertise required in the recruitment and exploitation phases.	Moderate costs and barriers depending on the form of exploitation. Low for recruitment and movement phases.	Nearly unlimited.
Extortion	Little expertise required.	Low costs and barriers, save	Nearly unlimited in areas where the

	Expertise required	Costs and barriers	Scale / Limitations
		for competing sources of private protection.	authority of the central government is poor.
Kidnapping	Little expertise required.	Low costs and few barriers.	Nearly unlimited.
Intellectual property theft	Moderate technical expertise required.	Moderate costs for access to technical equipment for production. Few barriers for distribution save costs of acquisition.	Nearly unlimited.
Counterfeiting	Moderate expertise required. Expertise dependent on the level of awareness of counterfeit instruments.	Moderate to high costs for access to technology and defeating anti-counterfeiting measures.	Limitations directly related to the quality of the counterfeit instrument.
Fraud	Little expertise required.	Low costs and few barriers.	Limited only by the prevalence of targets for the fraud.
Credit card theft	Little expertise required.	Low costs and few barriers.	Nearly unlimited.
Armed robbery	Little expertise required.	Costs related to measures required to defeat security measures.	Somewhat limited to the range of potential victims present in the area of operation.

cell's operations was an important way that terrorists could obtain the initial working capital to set up criminal enterprises of their choosing. This initial funding bought equipment, obtained technological advice, or helped sustain the terrorist cell while the members worked to make their illegal business viable. For terrorists without the luxury of initial funding, entry-level crimes can provide the capital needed to expand into more sophisticated crimes. Competition from criminal groups presents a significant barrier to entry in many cases, particularly in drug markets. As a result, terrorists seem to be gravitating toward less-saturated criminal markets in an effort to avoid turf wars with existing crime groups.

TERRORIST RELIANCE ON CRIME AS A SOURCE OF LOGISTICAL SUPPORT

Several of the criminal enterprises listed in table 3.1 may also be used to support the logistical needs of terrorist groups. Since passports and visas are critical to the movement of personnel within and across national borders, terrorist groups invest significant resources into obtaining these documents—usually through document fraud. For example, the French investigation of false passports given to a terrorist cell planning to assassinate the Turkish president revealed that their document source was the same cell that supported Ahmed Ressam's plot to bomb Los Angeles International Airport.[20] Likewise, electronic surveillance transcripts of Rabei Osman Sayed Ahmed's conversation from his al Qaeda support cell located in Milan recorded the following comment about false documents:

> Stay calm because I will buy you the documents, the documents are there but we have to be very careful. The documents have a value and we can easily find them, but if you don't know who used them it is dangerous, because if one was burnt then you are ruined. And you also have to look at the quality. There are documents that you only need to heat, like this one for example, you heat it, you change the picture and you're fine, even if the stamp is dry, but the important thing is that the name is not burnt.[21]

It is clear from this quotation that terrorists place a high priority on false documents and have developed the necessary skill to select and produce those documents or use the same suppliers as sophisticated criminal enterprises.

Another form of organized crime that supports the operations of terrorist groups is money laundering. Money laundering allows terrorist groups to retain and use funds acquired from illicit or non-traditional sources, while reducing the risk that such funds might trigger suspicion from regulators or businesses. While some methods, like wire transfers and *hawala* networks, have garnered significant interest, financial transfers are also made through offshore banks. The secrecy of these banks and their lack of cooperation with international law enforcement authorities had meant that money placed in offshore locales could not be traced. Yet as greater controls were established over this banking sector, terrorists are moving their funds in more underground ways or using non-traditional practices of money movement. Our research highlighted significant movements of cash, particularly in cross-border areas where little oversight exists, and in locations that are manned by corrupt customs and border guard officials. Anecdotal evidence also points to the use of auction houses and art dealers to store and move funds tied to terrorist groups.

Smuggling also provides logistical support. As mentioned earlier, while migrant smuggling can generate funds, the skills and methods employed can also provide a mechanism for moving terrorists across borders. Senior members of U.S. Customs and Border Protection patrolling the borders in the American Southwest revealed to us that dozens of terrorist suspects were apprehended in fiscal year 2004. Furthermore, arms smuggling is a critical requirement of terrorists, who have near constant need for a range of armaments and explosives. In return for payments of narcotics, the Basque nationalist organization ETA contracted with the Camorra's Genovese clan of Avellino in 2001 to secure missile launchers and ammunition.[22] Likewise, a major Balkan organized crime faction led by a Tunisian named Mohamad bin Saleh bin Hmeidi specializes in smuggling migrants, narcotics, and arms. He is wanted for supplying arms to the IRA, the ETA, Islamic terrorist groups, and Italian mafia families.[23]

Terrorists may also funnel money into their host countries to fulfill their operational goals. This can take the form of officially sanctioned payments to the host governments for their hospitality or of payoffs to corrupt lower-level officials. During the 1990s, Osama bin Laden made payments to Sudan to secure his safe haven there. When he fled to Afghanistan, he continued to pay off Taliban officials for allowing him safe haven and permission to set up terrorist training camps. In addition, terrorists have used corruption at a tactical level, bribing local law enforcement officials, border guards, or others to accomplish operational goals, which is often possible because such networks and practices have been previously established by criminal organizations.

All of these cases illustrate that the set of forces driving terrorist groups to crime is not the same as those in table 3.1, which listed opportunities, capabilities, and entry costs as the main factors shaping terrorists' decisions to engage in crime for fund-raising purposes. Crime for logistical purposes, however, is driven primarily by necessity, even if opportunity and capability might play a secondary role. In the next section, we take up some of the ramifications of this analysis.

Risks for Terrorists Engaging in Criminal Activity

Our analysis identified two types of risks for the terrorists who engage in criminal activity. First, terrorists who choose criminal enterprises to raise funds may become distracted from their perceived mission. Second, terrorists create another area of vulnerability to government authorities when they participate heavily in criminal activities. Terrorist groups may not fully evaluate the risks inherent in criminal activities until they are well caught up in their criminal careers. For example, the IRA's recent involvement in a $45 million bank robbery raises the question of whether the IRA's long-standing criminal activities have weakened its identity as an organization solely motivated by political goals.

EFFECTS ON ORGANIZATIONAL GOALS AND EFFICIENCY

While criminal enterprises provide a somewhat stable source of income, terrorist groups must manage the risks if they want to survive. The adage "one man's terrorist is someone else's freedom fighter" points to the enormous divergence of opinions over some of these politically motivated "terrorist" groups. The guerrillas in Colombia, some of the jihadists in the Middle East, and the IRA in Northern Ireland enjoy strong support from the communities in which they operate. Nevertheless, if their criminal activities become harmful to the community or introduce either increased violence or health risks to citizens in that community, terrorists may jeopardize the support of those local communities essential to their operational effectiveness.

Terrorist groups that traffic in drugs may harm the communities in which they operate. Few families want to see their children become addicted to drugs or fall victim to drug related violence. To counter this appearance, terrorists involved in the drug trade often pass on profits to peasants or even provide needed social services to the local community.

The use of corruption also brings into question the motives of terrorist groups. One of the greatest sources of strength for Islamic terrorist groups is their opposition to the corrupt governments aligned with the West. To maintain the integrity of their organizations and their political goals, they are thus hesitant to bribe officials and participate in other forms of corruption. When they bribe officials to allow drug shipments to move across borders, buy border guards to smuggle migrants, or pay off officials to avoid arrest, they are denying their very raison d'être: fighting the venal and corrupt states that rule their countries and regions.

Criminal involvement thus appears to be a double-edged sword. Research into al Qaeda and other Islamic fundamentalist groups highlights the *fatwa*s that have excused those resorting to crime as a necessary means of furthering jihad and its struggle with the infidel. In the case of al Qaeda, a 1998 *fatwa* stated that a Muslim could steal money from "the Infidel" so long as at least 20 percent of criminal earnings went to the jihadists. As a result, French cells associated with Salafist terrorist groups ramped up petty and organized crime, keeping 80 percent of their earnings and sending 20 percent along for operations.[24] However, there is some evidence of a decline in support for the FARC and Abu Sayyaf as these groups have come to be seen as divorced from their ideological goals by participating in criminal activities.

RISK OF INCREASED VULNERABILITY TO LAW ENFORCEMENT

Of course, criminal activities also increase the risk of detection. Terrorists come under the surveillance of not only those seeking to detect terrorists but also the full range of law enforcement bodies organized to fight crime. The risk from law enforcement has tended to be highest in narcotics trafficking, the most common means of financing terrorist activity. With increasing harmonization of laws and coordination of legal and intelligence efforts in the narcotics arena, there is an increasing risk of both detection of personnel and confiscation of assets. By engaging in a variety of illicit activities, terrorists diversify their sources of financial supply as well as diminish their risk of detection and confiscation of assets. Profits from criminal activities outside the narcotics arena are less likely to be seized by law enforcement. Furthermore, by committing a wide range of criminal activities, such as credit card fraud, cigarette smuggling, and counterfeiting of airline tickets, they fall under the scrutiny of different branches of law enforcement. Given the absence of information sharing among different law enforcement agencies outside the drug arena, terrorists can ensure the viability of their criminal activities and secure a steady flow of profits. In more general terms, there seems to be a growing tendency of terrorists to diversify the types of illicit activities in order to reduce their risk. In this way, they are responding to the same economic forces common to legitimate businesses that diversify to reduce risk.

The criminal activities engaged in by terrorists or in conjunction with criminals are often small scale. Therefore, the perpetrators are often apprehended as petty criminals, not recognized as terrorists, and are sent to prisons as small-time offenders. However, prisons provide terrorists with a new opportunity to recruit and organize their activities if the terrorists are not recognized and are mixed with the general prisoner population.[25]

Terrorists may also reduce their risk by outsourcing some of their activities, thus making it more difficult for law enforcement to establish a link between the law breaker and the terrorist organization. While both organized crime and terrorist groups normally avoid contact with external entities, these concerns are often set aside due to issues of pragmatism and opportunity. When the Provisional Irish Republican Army (PIRA), for example, needed a secure means to launder their funds into the licit economy, they used the services of four accountants.[26] None of the accountants were members or were previously associated with the PIRA.

The al Qaeda networks have also developed a strategy to reduce the risks associated with criminal activities. Al Qaeda cells are divided between support cells and operational cells. While the support cells exist by criminal activity, the operational cells do not. Therefore, those who are most vital to the execution of a terrorist act are not subject to the risk of exposure that participation in criminality raises.

Conclusion and Recommendations

Terrorists today use an increasing range of illicit activities to finance their activities and form links with criminals more frequently than many analysts have previously expected. While links between drug trafficking and terrorism draw the greatest attention, increasingly terrorists are diversifying their illicit activities to reduce risk and increase the dependability of financial flows. The forms of terrorist financing described in this chapter occur frequently in conflict zones and regions outside of the control of a central state. Yet many of these, including identity theft, document fraud, and credit card fraud, also occur in large urban centers. Terrorists in the United States have funded themselves through crime, even importing patterns of crime developed overseas. The Hezbollah involvement in cigarette smuggling in the Tri-Border Area in South America was replicated, for example, in North Carolina, as later chapters in this volume detail.

The challenges inherent in terrorist funding vary by location. In developed countries, this illicit activity of terrorists is often hidden under the shadow economies of immigrant communities. The cooperation of petty criminals and terrorist-motivated criminals—particularly within immigrant communities—often makes it hard to differentiate the phenomenon.

In developed countries, terrorist funding may involve even high-status individuals or institutions as money is moved through banks, high-priced real estate, and the sale and false invoicing of costly art or other artifacts. We have to be careful in assuming that terrorist funding operates only on the margins of society. Thus, understanding the diversity of crime activity of the terrorists is not enough; we must find its points of intersection with the legitimate economy.

Businesses outside the banking community, for example, are valuable sources of intelligence on suspicious financial movements. From our interviews and discussions with representatives of the business and intelligence communities, we see what appears to be a willingness to share information that might be related to terrorism. Both communities see real utility in establishing such a relationship. While significant issues related to privacy, liability, and trust affect this free sharing of information, businesses also recognize the costs of supporting terrorism and seem willing to cooperate in new ways to protect their reputations.

Those who seek to cut off terrorist funding find that the strategies that work in developed countries are rarely applicable in less-developed countries, which often suffer from the weakness of the state apparatus and the rule of law. Furthermore, they face even greater challenges when terrorist funds are commingled with other funding streams within the large shadow economies of conflict regions and failed or weak states. These challenges have far-reaching implications for international finance and investment, and the failure to address these problems may undermine the global economy or provoke poorly thought out and reactive government policies. We recommend a variety of strategies to target such challenges.

First, counter-terrorist agencies must begin to grapple with the centrality of criminal activity in the financing of terrorism. Law enforcement and the intelligence community have too often viewed terrorism and organized crime as separate phenomena and have ignored important warnings that have emanated from the criminal activities of terrorists. Therefore, they must give higher priority to analyzing and addressing the diverse range of criminal activities that fund terrorists. While still important, narcotics can no longer be seen as the predominant form of funding terrorism.

Second, the professional financial community must be educated as to their possible role in terrorist financing and their obligation not to be complicit. Many of the individuals who provide services unwittingly to terrorists do so because they are not asking sufficient questions or understanding the origins of their customers' assets. The USA Patriot Act establishes greater accountability in the U.S. financial system, but the United States needs to do more to export best practices in financial regulation and anti-money laundering mechanisms to other states with significant financial commodity markets. Professionals both inside and outside the banking sector should know and understand their customers.

Third, investigations into terrorist funding must also include the prosecution of high-status individuals. The U.S. government's failure after September 11 to investigate aggressively the role that Riggs Bank played in money laundering and possible terrorist funding suggests strategies that focused too heavily on the low forms of terrorist financing and the narcotics trade. Terrorist financing also involves bankers, art dealers, accountants, and others. These individuals must also be held responsible for their role in terrorist financing.

Fourth, governments need to encourage the development of a set of public-private partnerships to address terrorist financing. Currently, large financial service firms are simply writing off the cost of credit card fraud as the cost of doing business. Security specialists within these firms investigate only a small share of the criminal activities associated with these losses. Greater cooperation might lead to information sharing between private firms and law enforcement and intelligence officials, which might more effectively target credit card fraud and other terrorist criminal activity.

Fifth, law enforcement and intelligence should concentrate their attention on locating the logistical cells that provide support to terrorist operations groups. In the Ahmed Ressam case, Canadian authorities did not focus on investigating this cell because they thought of it as made up of petty criminals, even though the Canadians had been warned to the contrary by French authorities. Within the United States, the Los Angeles Police Department is at the forefront of addressing the criminal sources and connections of terrorist funding, and they should provide a model for American law enforcement in this area.

Sixth, we need to train and equip law enforcement agencies to better focus on the crime patterns of non-traditional criminal groups that may be allied with terrorists. The linkages between terrorists and criminals are strongest in conflict zones. Therefore, law enforcement should focus more closely on the crime activities of groups emanating from the Balkans, the Middle East, and the Afghan-Pakistani region. These groups may not be the largest or most powerful crime groups, but it is in these emerging crime areas that the terrorist funding link is most likely to be established.

Finally, tackling the financing of terrorism in conflict regions and in those regions outside of state control is enormously difficult. Embassies of the United States and other countries increasingly contain representatives from different law enforcement agencies. These representatives should be tasked to identify the terrorist crime patterns observed in these regions of greatest risk. Their observations could provide valuable assistance in identifying patterns and trends in terrorist financing and in the terrorist-criminal synthesis.

CHAPTER FOUR

Terrorist Organizations' Vulnerabilities and Inefficiencies

A Rational Choice Perspective

JACOB N. SHAPIRO

This chapter uses a rational choice approach to examine the political economy of terrorist financing. To date, much of the theoretical literature and almost all government-sponsored reports discuss terrorist organizations as though they are made up of ideologically driven purists who share a uniform commitment to the cause. This assumption is needed to explain how these organizations can both (1) efficiently distribute funds and (2) operate covertly without the checks and balances most organizations require. However, upon closer inspection, one often sees substantial differences in the preferences of key players in terrorist networks. Two selection processes explain why these differences exist, and a principal-agent framework shows how these differences lead to inefficiencies in terrorist financial systems. Terrorist organizations face a trade-off between enduring the inefficiency or employing corrective strategies that create vulnerabilities. Governments can undertake specific actions to make this trade-off more problematic.

With all due respect, this is not an accounting. It's a summary accounting. For example, you didn't write any dates, and many of the items are vague. The analysis of the summary shows the following:

1—You received a total of $22,301. Of course, you didn't mention the period over which this sum was received. Our activities only benefited from a negligible portion of the money. This means that you received and distributed the money as you please. . . .

2—Salaries amounted to $10,085—45 percent of the money. I had told you in my fax . . . that we've been receiving only half salaries for five months. What is your reaction or response to this?

3—Loans amounted to $2,190. Why did you give out loans? Didn't I give clear orders to Muhammad Saleh to . . . refer any loan requests to me? We have already had long discussions on this topic. . . .

4—Why have guesthouse expenses amounted to $1,573 when only Yunis is there, and he can be accommodated without the need for a guesthouse?

—Ayman al Zawahiri, e-mail to Yemeni cell, February 11, 1999[1]

Accountability

Standard accounts of terrorist financial and logistical systems stress the efficiency with which terrorist financial networks distribute funds while operating through a variety of covert channels. We are told that "Al Qaeda is notably and deliberately decentralized, compartmentalized, flexible, and diverse in its methods and targets. . . . Al Qaeda's financial network is characterized by layers and redundancies. It raises money from a variety of sources and moves money in a variety of manners."[2] Reports from the multinational Financial Action Task Force on Money Laundering,[3] the Asia/Pacific Group on Money Laundering,[4] and others provide a similar narrative.[5]

Because of the covert nature of their work, these networks must operate with fewer checks and balances than most financial organizations.[6] Indeed, the cellular structure of terrorist networks so often cited in the literature necessarily implies that leaders will be poorly informed about the actions of their subordinates.[7] If we assume that all members of the network are uniformly committed to the cause and all agree on how best to advance the group's political goals, then there is no inconsistency here. However, if leaders, middlemen, and operational cadres have divergent preferences over spending, then information asymmetries created by the secretive nature of terrorist networks lead to myriad opportunities for spending money differently than leaders would like.

While the evidence is mixed regarding disagreements between key terrorist leaders, there is good reason to believe that the preferences of middlemen are not always aligned with those of leaders and operational elements. For example, mid-level managers of organizations such as Harakat ul-Mujahidin (HUM), a Pakistani militant group focused on Kashmir, often live luxurious lives far beyond what their followers can afford.[8] Captured Palestine Liberation Organization (PLO) documents show that those who plan attacks are paid eight times as much as the families of those who die carrying out the attacks.[9] People running criminal fund-raising operations in the United States for Hezbollah drive luxury cars and live in upper-middle-class neighborhoods.[10] During the Christian-Muslim violence in Poso, Indonesia, in late 2000, a relatively senior Jemaah Islamiyah (JI) member arranged for funds raised from oil company workers to be channeled through one local militia, KOMPAK-Solo, to JI and another local militia, Mujahidin KOMPAK. The workers were so concerned about the probity of these transfers that they appointed an auditor to oversee the funds.[11] Arguments betweens moderates and extremists over strategy frequently occur in organizations contemplating making peace with the government.[12]

RATIONAL CHOICE

Several academic studies have noted that such variations in motivation can cause difficulties for terrorist groups.[13] However, none have explored the challenges such heterogeneity poses for terrorist financial systems.[14] This chapter offers a rational choice perspective, using agency theory, for analyzing these issues. The rational choice approach is particularly attractive for dealing with this type of problem because it presents the strategic and organizational dilemmas faced by terrorist groups in the starkest possible contrast. Doing so can help explain otherwise puzzling patterns of behavior.[15]

Terrorist groups face two adverse selection problems. The first is that those likely to survive for long periods in terrorist networks tend to be less ideologically committed and less likely to volunteer for the most dangerous missions.[16] The second is that, because participation as a financier or logistician is less risky than participating as a local leader or operator, middlemen in terrorist organizations tend to be less committed.

These two dynamics create a moral hazard problem for leaders. For security reasons, leaders (principals) have to delegate fund-raising and financial duties to middlemen (agents).[17] However, the agents can take advantage of the information asymmetries in the network to expropriate some funds, to shirk. Because the environment is noisy and security concerns prevent perfect monitoring, principals are uncertain whether the agents are passing on all the resources they bring in or are keeping a cut for themselves, a classic moral hazard problem. Leaders can solve this problem by providing enough money to middlemen so that, after the logisticians take their cut, the optimal amount still makes it to the operators. However, doing so is inefficient. Alternatively, leaders can try to reduce inefficiency.

Of course, the real-world division of labor is not always so stark. The level of specialization can vary over time and between groups. Al Qaeda and its affiliates used to have quite defined organizational roles with a strong distinction between support and operational roles.[18] However, since losing their refuge in Afghanistan, al Qaeda and its affiliates may have shifted to a less-hierarchical system. In Madrid and Casablanca, for example, the same members appear to have engaged in logistical tasks and conducted operations.[19] Moreover, the level of specialization can be a strategic choice. Resource-poor groups must be efficient to survive, while wealthy organizations may not be concerned with inefficiency so long as they can meet their political goals.

There are at least four inefficiency-reducing solutions to this moral hazard problem. First, leaders can engage in monitoring or auditing their middlemen. Second, leaders can provide incentive-based compensation, withholding payment for services until they have observed a signal—a successful attack, for example—telling them the agent has performed as promised. Third, leaders can engage in punishment strategies when they have evidence of shirking. Fourth, leaders can encourage members to enter into relationships that raise the costs of getting caught expropriating funds.

Unfortunately for terrorist leaders, each of those strategies creates vulnerabilities. The first two demand that the group conduct additional communications and keep records, both of which violate operational security concerns. The third strategy is risky because it entails additional communications and because the punished individual may decide to compromise the

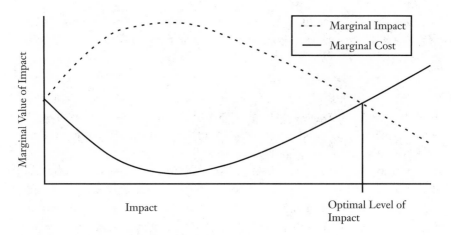

FIGURE 4.1 Value of Terrorist Attacks

network.[20] The fourth strategy creates additional interconnections, making the potential cost of any one compromise much greater. Thus, given the selection dynamics caused by government strategy, terrorists face an inherent trade-off between security and efficiency.

The Economic System of Terror

Decisions about spending are best understood in terms of the trade-off between achieving political impact and the fact that greater impact spurs greater government enforcement efforts. Figure 4.1 demonstrates this logic.[21] Leadership seeks a level of political impact where the marginal benefit of one more unit of impact matches the marginal cost in terms of government action.

Unlike in traditional economic organizations, this optimal point is not always determined by a spending constraint. Terrorist groups rely on five distinct sources of funding: (1) direct contributions from individuals; (2) intentional donations from charitable foundations; (3) state sponsorship; (4) profits from legitimate businesses—including tithing by the membership; and (5) profits from criminal enterprises—including skimming funds from legitimate organizations and extortion from individuals. Production decisions, choices about how many attacks to undertake or how much to spend providing social services, influence the first three sources. In general, the more attacks or social services a group provides, the more funds it can raise from individuals, charities, or state sponsors.[22] However, the last two sources enable some groups to produce at this goal-optimal level even if their financial system is inefficient.[23]

Whatever impact the leader desires, the financial system has three basic tasks. First, it must generate resources through fund-raising, taxing criminal activities, fraud, or some other source. Second, the system must preserve these resources and protect them from seizure. Finally, it must distribute money to operational cells. There are opportunities for middlemen to appropriate resources at each step in this chain.

SELECTION DYNAMICS AND DIVERGENT PREFERENCES

One of the most striking patterns to emerge from a close examination of terrorist organizations is that financial network members face dramatically lower risks than local leaders and tactical operatives. Beyond not being asked to participate in risky or inherently fatal ventures, they are less likely to be targeted by government forces. When targeted, they are less likely to be killed; when arrested, they face more lenient treatment.

Using Sageman's sample of 366 participants in the "global Salafi jihad"—al Qaeda, affiliated groups, and some individuals operating outside of formal organizations—I assessed the risks of participating at different levels. Using open-source material, I collected data on individuals' operational roles, when they left the jihad, and how they left.[24] According to these data, between 1997 and 2003, financiers were rarely killed, and their chances of being arrested were 10–20 percent lower than that of tactical operators, with 2002 being the only exception.

Even when governments succeed in capturing logisticians and other support network members, the members face dramatically lesser consequences than operators. Of the 33 financiers and logisticians removed from the global Salafi jihad between January 2001 and December 2003, only 1 was killed. While roughly 40 percent of the captured local operational leaders in the sample received life in prison or a death sentence, only 8 percent of support personnel received such sentences. A particularly telling example is the Jemaah Islamiyah (JI) cell broken up in Singapore in late 2001. The cell provided fund-raising services to JI and was making logistical arrangements for an al Qaeda attack in Singapore. Of the 30-plus people arrested, the 13 engaged in direct logistical support each received two years in prison. Those engaged in fund-raising activities were released but not permitted to leave the country.[25] This dramatic difference in risks leads to divergent preferences in terrorist organizations.

In our rationalist approach, individuals join terrorist organizations when the utility of doing so is at least as good as that provided by their next best option.[26] Utility is composed of two components. First, individuals get utility out of doing what they believe is right, in this case out of the impact of their actions in furthering the group's goals.[27] Second, individuals get utility out of monetary compensation. Each individual places a weight on these two components such that the sum of the weights is 1. The utility of an action is the probability it yields an impact, I, times the weight placed on impact plus the probability it yields wages, W, times the weight placed on wages.[28] We can then describe the population of potential members by the distribution of weights in the population. At the extremes are individuals who are purely motivated by impact, suicide bombers perhaps, and those motivated purely by money.

Within this framework, consider a hierarchical organization where individuals come up through the ranks, starting out in subordinate roles and moving into management roles as local leaders, financial facilitators, or logisticians.[29] Throughout their careers, these individuals will have opportunities to volunteer for risky missions.[30] Those most likely to do so will be those who place the greatest weight on impact. Thus, the longer individuals remain in the organization, and the further they move up in the management structure, the more likely they are to place a heavy weight on monetary rewards.[31] Of course, there is a countervailing dynamic. Assuming constant wages, those who are less committed will receive lower total utility from participating and will thus be more likely to quit the group.[32] Where the value of participating is only marginally greater than the value of the next best option, quitting should mitigate this particular adverse selection process.

Even without this adverse selection process, there is reason to expect divergence. The lenient treatment observed for support network members means that the threshold level of risk acceptance and commitment required for participation in support activities is much lower than for participation in tactical roles. Recall that there is a distribution of weights in the population of potential members. Thus, given set wages for different activities, individuals placing a certain weight on economic considerations might participate in support activities while balking at other roles within the organization. Seeking to maximize operational capability, a rational organization would concentrate such individuals in support roles, freeing up the true believers for riskier operational duties. These personnel decisions would then lead to consistent variance between levels of the organization.

A reasonable objection to the preceding logic is that groups would not engage in such centrally directed personnel movements because they create connections between cells. Because of this security consideration, terrorist organizations may actually recruit directly into specific positions with little opportunity for movement. Suppose that the organization in question filled these roles using a strategy of recruitment through existing social ties.[33] Any member tasked with the recruitment and early ideological training of potential members will have access to a limited population. From this population, they will need to fill various spots. If we make the reasonable assumption that belief in a group's ideology follows a bell-shaped distribution—the purely ideological or purely venal types are rarer than those who place moderate weight on both pecuniary rewards and impact—it will be harder for the recruiter to find potential tactical operatives than logisticians. Unless the recruiter knows a surfeit of potential members, he will place individuals in the riskiest position they will accept. Thus, individuals will rarely be more ideologically motivated than is necessary given the risk level of their occupation, leading to variance across levels.

A second, more significant, objection to the above logic is that if middlemen have scarce skills, their next best option will be much more valuable. Thus, their involvement in terrorism may actually suggest they are *more* committed than the foot soldiers who have no other employment options.[34]

Two responses are worth noting here. The first is that the modal profile of an operational terrorist is someone with better prospects than the average person in his society.[35] Moreover, that skills are rare among potential terrorist recruits does not necessarily imply that they are equally rare in the population, and it is the value of skills to the organization that drives the logic above. The second response is that the evidence from some conflicts is that middlemen do quite well. Middlemen in the PLO are paid relatively well compared to those who fight, and many middlemen in the Kashmiri jihad live relatively ostentatious lifestyles.[36] If these individuals were, in fact, more committed than those who fight and die, one would expect them to reject such large payments out of devotion to the cause.

Different levels of risk faced by those filling different roles will translate into different preferences within groups under three different sets of assumptions about how terrorist organizations make staffing decisions. This diversity of preferences, combined with the covert nature of terrorist organizations, creates a problem for terrorist leaders.

MORAL HAZARD IN COVERT ORGANIZATIONS

The relationship between terrorist leaders and their financial networks can be understood in terms of a principal-agent relationship wherein the principals, i.e., terrorist leaders, need to delegate certain tasks—raising funds and distributing them to operational elements—to their agents, the financial network. This delegation entails a risk. If the agents' preferences differ from those of the principal, the agents will not carry out their tasks exactly as the principal would like; they may "shirk." The moral hazard is that the agent can undertake actions that reduce the principal's utility, but the principal can neither perfectly monitor nor punish the agent with certainty.[37]

Traditional organizations use three general strategies to deal with this type of problem. First, they audit their employees, accepting monitoring costs to prevent shirking. Second, they create wage schemes that are attractive only to agents whose preferences are aligned with those of the principals. Third, they provide incentive pay or salary conditional on performance. There are many possible screening mechanisms and incentive-based contracts, but all involve making full payment conditional on not deviating too far from the principals' desires.

Both principals and agents hold five pieces of information. Principals know the amount passed to leaders through fund-raising activities, and each agent knows how much she has passed on. Likewise, principals know the amount given to financial network members to pass on to operational elements while each agent only knows how much she was given. Both principals and agents are able to observe the operational impact of their actions. They also share common beliefs about the amount of impact they can achieve given spending levels and the likelihood of achieving that amount.[38] Finally, both are able to observe how risky it is to fulfill certain roles.

There are three critical pieces of information known only to the agents, information that can be considered their "private information." Only they know the percentage of funds raised that is actually passed up to the leadership. Similarly, only they know the amount passed down to the operational elements.[39] Finally, only the agents know how much weight they place on impact. Impact dominates the leader's decisions, but he is not so myopic as to spend an infinite amount to achieve his ideal level of impact.

Given who knows what, there are three ways financial network members can take advantage of their private information. First, they can misrepresent their preferences over money and impact to pad their salary. Essentially, they can mislead the principal into thinking that he has to offer more compensation than he actually does. This problem will be ameliorated to the extent that there is a market for terrorist financial services.[40]

Second, the agent can appropriate some of the money from fund-raising activities. Because the environment is noisy and the network is covert, the principal will be poorly informed about the actual amount raised. Depending on the principal's beliefs about how accurately he can anticipate fund-raising levels, the agent will be able to get away with appropriating some amount without arousing suspicion. How large an amount will depend on the accuracy of the principal's beliefs, which depends in turn on where the funds are coming from. When money from legitimate enterprises is passed through the group to operational cells, the process can be relatively overt. Because the organization is putting good money to ambiguous purposes—at least until the cell commits an attack—the transactions are essentially indistinguishable from legitimate transfers.[41] As such, the principal will be better informed about the likely success of fund-raising efforts, and the agent will not be able to appropriate as large a percentage. However, when the organization is using money from illicit purposes to fund operations, some kind of laundering will be needed to prevent investigators who are tracking the original crime from finding out about impending operations. This is a riskier proposition, involving more financial machinations and a greater need for secrecy. Hence, the principal will be less well-informed about his returns from fund-raising. As such, the financiers will be able to appropriate a larger percentage without arousing suspicion.[42]

Third, the agent can appropriate money intended for operational cells. Whether these appropriations lead to underfunding of specific operations depends on the nature of the command and control structure.[43] Consider the case where the leaders decide how many attacks to carry out and allocate funds to each attack based on their beliefs about how to equate the marginal returns to impact with marginal costs.[44] Because the principal's ability to observe the impact to cost relationship is imperfect, members of the financial network can skim some of the money intended for operations and blame the reduction in observed impact on the noisy environment.

If opportunities for shirking exist in terrorist organizations, the next question is to ask whether financial agents will take advantage of these opportunities. Consider the case of an agent who is participating because her utility from wages and impact are better than her next best option. This agent knows she can appropriate some funds and get away with it, thereby increasing her utility.[45] Now, consider the leader. He has some optimal level of impact that we assume to be below the maximum he could achieve if he spent all his funds.[46] He is uncertain whether he is dealing with a good agent who will pass everything on or a bad one who will appropriate as much as she can get away with. Since the leader's utility function is heavily weighted towards impact, and since he can spend above the point of diminishing marginal returns, he is willing to provide some extra wages to the agent. He knows the agent will appropriate these funds, but he takes the efficiency loss because the agent will then pass the ideal amount on to the operational group. Thus, the leader should pay what he needs to for his optimal impact plus the minimum amount that can be appropriated without his becoming suspicious. The agent then appropriates this amount and passes the optimal amount of funds on to the operators. The leader remains unable to tell whether he is dealing with a good or a bad agent and the system moves on. In a more formal presentation, this would be the "shirking" equilibrium.[47]

In the terrorist leader's ideal world, where the agents share the leader's preferences exactly, all the money raised would be passed to the organization and all the money intended for operations would be used as desired. However, selection dynamics mean there is likely to be a difference between the weights placed on impact and wages at different levels of the organization. This difference can lead the agents in the financial network to shirk by appropriating some funds for personal use, introducing inefficiency into the financial system. A security trade-off arises from each strategy leaders use to deal with these problems.

CREATING VULNERABILITIES

Terrorist leaders can undertake a number of strategies to minimize inefficiency due to shirking. However, each of these strategies creates specific vulnerabilities. This section looks briefly at six of those strategies and discusses the security-efficiency trade-off in more detail. The first two strategies, auditing and providing funds on a need-to-have basis, apply primarily to the process of moving money to operators. The remaining four strategies apply more generally.

Auditing strategies, such as those apparently employed by Ayman al Zawahiri, require the agents to provide periodic, detailed reports on their spending. Such reports provide the leadership with more detailed information about how their money is being spent. This additional information effectively reduces the noisiness of the environment, narrowing the scope of cheating available to the agent. But this additional efficiency comes at the cost of additional communications. Because each communication entails a specific risk of compromise, these strategies effectively raise the marginal cost curve, reducing the total impact a group will desire. Thus, we should not expect groups who have a surplus of funds to employ such strategies.[48]

Providing funds only on a need-to-have basis is another way in which principals can inhibit cheating by their agents. By increasing the frequency of transfers and reducing their size, leaders build up better knowledge about the nature of the spending-impact relationship.[49] This reduces the size of appropriations the agents can get away with. However, because each additional transfer entails communications, the previous security trade-off applies and, again, leaders who have a surplus of funds are unlikely to employ this strategy.

Punishment strategies depend on the principal's ability to catch and credibly punish shirking. Getting the information needed to increase the probability of catching shirking has a clear security cost, so the focus here is on the second requirement, credible punishment. Punishment can be as simple as excluding the agent from future transactions. The agent then loses the difference between the future value of participation and that of her second-best option. Where economic opportunity is low, this difference could be quite substantial, so such a strategy may be sufficient. Because such a strategy is built into the shirking equilibrium, the principal may want to use the threat of additional violent punishment, a punitive strategy.

A punitive strategy is harder to implement because the agent in a covert system holds an inherent threat over the organization. If she is sufficiently incensed by her punishment, she can go to the authorities. For example, Jamal Ahmed Al Fadl, who testified in the African Embassy bombing trial, stole money from al Qaeda, got caught, went on the run, and approached the U.S. government in an attempt to save himself and his family. Because agents have exactly this option, the organization should employ punitive strategies only when it can wield a credible threat of violence over the agent. Financial agents operating in foreign countries, such as the Yemeni recipient of al Zawahiri's e-mail, will be less susceptible to this strategy. That agent responded to being called out by quitting the network, illustrating the difficulties transnational groups face in using punishment strategies.[50]

One common way to discourage shirking is to encourage members to enter into trust-inducing relationships such as marriage.[51] The logic is that those who have entered into such relationships will face a larger cost if they are caught cheating. Not only do they lose a future income stream, but they lose familial and community connections as well. For example, such a strategy is central to the success of the *hawala* funds transfer system.[52] Of course, if a member embedded in a dense network of strong ties is captured, myriad opportunities for compromise are created. Historically, governments have only worked aggressively through terrorists' non-operational relationships, targeting terrorists' friends and family, when the impact of a terrorist campaign is very large.[53] Thus, this strategy raises the slope of the marginal cost curve only at high levels of impact, where further attacks will trigger very aggressive government action. Think of this as bending the right side of the cost curve upwards. This is what happened to al Qaeda's cost curve following the September 11 attacks. If the optimal level of political impact is low— that is, if the curves cross where the marginal cost curve is not steep—then such a strategy will not reduce the acceptable impact, as it only affects the cost curve above the level of impact the terrorists seek.

However, when the cost curves intersect at higher levels of impact, the results are more conditional. In the first case, suppose that the curves intersect at high levels of impact when the slope of the cost curve is already quite steep. This would be the case where government enforcement is quite stringent but the political benefits to more attacks are still substantial. Here, requiring dense ties will not shift the equilibrium very much to the left since the cost curve is already steep. In the second case, suppose that the marginal political gains to attacks are rapidly decreasing. This could be because the group's supporters have gotten fed up with violence, or because the target population becomes inured to it.[54] In this situation, the cost curve has a small slope at high impact, and increasing that slope can shift the intersection dramatically to the left. This would yield a substantial decrease in the equilibrium level of impact. Only under this last condition would we not expect the strategy of trust-inducing relationships to be used.[55]

Incentive-based contracts offer another way for principals to reduce shirking. In the terrorism context, such an agreement could entail several different arrangements. One is that payments might be made only after successful attacks or other impact-producing activities.[56] Another strategy might entail allowing financiers a set wage once they raise a specific amount. This wage has to be greater than the expected utility of appropriations given the amount raised. Because the appropriation entails some risk of being caught, the incentive can be less than the amount the agent could appropriate. Thus, principals should prefer this strategy to overpaying to account for shirking. While these strategies do entail additional communications, they require fewer than the first two strategies. Thus, incentive-based contracts raise the cost curve less, and principals should employ them more often.

Finally, terrorist leaders may seek to screen their recruits for ideological purity, to ensure that they all place a very high weight on impact. Some accounts suggest that the training program in Afghanistan served as such a screening process for al Qaeda.[57] The lengthy ideological debates that form an essential part of the recruiting process in European Islamic expatriate communities also fulfill such a function. While this strategy does not generate additional risks, it does reduce the pool of potential participants. For groups recruiting from a limited recruiting population, this may be problematic. The best financiers are unlikely to be religious or ideological purists, as such individuals rarely spend time developing expertise in money laundering and covertly moving funds. This strategy, therefore, entails an efficiency loss. This loss may drop the feasible level of impact below that which could be achieved with less impact-driven agents.

Of the six strategies outlined above, all entail some cost for the groups. In five of the six, there was a specific security-efficiency trade-off. Only demanding ideological purity did not have a clear security cost. However, in the realm of terrorist financing the necessary expertise may not be available from highly ideological individuals.

Conclusion and Recommendations

In a principal-agent framework, leaders are considered the principals who delegate three stages of financial activity to their agents. These agents raise funds, store them for future use, and transfer them to operational elements.

Two selection processes cause those agents to have divergent preferences from the principals. First, terrorist organizations face an inherent adverse selection problem because those individuals who are less committed are likely to survive longer and rise into the mid-level positions. Second, because terrorist financiers face significantly lower risks than other members of their organizations, recruiting efforts will place more risk-averse, less committed individuals into financial roles.

Because of the information asymmetries inherent in covert networks, these individuals have opportunities to "shirk" by skimming money at all three stages. So long as terrorist financiers face lower risks than other members of terrorist organizations, these groups will suffer from a moral hazard problem. "Shirking" by the agents creates inefficiency in the financial system. Like any organization, terrorist groups can use a variety of strategies to control the moral hazard problem. But all these strategies come at a cost. In five of the six strategies examined, there was a specific security-efficiency trade-off. Strategies that reduce the moral hazard problem create operational vulnerabilities.

Terrorist leaders thus face an unpalatable choice. Where funding constraints do not bite, terrorists can make the trade-off in favor of security. Where funding constraints do bite, government can undertake some specific actions to make this trade-off even more problematic.[58]

This analysis leads to three distinct recommendations. First, governments should not publicize the freezing of funds. If funds are frozen without public statement, then financiers must explain how the money was lost. The organization will then achieve a lower impact. Seeing this, the principal will suspect the agent of shirking. If the freezing is made public, the agent has an excuse. If it is not, she has two choices: she can make up the frozen amount, or she can get blamed and forego the future value of her relationship with the organization.

Second, governments can make engaging in trust-inducing relationships riskier. Publicly targeting relatives and extended families for surveillance would increase terrorists' assessment of the probability that such relationships would lead to compromise. Government can achieve the same end by publicizing counter-terrorism successes based on tracing such relationships.

Third, government may actually reduce tensions within terrorist organizations by engaging in economic development activities. Greater development in recruiting areas effectively increases the value of an individual's second-best option. Thus, the wages terrorist principals need to pay to induce participation in terrorism will be higher. While this may make recruiting more difficult, the moral hazard problem becomes less problematic from the principals' perspective. Because the difference between the wage they must pay and the feasible appropriations—which depend only on the noisiness of the environment and the desired number of attacks—is smaller, the relative value of the inefficiency is reduced. Under this scenario, the group is less likely to engage in the inefficiency-reducing strategies that create vulnerabilities, making government's job more difficult.

Consider the following thought experiment. Suppose that for political reasons a leader wants to have two successful attacks. Given the success probabilities and economies of conducting an attack, the leader chooses to fund three attempts with $90 and pay someone $10 to serve as a middleman. To avoid detection as a shirker, the middleman must allocate $70 to the attacks, leaving a feasible appropriation of $20. Thus the boss pays $100 and gets $70 worth of attacks. Now suppose there is some economic development and the middleman's outside option increases in value to $20, but the boss still pays $100. The middleman must still devote $70 to attacks, so he captures only $10 in rents. Before development, the bad agent captured 20 percent of the expenditures in rents. After development, he is only able to capture 10 percent. Thus, the difference between a good and bad agent is smaller, and inefficiency is reduced. With this reduction, the leader has less incentive to engage in inefficiency-reducing behaviors. Whether this trade-off—difficulty recruiting but fewer security violations—is favorable to a government will depend on local conditions.

Each of these strategies impinges on other areas of counter-terrorism and cuts in several directions. For example, publicizing methods and causes of compromise may prevent terrorists from dealing with inefficiencies in their financial system, but it may also aid terrorists' efforts to improve operational security. This dilemma and others discussed above apply only when funds are restricted.

Based on this framework, clamping down on finances can have a host of benefits. So long as groups have excess funds, they do not need to face the trade-offs outlined above. However, when funding becomes scarce, terrorist leaders face a security-efficiency trade-off. Choosing efficiency-enhancing strategies creates vulnerabilities that governments can exploit. Choosing security means fewer operations and therefore less impact. In either case, government wins when funds are restricted.

CHAPTER FIVE

Warning Indicators and Terrorist Finances

PHIL WILLIAMS

The attacks of September 11, 2001, on the World Trade Center and the Pentagon were seen initially as a "bolt from the blue" but were, in fact, in the planning stage from 1995 onwards. Carefully adapted and refined over time, these plans were given a much higher level of funding than any other al Qaeda attack—an estimated $500,000. Though a trivial sum compared to the death and destruction that were caused, the half a million dollars was nonetheless a significant investment—one that involved the transfer of substantial sums of money to the hijackers prior to the attack. Had law enforcement and intelligence agencies been focused on these money flows or been sensitive to their potential significance, then the catastrophic surprise of September 11 might have been avoided.

This is not to suggest that financial transfers were the only indicator. Indeed, there were several other indications of the impending attacks that could have provided some degree of warning for the United States if there had been better inter-agency coordination and intelligence sharing and greater receptivity to the possibility that civilian airliners might be used as weapons. At the same time, it is important not to under-estimate the sheer difficulty of the intelligence process. We need to recognize what one management analyst termed "retrospective coherence."[1] All the indicators were, for the most part, scattered, fragmentary, incomplete, indeterminate, and surrounded by noise.[2] Discerning such signals is a difficult intelligence challenge. Nevertheless, in the aftermath of the attacks, the United States formulated a comprehensive strategy against al Qaeda that included an assault on the terrorist finances as well as efforts to strengthen other possible indicators and warnings of future terrorist attacks.

The dual United States response to al Qaeda involved developing better indicators and warnings on the one side and trying to freeze and seize terrorist assets on the other. This response created dilemmas, however, that have not yet been resolved. It also brought to light difficult and uncomfortable trade-offs that have yet to be made. The decision to freeze terrorist assets certainly weakened al Qaeda's immediate capacity to carry out further attacks, but at the same time it undercut the ability of anti-terrorist agencies to follow the terrorist money trail. Since frozen assets cannot be moved, intelligence and law enforcement agencies cannot monitor the movement or transfer of those funds. The justification for the freeze strategy, of course, is compelling. The United States and other countries felt that the loss of monitoring opportunities was outweighed by putative ability to deny terrorists access to funds. Yet it is unclear whether the attack on terrorist finances yielded the kind of results initially anticipated. In fact, the global campaign aimed at freezing terrorist assets is more accurately characterized as a dismal failure. Against this background, this chapter sets out to

- highlight some of the reasons why the freeze strategy has not been more successful;
- identify the various ways in which financial transactions of different kinds could provide indicators of potential attacks; and
- make recommendations about the optimum trade-off between freezing assets and following the money trail.

Attacking Terrorist Finances: A Failed Strategy?

In the months following the September 11 attacks, the international community, led by the United States, froze approximately $100 million of terrorist funding. Subsequent efforts over the next three years added only an additional $47 million to the total of frozen or confiscated funds.[3] The Office of Foreign Assets Control in the United States Treasury Department prepared the initial designated list of targets while the United Nations imposed sanctions on the Taliban and al Qaeda under resolution 1267 (subsequently superseded by resolution 1455). Constant additions have been made to the United States' target list, reflecting enhanced intelligence and an increasing appreciation of the challenge of targeting terrorist finances.

The results of this assault on the financial infrastructure of terrorism have been modest, if not mediocre. Not only has the strategy imposed only limited constraints on the flow of money to terrorist organizations, it has patently failed to stop terrorist attacks. Although al Qaeda has not mounted another attack on the scale of September 11, the Madrid train attacks, the frequency and scope of terrorist incidents in Iraq, the attacks in Turkey, the Bali nightclub bombing, and the attack on the Marriott Hotel in Jakarta, as well as a series of thwarted attacks in Western Europe, suggest that al Qaeda and its affiliates remain a potent threat.

At least four main reasons explain why the assault on terrorist finances has had limited impact on the capacity of al Qaeda and its associates to carry out attacks. First, the global financial regimes concerned initially with criminal money laundering and then the targeting of terrorist finances are wholly inadequate. Second, anti-terrorist forces have not been able to deal adequately with Islamic charities. Third, the terrorist networks have adapted to these financial attacks by appropriating the methods of organized crime. And last, the simple fact remains that terrorist attacks are cheap.

THE INADEQUACIES OF GLOBAL FINANCIAL REGIMES

In some respects, the effort to target terrorist financial assets was doomed to failure from the outset. The extension of the existing global anti-money laundering regime to cover terrorist finances only highlighted its serious shortcomings. Although the Financial Action Task Force (FATF) joined hands and expertise with the World Bank and International Monetary Fund (IMF) in its expanded mandate to counter-terrorist finances, the same old problems it had encountered in combating money laundering remained.

As with any multilateral effort of this kind, there are always weak links to be exploited. Both money laundering and terrorist financing are global in scope and transnational in operation. Criminals and now terrorists engage in jurisdictional arbitrage, exploit jurisdictional voids, and create jurisdictional confusion—all of which can only be combated through sustained and systematic international cooperation. Such cooperation is difficult to achieve and is limited in its impact even when it is achieved. The reasons are numerous and relatively clear.

First, the greater the effort to develop a global consensus, the weaker or more diluted the action is likely to be. In this connection, it is worth emphasizing that the United Nations effort to target the Taliban and al Qaeda has focused on freezing bank accounts but not their other assets.[4] Many states also lack the capacity to carry out their commitments to combat terrorist finances. As the United Nations Monitoring Group (UNMG) noted shortly before its dissolution:

> Efforts are still required to extend the measures to banks and financial institutions in many parts of the world that lack the resources, capability or political will to replicate such measures. . . . Al-Qaeda and other terrorist groups are adjusting to the new measures and have concentrated their activities in areas which still lack such effective controls. This includes, but is not limited to, the so-called list of failed or weak States. In fact, no terrorist assets at all have yet been located or frozen in a number of countries where Al-Qaeda is well established and known to operate.[5]

Second, some states lack the will to carry out their obligations in this area. There are several possible reasons for this: (1) they are sympathetic to the cause of al Qaeda and are therefore reluctant to implement measures against the network and its financial activities; (2) combating terrorism is a low priority given their other problems and challenges; (3) they are reluctant to comply with overt actions that might make them a target for al Qaeda or its affiliates. Whatever the specific reasons, it is clear that many states are not fulfilling their obligations under the United Nations mandate in this area. For example, as of October 2003, only 83 governments had responded to UN requests for reports on their efforts to implement sanctions against al Qaeda and the Taliban; 108 states had not reported, and 25 of these were known to have an al Qaeda (or associate group) presence.[6] In some cases, states used the exemption clause that a release of names would

compromise existing investigations—but the monitoring group was skeptical of these claims.[7] In other instances, states covertly defect from the international effort. Many governments have agreed to combat terrorism
finances and have even created new laws that appear to meet the demands
of the United States and the United Nations. Yet they have done little to
implement these laws. Moreover, the way in which al Qaeda has beaten the
U.S. government in winning the "battle of the story" suggests that cosmetic
conformity and tacit defection is likely to be the norm in a large part of the
Islamic world.[8]

Third, it is certainly the norm where money is to be made. This explains
the continued existence of financial safe havens that can be exploited by terrorists and criminals alike. The FATF's "name and shame" campaign succeeded in compelling some offshore financial jurisdictions to clean up their
acts and provide greater transparency. At the time, other jurisdictions continue to offer bank secrecy and demonstrate little inquisitiveness into either
the source or the purpose of funds flowing into or through their financial
institutions. As the UNMG noted,

> many of the offshore business centers that have been deemed to be com-
> plying continue to pose serious obstacles in the war on terrorist financing.
> They still serve to mask potential terrorism-financing activities, and make it
> difficult to locate and deal with terrorist-related financial assets other than
> bank accounts.[9]

THE DIFFICULTIES OF ATTACKING CHARITIES

Islamic charities linked to international terrorism continue to make it
difficult for the United States and the international community to attack
terrorist finances. The difficulty is two-fold. First, there is what the UN
Monitoring Group described as a

> general reticence to act against charities, even those suspected of channeling
> funds to Al-Qaeda, unless strong evidence is presented and judicial findings
> can be obtained. This higher standard of proof has inhibited the designation
> of charities and their inclusion in the list. . . . Even when such charities have
> been listed there has been an even stronger reticence to go behind the char-
> ities, to reach to their directors, donors and fund-raisers.[10]

Second, terrorist financial support structures are not static targets. Even when they have been included on the United Nations list, Islamic charities have adapted in a variety of ways. In some cases, the head office has closed but branch operations continue to operate unhindered. In other cases, the charities have simply re-registered and re-opened under new names but with the old infrastructure intact. Another approach has been to support terrorists less through direct contributions than through logistical support (such as employment in a charity branch office).[11]

In other words, the charities linked to terrorist organizations have displayed a degree of resilience and a capacity for adaptation, thereby limiting the ability of the international community and the United States to inhibit their continued involvement in terrorist financing. Of course, the international strategy to combat terrorist financing has had some impact. Clearly such financing is more problematic than it was, and funds from these charities are neither as plentiful nor as easily moved as in the past.

ALTERNATIVE MEANS OF FUNDING TERRORISM

Terrorist organizations themselves have also compensated with their own form of adaptability and emergent behavior. They have appropriated the practices of organized crime and used these new sources of funding to make up the shortfalls in funding from the charities. Kidnapping, extortion, drug trafficking, other forms of smuggling, credit card theft and fraud, document fraud, and robbery have thus become staple features of the terrorist fund-raising repertoire. This is not surprising. Most organized crime activities do not have a steep learning curve, nor do they require significant upfront investments. Given the low entry costs on the one side and the gains that can be made on the other, the exploitation of organized crime methods by terrorist networks from the Philippines to Western Europe is a natural development—one that has partially neutralized the "global" effort to undermine terrorist finances. In addition, terrorists continue to use *hawala* and other informal value transfer systems, as well as transforming some of their funds into easily transported commodities.

OPERATIONS ARE CHEAP

The strategies designed initially to attack the profits of organized crime confront other significant challenges when directed against terrorist financing. First, the success level has to be much higher when dealing with terrorists—even though the target profile is so much smaller. Indeed, the inherent advantage lies with the terrorists. Most terrorist attacks can be carried out without large expenditures of money. As the UN Monitoring Group noted,

> The simultaneous truck bombings of the United States embassies in Kenya and the United Republic of Tanzania in August 1998 are estimated to have cost less than $50,000; the October 2000 attack on the USS *Cole* in Aden less than $10,000; the Bali bombings in October 2002 less than $50,000; the 2003 bombing of the Marriott Hotel in Jakarta about $30,000; the November 2003 attacks in Istanbul less than $40,000; and the March 2004 attacks in Madrid about $10,000.[12]

In fact, the Spanish investigation of the Madrid bombings revealed that the attack cost about five times the UNMG estimate. Nevertheless, the point remains that attacks are relatively cheap.

Thus, unless efforts to constrict the flow of finances to operational cells are extremely successful, they are unlikely to degrade the capacity of terrorist networks to carry out new attacks. Significantly, the explosives for the Madrid attack were purchased with hashish, which once again highlights the role of organized crime activities in funding terror.[13] In other words, stopping the relatively modest flows of money to the sharp end of terrorist networks is almost impossible. And these terrorist cells are increasingly likely to become financially self-sufficient.

The implications of all this are far-reaching. The freeze strategy, combined with the adaptations initiated by the terrorist networks and supporting charities, now make it even more difficult to follow the money and use its trail as a critical warning indicator. Even before this occurred, of course, following the money had been a formidable task. Nevertheless, it is also clear that the financial dimensions of terrorist activity offer opportunities for intelligence collection and analysis that might help provide warning of impending attacks. Indeed, with the rationale for the freeze campaign undermined by a continued lack of effectiveness, there is a strong case for resolving tensions between "freezing and following" in favor of the latter.

Financial Transactions as Warning Indicators

Though financial transactions rarely provide the critical indicator, they are part of a broader picture and can sometimes illuminate and crystallize what had hitherto been uncertain. Realizing that the broader picture often remains murky and diffuse, there are several dimensions of financial transactions that need to be considered.

- Financial movements and expenditures remain a critical component of attack preparations.
- Money often connects a known part of the terrorist network with an unknown part.
- Changes in the predominant patterns of financial transactions within and by a terrorist network may signal an extension of terrorist activities and/or indicate a new set of targets.
- Terrorist cells use criminal activities to fund terrorist action by the cell itself or to provide support for a cell planning an attack.
- Suspicious financial transactions include financial transfers, deposits, or withdrawals of whatever amount that either appear to have no economic rationale or that, for whatever reason, arouse the suspicions of banking personnel.

Obviously, some overlap exists among these various indicators. Criminal activities at the cell level might lead, for example, to increased financial expenditures in anticipation of an upcoming attack. Nevertheless, it is worth distinguishing between these various indicators, recognizing that in practice the greater the concentration of indicators, the more confident the judgments and warnings that are based on them. With this in mind, we will explore each of the possible indicators.

FINANCIAL EXPENDITURES AS A CRITICAL COMPONENT OF ATTACK PREPARATIONS

As suggested above, terrorist attacks, being relatively inexpensive, represent a form of asymmetric warfare in which a weapon of the weak is used against the strong. In the planned al Qaeda suicide bombings on the United States embassy in Paris and the consulate in Marseilles in the summer of 2001, Jamal Beghal, the cell leader was scheduled to go to Morocco to pick up a mere $50,000 for the operation.[14] The cost of the abortive attack on the Christmas market in Strasbourg in December 2000 was estimated at between $20,000 and $30,000. Although the costs will depend in crucial ways on the precise nature of the operation, it seems likely that they fall into several categories:

- *Subsistence for the perpetrators as they prepare for their actions.* The day-to-day living expenses are not trivial even if the terrorists live a very frugal lifestyle. As they attempt to blend in by frequenting social events and clubs, their expenditures increase. The costs also vary depending on the location of the targets and the proximity of the terrorists to these targets. The costs of operations in the United States or Western Europe will obviously be considerably greater than operations in countries such as Tanzania, Kenya, and Yemen.

- *The cost of special training and the development of expertise that is critical to the successful completion of the mission.* Although many of the skills necessary for an operation have been developed at terrorist training camps, more specialized requirements can only be met through more legitimate and more costly avenues such as attendance at flight schools.

- *The purchase of any weapons or explosive materials that are to be used in the attack.* The September 11 hijackers were relatively unusual in that they were so lightly armed. In other cases, however, the acquisition of explosives or weapons is more costly—especially if combined with efforts to disguise the activities. In an attempt to avoid suspicion, the Frankfurt terrorists who were planning an attack in Strasbourg traveled extensively to procure raw materials in small amounts. This increased the costs of the operation and required them to make purchases with stolen credit cards provided for them by a support cell in Milan.

- *The cost of travel for meetings related to the plan.* In most cases of planned or actual attacks by terrorist networks operating in the United States and Western Europe, there was considerable travel prior to the event itself. Often, terrorists traveled to meet with co-conspirators or with senior people in the network or support cells. Mohammed Atta's trip to Spain in July 2001, for example, probably included meetings with the Spanish cell that provided support to his group while they were in Hamburg.

- *The cost of communications among those involved.* Communications costs, of course, have declined enormously with cell phones, pre-paid telephone cards, and e-mails (often from public libraries and internet cafes). Nevertheless, these costs still have to be included in the overall cost of the mission. Moreover, even though cell phones and pre-paid telephone calls are relatively cheap, the tendency to use them and quickly dispose of them in order to maintain operational security adds to the operational costs.

In other words, certain kinds of expenditures have to be met—and therefore have to be funded—either by those directly involved in the operation or by their supporters. In some cases, the payments for such purchases (whether materiel or services such as training) can be an indicator. In other cases, the transfer or raising of money to fund purchases and meet other costs for the terrorists can help to reveal attack preparations.

MONEY AS A CONNECTION BETWEEN KNOWN AND UNKNOWN PARTS OF TERRORIST NETWORKS

Mapping a terrorist network is an enormously complex task. Networks are inherently dynamic and expansive, especially when recruiting new members. Although parts of the network might be well known, other loosely coupled components remain at some distance from the core of the network, both geographically and in social network terms. Such detached components are inherently difficult to trace or identify, given that terrorists take deliberate efforts to maintain a low profile.

By monitoring the communications of known members, however, counter-terrorism agencies hope to find additional clues about unknown members of the network. Although terrorists deliberately limit their communications to avoid detection, communication is still essential. Indeed, these communications often involve effort to secure adequate funding for a planned operation. Monitoring such communications might provide missing pieces of the puzzle, allowing law enforcement and intelligence agencies to map the terrorist network in ways that better enable them to take decisive action in forestalling an attack. For example, the Meliani terrorist cell in Frankfurt was planning an attack on the Strasbourg Christmas market and cathedral. Already under surveillance by German law enforcement, the cell appeared suspicious—but German authorities had no clear reason to apprehend them. Using stolen credit cards supplied to them by a support group in Milan, the Frankfurt cell bought chemicals for making explosives. With "almost $14,000 in cash—some of it . . . raised by drug dealing on the streets of Frankfurt," they still needed more money.[15] So, they "went back to their paymasters. It was the mistake that destroyed the mission."[16] A member of the Frankfurt cell called a key al Qaeda operative in Britain known as Abu Doha, or "the Doctor," asking for more money and informing him that the operation would be carried out before the end of the year. British intelligence agents had Doha under surveillance and monitored the call. They then informed the German authorities, providing a critical piece of information that enabled the Germans to act preemptively and forestall the planned attack.[17]

In this case, not only was an additional segment of the network identified but the information was so good that it facilitated action preventing the planned attack. In effect, the financial transactions that had earlier been difficult to explain or understand were seen as part of the recognized pattern of attack preparation. They provided enough of an indication to justify decisive action. The importance of money as a link or connector between the known and the unknown segments of the network transcends this particular case. At the very least, this case shows that following money flows can assist in mapping the network and identifying previously obscure or unknown nodes and connections.

CHANGES IN THE PREDOMINANT PATTERNS OF FINANCIAL
TRANSACTIONS BY TERRORIST NETWORKS

As more details have been uncovered about Islamic terrorist finances in general and al Qaeda finances in particular, it is clear that one important and recurring pattern has been the use of Islamic charities for both raising and moving money. By carefully monitoring these charities, anti-terrorists agencies may acquire good tactical intelligence. Changes in financial flows within terrorist networks, for example, might suggest that new targets have been identified or that the terrorist network and its leadership have shifted their priorities. Channeling of funds in an otherwise unexpected direction can be a clue to an impending operation. When known or reconstituted Islamic charities suspected of being covers for terrorist networks appear in new countries, this may indicate that new targets are either under consideration or have already been selected. If the charities are already present, then serious shifts in funding levels or a surge of funds into the charity in general, or its country office in particular, can be another important indicator. Sudden surges might be particularly revealing, but even more gradual surges could offer a degree of warning and, at the very least, impel much closer scrutiny.

After the September 11 attack, the speculation that al Qaeda had sold stock it owned prior to the attacks on Washington and New York proved inconclusive. Nevertheless, the rationale for such speculation was sound. What actually occurred seemed to have been some kind of deviation from an established pattern of investment, possibly caused by prior knowledge. As such, it clearly merited attention. Moreover, in the financial world, surge activity of one kind or another requires careful scrutiny. The problem, of course, is that such surges of activity are often caused by rumor or by some shift in the political or economic context. Nevertheless, close human scrutiny combined with innovative data-mining techniques might uncover indicators that would otherwise be missed.

CRIMINAL ACTIVITIES TO FUND TERRORIST ACTION

As suggested above, what can be termed do-it-yourself organized crime by terrorist networks has evolved into an important and almost ubiquitous tool for terrorists, regardless of their ideological or religious roots. In some instances, criminal activities are used at a strategic level to provide the overall funding mechanism for the terrorist organization as a whole. Hezbollah supporters or its members have been involved in cross-state cigarette smuggling in the United States, sending the proceeds to the home organization.[18] Similarly, Tamils in Canada have sent a significant part of the profits made in drug trafficking and credit card fraud back to Sri Lanka for the Liberation Tigers of Tamil Eelam.[19]

In other cases, however, criminal activities undertaken at the tactical or cell level have been used to fund specific terrorist activities. In the al Qaeda network, despite the presumed wealth of the organization and of bin Laden in particular, most cells planning terrorist operations have received very little money from the leadership. Instead, they have been compelled to engage in petty crime and minor forms of organized crime to acquire the necessary funding. Ahmed Ressam, for example, robbed hotels and unsuccessfully attempted to hold up a currency exchange office. When his request for more money from al Qaeda was turned down, he opened a store in Montreal where he collected credit card information that was then passed to associates for fraud.[20] Similarly, the cell in Frankfurt engaged in drug pushing as a source of sustenance while planning the Strasbourg attack. Other groups engaged in selling false identities as a means of raising money. From this perspective, the criminal activities of a terrorist cell designed to maintain the cell and provide operational funding can be an indicator that the cell is preparing for action.

Yet there is a complicating twist. Between 2000 and 2002, the European al Qaeda network divided the labor among different cells, with some clearly designated as operational while others provided financial support. The cell in Milan under Ben Khemais, for example, stole the credit cards subsequently used by the Frankfurt group to purchase chemicals for explosives. In other words, criminal activities of one cell may be part of the support structure for another cell. This division of labor within a small matrix generally results in a one-way flow of money, which may indicate which cell is actually planning an operation. Moreover, in some cases, criminal activities leave a trail that investigators and intelligence analysts can follow to obtain a more accurate picture of at least one segment of the overall terrorist network.

As al Qaeda has evolved in ways that place greater reliance on local initiatives, so cells have become more autonomous and consequently have to be more self-sufficient. This was certainly the case in the Madrid bombings of March 2003. In fact, the operations were funded exclusively by money from Moroccan drug traffickers who had converted to Islam and, in effect, had transformed themselves from criminals interested in profit to terrorists pursuing a political agenda. As part of this transformation they became integrated into the local terrorist network that carried out the train bombings. The radicalized Moroccan drug traffickers provided the finances, the logistical support, network contacts to obtain the explosives, and the organizational skills to plan and implement the attack.[21] They spent somewhere between €41,000 and €54,000, had a contingency fund of €52,295, and had drugs worth between €1.35 and €1.53 million as the basis for a "war chest" to fund a sustained campaign of terror.[22]

SUSPICIOUS FINANCIAL TRANSACTIONS

To make it more difficult to launder money through the financial system undetected, the United States government, in effect, co-opted the banks. Regulations were established to ensure that all cash deposits of $10,000 or more were accompanied by a cash transaction report (CTR)—which the bank subsequently had to submit to the Treasury Department's Financial Crimes Enforcement Network (FinCEN). In addition, any transaction that aroused the suspicion of bank employees—irrespective of the amount involved—had to be passed to law enforcement in a suspicious activity report (SAR). While some critics suggest that the effort involved does not yield commensurate payoffs, the SAR mechanism in particular offers a way of identifying activities worth investigating further. Although initially designed to assist in combating drug-related money laundering by organized crime, this mechanism has broader application. Suspicions may arise from the behavior, character, or origin of the person (or persons) involved in the transaction or simply from the fact that no obvious commercial or financial basis exists for the transaction. Indeed, the requirement to report suspicious activities or transactions has become a standard not only for the United States but also for most countries with well-developed financial systems. When accompanied by provisions for due diligence and the "know your customer" requirements, the SAR system provides opportunities for warning about criminal activity.

Although this has some relevance to terrorist activity, terrorist financial transactions cannot simply be equated with money laundering—in spite of the tendency of many commentators to make such an equation. In fact, the two phenomena are basically different. Money laundering takes dirty money, hides its origins and ownership, and makes it appear to be the proceeds of legitimate economic activity. Terrorist operational financing, in contrast, takes money and simply uses it for terrorist attacks and their preparations. More often than not, it is a case of clean money being used for nefarious purposes. Terrorism financing may encompass money laundering, especially when the money involves the proceeds of crime. Yet most dirty money is simply spent by terrorists rather than put through an elaborate laundering process. Terrorists do not actually launder much money.

Terrorist networks do, however, want to move their money covertly and with the same lack of attention from the authorities that criminals seek when they move the proceeds of their crimes. In this sense, some terrorist groups engage in financial activities that clearly have a functional resemblance to money laundering and employ many of the same mechanisms and modalities for moving money as do transnational criminal organizations. In some respects, terrorists have even added to the repertoire of options for moving money by supplementing or even supplanting front companies with charities. Al Qaeda has also made extensive use of underground banking such as the *hawala* system to move money without leaving a significant paper trail. Yet al Qaeda still uses the normal banking system, disguising the transactions as legitimate business activities and financial transfers.

There are occasions, therefore, when the SAR system can trigger a warning that might be linked to terrorist activity. The SAR system flags all suspicious transactions and is not limited only to those involving money laundering. In the aftermath of the September 11 attacks, as investigators sought to discover the activities and movements of the hijackers, they learned that a money transfer from the United Arab Emirates to Sun Trust Bank in South Florida provided crucial funding support to several of the hijackers. That transfer reportedly had also prompted a suspicious activity report. If this was the case the report was not evaluated in time or followed up with a further investigation. Nevertheless, it suggests that the SAR system could, on occasion, indicate a money transfer linked directly to support of terrorist operations.[23]

Following the money is certainly no magic bullet leading to early detection and warning. As with all other aspects of counter-terrorism intelligence, attempts to use the movement and disbursement of money as a warning indicator will involve false leads, false positives, and false alarms. At the same time, leads that could offer warning indicators might appear so innocuous that they are overlooked or discounted. Signals and noise are often distinguishable only in retrospect. Moreover, linking finances to operational planning and attacks by terrorists proves problematic because only a relatively small part of terrorists' financial resources are actually devoted to operations, as opposed to recruitment and training. In other words, the financial signals themselves are intrinsically quiet, modest, and a very small part of the overall financing effort.

Most financial transactions are neutral in the sense of setting off alarms. They take on real significance only when they are carried out by or involve people who are themselves regarded as an actual or potential threat, either because they are known or suspected terrorists or because they have strong associations with terrorists. It is the marrying of the person or persons and the transaction that is critical, rather than the transaction itself.

Such limitations on the use of financial flows and financial transactions as warning indicators, however, do not mean that this dimension of activity can or should be ignored. In combating terrorism, financial scrutiny is a key component of a much broader process. That process must include network analysis, travel analysis, and telephone toll analysis, as well as fusion of open sources and covert intelligence such as electronic intercepts and information from defectors.

Conclusions

The implication of all this is that terrorist financial transactions can be an important, if elusive, indicator of a planned or impending attack. Such indicators must be combined with other intelligence as part of an overall assessment. While financial transactions alone are unlikely to provide definite and unequivocal warning, they sometimes spark a search for other parts of the puzzle, providing a stimulus for a tighter focus or simply a heuristic for a shift in direction. If their value as indicators is to be maximized, however, several other things need to be done as part of the intelligence process. Some of these occurred in response to September 11 but need to become standard operational procedures.

- Establish a baseline of understanding about terrorist finances that encompasses knowledge of established patterns and sensitivity to deviations, anomalies, and the possible emergence of new patterns. The deeper the knowledge base and the greater the level of understanding of terrorist finances, the greater the chance of detecting activities or shifts in activities that provide warning indicators.

- Bring together combinations of expertise from disparate fields. In examining financial transactions, national security intelligence personnel and even law enforcement agents need accountants and banking and financial experts who are familiar with the often arcane practices of the financial world and are adept at following money trails and identifying anomalies.

- Recognize that analysis is as important as collection. If the information has been reported but not analyzed, the result is the same as if it had not been reported in the first place. This has been particularly the case with SARs. The analysis of SARs needs to be expedited and the results shared with the wider intelligence community on a timely basis.

- Information needs to be pooled, shared, and widely examined in the intelligence community to ensure that financial indicators are seen in a broader context and considered along with other possible indicators of a forthcoming attack. In attempting to combat terrorist networks, government itself needs to operate as a network, transcending the bureaucratic turf wars and obstacles to information sharing that characterized the intelligence process prior to September 11. Information is not a resource to be guarded but one to be shared as widely as possible within the bounds of an intelligence community that goes well beyond the traditional agencies.

- Information needs to be widely diffused not only within the federal government but also at the state and local levels—albeit with sensitivity to security concerns. As a study of the ecology of warning carried out by Global Futures Partnership at the Central Intelligence Agency noted, the consumers for warning go well beyond the traditional national security community.[24] As terrorist organizations engage in organized crime, the people best placed to detect specific examples of this are in local law enforcement. The broadening of the information customer base can provoke a further search for indicators that can augment and refine the whole intelligence process.

- Since following the money effectively requires the cooperation of multiple governments, transnational intelligence sharing with trusted allies is essential. Even though these governments might not have the same capacity for following the money, their willingness to allow the United States some kind of access to their financial systems could be critical.

No single one of these measures is a palliative. Nor will financial indicators always be identified and understood as such. Much of the time the intelligence task is an attempt to know the unknowable. And even when something is known, its significance is not always fully understood or appreciated. Nevertheless, these kinds of changes—which are really about attitude, procedure, and bureaucratic norms and practices rather than about bureaucratic structures—are essential to ensure that financial indicators become an integral part of the indicator and warning process.

The other thing that needs to be done—and this can be tacit rather than explicit—is to back away from the effort to freeze terrorist assets. While frozen funds provide a tangible measure of effectiveness, the strategy has been given more significance than it deserves. Freezing terrorist assets obscures more than it reveals and gives a misleading impression of the success of the counter-terrorism strategy. Moreover, the unintended consequence of the freeze strategy is to make terrorist networks such as al Qaeda even better at hiding their money, thereby making it more difficult to follow the money and perhaps obtain the level of warning that is necessary. The tacit abandonment of the freeze strategy, therefore, might be an important contribution to the detection of financial indicators that would otherwise be elusive and the achievement of a degree of warning that would otherwise be unobtainable.

The good news is that there has been some progress in these directions. The staff report of the 9/11 Commission on the financing of terrorism, which was released in August 2004, noted that following the money was a very powerful tool, an assessment that contrasted with its rather lukewarm assessment of the freeze campaign.[25] The bad news is that the tracking efforts have become both very public and very controversial. In June 2006, the *New York Times* revealed that the Bush Administration had obtained access to financial transactions going through the Society for Worldwide Interbank Financial Telecommunication (SWIFT), headquartered in Belgium. SWIFT, the Clearing House Interbank Payments System (CHIPS), and Fedwire, the payments system run by the Federal Reserve, handle the vast bulk of international funds transfers. Access to SWIFT, therefore, was critical to any attempt to follow terrorist money. Indeed, the administration claimed that the Terrorist Finance Tracking Program, as it was now called, had achieved major successes and had led to several key arrests. It was also very critical of the disclosure, claiming that the revelations about SWIFT, in effect, provided al Qaeda with critical knowledge about U.S. intelligence sources and methods and therefore made it less likely that the program would retain its effectiveness.[26] The issue is both difficult and complex. Trade-offs have to be made between privacy rights and the public right to know about such initiatives on the one hand and the importance of secrecy to the effectiveness of a follow-the-money program on the other. From the perspective of this chapter, however, an effective tracking program could be crucial in providing warning of another major attack. As such, it is at least comforting to know that such a program has been a key part of the effort to combat terrorism—and will continue to be so.

PART II

Case Studies of Terrorism Financing and State Responses

CHAPTER SIX

Financing Afghan Terrorism

Thugs, Drugs, and Creative Movements of Money

THOMAS H. JOHNSON

The September 11, 2001, attacks on New York City and Washington refocused attention on Afghanistan for the first time since the end of the Soviet intervention in 1989. Afghanistan, an ethnically, linguistically, religiously diverse country, has been in continual and violent conflict since the 1970s. "By 1992 there were more personal weapons in Afghanistan than in India and Pakistan combined. By some estimates more such weapons had been shipped into Afghanistan during the previous decade than to any other country in the world."[1] An entire generation of Afghans has known little other than conflict. This nearly continuous conflict and Afghanistan's remoteness make it attractive to extremists and terrorists in search of a relatively safe and secure haven for refuge, training, and basing operations.

In the decade following the Soviet Union's invasion of 1979, the country became a battlefield and training ground for Islamist extremists and terrorists. Muslim volunteers, who became known as Afghan Arabs—a focus of this chapter—flocked to join Afghan resistance movements and fight in what was viewed as a "holy war," or *jihad*, against the Soviet invader. Among these volunteers was Osama bin Laden, who would eventually recruit, train, and deploy jihadists and terrorists from Afghanistan. During the anti-Soviet jihad bin Laden "built al-Qaeda's financial network from the foundation of a system originally designed to channel resources to the mujahideen."[2] The Taliban, and especially its leader, Mullah Omar, became the initial focus of the global war on terrorism after 9/11, due to its close ties to al Qaeda and the sanctuary they provided to Islamic terrorists of many nationalities. Egyptians, Algerians, Lebanese, Chechens, Saudis, Gulf Arabs, Palestinians, Sudanese, Filipinos of the Abu Sayyaf Brigade, and even Bosnian Muslims all perfected their skills in Afghan training camps. Abu Musab al Zarqawi, who became the leader of al Qaeda in Iraq, was one of those who refined their skills in Afghan training camps.

Two other Afghan leaders, Gulbuddin Hekmatyar and Abu Sayyaf, have also played prominent roles in Afghan terrorism networks in recent years. Hekmatyar's faction, Hizb-e-Islami Gulbuddin (HIG), is allied with al Qaeda and Taliban remnants. On February 19, 2003, the U.S. government formally listed Hekmatyar as a Specially Designated Global Terrorist under the authority of Executive Order 13224.[3] Sayyaf represents a hard-core Islamic fundamentalist element that is anti-West, anti-American, and closely allied with the Muslim Brotherhood. The U.S. State Department states that Sayyaf provides logistical support and training facilities to Islamic extremists who have been involved in terrorism and insurgencies in Bosnia and Herzegovina, Chechnya, Tajikistan, Kashmir, the Philippines, and the Middle East.[4]

Afghan terrorism and its financing are best understood by examining the historical process by which the early insurgents against the Soviet Union developed into terrorist organizations connected to a transnational jihadi network and thereby became part of an international terrorist financial network. Afghanistan's history is replete with what the CIA calls "blowback," or the unintended consequences of intervention for the external powers that have attempted to shape this country's future.[5]

The Taliban: The Harbinger of Afghan Terrorism

By late 1985, it was clear to the new Soviet leader, Mikhail Gorbachev, that the Soviets' occupation of Afghanistan, which began in December 1979 when the Soviets invaded to prop up a failing Afghan Marxist regime, was a quagmire. Gorbachev stated that he planned to withdraw troops from Afghanistan, which had become a "bleeding wound" to his country and administration. In 1989, after suffering over 26,000 killed and 50,000 wounded, the Soviets completed their troop withdrawal across the Amu Darya according to the terms of their peace agreement with the United States, Pakistan, and Afghanistan.[6] The withdrawal of the Soviets left a power vacuum in the country, especially in Kabul, a vacuum that would have important implications for the evolution of Afghan radicals, jihadists, and terrorists.

Most observers expected the Afghan regime to quickly collapse after the Soviet withdrawal. Surprisingly, the Soviet puppet regime headed by Mohammad Najibullah fought on without direct Soviet military involvement until April 1992, when *mujahidin*[7] finally entered Kabul and forced Najibullah's resignation. While the fall of Najibullah brought the *mujahidin* parties to power, it also exposed the serious differences among them, eventually resulting in a new civil war and the near destruction of Kabul. The *mujahidin* rivalries reflected divisions of ethnicity (primarily between the Pashtun, Tajik, Hazara, and Uzbek), religion, region, clan, and tribe.

In 1994 the Taliban arrived on the Afghan scene with little warning, vowing to install a traditional Islamic government in Afghanistan and end the fighting among the *mujahidin*. Formed by theology students studying in the neighboring provinces of Pakistan and devout Pashtun Sunni Muslims, the Taliban were led by Mullah (Sunni Muslim cleric) Muhammad Omar, who had fought in the anti-Soviet war. The predominantly Pashtun (and southern) Taliban overthrew the largely Tajik (and northern) *mujahidin* Kabul regime, capturing Kabul in September 1996. The Taliban viewed this regime as responsible for the continued civil war and the deterioration of security in the major cities, as well as for discrimination against Pashtuns.

The war-weary Afghans, particularly fellow Pashtuns, initially welcomed the Taliban because they believed Taliban promises to bring peace and stability to their ravaged country. However, the Taliban represented a radical departure from traditional Afghan norms of social behavior, instituting a religious police force, Amr Bil Marof Wa Nai An Munkir (Promotion of Virtue and Suppression of Vice), to brutally uphold its hard-line interpretations of Islam. They banned women from work and education and used extreme punishments, such as stonings and amputations, to enforce its new laws.

After the Taliban seized Kabul, the *mujahidin* government of Burhanuddin Rabbani (a Tajik and leader of the *mujahidin* Jamiat-i-Islami, Islamic Society Party) fled north and formed the anti-Taliban Northern Alliance that would fight the Taliban regime over the next five years, eventually teaming with the United States to defeat the Taliban in December of 2001.

THE TALIBAN AND PAKISTAN: SUPPORT AND FINANCING

There is little doubt that Pakistan significantly aided the Taliban's swift rise to power in Afghanistan between 1994 and 1996. The Taliban movement was partly a manifestation of Pakistan's desire to support Islamist rule rather than Afghan nationalism. In fact, some have argued that the Taliban basically became a proxy for Pakistan—and to a lesser extent, Saudi Arabia.[8] While both of these countries influenced the Taliban, they did not control them, in part because of the diversity of funding sources on which the Taliban relied.

Pakistan's overriding interest in Afghanistan included a stable government that Pakistan could manipulate, strategic depth, a training area for Kashmiri militants, and secure trade routes to Central Asia. Pakistan provided military support, including arms, ammunition, fuel, and military advisers, to the Taliban through its Directorate for Inter-Services Intelligence (ISI). In addition, Pakistan provided the Taliban with diplomatic support and considerable financial support.

Pakistani interest in Afghanistan was renewed following the 1990 popular revolt that broke out in Indian-controlled Kashmir. Under protest from India and the United States, Pakistan was forced to remove Kashmiri insurgent groups that had originally trained on its territory. Pakistani leaders began to see the importance of a friendly Afghanistan as a place for Kashmiri fighters to train, and government policy toward Afghanistan was increasingly shaped by the situation in Kashmir.[9] This led to Pakistan shifting its support, financial and military, away from Gulbuddin Hekmatyar—the main beneficiary of Pakistan aid and policies during the anti-Soviet jihad—to the Taliban movement in 1994. In addition to needing shelter and training for the Kashmiri insurgents, Pakistan was frustrated with Hekmatyar's failure to gain control of Kabul and secure the country.

Pakistani politicians also viewed support for the Taliban as a means to rein in its country's powerful intelligence services. During the 1980s, the United

States and other Western nations, as well as Saudi Arabia and Gulf States, channeled enormous sums of money through Pakistan in support of the most radical Islamist groups in Afghanistan. This money was funneled and distributed to groups in Afghanistan through the ISI, but substantial portions were used to fund the ISI itself. The result was an influential and powerful ISI that not only was running Pakistan's Afghan policy but also had extensive influence on Pakistan's domestic politics, economy, and media.[10] With the election of Benazir Bhutto in 1993 and the end of outside assistance to the Afghan *mujahidin*, it became increasingly difficult for the ISI to retain its totality of power. Bhutto, who had been forced from office by the ISI in 1990, supported the Taliban over the ISI-supported Hekmatyar as another strategy to undermine the intelligence services.[11]

Another important incentive for Pakistani support to the Taliban stemmed from its desire to open a secure trade route between Pakistan and Central Asia. With the highway between Kabul and Uzbekistan blocked by fighting, Pakistan made known in June of 1994 its desire to open a route to Central Asia through Kandahar and Herat.[12] Islamabad believed that truck trade from Pakistan through Afghanistan to Central Asia would help their ailing economy. In addition, Pakistan had plans for a railway linking Pakistan and Central Asia, as well as oil and gas pipelines from Central Asia through Afghanistan.[13] At the time, the biggest roadblock to trade with Central Asia was instability throughout Afghanistan. The Bhutto government would call upon the Taliban to address its security concerns. The subsequent success of the Taliban in opening truck travel and its simultaneous capture of Kandahar were perhaps beyond anything their Pakistani supporters could have imagined.

Pakistani logistical support to the Taliban was extensive. Pakistan provided vehicles, ammunition, fuel, and spare parts. Although some have claimed that logistical support to the Taliban was restricted to secret exchanges through mountain passes and trails, the extent of the support makes this nearly impossible. Instead, it is very likely that logistical support for the Taliban was in the open, with equipment carried on highways in large convoys.[14] Further support for the Taliban was probably offered by Pakistan in the form of military training. New recruits to the Taliban were indoctrinated through a two-month training program just over the border from Pakistan throughout the mid-1990s.

Pakistani operational military support to the Taliban was also important.

Several Taliban offensives in Afghanistan were extremely well planned and executed. The Taliban forces exhibited a swift, effective style of warfare that could only have come with the assistance of the Pakistani military and the ISI.[15] On several occasions between 1994 and 1995, the Taliban attempted to take over cities and towns, only to be severely defeated. These same defeated forces came back a short while later displaying capabilities, gained through Pakistani assistance, which they had previously lacked. It also seems likely that Pakistan provided direct military assistance to the Taliban on limited occasions.

Despite sanctions and an ailing economy, Pakistan managed to provide substantial financial aid to the Taliban movement. During a budget crisis in 1997, Pakistan still provided $6 million to pay the salaries of the Taliban leaders, and this assistance later increased to $30 million in fuel, food, ammunition, military equipment, and spare parts in 1998.[16]

For as much support as Pakistan offered the Taliban movement, however, the Taliban movement was not a mere puppet of Pakistan.[17] While the vast majority of the Taliban came from the Pashtun tribal areas along the Afghan-Pakistan border, Taliban leadership was indigenous to Afghanistan, and they pursued their own independent agenda.[18] The Taliban exploited divisions within the Pakistani power structure through its use of extensive social, political, and economic ties to this network.[19] Whereas Afghan warlord Gulbuddin Hekmatyar was completely dependent on the ISI for support, the Taliban had numerous connections throughout the Pakistani government and business circles. These connections were especially important because they cushioned the impact of sudden changes in Pakistani government policy.

TRUCK TRADE AND SMUGGLING — FINANCING THE TALIBAN

Pakistani trade with Central Asia, alluded to above, helped to create additional sources of financial support for the Taliban. By December 1994, regular deliveries of cotton from Central Asia were arriving in Quetta after paying the Taliban a transit fee of $5,000.[20] According to a World Bank study, by 1997 the Taliban was receiving $75 million from the smuggling trade between Afghanistan and Pakistan. Although smuggling resulted in the loss of millions of dollars in revenues annually to Pakistan, the government did very little to control it. Corruption emanating from Pakistani-Taliban relations was rampant. Pakistani army officers at the border received significant bribes to allow smugglers to transit the border. The traders who profited from the smuggling contributed significant sums of money to the *madrasahs* where the Taliban recruits trained, as well to officials in the provincial governments of Baluchistan and the Northwest Frontier Province in exchange for amnesty.[21]

The provincial governments in the border areas of Pakistan had reason to support the Taliban. During the war with the Soviets, many of the Pashtun tribal leaders received money and arms from the ISI and the provincial governments in exchange for allowing *mujahidin* fighters to pass on their way to Afghanistan. Pashtun tribes on the border were allowed to purchase food in Pakistan and sell it across the border to the *mujahidin* in Afghanistan for a significant profit. With the end of the Soviet intervention, many refugees returned to Afghanistan, and the Pakistani government permitted the continued sale of food and supplies to Afghanistan, resulting in a rapid increase in organized groups in Pakistan that were tied to the Taliban.[22] The sale of fuel to the Taliban, especially in the border areas, made huge profits for some Pakistani politicians.[23] When the Taliban swept to power in Afghanistan, it received much of its supplies from this cross-border trade.

Private traders in Pakistan and along the Pakistan-Afghanistan border also had reason to support the Taliban movement. The group that Ahmed Rashid has come to call the "transport mafia" in and around the Quetta and Chaman areas in Baluchistan had become very frustrated with the lack of stability in Afghanistan. Profits from smuggling were curtailed due to fighting in and around Kandahar, and expansion of smuggling routes to Iran and Central Asia was put on hold. There were extensive links between the transport mafia and the Taliban leadership since they came from the same tribes, and intermarriage further cemented relationships.

Not surprisingly, the Taliban received huge portions of its funding from the transport mafia. Sources claim that the Taliban received $450,000 from the Quetta-Chaman transport mafia over the course of just a few days in 1995.[24] Shortly after the Taliban takeover of Kandahar, smuggling traffic began to increase dramatically as routes extended into Iran and Turkmenistan, and members of the smuggling mafia encouraged further Taliban conquest in western Afghanistan. Largely based on this pressure, the Taliban rejected the advice of the ISI and launched a failed attack on Herat in May 1995.[25] This influence would only grow with the increase in drug smuggling in the mid-1990s.

THE TALIBAN AND OPIUM PRODUCTION AND TRANSPORT

During the first three and a half years of Taliban rule, the opium crop flourished in Afghanistan, and the Taliban became heavily involved in narcotics production.[26] Taliban forces were able to secure the trade routes, allowing for opium to flow without the threat of banditry or illegal checkpoints. In 1996, opium production increased in Kandahar province alone from 74 to 120 metric tons. In 1997–1998, overall production totaled 2,700 metric tons, an increase of 43 percent over the previous year.[27] From 1996 to 2000, opium cultivation increased from 57,000 hectares to 91,000 hectares (with a yield of 4,600 metric tons of opium in 1999).[28] Besides expanding the area in which Afghan opium was grown, the Taliban also significantly expanded transport and distribution routes. In addition to various land routes to Pakistan and Central Asia, the Taliban also began flying out opium in cargo planes from Kandahar and Jalalabad to Abu Dhabi and Sharjah in the Gulf.[29]

The Taliban were well aware of the importance of opium production in raising badly needed revenue. The Taliban imposed an opium transport tax of as much as 20 percent of each truckload of the drug.[30] The Taliban justified its policies towards narcotics in classic Orwellian "double-speak." The head of the Taliban's anti-narcotics control forces in Kandahar was quoted as saying that the Taliban imposed a strict ban on hashish production because "it is consumed by Afghans and Muslims," but "opium is permissible because it is consumed by *kafirs* (unbelievers) in the West and not by Afghans or Muslims."[31]

In 2000, under mounting international pressure and in its attempt to garner diplomatic recognition, the Taliban banned opium production. Draconian measures brought immediate results.[32] Opium production fell from 3,300 metric tons in 2000 to 185 metric tons in 2001.[33] While poppy cultivation largely vanished from the areas of Afghanistan under Taliban control, opium and its derivatives continued to flood out of the northeastern corner of Afghanistan under the control of the Northern Alliance, with production growing by 162 percent in 2001.[34]

While explicit supporting evidence is scarce, the Taliban may have also curtailed the opium trade in an effort to inflate prices, which had plummeted because of over-production in previous years. Prices for opium were $60 per kilogram in 1998 but had plunged to $20 per kilogram in 2000. Most analysts, however, point to the ultimate role of Mullah Omar in mitigating the drug trade in Taliban-controlled Afghanistan. In 1999 he issued his first edict, calling for the opium trade to be reduced by one-third. In 2000, Mullah Omar called for a ban on all poppy cultivation, citing it as un-Islamic, and the ban was largely successful.[35]

THE TALIBAN AND SAUDI ARABIA: SUPPORT AND FINANCING

Saudi Arabia was critical for the success of the Taliban. Saudi Arabia was among the first countries to recognize the Taliban regime in May 1997, despite the fact that Osama bin Laden, a committed enemy of the Saudi regime, had returned to Afghanistan a year earlier. Support for the Taliban even continued after the passage of UN Security Council Resolution (UNSCR) 1267 on October 15, 1999, which demanded the rendering of bin Laden to justice within 30 days.[36] Even with Saudi Arabia in compliance with international efforts to freeze Taliban assets, the two regimes continued to enjoy close relations, which ended only when the Taliban refused to hand over bin Laden in September 2001.

Zakat was a key funding source for Saudi aid to the Taliban and its allies. The international relief agencies that channel *zakat* to international recipients are regulated by the Saudi Ministry of Islamic Affairs, which used *zakat* as a kind of foreign aid for Wahabbi organizations.[37] Saudi financial aid was especially important for the Taliban because in addition to providing direct aid to the movement, it was also a major source of support for mosques and *madrasahs* in Pakistan.[38] Students of these *madrasahs* served as an important military reserve for the Taliban in their continuing conflict with the Northern Alliance.

Afghan Arabs and Osama Bin Laden: The Operational Agents of Afghan Terrorism

During the 1980s, thousands of Middle Eastern and North African Arabs (as well as others), often with the assistance of their home governments, flocked to Afghanistan and fought the Soviets together with the Afghan *mujahidin*. Many of these jihadists would eventually play a central role in international terrorist operations in the decades that followed the Soviet withdrawal.

Osama bin Laden was one of the first Arabs to join the Afghan resistance and an early key participant in the development and funding of the Afghan Arabs.[39] During this time bin Laden developed relationships with some of the more radical Islamist members of the *mujahidin*, such as Gulbuddin Hekmatyar, Abu Rasul Sayyaf, and Mullah Mohammed Omar, who later emerged as the Taliban's supreme leader.

By 1984, bin Laden had carved out a significant role in recruiting and funding non-Afghan *mujahidin* during the war by running an organization known as the "Bureau of Services," or MAK (Maktab al-Khidamat). His privileged background as a member of an extremely affluent and important Saudi family made him an important piece of the financial and logistical support network for the Afghan resistance, and partly for this reason MAK was nurtured by Pakistan's ISI.[40] Bin Laden's most important role in the anti-Soviet Afghan jihad was recruiting and funding jihadists from mosques around the world. It is estimated that the 30,000 who joined the jihad during the 1980s consisted of an almost equal number of Arabs and non-Arabs. Bin Laden, who attracted 4,000 volunteers from Saudi Arabia alone,[41] eventually became the nominal leader of the Afghan Arabs. He reportedly paid Arabs expenses of $300 per month to fight in Afghanistan.[42]

The actual importance of the Afghan Arabs as a military force supporting the *mujahidin* has been controversial. Many observers argue that they played a minimal role in anti-Soviet operations,[43] and in fact many Afghan *mujahidin* found the Arabs an annoyance. The Afghan Arabs dressed, prayed, spoke, and basically behaved in ways foreign to Afghans, and thus represented a group alien to their traditions.[44] While the actual number of Afghan Arabs serving in Afghanistan during the anti-Soviet jihad is another source of debate, Ahmed Rashid has estimated some 35,000 Afghan Arabs served in Afghanistan between 1982 and 1992.[45]

Afghan Arabs played a critical political role in the evolution of terrorism in Afghanistan. Many of the Afghan Arabs joined either the Islamic party of the Hizb-e-Islami (Party of Islam) led by Younus Khalis or Harakar-i-Inqilab-i-Islami (Islamic Revolutionary Forces) led by Nabi Muhammadi. Many of the senior leaders of the Taliban came from this latter jihadist group that represented the party of the majority of traditional Afghan clerics. Other Afghan Arabs became the staple of al Qaeda.

The 1989 Soviet withdrawal from Afghanistan led to the dispersion of Afghan Arabs, including bin Laden, across the Middle East, although some continued to participate in Afghan politics.[46] As a group, these jihadists were changed men. They had helped defeat the Soviet Union, and they had been radicalized through their Afghan experiences with heightened political consciousness and radicalism married to their guerrilla warfare skills. Having defeated Soviet imperialism in Afghanistan, they felt that they could do the same to U.S. imperialism. These Afghan Arabs would eventually join jihadist operations, including those in Bosnia, Chechnya, China, Kashmir, the Philippines, and Tajikistan. These operations clearly suggest the desire of these radical Afghan-trained Islamists to internationalize their campaign."[47]

Bin Laden used a variety of sources to fund the recruitment of the Afghan Arabs during the anti-Soviet jihad. An important source was bin Laden's use of the Golden Chain—an informal financial network of prominent Saudi and Gulf individuals established to support the Afghan resistance. This network collected funds through Islamic charities and other non-governmental organizations.[48]

This financial network would later be complemented by the Bureau of Services, or Mekdat al Khidmat (MAK), organized by bin Laden and his allies. This bureau operated not only as a recruiting network in Muslim communities throughout the Middle East, Southeast Asia, Western Europe, and the United States, but it also provided travel funds and guest houses in Pakistan for recruits and volunteers on the road to the Afghan battlefield.[49] Bin Laden used MAK and the Golden Chain to finance training camps and procure weapons and supplies for Afghan Arabs. Bin Laden also drew on the network of Islamic charities, NGOs, and educational institutions to recruit volunteers.[50]

Bin Laden created a number of other organizations to fund the Afghan Arabs. For example, bin Laden with his brother Khaled founded the Islamic Salvation Foundation in Saudi Arabia, through which he financed the Afghan *mujahidin*. Funding from this foundation was later extended to support other radical Islamic groups and terrorists around the Arab world. One analyst estimates that the returning Afghan Arabs included "some 5000 Saudis, 3000 Yemenis, 2000 Egyptians, 2800 Algerians, 400 Tunisians, 370 Iraqis, 200 Libyans, and scores of Jordanians."[51] The considerable worldwide support, especially public opinion, for the Afghan *mujahidin* in their fight against the Soviets provided a useful cover under which bin Laden could organize the financial networks that funded the Arab fighters in Afghanistan. According to the U.S. Department of the Treasury,[52] other organizations supporting Afghan Arabs included the Aid Organization of the Ulema (AOU) based in Pakistan, also known as the Al Rashid Trust Afghanistan; the Al Akhtar Trust; al Haramain (Pakistan branch); and Reconstruction of the Islamic Community, also known as Ummat Tamir-i-Pau (Nau).

Osama Bin Laden and the Taliban: A Key Connection for Afghan Terrorism

In May of 1996 bin Laden left Khartoum, Sudan, to return to Jalalabad, Afghanistan.[53] Bin Laden was accompanied by a large number of well-equipped jihadists who would later become the core of the so-called "bin Laden brigade" or Brigade 55.[54] This brigade played a key role for the Taliban on the front lines fighting against the Northern Alliance. It is estimated that bin Laden personally spent $20 million annually on this brigade. While the Taliban suffered a high international cost for hosting bin Laden and his fellow jihadists, this was offset by the domestic benefits the regime gained. In particular, Brigade 55 proved to be instrumental in the Taliban's fight against the Northern Alliance.

Al Qaeda and the Taliban were distinct organizations with their own identities and goals. After 1996, however, the differentiation between bin Laden and the Taliban became less clear because of the complementary nature of their roles in the transnational jihadi terrorist network. The Taliban created an indispensable haven in Afghanistan where extremists like bin Laden and others could meet and plan jihadist attacks in relative safety.

Afghanistan holds great symbolic importance for bin Laden, and he developed a strong relationship with Taliban leader Mullah Omar. As Scheuer argues,

Afghanistan . . . remains at the center of bin Laden's concerns and priorities. The West has largely missed the affection with which bin Laden regards Afghanistan, and the debt of personal honor and religious duty he feels toward Mullah Omar and the Taliban for hosting al Qaeda and refusing U.S. demands to surrender him. . . . Beyond the personal debt to the

Taliban, bin Laden and other Islamic leaders view Afghanistan as the "the only Islamic country" in the world, and the battle going on there against the United States will decide the Muslim world's future and therefore "is one of Islam's immortal battles."[55]

When other Taliban leaders raised concerns and objections about bin Laden or his actions, Omar supported him, partly because bin Laden offered the Taliban financial benefits through the financiers of the Golden Chain as well as his personal finances. Ultimately bin Laden and al Qaeda provided important financial support to its host state. Bin Laden in return was allowed freedom of movement that he had lacked previously in Sudan.[56]

From Afghanistan bin Laden directed a number of terrorist operations that included the 1998 bombings of the U.S. embassies in Kenya and Tanzania, the October 2000 attack on the USS Cole,[57] and the 9/11 attacks on New York and Washington. Bin Laden's safe haven in Afghanistan ultimately allowed him to finance and support numerous jihadist organizations worldwide, including an insurrectionist group in Kashmir, the Abu Sayyaf Brigade and Moro Islamic Liberation Front in the Philippines, and Jemaah Islamiyah in Indonesia. The support also included assistance for Islamist insurrections closer to his safe haven, such as his direct aid to Tajik Islamists in Central Asia.[58]

Afghanistan also offered al Qaeda and associated organizations an invaluable training venue. Bin Laden had established a variety of training facilities in Afghanistan that were used to train Afghan Arabs during the Soviet jihad. Upon his return to Afghanistan in 1996, he regained control of these camps and built others. These camps, funded by bin Laden and contributions from a variety of Arab patrons, were used for training newly recruited Afghan Arabs as well as Taliban fighters. These camps were also used for recruiting and training fighters for Islamist insurgencies in Tajikistan, Kashmir, and Chechnya, among other places.[59] U.S. intelligence estimates that 10,000 to 20,000 fighters underwent instruction in bin Laden–supported camps in Afghanistan from 1996 through 2001.[60] The importance of bin Laden's Afghan camps cannot be overestimated, as they served as a major indirect source of financial support for numerous international terrorists and groups.[61]

Abu Musab al Zarqawi, the leader of al Qaeda in Iraq until his death in 2006, represents an example of how al Qaeda financial support and Taliban collaboration fostered international terrorist networks. Al Zarqawi was one of many Salafi Jordanians who left Jordan to join the Afghan jihad.[62] He eventually became a key bin Laden lieutenant in charge of operations planning and the leader of several dozen militants with the financial support of al Qaeda.[63] Zarqawi was quickly given broader responsibilities and was put in charge of the al Qaeda training camp in Herat, Afghanistan, near the Iranian border, a camp that housed and trained recruits from 18 different Arab countries.[64] Many of the individuals trained in Herat would later prove invaluable to Zarqawi's operations against the American occupation in Iraq as well as his European terrorist operations.

Bin Laden's political support and financial aid would prove pivotal for Zarqawi's operations until he fled Afghanistan to Iran and later Syria after the commencement of the U.S. intervention in Afghanistan in fall 2001. It was only after this departure from Afghanistan that Zarqawi was able to end his dependence on al Qaeda and begin to develop his own financial support from networks in Europe, especially from individuals in Germany and Italy, and from the Middle East. On the eve of the American offensive in Iraq, Zarqawi had over 600 Afghan Arabs under his leadership in Iraq.[65] Despite his new financial independence, Zarqawi remained publicly loyal to bin Laden, creating a new terrorist entity named the al Qaeda Committee for Jihad in Mesopotamia (Iraq).[66]

Gulbuddin Hekmatyar: Other Paths from Mujahidin *to Terrorist*

Al Qaeda was not the only important terrorist organization to take refuge in Afghanistan. On February 19, 2003, the United States designated Gulbuddin Hekmatyar a Specially Designated Global Terrorist.[67] Since the early 1980s it has been quite clear that Hekmatyar was a radical Islamist who despised the United States. One of the great ironies of the American covert aid program to the *mujahidin* in their jihad against the Soviets is that the vast majority of this U.S. aid went to Hekmatyar—a sworn enemy of the United States. Since the fall of the Taliban and the U.S. presence in Afghanistan, Hekmatyar has been accused of numerous attacks on U.S. troops, U.S Afghan allies, and the International Security Assistance Force (ISAF), as well as others.[68] Hekmatyar has repeatedly called for a jihad against the coalition forces in Afghanistan and those who cooperate with them—including the current Karzai government.[69]

A Ghilzai Pashtun from Kunduz, Hekmatyar became a radicalized Islamist during his studies at Kabul University in the late 1960s. After a brief period of involvement with Afghan communists, he became a disciple of Sayyed Qutb and the Ikhwan ul-Muslimeen (Muslim Brotherhood) movement. Ever since, he has been one of the most outspoken and extreme of all Afghan leaders. He was known, for example, to patrol the bazaars of Kabul with vials of acid, which he would throw in the face of any woman who dared to walk outdoors without a full burka covering her face. His insurgency movement—Hizb-e-Islami (HIG)—is built on the Ikhwan model of Islamic revolution, which stresses the establishment of a pure Islamic state and utilizes a highly disciplined organizational structure built around a small cadre of educated elites. With the support of Pakistan, Hekmatyar and HIG would become infamous during the anti-Soviet jihad for assassinations, purges, and infighting with rival groups, especially Rabanni's Jamiat-i Islami, and other *mujahidin* personalities. Many have claimed that he killed more Afghans than Soviets.

Early in the anti-Soviet jihad, Pakistan's ISI chose Hekmatyar as its Afghan favorite. From the 1980s to the early 1990s Hekmatyar's HIG received more funds from the ISI than any other *mujahidin* faction.[70] In 1994, Hekmatyar started training foreign volunteers with ISI backing to support Pakistan's new covert jihad in Indian-held Kashmir.[71] When it later became clear that Hekmatyar was not achieving Pakistan's goals, the new Pakistani government of Benazir Bhutto switched allegiances and helped to organize the Taliban movement.

Despite sharing the Taliban's ideology and Pashtun ethnicity, Hekmatyar was a bitter enemy during the Taliban's initial reigning years. There are also important differences between his vision of an Islamic state and the distorted view of Deobandi thought held by Mullah Omar. Hekmatyar's forces fought the Taliban until they ousted him from his power base around Jalalabad, after which he fled to Iran before returning to Afghanistan in early 2002. Despite residual animosities, however, on the principle that "the enemy of my enemy is my friend"—at least temporarily—he has recently negotiated a truce with the Taliban and an agreement on limited cooperation in destroying the government of Hamid Karzai.

HEKMATYAR'S FINANCIAL SUPPORT

Pakistan's ISI was able to control the flow of funding to the numerous *mujahidin* factions in Afghanistan, with estimates of support from the United States, China, and Saudi Arabia totaling between $6 and $12 billion,[72] and Hekmatyar received more of these financial resources (and supplies) than any other Afghan mujahid. It is also reported that the United States and other foreign supporters paid "stipends" to several HIG commanders.[73] In the 1990s, bin Laden also provided support for Hekmatyar.

Hekmatyar was also the recipient of vast *zakat* from Saudi mosques and wealthy Saudi sheiks. The importance of this source of financial support is indicated by the fact that Hizb-e-Islami (HIG) had offices in Saudi Arabia to facilitate the receipt of such charity.[74] During the anti-Soviet jihad, Hekmatyar maintained close relationships with the Saudis.

The Muslim Brotherhood was also an important financial supporter of Hekmatyar, especially in the early years of the anti-Soviet jihad. The Brotherhood raised monies for him and helped to network a variety of humanitarian volunteer organizations such as the Saudi Red Crescent, the World Muslim League, the Kuwaiti Red Crescent, and the International Islamic Relief Organization. The Muslim Brotherhood's role in recruiting organizations to support Hekmatyar and others (often through intermediaries) represented a dynamic that "intertwined . . . political-religious networks . . . [with other organizations] that raised money and guns."[75]

An additional and important source of financial support for Hekmatyar came from his involvement in the trade and production of narcotics, especially opium and heroin, beginning in the 1980s.[76] The *Washington Post* has reported that Afghans in Pakistan have given U.S. officials accounts of extensive heroin smuggling by commanders under Hekmatyar. According to Barnett Rubin, Hekmatyar was the only Afghan leader to exploit opium profits systematically as a basis for funding a party and a conventional army during the anti-Soviet jihad. Most *mujahidin* commanders were content in selling raw opium, but Hekmatyar also invested in laboratories in partnership with Pakistani heroin syndicates.[77] The ISI cooperates in heroin operations, according to the Afghan accounts given to U.S. officials.[78] It has also been reported that bin Laden greatly strengthened Hekmatyar's opium smuggling operations.[79]

From the early stages of the Afghan resistance to the Soviets, Hekmatyar accumulated and hoarded considerable financial aid and associated support for the fights he envisioned developing with other *mujahidin* after the Soviets left Afghanistan. Once it was clear that Hekmatyar was not going to succeed in his ambitions to rule Afghanistan, he turned the resources he had accumulated to pursue other strategies, many of which involved terrorism. These terrorist activities accelerated after October 10, 2001, when he joined the Taliban to fight the United States and the new Afghanistan of Hamid Karzai.

Wahabbism and Afghan Terrorism

As part of the anti-Soviet effort of the 1980s, Saudi Arabia played a vital role in sponsoring individuals and parties that eventually became involved in Afghan terrorism. In the early stages of the anti-Soviet jihad, Saudi Arabia sent Abu Rasul Sayyaf, an Afghan Islamic scholar, back to Afghanistan to establish a Wahabbi party,[80] Iittihad-i-Islami (Islamic Unity), which would become one of the seven Sunni *mujahidin* parties based in Peshawar, Pakistan. Iittihad-i-Islami was to become the Saudis' favorite Afghan jihad party. This faction, along with HIG, was the principal recipient of U.S.-supplied weaponry during the war against the Soviet occupation of Afghanistan.[81] Arab volunteers became very important to Sayyaf's party. When bin Laden first went to Afghanistan in the early 1980s, Sayyaf was one of the first *mujahidin* leaders he sought out.[82] The personal relationship between the two leaders would continue over two decades[83] with Sayyaf playing a central role in the establishment of the al Qaeda training camps that catered to the Afghan Arabs.[84]

Despite considerable Saudi patronage and the U.S. aid he received through the Pakistani ISI, Sayyaf made his hardline anti-Western views explicitly known. He, for example, denounced the United States during the first Gulf war against Iraq.[85] Even while accepting U.S. aid via the ISI during the anti-Soviet jihad, he made his disdain for the United States well known through his preaching and writing.[86]

Sayyaf would eventually become a member of the Northern Alliance in its fight to oust the Taliban, but there have been continuing questions concerning his real motives. It is reported that Sayyaf was responsible for arranging the meeting that resulted in the assassination of the famous Afghan guerrilla leader and head of the Northern Alliance, Ahmed Shah Massoud, on

September 9, 2001.[87] Many believe that Massoud's assassination was the pre-cursor to what was going to happen two days later—September 11, 2001—arguing that bin Laden and some in the Taliban expected that the United States would most certainly take direct action against them in the wake of the attacks; hence they wanted to eliminate the most effective leader of the resistance to their regime. In addition, the Taliban were planning to start a new long-delayed offensive against the Northern Alliance, which was led by Massoud, on September 10.[88]

Sayyaf's greatest contribution to international terrorism appears to be in the prominent role his organization has played in terrorist training. Beginning in the mid-1990s with ISI and Saudi financing, Sayyaf's terrorist "university," Dawal al-Jihad, located north of Peshawar, Pakistan, has trained jihadists involved in actions in Bosnia and Herzegovina, Chechnya, Tajikistan, Kashmir, the Philippines, and the Middle East.[89] A senior Pakistani military officer has claimed that this one terrorist facility has trained 20,000 volunteers.[90] A Philippine terrorist organization with alleged al Qaeda connections calls itself the Abu Sayyaf Brigade, apparently named after the Afghan Wahabbi jihadist.[91] This Philippine terrorist organization—responsible for kidnapping and killing of many by decapitation in the Southern Philippine island of Mindanao—"actually swore loyalty" to Sayyaf.[92] Sayyaf also report-edly served as Khalid Sheikh Mohammed's mentor and provided the architect of the 9/11 operation with military training at his Sada training camp in Afghanistan.[93]

SAYYAF'S FINANCIAL SUPPORT

Sayyaf was Saudi Arabia's most important client among all of the Afghan *mujahidin* for sectarian reasons. To understand the financing of Sayyaf one need not look far beyond the Saudis. Saudi Arabia was one of the first countries to embrace and support the anti-Soviet jihad in Afghanistan, and both the monarchy and individual financiers played a role in providing assistance. This money would eventually be used to support terrorism by Afghan jihadists, primarily Afghan Arabs, after the end of the Soviet occupation. Since the early 1980s wealthy Saudi businesspeople, bankers, and institutions have supplied the *mujahidin* with financial resources, much of which was fun-neled to bin Laden and eventually served as the financial seed money for al Qaeda and its terrorist operations. Especially important anti-Soviet *muja-*

hidin funding came via a U.S.-Saudi agreement where the Saudis matched U.S. support to the *mujahidin* on a dollar-for-dollar basis. The Saudis gave nearly US$4 billion in official aid to the *mujahidin* during 1980–1990, in addition to more than $3.3 billion spent by the United States.[94] U.S. support continued well into the mid-1990s, even after the success of the Taliban in seizing control over most of Afghanistan. Although the Taliban victory caused concern for most Central Asian states, at the time the United States perceived this regime as a useful bulwark against Shi'a Iran. As Rashid points out, it was only after 1997 that domestic interest groups in the United States successfully drew attention to the fundamentalism of the Taliban, particularly in their treatment of women, which led to a shift in the U.S. attitude towards this regime.[95]

Saudi financial support was given to individual *mujahidin* leaders such as Abu Rasul Sayyaf and his Iittihad-i-Islam, or Islamic Unity party, and Hekmatyar's Hizb-e-Islami party, both of which promoted Wahabbism.[96] This assistance fit into U.S. and Pakistani plans for supporting the most militantly anti-Soviet insurgents, who were also often the most radical Islamic organizations. Sayyaf had close ties to Saudi intelligence, which perceived him as a direct channel to the *mujahidin*, bypassing the Pakistani ISI.[97]

Saudi financing was of paramount importance to Sayyaf. Like Hekmatyar, Sayyaf retained offices in Saudi Arabia to collect *zakat* that was funneled back to Iittihad-i-Islami in Afghanistan. Sayyaf also was the beneficiary of financial resources and support from Pakistan's Jamaat-i Islami party—another organization that has been prone to support radical jihadist organizations. Finally, many of the Afghan Arabs that were funded by bin Laden were members of Sayyaf's Iittihad-i-Islami. Hence, it can be argued that bin Laden indirectly helped to finance Sayyaf.[98]

Assistance to Afghan Terrorism from Sympathetic States

Over the course of the anti-Soviet jihad and its aftermath, the *mujahidin* morphed into radical jihadist and terrorist organizations. These same *mujahidin* received considerable financial aid and at least implicit sponsorship from a wide variety of states, including the United States, Pakistan, Saudi Arabia, China, and others, who extended aid without considering who the *mujahidin* really were or what their ultimate politics might be. Many veteran *mujahidin*, especially Afghan Arabs, then reemerged in unexpected places and became key lieutenants of bin Laden's and other terrorist networks. Blowback[99] has become the shorthand for the unintended consequences of these states' initial financial support and encouragement. In the Afghan case, this blowback surprised the original financiers of the anti-Soviet Afghan jihad, reflecting a "blind spot" in U.S. intelligence.[100]

The United States initially funded the *mujahidin* with a primary goal in mind: "bleeding" the Soviet Union with the hope of forcing them to withdraw in humiliation from Afghanistan. Very few in the U.S. government thought that the *mujahidin* could actually defeat the Soviets, and the United States simply wanted to turn Afghanistan into a Soviet "Vietnam." This led the United States to use Pakistan to distribute financial aid and supplies due to their ideal position as a transit country. Pakistan, in turn, used this opportunity to pursue its own strategic interests.

Pakistan used its support for the *mujahidin* as the means to further its goals to be the dominant player in Afghanistan and turn Afghanistan into a cooperative neighbor. Pakistan was able to control the flow of funding to the numerous *mujahidin* factions in Afghanistan and promote those that furthered its own goals. While the perceived threat from India and fear of a two-front war has shaped Pakistan's relationship with Afghanistan, the desire for "strategic depth" is not the only driver of Pakistan's foreign policy towards Afghanistan. The relationship has also been affected by Pakistan's strategy towards India-controlled Kashmir. Camps in Afghanistan created for training Afghan Arabs during the anti-Soviet jihad have been recycled to train guerrilla forces for fighting in Kashmir. Pakistan has used these jihadi forces as a bargaining chip with India in an attempt to gain more autonomy and even independence for Kashmir.

Saudi Arabia was most interested in pursuing an Afghan strategy that promoted Wahabbism. The vast majority of their financial aid went to Sayyaf's Iittihad-i-Islami, their Wahabbi Afghan representative. The Saudis were also instrumental in funding and recruiting bin Laden's Afghan Arabs. And, of course, the Saudis also supported and helped finance the Taliban as well as Hekmatyar. The Saudis have been a financial backer, to one degree or another, of all Afghan jihadists.

Once it became clear that some *mujahidin* had transformed into radical jihadists and terrorists, the United States, Saudi Arabia, and Pakistan ended any official financial support. However, the financial aid from Saudi Arabia—

and to a lesser extent from Pakistan—that had originated as *zakat* continued to fund new jihadists and terrorists. Years of supporting the *mujahidin* resulted in a kind of inertia that continued even after these groups were clearly identified as terrorists or accused of harboring terrorists. State financial support helped to establish the *mujahidin*, but financial resources emanating from private citizens, especially in Saudi Arabia in the form of *zakat*, enable the groups to prosper even after the end of Soviet activities in Afghanistan.

Conclusion

There is little doubt that Afghanistan has been a central front in the global war on terrorism. While the defeat of the Taliban regime and the unprecedented elections that followed would suggest a brighter future, Afghanistan could again become a haven for international terrorists. Warlords continue to control much of the country despite President Karzai's policies aimed at marginalizing them. Moreover, the Taliban have reemerged as a political and military force, and Afghanistan is now embroiled in an intense, violent, and growing insurgency. The country remains awash in weapons and economically depressed, with most of its people living in abject poverty. Economic recovery and development remain distant goals and, most troubling, narcotics production and trafficking are once again driving the economy, with Afghanistan producing approximately 87 percent of the world's heroin.[101] Mullah Omar, Osama bin Laden, Gulbuddin Hekmatyar, and Abu Rasul Sayyaf all remain alive and committed to Afghan terror to one degree or another.

By 2005, it had become apparent that Afghanistan's Taliban Islamic militants had regrouped and resumed attacking the Afghan government, the U.S. military, and "soft targets" with new vigor. Especially troubling is evidence suggesting that Afghan insurgents are emulating the tactics of insurgents in Iraq—such as the use of suicide bombers, roadside bombs, assassinations, and kidnappings. Foreign financial assistance and, to a lesser extent, the opium trade continue to provide funds for terrorism in Afghanistan. There are reports of jihadists returning from Iraq to Afghanistan and the Pakistani tribal areas. It is also reported that terrorist training camps along the desolate Pakistani-Afghan border have reopened.[102]

If Afghanistan does falter, and the events of 2006 indicate such a trend, the financial channels currently supporting terrorism within Afghanistan could be used once again to support international terrorist organizations. There remains a network of Islamic charities that could be exploited to serve as the financial foundation of such terrorism, a booming narcotics industry, and a number of regional actors who would benefit from such resurgence. The United States and the international community must make a long-term commitment to a secure and stable Afghanistan. The international resources required to secure and stabilize Afghanistan are but a fraction of the opportunity costs associated with an Afghanistan dominated by terrorists or radical jihadists.

CHAPTER SEVEN

Al Qaeda Finances and Funding to Affiliated Groups

VICTOR COMRAS

Considerable mystery and intrigue surround the al Qaeda terrorist network and its funding sources. We know more today than we did five years ago about its financial tools and structure, but there is much about its sources of supply and funding that we still do not know. The CIA estimated that it cost al Qaeda some $30 million per year to sustain itself in the period preceding 9/11. But there are no clear estimates as to what al Qaeda and the loosely connected network of terrorist cells associated with it actually need or spend today. And we still do not know how much money these groups raise or from whom.[1]

The roots of al Qaeda's financial network trace back directly to the extensive recruiting and financing networks that were originally established to support anti-Soviet jihad activities in Afghanistan. These networks grew in sophistication during and after the Bosnia war.[2] Al Qaeda established and infiltrated several international Muslim charities, using them to collect and mask their funds. These charities disbursed funds not only for legitimate humanitarian relief but also for al Qaeda activities, including the establishment and maintenance of new, radical Islamic centers. These centers propagated a virulent theology and strong opposition to Western culture and values, and they provided al Qaeda and other Salafist groups the means to undertake extensive worldwide indoctrination and recruitment activities. Al Qaeda also relied heavily on sympathetic financial facilitators and on other deep-pocket donors to obtain and channel the funds necessary to meet its logistical and operational requirements. The 9/11 Commission Report concluded that a core group of these financial facilitators was responsible for a substantial part of its funding. The facilitators obtained funds from various donors in the Gulf countries, in particular Saudi Arabia. "Some individual donors surely knew," the Commission report says, ". . . the ultimate destination of their donations. . . . These financial facilitators also appeared to rely heavily on certain *imams* at mosques who diverted *zakat* donations to the facilitators and encouraged support of radical causes."[3]

Considerably less certainty surrounds other sources of al Qaeda funding. The 9/11 Commission indicated that it had been presented no credible evidence supporting allegations that bin Laden used his own money to fund al Qaeda, or that al Qaeda was funded by foreign governments, or that it ran its own businesses, dealt in conflict diamonds, or profited from the international drug trade.[4] The 9/11 Commission admitted, however, that this lack of credible evidence might be due to the absence of hard intelligence regarding al Qaeda's finances.[5] Despite these assertions, many international experts and observers continue to believe that al Qaeda has drawn, and continues to draw, on all of these sources of funding.[6]

The overthrow of the Taliban regime and the elimination of al Qaeda's bases and safe haven in Afghanistan resulted in al Qaeda splintering into scores of independent and copycat cells increasingly responsible for their own funding and maintenance. Many of these groups now rely on local donations, internet solicitations, petty crime, and the drug trade to sustain themselves.[7]

In the aftermath of 9/11 al Qaeda reportedly experienced some difficulties in raising funds, and, according to the report of the 9/11 Commission, had to cut back significantly on its expenditures.[8] This was due, in large part, to the presumed success the United States and certain other governments had in identifying and closing down many of al Qaeda's traditional resource bases. However, there is some reason to question these assumptions.[9]

There is mounting evidence that large sums are still being raised and transferred to al Qaeda–inspired terrorists, including the insurgents in Iraq and Afghanistan. This includes reports of money flowing from Saudi Arabia and other Muslim states into the hands of Iraqi Sunni insurgents, including so-called "foreign fighters" such as those previously led by Abu Musab al-Zarqawi.[10] And there are further indications that the number of self-sustaining local al Qaeda–like cells is continuing to grow in Europe and elsewhere.[11] New training camps have also been established in remote areas in the Middle East, Southeast Asia, Africa, and several countries of the former Soviet Union.[12] Indications are that the pace of funds being provided to radical fundamentalist teaching centers around the world has also continued to increase.[13]

Much of the investigation and research related to al Qaeda has dealt with its funding mechanisms and not with the motivation and dedication that have generated the donations. After four decades of fundamentalist Islamic expansion, a good part of this dedication comes from radical Islamic conviction and its associated absence of tolerance towards other ethnic or religious customs and beliefs. It has generated a growing resentment and alienation towards Western cultural influences in the Muslim world. The continuing Israeli-Palestinian conflict and the war in Iraq have also served as motivations for recruitment and support of a new generation of al Qaeda–related jihadists. A clearer understanding of these and other factors driving jihadi recruitment is essential to developing an effective strategy to counter this trend.

Al Qaeda's Financial Facilitators

The 9/11 Commission pointed to a core number of financial facilitators involved in raising, moving, and storing the money al Qaeda used for its maintenance and logistical and operational requirements. These facilitators raised funds from donors primarily in the Gulf region but also from other countries around the world. Using bogus and legitimate charities and businesses as covers, they enabled al Qaeda to develop a substantial financial network in Southeast Asia, Europe, Africa, and Asia.

The capture of Sheikh Mohammed and several other senior al Qaeda officials dealt a serious but far from knockout blow to al Qaeda's financial network. These al Qaeda leaders reportedly divulged names and information that led to the identification of other facilitators and funding sources.

Credible information and leads were also obtained from past al Qaeda financial operatives such as Omar al-Faruq and Jamal Ahmed Al-Fadl, who broke with al Qaeda in the mid-1990s.[14] Several of the individuals identified by these sources have been designated by the U.S. Treasury and the United Nations al Qaeda and Taliban Sanctions Committee. But despite the freezing orders against their assets, many continue their financial and business operations. Knowing the names of al Qaeda's financial facilitators, and designating them, has not been enough to put them out of business!

Saudi Arabia has been heavily criticized in the media for allowing certain identified al Qaeda financiers, such as Osama bin Laden's brother-in-law, Mohammed Jamal Khalifa, and Wael Hamza Julaidan—both of whom were very active in raising funds for al Qaeda—to continue to conduct business affairs in Saudi Arabia.[15] Similarly, Youssef Nada and Idris Nasreddin, both designated as al Qaeda financiers by the U.S. Treasury Department and the United Nations, continue to manipulate their assets from their headquarters in Campione d'Italia and Rabat, Morocco.[16] Although Saudi millionaire Yasin Al-Qadi was designated by the United States and the United Nations for funding al Qaeda through his Muwafaq charity, he continues today to run a billion-dollar business empire.[17] A high court in Turkey recently ordered the unfreezing of Al-Qadi's assets in Turkey, disregarding his UN designation, on the basis that there was insufficient evidence to establish that he had engaged in financing terrorism.[18]

CHARITIES

Al Qaeda's use of charities to raise, mask, transfer, and distribute the funds it needs has also come under close scrutiny by counter-intelligence and enforcement agencies. The charities used by al Qaeda, the agencies discovered, included several major Islamic umbrella organizations headquartered in Saudi Arabia. Among them were the International Islamic Relief Organization (IIRO), the Benevolence International Foundation, the al Haramain Islamic Foundation, the Blessed Relief (Muwafaq) Foundation, and the Rabita Trust. These organizations have branches worldwide engaged in religious, educational, social, and humanitarian activities. But we now know that they were also used, knowingly or unwittingly, to channel funds to al Qaeda.

Charity forms a very important part of Muslim law and tradition. There is a recognized religious duty in the Muslim world to donate a set portion of one's earnings or assets to religious or charitable purposes (*zakat*) and, additionally, to support charitable works through voluntary deeds or contributions (*sadaqah*).

In countries that have no established income tax system, like Saudi Arabia or the United Arab Emirates, the *zakat* substitutes as the principal source of funding for religious, social, and humanitarian organizations. The funds are collected by the government, local mosques, or religious centers. *Sadaqah* contributions are made directly to established Islamic charities. Because both *zakat* and *sadaqah* are viewed as personal religious responsibilities, there has traditionally been little or no government oversight of these activities. Donations in large measure remain anonymous.

Al Qaeda took full advantage of this lack of oversight to open its own front charities and to solicit funds through collection boxes at mosques and Islamic centers. It placed operatives in key positions within these and other established charities to do its bidding. Funds raised for, or allocated by, al Qaeda could then be co-mingled, maintained, and transferred with funds designated for legitimate religious, cultural, relief, and development activities—their ultimate use by al Qaeda only becoming known once the monies were transferred or diverted to al Qaeda-related recipients.[19]

In 1962, the Saudi Royal family established the Muslim World League in Mecca and provided it with funds to support the propagation of Wahabbi Islam. The Muslim World League funded institutions outside of Saudi Arabia, especially in Afghanistan, Pakistan, Southeast Asia, and the Middle East. The organization also became active in Europe—including countries of the former Soviet Union—and North America. Saudi public and private support for these activities during the last four decades has, according to some estimates, exceeded $75 billion.[20] One can draw a link between this conversion effort and the rapid rise in appeal of al Qaeda throughout the Muslim world.

The International Islamic Relief Organization (IIRO) is another Wahabbi-sponsored charity. Established in 1978, it has branch offices throughout the world, including 36 in Africa, 24 in Asia, 10 in Europe, and 10 in Latin America, the Caribbean, and North America. The bulk of its financial contributions come from private donations in Saudi Arabia, including a long-standing endowment fund (Sanabil al-Khair) that generates a stable income for its various activities. The IIRO continues to be closely associated with the Muslim World League. Prominent Middle East figures and financiers have supported this mainstream Islamic charity.[21]

According to a CIA report, funds raised through the International Islamic Relief Organization were used to support at least six al Qaeda training camps in Afghanistan prior to 9/11.[22] Evidence produced in Canadian court proceedings linked the IIRO directly to groups responsible for the 1998 bombings of the American embassies in Dar es Salaam and Nairobi.[23] The former head of the IIRO office in the Philippines, Mohammed Jamal Khalifa, was also accused of links to al Qaeda and terrorist activities.[24] On August 3, 2006, the U.S. Treasury Department finally took steps to designate the IIRO branch offices in the Philippines and Indonesia, charging that they had long been involved in fund-raising for al Qaeda and affiliated terrorist groups. Treasury also designated Abd Al Hamid Sulaiman Al-Mujil, the Executive Director of the Eastern Province Branch of IIRO in Saudi Arabia. According to the designation order, Al-Mujil used his position in the IIRO to bankroll al Qaeda's operations in Southeast Asia.[25]

The Benevolence International Foundation (BIF)is another Saudi umbrella charity organization that has helped fund al Qaeda. Benevolence was established in the late 1980s as two separate organizations. One, the Islamic Benevolence Committee, was a charity based in Peshawar, Pakistan, and Jeddah, Saudi Arabia. Its titular founder was Sheikh Adil Abdul Batarjee. Its sister organization, Benevolence International Corporation, was set up as an import-export business in the Philippines by Mohammed Jamal Khalifa, also the head of the Philippines' IIRO office and bin Laden's brother-in-law. Both organizations were engaged in fund-raising efforts for the *mujahidin* in Afghanistan, but they appeared to work separately until the early 1990s. In 1992, they became the Benevolence International Foundation and opened new branches throughout Southeast Asia, Europe, and America.

The U.S. Treasury Department took action in December 2001 to designate Benevolence International Foundation as financiers of terrorism. The United States subsequently asked the UN al Qaeda and Taliban Sanctions Committee to add Benevolence to its list of entities associated with al Qaeda. The Treasury Department maintained that BIF and its chief executive officer, Enaam Arnaout, were involved in "the purchase of rockets, mortars, rifles and offensive and defensive bombs, and . . . [their distribution] to various mujahideen camps, including camps operated by al Qaeda."[26] The Treasury document also cited direct links between Arnaout and bin Laden through one of his lieutenants, Mamdouh Mahmud Salim. Testimony at the 2001 trial *United States v. Bin Laden et al.* implicated Salim in efforts to develop chemical weapons and obtain nuclear weapons components for al Qaeda.[27]

The al Haramain Islamic Foundation, based in Jeddah, has been one of Saudi Arabia's most active charities in the spread of Islamic fundamentalism. Al Haramain reportedly funded some 3,000 Wahabbi missionaries around the world and concentrated on establishing new Wahabbi mosques in Southeast Asia, the Balkans, and Africa. According to its website, al Haramain maintained operations in some 49 countries. After 9/11, al Haramain was put under close international scrutiny as a conduit for al Qaeda funding. During the pre-9/11 period, al Haramain reportedly raised some $30 million per year, drawing its funding largely from Saudi donors, including the Saudi government. In fact, its founding General Manager, Shiek Aqeel al-Aqeel, maintained a close relationship with the Saudi Ministry of Islamic Affairs.

On March 11, 2002, the United States and Saudi Arabia jointly designated the Bosnia and Herzegovina and Somalia offices of al Haramain as al Qaeda funding sources. Al Haramain Somalia had funneled money to Al-Ittihad al-Islami, a designated terrorist group, by disguising the funds as contributions for an orphanage project, an Islamic school, and mosque construction.[28] The Bosnia office was linked to Al-Jemaah al-Islamiyah al-Masriyah and to Osama bin Laden. Further investigation implicated branches in Albania, Croatia, Ethiopia, Kenya, Kosovo, Indonesia, Pakistan, and Tanzania. The Russian government also complained to Saudi Arabia about alleged al Haramain funding for Chechen rebels.[29] The Saudi government has removed Shiek Al-Aqeel as al Haramain's General Manager and ordered the closing of 15 branches outside Saudi Arabia.[30] It does not appear, however, that Saudi Arabia has taken any other actions against him. Shiek Aqeel al-Aqeel was designated a terrorist by the U.S. Treasury in June 2004, and his name was added to the United Nations Consolidated al Qaeda associate list.[31]

The Blessed Relief charity, also known as the Muwafaq Foundation, was established in 1991 by Yasin al-Qadi, who was subsequently identified as an associate of Osama bin Laden. The stated purpose of the charity was to "relieve disease, hunger and ignorance." It was active in Bosnia during the Balkan wars, but was closed in 1998 following allegations of fund-raising and transferring funds on behalf of al Qaeda and other terrorist organizations. Al-Qadi was designated a terrorist financier by the U.S. Treasury Department on October 12, 2001,[32] and was added to the UN-designated list on October 17, 2001.[33]

The Rabita Trust, begun in Pakistan in 1988, ostensibly worked to repatriate and rehabilitate stranded Pakistanis from Bangladesh. Its stated aims were to disseminate *dawah* (culture) to expound the teachings of Islam, "and to 'defend' Islamic causes in a manner that safeguards the interests and aspirations of Muslims, solves their problems, refutes false allegations against Islam, and repels inimical trends and dogma which the enemies of Islam seek to exploit in order to destroy the unity of Muslims and to sow seeds of doubt in the Muslim brethren."[34] Members of the trust included Pakistan's ministers of Finance and Interior, Saudi Prince Talal ibn Abdul Aziz, the secretaries general of the Muslim World League and the International Islamic Relief Organization, and the president of the Council of the Saudi Chamber of Commerce. Most of its funding was secured from Saudi businesspeople. Funds from the trust reportedly were used for a number of al Qaeda–related activities, including recruitment and training in Afghanistan, Pakistan, and elsewhere. The Rabita Trust was run by Wael Hamza Julaidan, who the U.S. Treasury Department charged was an associate of bin Laden and Ayman al-Zawahiri. He was formally designated by the United States and the UN as an al Qaeda associate in late 2002.[35] The government of Pakistan has suspended the activities of the Rabita Trust in accordance with its designation by the United Nations as a source of al Qaeda funding.[36] Wael Hamza Julaidan remains active in Saudi Arabia.

These are but a few of the charities that al Qaeda has used to support indoctrination, recruitment, training efforts, logistical maintenance, and terrorist activities. The current status of many of these charities is unclear. Some remain in operation. The International Islamic Relief Organization has new top leadership in Saudi Arabia, but many of its local chapters retain their past management and structure. Likewise branches of al Haramain, despite closing orders from Saudi Arabia, continue to be active in many countries, including Somalia and Indonesia. Other closed charities have merely reopened under new names.

Many of the charities that have been designated are deeply embedded in the social and humanitarian fabric of the communities they serve. They provide critical services that are not easily replaced. Lajnat al Daawa Al Islamiya

(LDI), a Kuwait charity active in Pakistan and Afghanistan, is a case in point. Although it had been linked with al Qaeda, its activities were considered critical to ongoing Afghan relief activities. The charity ran five medical clinics, three Islamic schools, and an orphanage in different parts of Pakistan. At the time, the UN Special Representative to the Secretary General for Afghanistan, Lakhdar Brahami, indicated that, given the important role that LDI has played in Afghan relief activities, some consideration should be taken to de-listing this charity.[37] Lashkar-e-Taba, another designated charity, remained in operation under the name Jamaat-Ud-Dawa and played a critical role in bringing relief to the Pakistan-Kashmir-India earthquake victims.[38] Many of the charities used by al Qaeda were only shams, serving to hide al Qaeda fund-raising and fund-transferring activities.[39] But in many cases the charities, as well as their sponsors, were simply the victims of infiltration and abuse. Field auditing of charities in conflict zones is a very difficult task. And while there have been numerous reports of funds being diverted in the field from their intended purpose, it is often impossible to determine the extent to which such diversions were hidden from senior home charity officials.[40] Another difficult area is the use of these charities to proselytize for al Qaeda and similar Salafist terrorist groups. Defenders of these charities argue that their alleged support for the teaching and preaching of radical Islamic theology or jihadism should not be enough to link them to terrorism.[41] But while it may not always be clear when the line between preaching theology crosses into indoctrination for terrorism, hate, and violence, it is clear that such groups must be closely scrutinized and held accountable when they do cross that line.[42]

BUSINESS SUPPORT FOR AL QAEDA

There is considerable anecdotal information that al Qaeda and its sympathizers continue to raise money through their own business activities. Shortly after September 11, U.S. investigators looked at several businesses in Yemen that were implicated in providing funding to al Qaeda. They named the Al Hamati Sweet Bakeries and two honey businesses, Al Nur Honey Press Shops and Al Shifa Honey Press for Industry and Commerce. Despite the Treasury Department's charge that these companies knowingly funneled money to bin Laden and helped transport arms for al Qaeda, both these businesses are still operating.

Al Qaeda's financial facilitators also make use of networks of companies and shell companies, shell banks, and offshore trusts to raise money, hide assets, and protect their identity and the identity of other financial contributors. Some progress has been made in tightening regulation and oversight over such shell companies and trusts, but several countries continue to retain a liberal "no look" policy in the belief that it will stimulate new business or investment activity within their territory. During the early 1990s, al Qaeda ran a series of international businesses out of its safe haven in Sudan. According to testimony given in U.S. court by Jamal Ahmed al-Fadl, many of these businesses were part of a shell corporation named Wadi al-Aqiq. Other companies al-Fadl mentioned included the Laden International Company, an import-export concern; Taba Investment, a currency trading firm; Hijra Construction, which built bridges and roads; and the Themar al-Mubaraka Company, which grew sesame, peanuts, and white corn on a farm in Sudan for the group. The 9/11 Commission Report indicates that these businesses were closed down by the Sudanese government when al Qaeda was expelled in 1998. Nevertheless, little information was made available concerning the disposition of these assets, and the possibility remains that the shell companies involved continued to possess assets outside Sudan.[43]

In a report submitted to the United Nations al Qaeda and Taliban Sanctions Committee, the government of the Philippines indicated that Mohammed Jamal Khalifa, Osama bin Laden's brother-in-law, had established a network of businesses and charitable institutions that provided funds to the Abu Sayyaf group and other extremist organizations.[44] These reportedly included the Khalifa Trading Industries, ET Dizon Travel Pyramid Trading, Manpower Services, and Daw al-Iman al-Shafee Inc.[45]

Another al Qaeda operative, Wali Khan Amin Shah, established several shell companies in Malaysia, as did Hambali, who founded the import-export company Konsojaya Trading Company to hide terrorism-funding transactions.[46]

In Europe, Youssef Nada and Idris Nasreddin established a series of shell companies in Liechtenstein, Switzerland, and Italy to hide and protect their transactions and holdings and to move al Qaeda money. Nada and Nasreddin were able to continue to manage these assets well after they had been ordered frozen pursuant to UN Security Council resolutions.[47] In order to circumvent the sanctions against him, Nada changed the registered name of two companies in Liechtenstein and used them to begin a process of liquidation. Liechtenstein was unable to identify which assets were being liquidated, as it had not required the shell company to maintain any list.[48] In mid-2005, an NBC News investigation highlighted the continuing activities of Nasreddin's NASCO conglomerate in Northern Nigeria, where little oversight is provided over the use and destination of the funds generated.[49]

These activities point also to an interesting nexus between businesses run for and on behalf of al Qaeda, its deep-pocket donors, and the charities that provide these businesses and deep-pocket donors deniability, protecting them from charges of knowingly financing terrorist organizations. The charities also provide an ideal conduit to mask the transfer of funds to al Qaeda. On the flip side, it is not uncommon for large and small Islamic charities alike to own and control their businesses in order to use these unregulated funds as they please. These businesses may have also been used to fund al Qaeda operations. Operation Green Quest uncovered such links in its investigation of Yasin al-Qadi and his involvement with BMI, the Arabic Beit ul Mal, or House of Finance. Green Quest established that there were links between BMI and an Islamic charity called Mercy International. Mercy, in turn, was tied in with al Taqwa and was implicated in several al Qaeda operations, including the bombing of the American embassies in Kenya and Tanzania.[50]

An investigation into the activities of a number of Saudi and other Middle Eastern businesspeople working out of Herndon, Virginia, also unveiled a network of some 100 intertwined companies and charities funding al Qaeda and other terrorist groups. These included Islamic educational, cultural, and charitable organizations, as well as for-profit business and investment firms. Most of the educational and charitable organizations were "paper" organizations, all registered at a common address but having no apparent physical structure. This network became known as the Safa Group.[51]

The Safa Group was closely associated with the SAAR Foundation, a charity funded by Saudi billionaire Salaeh Abdul Aziz-al Rajhi with branches in both Canada and the United States. Evidence showed that the Safa Group, using the various affiliated charities and companies under its control, transferred money in convoluted transactions designed to prevent investigators from tracking the ultimate recipients. Collateral evidence supported the view that these recipients included al Qaeda, Hamas, and other associated terrorist groups.[52]

OTHER AL QAEDA FUNDING SOURCES

Attention is also being focused again on al Qaeda's and the Taliban's use of the international drug trade operating out of Afghanistan and Pakistan's northwest territory. How much of this money may still reach al Qaeda is uncertain. The Taliban was known, pre-9/11, to take a large cut from this $6 billion per year drug trade. While the 9/11 Commission was dubious that any of these funds reached al Qaeda, other experts maintain that they remain critical to funding al Qaeda's continuing presence in remote areas of Afghanistan and neighboring regions.[53] Some experts believe that al Qaeda's reliance on drug money has increased as a result of the crackdown on charities. Admittedly, evidence linking al Qaeda directly to the drug trade is scarce. Yet Mirwais Yasini, head of Afghanistan's Counter Narcotics Directorate, maintains that the Taliban and its allies derived more than $150 million from drugs in 2003. He believes that there is still a "central linkage" between many of the drug traffickers, Mullah Omar, and bin Laden.[54] Drug funds are also reported to be crucial in al Qaeda's operations in areas of the former Soviet Union, including Chechnya.[55]

THE NEW AL QAEDA

Since 9/11 and the United States-led coalition victory in Afghanistan, al Qaeda has gone through a transformation. Its network structure has splintered. Al Qaeda's *shura*, or high command council, no longer plays a central role in soliciting funds or allocating expenditures. Rather, al Qaeda's largely compartmentalized cells have become responsible for much of their own financial support. These local cells now operate autonomously, raising funds through local businesses, charities, and petty crime, such as extortion, drug and cigarette smuggling, and credit card and coupon fraud.[56] They are also increasingly using internet sites and chat rooms to raise funds and stimulate support for their radical jihadi cause.[57] The crackdown on al Qaeda financing following 9/11 may have led al Qaeda to transfer a portion of its exposed assets into untraceable precious commodities. By some accounts, this process began as early as 1998, when freezing actions were first initiated in the United States and Europe against the Taliban. The commodities used by al Qaeda allegedly included gold, diamonds, and tanzanite. These are small, easy to store and transport, and hold their value over time. They can also be released in small quantities in the market without attracting attention.[58]

More controversy surrounds allegations that al Qaeda was involved in the Central and West Africa conflict-diamond trade. Numerous credible reports of such activity surfaced in 2003 but were challenged by CIA and FBI analysts who were unable to substantiate such reports.[59] The 9/11 Commission Staff Monograph on Terrorism Financing concluded that "no persuasive evidence exists that al Qaeda . . . had any substantial involvement with conflict diamonds."[60] Yet the stories persist.[61] And a court in Belgium convicted two alleged al Qaeda associates of illegally importing conflict diamonds into the country.[62] Whatever al Qaeda's involvement, it is clear that it has become increasingly active in Africa south of the Sahara. There it has found several areas that are fertile for recruitment, including those engaged in conflict and in diamond smuggling.[63]

BANKING FOR AL QAEDA

From the beginning, al Qaeda made use of the international banking community to conduct many of its financial activities. Osama bin Laden, other top leaders of al Qaeda, and many of its financial facilitators maintained bank accounts in Europe, North America, and other international banking centers. Starting after the 1998 embassy bombings, and again after the September 11, 2001, attacks, banks began to increase their vigilance over suspect accounts. New regulatory doctrines, including enhanced "due diligence" and "know your customer" rules were put in place in many countries, as were new requirements that banks and other financial institutions report all "suspicious transactions." Freezing orders were also placed against identified al Qaeda and Taliban funds—as well as the funds of those associated with them. These steps served, to some degree, to drive al Qaeda away from the traditional international banking system and to seek means to mask such transactions. Despite this new regulatory environment, well-heeled financiers and established charities and businesses with links to al Qaeda continue to make careful and prudent use of the international banking system. They have simply become more adept at masking these transactions and at using intermediaries to act on their behalf.[64]

Al Qaeda's facilitators initially were also very active in establishing their own banking networks to handle and hide financial transactions. Two such networks uncovered by investigators, al Barakaat and al Taqwa, provide good examples of such activities.

Al Barakaat was founded in Mogadishu, Somalia, by Ahmed Nur Ali Jim'ale, and its headquarters was established in Dubai. Its principal activities include a telecom service in Somalia and several other countries, a bank, and a money remittance (or *hawala*) system. The U.S. Treasury Department charged that the company skimmed fees from remittances sent by expatriate Somalis and used that money to finance al Qaeda terrorist activities. Al Barakaat offered *hawala* services in some 40 countries, handling an estimated $140 million per year in transmitted payments. Service charges ranged from 2 to 5 percent, generating revenues in the millions for al Qaeda. Additionally, al Barakaat provided a discreet channel for the transfer and distribution of al Qaeda funds.[65]

Al Taqwa, founded by Youssef Nada, an Egyptian-born businessman close to the Muslim Brotherhood, was also one of the first financial networks to be designated for its links with al Qaeda and terrorism. With offices in Switzerland, Liechtenstein, Italy, and the Caribbean, al Taqwa provided important transfer and banking facilities for al Qaeda. According to the U.S. Treasury, the network acted largely as a money laundering facility and provided "indirect investment services for al Qaeda investing funds for bin Laden and making cash deliveries on request to the al Qaeda organization." According to one report, al Taqwa even provided a clandestine line of credit for a close associate of bin Laden.[66]

HAWALA

With the crackdown on international banking transfers, al Qaeda and its brethren have increasingly turned to the use of *hawala*s and similar alternative remittance systems. These systems abound throughout the Middle East, Asia, the Pacific region, and Latin America. They also have well-established branches in Europe and North America. *Hawala* provides a critical remittance function for guest and other migrant or itinerant workers. It provides bank-like services to groups or areas lacking access to traditional banks. By some estimates, *hawala* handles more international transactions in the Middle East, Asia, and the Pacific than the established banking system combined. Certainly, it services a larger client base.

Hawala operations are now coming under greater scrutiny than ever before, and numerous countries have imposed new regulatory measures to curb or oversee their activities. But it has proved exceedingly difficult to implement these regulations effectively, and unregulated *hawala* operations continue to abound. Few records are kept, and transfers are handled informally outside the purview of regulatory oversight. This makes the use of these *hawala* systems attractive to terrorist groups as a principal vehicle for handling money transfers.[67]

Many *hawaladar*s hold accounts at banks in Southeast Asia, South Asia, and the Middle East. They use these accounts, and the facilities offered by correspondent account banking, to support their activities and to hide the identity of the originator and ultimate receiver of the funds. This has led the United States and the European Union to take new steps to regulate correspondent account activity, including requiring the identity and location of the ultimate transferor and transferee.[68]

Using Al Qaeda Money

Figuring out what al Qaeda needs and spends today is certainly no easy task. The demands placed on terrorism funding by al Qaeda's leadership in hiding, the insurgencies in Iraq and Afghanistan, and the proliferation of al Qaeda–like cells around the world are certainly substantial and demonstrate that terrorism financing is still very big business. Before 9/11 the funds required by al Qaeda were used in large part for logistics, training, maintenance, and operations. According to the 9/11 Commission study, al Qaeda funded jihadists' salaries, training camps, airfields, vehicles, arms, and the development of training manuals. Indoctrination and recruitment remained the responsibility primarily of Islamic fundamentalist teachers sympathetic to al Qaeda's cause. And these groups had their own sources of support and funding. Al Qaeda also contributed to supporting the financial requirements of the Taliban regime—although the extent of this support remains also in the realm of conjecture. This may have included up to $10 million to $20 million per year from bin Laden's personal funds. Some funds were also used to support local social, cultural, and humanitarian programs aimed at winning a base of local support in Afghanistan and elsewhere.[69]

The 9/11 Commission Report tells us that before 9/11 al Qaeda was active in establishing alliances with other Islamic terrorist organizations—groups in Southeast Asia such as Jemaah Islamiayah and Abu Sayyaf. They also developed ties with the Salafist groups of North Africa and other emerging Islamist groups in areas of the former Soviet Union. Al Qaeda provided other jihadi groups with start-up funding and additional funding for selected operational activities. Many of these groups developed common resource and funding sources with al Qaeda.

The assumption made by the 9/11 Commission was that al Qaeda's financial support for other groups waned after 9/11.[70] On the other hand, there is much anecdotal information that al Qaeda continued to provide at least some financial and logistical assistance to allied groups in Chechnya, North Africa, and Southeast Asia. According to Indonesian investigators, al Qaeda was responsible for funding Jemaah Islamiayah's Bali bombing operation as well as the August 2003 bombing of the Marriott Hotel in Jakarta.[71] Al Qaeda is also believed to have helped finance the establishment of terrorist training camps in remote areas of Indonesia, Malaysia, the Philippines, and Thailand as recently as the spring of 2003.[72] Al Qaeda also reportedly retained substantial financial links with the Salafist Group for Call and Combat in North Africa and was suspected of providing new financial support to emerging groups in both East and West Africa.[73]

Today, it is the al Qaeda brand name, rather than al Qaeda's own funds, that serves as the most potent source of financing for al Qaeda-linked terrorism. Insurgents and local groups use al Qaeda's banner to raise their own funds directly from both deep-pocket and small-pocket donors, in mosques, Islamic centers, over the internet, and elsewhere. They continue to rely also, in large measure, on the funds made available by government-sponsored and -supported charities whose principal aim is to propagate their fundamentalist doctrines.

Assessing Government Responses

The fight against terrorism has benefited significantly from increased intelligence gathering in the wake of 9/11. Information has been gleaned from forensic banking investigations, from suspicious transaction reports, from seized computers and documents, and from captured al Qaeda operatives or associates. As a result, several terrorist financing schemes have been closed down and those responsible for them arrested.

Steps were taken in a number of countries to designate individuals and entities, including charities, as implicated in al Qaeda and associated terrorism financing. Many of these designations were submitted to the UN for addition to its consolidated list of al Qaeda- and Taliban-associated individuals and entities. The Security Council also passed a series of resolutions imposing on all countries the obligation to freeze the assets of such individuals and entities and to prevent their nationals from providing them any economic resources. To date, some $147 million, most of it belonging to the Taliban in Afghanistan, has been reported frozen by banks in 30 countries. Another $59 million appears to be associated directly with al Qaeda and those supporting it.[74]

Despite these successes, shortcomings in the way the asset-seizure regime has been implemented have limited its effectiveness. The United Nations Consolidated List of Designated Individuals and Entities, which provides the basis for freezing actions and for halting possible terrorism-related transactions, remains woefully inadequate and out of date. Although UN Security Council Resolutions[75] call upon all countries to identify al Qaeda members and associated organizations for inclusion on the list, many countries are reluctant to provide the names of their nationals or residents. The largest percentage of persons and entities listed to date was provided by the United States. The UN list of al Qaeda-related individuals and entities, contains around 210 individuals and 120 entities; that leaves the vast majority of al Qaeda members and associates relatively free to roam and support al Qaeda activities.[76] The UN list must either be expanded rapidly or replaced by a new formula that requires all countries to take the appropriate action against those who finance and actively support al Qaeda terrorism.

Although most countries now have provisions in place authorizing them to freeze assets, these regulations tend to apply only to the individuals or entities designated on the UN Security Council's consolidated list.[77] In some countries, further evidential requirements must be met before freezing actions can be implemented. In addition, most countries have limited their freezing actions to bank accounts, leaving untouched other tangible assets (such as businesses and other income-producing assets) that are in the hands of identified al Qaeda supporters.[78] Several countries have indicated that they lack the means or authority to reach beyond bank accounts. Many others are loathe to target assets that may be owned and administered jointly with non-designated persons, including family members.[79]

Before 9/11, few countries regulated charities other than determining their tax status. Since 9/11, a number of countries have imposed oversight procedures. Reportedly, some 50 charities were shut down in Gulf countries; 40 were reportedly put under official surveillance. Saudi Arabia announced that it has audited some 245 domestic charities and has taken steps to monitor transfers to their overseas branches. It also claims to have shut down 12 charities, and banned donation boxes at stores and mosques. Despite this reported crackdown, Saudi Arabia has submitted few of these charities to the United Nations for official designation, and it continues to take heavy criticism for not yet doing enough to rein in these charities and their support for radical Islamic activities.

Overall, there continues to be a general reticence to act against charities, even those suspected of channeling funds to al Qaeda, unless overwhelming evidence is presented and judicial findings can be obtained. But meeting this high standard of proof is severely inhibited by sensitivities associated with sharing or divulging intelligence information and sources and methods. Only some 24 charities or branches of charities have been designated so far by the UN al Qaeda and Taliban Sanctions Committee. These represent only the tip of the iceberg according to most experts in the field. Even when such charities have been listed, there has been an even stronger reticence to go behind the charities to reach to their directors, donors, and fund-raisers. Yet, this is the crucial step that must be taken to curb the use of such charities for terrorism financing purposes.

International cooperation in support of the effort to combat terrorist financing is still patently inadequate. Most cooperation takes place only on a bilateral basis. While the United States has developed some effective channels for working with other countries, multilateral cooperation remains quite limited. We need a much better forum for providing mutual support and for exchanging information. Neither the UN's Counter-Terrorism Committee nor the Group of Eight's (G8's) Counter-Terrorism Action Group has yet provided an effective platform for cooperative counter-terrorism efforts.[80] In particular, we must find a better way to use intelligence information in freezing assets and in pursuing criminal prosecutions. Too many known terrorist financiers remain free to carry out their trade because of reticence to share intelligence and other evidentiary information.

Finally, we need to focus greater attention on the funding that supports the propagation of radical Islam—the very foundation that al Qaeda and like-minded groups use to indoctrinate and recruit new adherents. We must put much greater pressure on all countries and entities that fund hate or religious intolerance. This should be considered both a foreign policy and public diplomacy initiative.

CHAPTER EIGHT

Hezbollah Finances

Funding the Party of God

MATTHEW LEVITT

It is a painful reality that no counterterrorism effort, however extensive, international, or comprehensive, will put an end to terror attacks or uproot terrorism. There will always be people and groups with entrenched causes, an overwhelming sense of frustration, a self-justifying worldview, and a healthy dose of evil who will resort to violence as a means of expression.

The goal of counterterrorism, therefore, should be to constrict the environment so that it is increasingly difficult for terrorists to carry out their plots. This includes cracking down not only on operational cells but on their logistical and financial support networks as well. In fact, one can so constrict a terrorist group's operating environment that it will eventually suffocate. September 11th illustrated the central role logistical and financial support networks play in international terrorist operations. Clearly, individuals who provide such support must be recognized as terrorists of the same caliber as those who use that support to execute attacks.

Since September 2001, the United States, together with many of its allies, has spearheaded a groundbreaking comprehensive disruption operation to stem the flow of funds to and among terrorist groups. Combined with the unprecedented law enforcement and intelligence efforts to apprehend terrorist operatives worldwide, cracking down on terrorist financing denies them the means to travel, communicate, procure equipment, and conduct attacks. Though the amount of money frozen internationally remains negligible, the impact of freezing terrorists' assets can be significant if the right accounts, companies, or front organizations are shut down. Denying terrorists access to their preferred means of raising, laundering, and transferring funds complicates their efforts to conduct their activities.

However, al Qaeda is not the only international terrorist network that poses a serious threat. Former Deputy Secretary of State Richard Armitage identified Hezbollah as "the 'A-team' of terrorism," and warned that "their time will come, there's no question about it."[1] Semantics aside, such statements are more than just tough talk. Highlights of Hezbollah's record of terror attacks include suicide truck bombings targeting U.S. and French forces in Beirut (in 1983 and 1984) and U.S. forces in Saudi Arabia (in 1996); suicide bombing attacks targeting Jewish and Israeli interests such as those in Argentina (1992 and 1994) and Thailand (attempted in 1994); and a host of other plots targeting American, French, German, British, Kuwaiti, Bahraini, and other interests in plots from Europe to Southeast Asia to the Middle East.[2] Moreover, Hezbollah cross-border operations have spiked since the Israeli withdrawal to the Blue Line in May 2000, as has its proactive support for Palestinian terrorist groups targeting Israel. This activity eventually provoked an all-out war between Hezbollah and Israel in the summer of 2006.

According to U.S. authorities, concern over the threat posed by Hezbollah is well-grounded. FBI officials testified in February 2002 that "FBI investigations to date continue to indicate that many Hezbollah subjects based in the United States have the capability to attempt terrorist attacks here should this be a desired objective of the group."[3] Similarly, CIA Director George Tenet testified in February 2003 that "Hezbollah, as an organization with capability and worldwide presence, is [al Qaeda's] equal, if not a far more capable organization."[4]

Still, some maintain that Hezbollah is merely a "resistance" organization responding to Israeli occupation of disputed land. The distinction is lost on most Western experts given that the group in question employs acts of terrorism such as suicide bombings to achieve its goals. Moreover, many of the operatives in such groups go back and forth between guerrilla units in South Lebanon and international terror cells plotting bombings abroad.[5] In any event, no goal, however legitimate, justifies the use of terrorist tactics and the killing of innocent civilians.

U.S. intelligence officials also expressed concern over possible links between Hezbollah and the now-deceased Iraq insurgent leader Abu Musab al Zarqawi, highlighting the ad hoc tactical relationship brewing between Iran's Shi'a proxy and the loosely affiliated al Qaeda network. In September 2003, when U.S. authorities designated al Zarqawi and several of his associates as Specially Designated Global Terrorist entities, the Treasury Department said that al Zarqawi not only had "ties" to Hezbollah, but that plans were in place for his deputies to meet with both Hezbollah and Asbat al Ansar (a Lebanese Sunni terrorist group), "and any other group that would enable them to smuggle mujaheddin into Palestine." The Treasury Department claimed that al Zarqawi received in excess of $35,000 in 2001 to facilitate the entry of suicide attackers into Israel and provide these missions with the required logistical and material support to ensure their success.[6]

Similarly, while the 9/11 Commission found no evidence that Iran or Hezbollah had advance knowledge of the September 11th plot, the commission's report does note that Iran and Hezbollah provided assistance to al Qaeda on several occasions. For example, al Qaeda operatives were allowed to travel through Iran with great ease. Entry stamps were not put in Saudi operatives' passports at the border, though at least eight of the September 11th hijackers transited the country between October 2000 and February 2001. The report also noted a "persistence of contacts between Iranian security officials and senior al Qaeda figures" and drew attention to an informal agreement by which Iran would support al Qaeda training with the understanding that such training would be used "for actions carried out primarily against Israel and the United States." Indeed, al Qaeda operatives were trained in explosives, security, and intelligence on at least two occasions, with one group trained in Iran around 1992 and a second trained by Hezbollah in Lebanon's Beka'a Valley in the fall of 1993.[7]

In the final analysis, whether suspected ties between Hezbollah and global jihadist elements such as the 9/11 plotters are proved or not, Hezbollah warrants being designated a terrorist group of global reach on the merits of its own activities. The means by which the group finances its vast and varied activities is, therefore, of paramount concern to U.S. intelligence officials and policy makers.

Iran: State Sponsorship of Hezbollah

Iran is believed to fund Hezbollah to the degree of at least $200 million per year,[8] and Hezbollah serves as Iran's proxy to further undermine the prospects for Israeli-Palestinian peace. In the wake of the death of Palestinian leader Yasser Arafat, Hezbollah reportedly received an additional $22 million from Iranian intelligence to support Palestinian terrorist groups and foment instability.[9] This increase in funding may be explained not only by Iran's interest in Palestine but by Hezbollah's success in funding and training Palestinian groups. Iran is known to employ a results-oriented approach to determining the level of funding it is willing to provide terrorist groups. As a U.S. court noted in *Weinstein v. Iran*, the period of 1995–1996 "was a peak period for Iranian economic support of Hamas because Iran typically paid for results, and Hamas was providing results by committing numerous bus bombings."[10] Iranian funding to terrorist groups like Hamas and Islamic Jihad (most often funneled via Hezbollah) increases when they carry out successful attacks and decreases when they fail or are thwarted or are postponed due to ceasefires or other political considerations.

Some of this financial support comes in the form of cash, while much is believed to come in the form of material goods such as weapons. Iranian cargo planes deliver sophisticated weaponry, from rockets to small arms, to Hezbollah in regular flights to Damascus from Tehran. These weapons are offloaded in Syria and trucked to Hezbollah camps in Lebanon's Beka'a Valley. Iran also funnels money to Hezbollah through purportedly private charities closely affiliated with the revolutionary elite led by Supreme Leader Khamenei. This elite controls such key Iranian institutions as the intelligence and security services, the judiciary, and the Revolutionary Council. Mohammed Raad, leader of Hezbollah's Loyalty to the Resistance Bloc in the Lebanese parliament, readily accedes that the group receives funds from Iran, but he maintains that these are only for "health care, education and support of war widows."[11]

Beyond this tangible support, Iran also provides Hezbollah less-quantifiable financial support through training and logistical assistance. Indeed, the most significant modus operandi apparent in all Hezbollah's global activities—financial, logistical, and operational—is that, at some level, all Hezbollah networks are overseen by senior Hezbollah and/or Iranian officials. For example, Hezbollah operatives in Charlotte, North

Carolina, responded directly to Sheikh Abbas Haraki, a senior Hezbollah military commander in South Beirut. At the same time, Hezbollah procurement agents in Canada, who coordinated with the Charlotte cell, worked directly with Hezbollah's chief procurement officer, Haj Hasan Hilu Laqis. Laqis works closely with Iranian intelligence.[12] In Southeast Asia, a Hezbollah network made up almost entirely of local Sunni Muslims was led by Pandu Yudhawitna, a terrorist recruited by Iranian intelligence officers stationed in Malaysia in the early 1980s.[13] This network was behind a failed truck-bombing targeting the Israeli embassy in Bangkok in 1994, as well as a series of other terrorist plots in the region throughout the 1990s. Other examples include senior Hezbollah operatives and Iranian agents involved in the 1996 Khobar Towers bombing in Saudi Arabia, in Hezbollah's efforts to smuggle weapons to Palestinian terrorists through Jordan since 2000, in Hezbollah operations in South America (including the 1992 and 1994 bombings), and in the recruitment of Shi'a students in Uganda.[14] Throughout these and many other cases, a key common thread is the direct contact each cell maintains to senior Hezbollah and/or Iranian intelligence operatives.

It is well-known that Hezbollah operatives often receive training in Iran.[15] In addition, Hezbollah prefers outside operatives to local contacts when running its major operations in other countries. These operatives generally are more trustworthy and better trained.[16]

Iran has also supported Hezbollah's involvement in the Palestinian-Israeli conflict and support of Palestinian militants. U.S. officials contend that, shortly after Palestinian violence erupted in September 2000, Iran assigned Imad Mughniyeh, Hezbollah's international operations commander, to help Palestinian militant groups, specifically Hamas and Palestinian Islamic Jihad (PIJ). According to a former Clinton administration official, "Mugniyeh got orders from Tehran to work with Hamas."[17] In fact, in the March 27, 2002, "Passover massacre" suicide bombing, Hamas relied on the guidance of a Hezbollah expert to build an extra-potent bomb.[18]

Iran has also demonstrated consistent financial and logistical support of Hezbollah and other terrorist groups by establishing terrorist training programs and camps. As of August 2002, Iran was reported to have financed and established terrorist training camps in the Syrian-controlled Beka'a Valley to train Hezbollah, Hamas, PIJ, and the Popular Front for the Liberation of Palestine-General Command (PFLP-GC) terrorists to use short-range rockets. The 2006 conflict between Israel and Hezbollah suggests that this train-

ing also extended to the use of longer-range Syrian- and Iranian-manufac-
tured rockets and other sophisticated guided missile systems. The camps,
including one in Khuraj near the Syrian border, were reported to be under
the command of Iranian Republican Guard Corps (IRGC) General Ali Reza
Tamzar, commander of IRGC activity in the Beka'a Valley.[19] According to a
Western intelligence agency report, which puts the cost of the Iranian program at $50 million, Tamzar's IRGC detachment also trains the Lebanese
and Palestinian terrorists to carry out "underwater suicide operations."[20]
The Iranian terrorist training program was the result of a secret meeting
held in the Tehran suburb of Darjah on June 1, 2002, in advance of a two-day
conference in support of the Palestinian Intifada held in Tehran on June 1–
2, 2002.

Beyond training and arming Hezbollah, Iran bankrolls the group's well-
oiled propaganda machine as well. Al Manar is the official television mouth-
piece of Hezbollah. Called the "station of resistance," it serves as Hezbollah's
tool to reach the entire Arab Muslim world to disseminate propaganda and
promote terrorist activity. At the time of al Manar's founding in 1991, the
station reportedly received seed money from Iran and had a running budget
of $1 million.[21] By 2002 its annual budget had grown to approximately $15
million.[22] Middle East analysts and journalists maintain that most of this
funding comes from Iran.[23]

Syria: Patronage, Headquarters, and Sanctuary in Lebanon

Practically, there is no dealing with Hezbollah without first dealing with
Syria. According to press reports from 2002, Syria actually integrated elements of Hezbollah's military units into the Syrian army formerly stationed
in Lebanon. Also, in a sharp break from the caution exercised by his father,
Syrian President Bashar al Assad has supplied Hezbollah with heavy arms (in
addition to Iranian arms transshipped via Damascus), including a new 220-
millimeter rocket, as became evident during the 2006 Israel-Hezbollah
war.[24] There is strong evidence that, since al Assad inherited the presidency
from his father, Syrian-backed Hezbollah has moved energetically into the
Palestinian arena, both by sending its own operatives to attempt terrorism
inside Israel—as in the case of Jihad "Gerard" Shuman, arrested in January
2001—and by establishing links with terrorist groups in the West Bank,

Gaza, and among Israeli Arabs.[25] For example, Hezbollah operatives working with Force 17 Colonel Masoud Ayad in Gaza reportedly directed small arms and mortar attacks against Israeli civilians in Gaza.[26] In June 2002, Israeli authorities conducting a search in Hebron arrested a Hezbollah operative who had entered the country on a Canadian passport. The arrest of this individual coincided with the discovery in Hebron of mines previously only used by Hezbollah in Lebanon.[27]

Hezbollah and the Iranian Revolutionary Guard Corps were immensely active and involved in Syrian-controlled Lebanon. For example, both groups recruited, trained, and dispatched a cell of Palestinians that killed seven Israelis in a cross-border raid on the northern Israeli community of Metsuba in March 2002.[28] In February 2002, Israeli Foreign Minister Shimon Peres told a press conference outside the UN in New York that, with Syria's blessing, Hezbollah had deployed 10,000 rockets capable of penetrating well into Israel from southern Lebanon. This report proved to be correct, as demonstrated by Hezbollah's ability to repeatedly fire barrages of missiles into northern Israel during July and August of 2006. The *Christian Science Monitor* reported in February of 2002 that "well-informed sources" referred to "truck[load] after truckload" of weapons that arrived in southern Lebanon from May 2000 to December 2001.[29] According to senior U.S. officials, Hezbollah leader Sheikh Hassan Nasrallah and Imad Mughniyeh worked together in planning terrorist attacks globally and across the UN-certified Blue Line separating Israel and Lebanon.[30] Asked if Syria would now allow Lebanon to "trace and hand over" Mughniyeh—who is prominently listed on the FBI's "most wanted terrorist" list—to U.S. authorities, Syrian spokeswoman Buthaina Shaaban responded, "I don't think this is the issue of the moment."[31]

Hezbollah has also engaged in a proactive effort to recruit Israeli Arabs to provide intelligence on Israel and logistical support for terrorist operations. Israeli authorities have broken up several cells of Israeli Arabs associated with Hezbollah and other "Lebanese groups." One such group was a four-person cell suspected of passing "computer programs, maps, various objects and documents which may constitute intelligence" through Ghajjar, a village that straddles the Blue Line, to groups in Lebanon in exchange for drugs and weapons.[32] Similarly, a Hezbollah operative recruited a terrorist cell of Israeli Arabs from the Galilee village of Abu Snan. Israeli authorities uncovered the cell as it was planning kidnapping operations against Israeli soldiers.[33] In July 2002, Israeli authorities arrested Hussein Ali al-Khatib and Hatem Ahmad al-Khatib, two Syrians from the Golan who, in addition to smuggling weapons and drugs, were spying on Israel and passing classified information to Hezbollah contacts.[34] In fact, Hezbollah operatives are known to have gone to Europe, where they picked up false identification and travel documents and continued on to Israel, the West Bank, and Gaza to train and assist Palestinian terrorist groups.[35]

Syria and Lebanon host the greatest concentration of terrorist training camps, particularly for Hezbollah and the PFLP-GC, with Iran running a close second. In them, Hezbollah and Iranian trainers have schooled a diverse crew of Palestinian, Kurdish, Armenian, and other recruits in a variety of terrorist and intelligence tactics. For example, several of the terrorists who carried out the 1996 Khobar Towers bombing were recruited in Syria and trained in Hezbollah camps in Lebanon and Iran.[36]

To a group like Hezbollah, which maintains parallel and intertwined terrorist, guerrilla, political, and social-welfare wings under the banner of one large movement, the multiple and varied forms of support that Iran (and to a lesser degree Syria) offers are at least as significant as the cash that Tehran deposits in the group's bank accounts. Not only does such support provide Hezbollah with technical know-how and material it would otherwise be hard-pressed to find, it also frees up funds Hezbollah raises from other sources, including expatriate remittances, charities and front organizations, and criminal enterprises.

Foreign Expatriate Remittances

Hezbollah receives significant financial backing from the contributions of supporters living abroad, particularly from Lebanese nationals living in Africa, South America, and other places with large Lebanese Shi'a expatriate communities. Hezbollah's main income, according to Hezbollah Parliamentarian Mohammad Raad, comes from the group's own investment portfolios and wealthy Shi'a.[37]

Take the example of Union Transport Africaines (UTA) Flight 141, bound for Beirut, which crashed on takeoff from Cotonou in Benin, West Africa, on December 25, 2003. According to accounts in the Arab press, a "foreign relations official of the African branch of the Lebanese Hezbollah party and two of his aides" were among those killed. Arab press reports also claim the Hezbollah officials were carrying $2 million in contributions, raised from wealthy Lebanese nationals living in Africa, to the organization's headquarters in Beirut, and they note that "this amount represented the regular contributions the party receives from wealthy Lebanese nationals in Guinea, Sierra Leone, Liberia, Benin, and other African states."[38] The fact that Hezbollah immediately sent an envoy to Benin "to console the sons of the Lebanese community" demonstrates the value that the group places on these expatriate communities.[39] The last known transfer of this size occurred in 1998, when Lebanese expatriates in Senegal attempted to smuggle approximately $1.7 million to Lebanon. An Israeli intelligence report focusing on Hezbollah fund-raising operations in the Ivory Coast, Senegal, the Democratic Republic of Congo, and South Africa estimated that the organization raises "hundreds of thousands of U.S. dollars yearly" on the continent.[40] As is the case with all terrorist groups that raise funds under the cover of charitable giving, some donors are defrauded unwittingly into funding terrorism while others are willing participants in Hezbollah's financing schemes.

Hezbollah supporters living in the United States also send remittances to Lebanon to fund Hezbollah activities. For example, in Charlotte, North Carolina, Hezbollah support networks organized regular parlor meetings in members' homes where a collection basket was passed around after watching Hezbollah propaganda videos, usually produced by al Manar.[41] As David Sanchez and John Lombardi point out in chapter 13, similar activity has been documented in South America, particularly in the Paraguayan city of Ciudad del Este in the Tri-Border Area with Brazil and Argentina.

CHARITIES AND FRONT ORGANIZATIONS

Hezbollah uses charities and front organizations to conceal its fund-raising activities. The Al Aqsa International Foundation—a charity that is now banned in the U.S., Germany, and the United Kingdom as a terrorist front—mostly raised funds for Hamas but also raised funds for Hezbollah and al Qaeda.[42] The Martyr's Organization (Bonyad-e Shahid), headed by Mohammad Hasan Rahimiyan, admittedly supplies charitable funds for the families of suicide bombers. In 2001, Paraguayan police searched the home of Hezbollah operative Sobhi Mahmoud Fayad in Ciudad del Este in

Paraguay and found receipts from the Martyr's Organization totaling more than $3.5 million for donations Fayad had sent.[43] Authorities believed Fayad had sent over $50 million to Hezbollah from 1995 until 2001. According to press reports, Iran has traditionally funded Palestinian dissident groups in the Lebanese refugee camps, including al Maqdah, through the Institute of the Palestinian Martyrs.[44]

Another example is the al Mabarrat Charity Association headed by Sheikh Mohammed Hussein Fadlallah. Formerly the spiritual leader for Hezbollah, Fadlallah maintains intimate ties with the organization and remains on the U.S. Treasury's list of Specially Designated Terrorists. In 2003, Lebanese Finance Minister Fuad Siniora was barred from entering the United States because of a donation he made to the al Mabarrat Charity Association in 2000.

In some cases, foreign remittances are funneled to Hezbollah through the group's charities. Members of the Hezbollah cell in Charlotte received receipts from Hezbollah for their donations, including receipts from the office of then–Hezbollah spiritual leader Sheikh Mohammad Fadlallah.[45] One receipt, signed by Ali Abu al Shaer, the financial manager of "the office of his Excellency Ayat Allah Mr. Mohammed Hussein Fadlallah," thanked "brother Mohammed Hammoud," the subsequently convicted leader of the Charlotte cell, for a $1,300 donation.[46]

According to a declassified research report based on Israeli intelligence, Hezbollah also receives funds from charities that are not directly tied to it but are radical Islamist organizations that donate to it out of ideological affinity. "Besides operating a worldwide network of fundraisers, funds are also raised through so-called 'charity funds.' Some of these are extremist Islamic institutions that, while not directly connected to Hezbollah, support it, albeit marginally, in view of their radical Islamic orientation."[47] The report cites many such charities worldwide, including four in the Detroit area alone: the Islamic Resistance Support Association, the al-Shaid Fund, the Educational Development Association (EDA), and the Goodwill Charitable Organization (GCO). Also cited are the al Shahid Organization in Canada, the Karballah Foundation for Liberation in South Africa, the Lebanese Islamic Association, the al Shahid Social Relief Institution in Germany, the Lebanese Welfare Committee, the Help Foundation, and the Jam'iyat al Abrar (Association of the Righteous) in Britain.

While some of these funds undoubtedly pay for Hezbollah's military and terrorist operations, other funds enable the group to provide its members with day jobs, to drape itself in a veil of legitimacy, and to build grassroots support among not only Shi'a but also Sunni and Christian Lebanese. For example, Hezbollah runs the al Janoub hospital in the southern Lebanese city of Nabatiyah. It is one out of a network of some 50 hospitals the group runs throughout the country. The hospital receives $100,000 a month from Hezbollah and is run by Ahmad Saad, the hospital director, who is also a member of Hezbollah's "national health committee."[48]

In light of its support from Iran, Hezbollah does not need to rely on charities to raise funds as much as other groups like al Qaeda or Hamas do. Nonetheless, as Assistant Secretary of State E. Anthony Wayne testified before Congress in September 2003, donating money to charities affiliated with terrorist groups like Hamas or Hezbollah frees up existing funds to support the group's terrorist activities. "If you are funding the organization, even if there are many charitable activities going on, there is some fungibility between funds. You are strengthening the organization."[49] Moreover, such funds are objectionable in their own right when they build grassroots support for terrorist organizations and subsidize the families of suicide bombers.

According to U.S. intelligence officials, "Hezbollah maintains several front companies in sub-Saharan Africa." Little information is available on these purported fronts, though they are widely assumed to include import-export companies (an established terrorist modus operandi). These officials say that many Hezbollah activists in the Tri-Border Area of South America relocated to Africa and other locations as a result of increased attention from authorities due to Hezbollah's role in the 1992 and 1994 truck bombings in Argentina. In an effort "not to have all their eggs in one basket," one analyst adds, some Hezbollah operatives have moved on from locations in South America and Europe and set up shop in Africa, Asia, and less conspicuous parts of South America.[50]

CRIMINAL ENTERPRISES

Hezbollah depends on a wide variety of criminal enterprises, ranging from smuggling to fraud to the drug trade and diamond trade, to raise money to support its activities. These enterprises operate in regions across the world, including North America, South America, and the Middle East. Published reports even suggest that al Qaeda and Hezbollah have formed additional tactical, ad hoc alliances with a variety of terrorist organizations to cooperate on money laundering and other unlawful activities.[51]

In the United States, law enforcement officials are investigating a variety of criminal enterprises suspected of funding Middle Eastern terrorist groups, including those engaged in the theft and sale of baby formula; food stamp fraud; and scams involving grocery coupons, welfare claims, credit cards, and even unlicensed T-shirt sales. U.S. officials believe "a substantial portion" of the estimated millions of dollars raised by Middle Eastern terrorist groups comes from the $20 million to $30 million annually brought in by the illicit scam industry in the United States.[52] Recent examples include an Arab-American in Detroit caught smuggling $12 million in fraudulent cashiers checks into the United States, and a fitness trainer in Boston accused of providing customers' social security and credit card numbers to Abd al Ghani Meskini, an associate of Ahmad Ressam, the Algerian convicted of plotting to blow up Los Angeles International Airport in 2000.[53]

The most prominent case in North America is the Charlotte, North Carolina, cell run by two brothers, Mohammed and Chawki Hamoud. In June 2002, the Hamoud brothers were convicted of a variety of charges, including funding the activities of Hezbollah from the proceeds of an interstate cigarette smuggling ring. Seven other defendants pled guilty to a variety of charges stemming from this case, including conspiracy to provide material support to terrorists, cigarette smuggling, money laundering, and immigration violations.[54] Mohammed Hassan Dbouk and his brother-in-law, Ali Adham Amhaz, ran the Canadian portion of this network under the command of Haj Hasan Hilu Laqis, Hezbollah's chief military procurement officer. Their activities were partially funded with money that Laqis sent from Lebanon in addition to profits from their own criminal activities in Canada (e.g., credit card and banking scams).[55] Among the items they purchased in North America and smuggled into Lebanon were night-vision goggles, global positioning systems, stun guns, naval equipment, nitrogen cutters, and laser range finders. The Canadian Hezbollah network also sought to take out life insurance policies for Hezbollah operatives committing acts of terrorism in the Middle East.[56] Members of the Charlotte cell entered the United States from South America using false documents, entered into sham marriages in Cyprus, and conducted their activities under multiple identities. Cell members paid indigent Americans to travel to

Cyprus at Hezbollah's expense and engage in sham marriages so additional operatives could get visas to come to America.[57]

In South America, Hezbollah operatives engage in a wide range of criminal enterprises to raise, transfer, and launder funds in support of their terrorist activities. These enterprises include mafia-style shakedowns of local Arab communities, sophisticated import-export scams involving traders from India and Hong Kong, and small-scale businesses that engage in a few thousand dollars worth of business, but transfer tens of thousands of dollars around the globe.[58] The Tri-Border Area of South America is especially important to Hezbollah, where the group raises close to $10 million a year.[59]

Hezbollah activities in Latin America, however, are by no means limited to the Tri-Border Area. Chilean officials have identified several import-export companies, primarily located in free trade zones, such as the Iquique Free Trade Zone (ZOFRI) in northern Chile, that are suspected of being either front organizations or shell companies for Hezbollah. According to Chilean law enforcement officials, "starting in 1980 Lebanese members of Hezbollah have been expanding its presence in South America and continue developing its network of contacts in the Triple Border area." In 1994 and 1995, these officials note, Hezbollah operatives began visiting Chile "to establish a new operational center for the development of their activities since the authorities of the Triple Border countries initiated greater and more rigorous control with respect to the activities of these foreigners, especially the Lebanese, who, according to information provided by international security services, are associated with terrorist members of Hezbollah."[60] Hezbollah members in Venezuela—centered within the large Lebanese expatriate community on Margarita Island—helped several members of the Hezbollah cell in Charlotte enter the United States through Venezuela in 1992. In the free trade area of Maicao, Colombia, Hezbollah is believed to participate in cigarette smuggling and may have operated a clandestine radio station broadcasting the group's propaganda.[61] According to Taylor, the U.S. Southern Command believes that between $300 and $500 million is raised in South America to support Islamic fundamentalism throughout the world.[62]

Hezbollah also raises money from smuggling to support its operations. Hezbollah benefits both financially and operationally from the Beka'a Valley's poppy crop, which the group trades to Israeli Arabs for intelligence on Israeli infrastructure and placement of Israeli soldiers. Israeli authorities have broken up a series of Israeli Arab cells working for Hezbollah in return for money and, frequently, drugs. Some of these cells, like one operating out of the Galilee village of Abu Snan, were planning to kidnap Israeli soldiers. In September 2002, an Israeli military court indicted a lieutenant colonel in the Israeli army, part of a 10-member gang, for spying for Hezbollah. The officer passed classified information to Hezbollah operatives in return for money, hashish, and heroin.[63]

Hezbollah and other terrorist groups also traffic narcotics in North America to fund their activities in the Middle East. A Drug Enforcement Administration (DEA) investigation into a pseudoephedrine smuggling scam in the American Midwest led investigators to bank accounts as far as Jordan, Yemen, Lebanon, and other Middle Eastern countries that were tied to Hezbollah and Hamas. DEA chief Asa Hutchinson confirmed, "a significant portion of some of the sales are sent to the Middle East to benefit terrorist organizations."[64]

Hezbollah is also believed to raise a significant amount of funds by dealing in so-called "conflict diamonds" in Sierra Leone, Liberia, and Congo, a practice that al Qaeda has reportedly copied using the model and contacts established by Hezbollah.[65] According to David Crane, prosecutor for the Special Court in Sierra Leone: "Diamonds fuel the war on terrorism. Charles Taylor is harbouring terrorists from the Middle East, including al Qaeda and Hezbollah, and has been for years." As of late 2006, Liberian former president Charles Taylor is awaiting trial by this very court, and new information regarding these links may emerge during his trial.[66] Moreover, a July 2000 Belgian intelligence report stated that "there are indications that certain persons, the 'Lebanese connection' mentioned in the diamond smuggling file, also put in an appearance in files on money laundering, the drugs trade and the financing of Lebanese terrorist organisations such as Amal and Hezbollah."[67] Belgian intelligence reports also tie the Congolese diamond trade to the financing of various terrorist groups including Hezbollah.[68]

Speaking in the context of the diamond trade and its links to Middle Eastern terrorist groups, one official noted in 2001 the "influx of hard-core Islamist extremists" in the Congo, over the past three years. He added, "We know Hezbollah is here, we know other groups are here, but they can probably operate a long time before we know enough to stop them."[69] The movement of Hezbollah operatives to Congo in the late 1990s and early 2000s is significant, given the rebellions that divided the country after the end of Mobutu Sese Seko's dictatorship in 1997.

Hezbollah operatives also run otherwise legitimate business enterprises that function as shell companies or fronts for raising, laundering, and transferring large sums of money. The most egregious example appears to be the use of Western Union offices by local Hezbollah operatives. Though Western Union officials were not complicit in this activity, the company failed to make any real efforts to vet local operators even as their international operations grew exponentially over a few short years, especially in areas of conflict.[70] According to Israeli officials, Hezbollah operatives run several Western Union offices in Lebanon and use the co-opted services of others worldwide, especially in Southeast Asia. In some cases where the local Western Union agent is a Hezbollah member or supporter, experts believe Hezbollah gets a cut of the 7 percent service fee split between Western Union and the local agent. In other cases, Hezbollah simply uses the money-wiring company to launder and transfer funds. For example, Hezbollah funding to Palestinian terrorist groups in the West Bank is almost entirely transferred via Western Union—including some $3 million in 2003–2004 alone.[71]

TRENDS IN RAISING AND SPENDING FUNDS

Unlike most terrorist groups, which need to focus much time and attention on raising, laundering, and transferring funds, Iran's largesse provides Hezbollah with a sizable and constant flow of reliable funding. By all accounts, Hezbollah operates under no revenue constraints; indeed, it often serves as a middleman funneling funds from Iran to other terrorist groups such as the Palestinian Islamic Jihad, Fatah Tanzim, and others. Still, despite not having the need to be particularly successful at independent fund-raising, the organization is very adept at raising, laundering, and transferring funds on its own through a wide array of activities. It remains unclear whether funds raised independently go toward specific, more clandestine purposes, and funds received from Iran go toward other more overt purposes. What little evidence is available suggests that funds from all sources finance a wide array of needs, including both overt and covert activities. In any event, attempts to make such distinctions are hollow, since money is fungible, and therefore funds provided for any one function free funds for other functions.

Hezbollah's fund-raising activities can often be boiled down to simply taking advantage of opportunities that arise from having a vast expatriate Shi'a population sympathetic to the group. Lebanese expatriate support for parties and militias back home is an age-old phenomenon. But the group's independent fund-raising, conducted alongside its generous subsidies from Iran, is also intended to guarantee the group's future independence through diversified funding no matter what happens to Iran. That is, Hezbollah likely wants to ensure that, even in the event that Iran were to ever strike a "grand bargain" with the West (trading its support for international terror, proliferation activities, and pursuit of a nuclear weapon for full economic and diplomatic relations with the West), the group would continue to be able to exist and function on its own.

Interestingly, although engaging in criminal activity often increases a group's vulnerability by exposing it to the scrutiny of law enforcement authorities, Hezbollah's reliance on fellow sympathizers and members of local expatriate communities minimizes that potential exposure. Still, as Hezbollah criminal activity in South America makes clear, the group does engage in criminal activities—including mafia-style shakedowns of local store owners, illegal pirating of multimedia, and the international drug trade—that gave rise to the unwanted attention of local and international authorities.

Hezbollah's funds are spent primarily on furthering the group's overall agenda of establishing a Shi'a entity in Lebanon and radicalizing Muslims against the West. To that end, the majority of its funds finance social welfare and political activities that support terror in a more indirect fashion (e.g., by freeing funds for other purposes, radicalizing and spotting future recruits, serving as a financial and logistical support network for the group's clandestine guerrilla and terrorist activities). "Annuities" are paid to the families of killed or captured Hezbollah operatives, and the group aims to provide its members with jobs through its vast social welfare and political infrastructure.

Although the attacks of September 11 raised public awareness of terrorism and created a surge in international counterterrorism efforts, Hezbollah financing efforts continue unabated. A small number of Hezbollah charities have been designated as terrorist entities by the United States, and fewer still individual Hezbollah operatives have been added to European lists. Hezbollah's reliance on local Shi'a communities—with ties among members and supporters often as tight as family relations or shared neighborhoods from childhoods in Beirut—has made it a particularly difficult group to penetrate. Iranian largesse alone provides the group with plenty of funds, and international fund-raising tied to social welfare and political activities is still considered untouchable in European capitals.[72]

Policy Recommendations

Efforts have been made by U.S. policy makers to hold states accountable for their support of designated terrorist groups such as Hezbollah. The Syria Accountability Act represents a long overdue effort to hold Syria accountable for its sponsorship of terrorism, development of chemical weapons, illegal smuggling of $1.1 billion in illicit Iraqi oil in violation of UN resolutions, procurement of military hardware and spare parts for the Iraqi military, and the now-concluded occupation of Lebanon. Despite this activity, Syria remains the only state sponsor of terrorism not subject to trade and investment bans, nor are Syrian diplomats subject to the same travel restrictions as diplomats from other states listed as sponsoring terrorism.[73]

In the wake of September 11, the goal of compelling change in Syrian support for terrorism must become a higher U.S. priority than ever before in order to check Syria's, and cut off Iran's, outlet to terrorist groups in Lebanon. Only with creative and persistent effort can Washington compel Damascus to discard its use of terrorism-by-proxy. Any such effort must incorporate measures to allow Syria to save face while still demanding it jettison terrorism as a state policy and shut down local terrorist groups. Having said that, Syria must be held accountable for any continued double-dealing, i.e., providing some measure of cooperation in the war on al Qaeda while fanning the flames of other terrorist groups of global reach. As the United States considers what carrots and sticks to apply in its efforts to motivate Syria, it should consider the need to apply inducements and consequences in tandem and in gradations: small carrots for small gestures, large sticks for large infractions. The 2006 war between Israel and Hezbollah only strengthens the case for such measures.

Additionally, after significant pressure and lobbying by both Israeli and American authorities, several individual European countries (but not the European Union) have joined the United States in banning the al Aqsa International Foundation, a Hamas front organization that is also suspected of sending money to Hezbollah. The head of the foundation's office in Yemen was arrested in Germany, not for fund-raising on behalf of Hamas but for sending weapons and millions of dollars to al Qaeda operatives well after September 11th.[74] Banning Hezbollah in Europe would mark a significant step forward in the effort to stem the group's international financial activity. The first sign that movement in that direction may be possible occurred in Germany on January 5, 2005, when a Düsseldorf court denied a Hezbollah member a German visa because he was "a member of an organization that supports international terrorism." In a statement, the court said that "Hezbollah is waging a war with bomb attacks against Israel with 'inhumane brutality' and against civilians."[75] Shutting down organizations such as front companies and charities found to be facilitating financial support of international terrorist networks will go a long way toward stemming the flow of funds to and among terrorist groups.

The foreign funding of subversive domestic organizations linked to designated terrorist groups poses immediate dangers to the national security of the United States. This much is clear: should the United States fail to adapt the culture of its law enforcement and intelligence community, to enact appropriate laws and procedures, and to commit the necessary resources and resolve, it will find the war on terror that much harder to fight, lasting that much longer in duration, and exacting that much higher and more tragic a cost in human life.

CHAPTER NINE

Arab Government Responses
to the Threat of Terrorist Financing

MOYARA DE MORAES RUEHSEN

After September 11, 2001, most governments throughout the Arab world came forward to express their deepest sympathies and condolences to the American people and government. Implicit in those messages was an understanding that those governments would be ready and willing to assist the U.S. government with follow-up investigations of al Qaeda and its finances. In practice, Arab government responses have ranged from being sincere and earnest, to being muted, and even hostile at times. This schizophrenic response can largely be explained by Arab perceptions of U.S. policy in the region, U.S. government pronouncements, and other related developments and pressures. This chapter seeks to clarify the tenor and substance of Arab government responses on the terrorism financing front, looking at both legislative and policy responses, and the extent to which those laws and policies have been implemented and enforced in the four years since the attacks.

After a discussion of initial reactions, the first part of this chapter focuses on legislative responses in the Arab world,[1] specific policy measures designed to address *hawala* and charities, and how new laws and regulations are being implemented and enforced. The second part of the chapter looks at how terrorism financing is defined and viewed in the Arab world and how that might shape the West's future strategy to stop terrorist groups like al Qaeda.

Initial Arab Reactions Following September 11th

Once the initial shock and sympathy wore off in the days and weeks following the attacks of September 11th, the media spotlight turned to the Middle East—specifically Egypt, Saudi Arabia, and the United Arab Emirates (UAE)—although all of the Arab world began to get unwanted negative attention. The instinctive reaction from most governments in the region, and their publics, was denial. There was a general unwillingness to believe that Muslims, of their own free will, could have committed such acts, let alone Muslims from their countries. And there was a clear unwillingness to believe that any of their citizens would have wittingly *funded* such acts.

In the weeks that followed, one Arab official after another publicly declared that their country's financial system was free of money laundering and/or terrorist financing, although in many cases it was ambiguous whether they were talking about one or both. Three weeks after the attacks, for example, Lebanon's Prime Minister insisted, "We have no money laundering in this country because money laundering is a very large operation, worth hundreds of billions of dollars. The entire volume of funds now available in the Lebanese banking sector is less than $40 billion. That money has been there for several years and belongs to Lebanese who have worked hard to earn it."[2] At the end of October, the Governor of the Central Bank of the UAE, insisted that there were "no money laundering operations in the UAE."[3] Two months later, he clarified by saying, "We have no laundering activities in the UAE economy, but we cannot guarantee money coming from outside."[4] And in early November, the Governor of Kuwait's Central Bank declared at a conference on Islamic Banking that "there are no banks in Kuwait that deal with terrorist acts."[5] This tone of denial continued well into 2002, with a representative of Kuwait's Banking Studies Institute insisting that "money laundering does not exist in Kuwait."[6] Egypt's Central Bank Deputy Governor also declared that "Egypt has no money laundering operations."[7] And later in the year, an official from Oman's Central Bank publicly declared that "the Sultanate has so far remained untainted by the scourge of money laundering."[8]

In this climate of denial, there was some initial intransigence on the part of Arab officials to provide assistance to investigators. This was perceived by Western investigators as a stubborn refusal to cooperate. But it is likely that much of this seemingly obstinate response was the result of cross-cultural clashes. Saving face is extremely important in Eastern cultures, and there was undoubtedly some degree of shame and embarrassment among Muslims and Arabs that other Arab Muslims could have committed these atrocities. Western investigators, from the start, should have made a concerted effort to reassure their Arab counterparts that the events of September 11th were the act of criminals, or "deviants" as some Arab governments described them, and did not reflect badly on Arabs or Islam. Instead, public officials in the Arab world felt guilty by association until proven innocent. They were not treated with equal respect and felt persecuted in the media. Many surmised that the Western media was deliberately trying to undermine the region's financial institutions and smear Islam.[9] And the frantic rush on the part of financial institutions and investigators to find and freeze suspected terrorist accounts in the first few months after the attacks seemed like a witch hunt at times. Indeed, many Arab investors, alarmed by the rush to freeze suspect accounts without due diligence, began to liquidate their U.S. assets.

The prevailing attitude in the Arab world shifted from sympathy to defensiveness and a reluctance to cooperate with Western investigations and strengthen financial sector regulations. With hindsight it is not hard to understand why Arab governments might have taken umbrage at the assertive threats made by U.S. officials.[10] But Western officials realized too late that their aggressive approach was backfiring.

By 2002 the United States had few remaining Arab allies in its fight to curtail terrorist financing. In January, when the United States abruptly rejected Egypt's draft anti-money laundering law and threatened sanctions, an Egyptian columnist for the newspaper *al-Wafd* summed up the views of many in the region. "Why does the United States poke its nose in our affairs? Who gave it that right? . . . Washington treats us as schoolchildren. It gives us an examination to test our obedience. It also gives us marks depending on its degree of satisfaction."[11] In a July 2002 interview, Dubai's chief of police explained that "it would be wrong for any nation to try to apply any pressure on the Arab kings and heads of state and princes to wrest further concessions from them. This is because they have made as many concessions as they possibly could and so they [can] not go any further. If the United States, after all, tries to apply yet more pressure on the Arab leaders, there is going to be a popular backlash that could spin out of control."[12] The backlash had already begun. It was time for damage control.

Realizing, perhaps too late, that "the highhanded manner in which pressure was brought to bear"[13] would not elicit the cooperation they desired, officials from the U.S. Treasury Department began to take a more conciliatory approach with their Arab counterparts by early 2002. U.S.-Saudi cooperation started to take the form of less-publicized, behind-closed-doors cooperation to avoid giving the impression that the Saudis were merely doing the U.S. government's bidding. And in March 2002, former Treasury Secretary Paul O'Neill visited Saudi Arabia to hold talks on terrorist financing. Secretary O'Neill was careful not to offend. He went out of his way to praise the Saudis for the steps they had taken and assured them that the United States was refining its intelligence to avoid needlessly damaging the reputations of wrongly accused charities and individuals.[14] This softer approach mollified Arab reactions somewhat, but there still remained the intractable problem of the Palestinian-Israeli dispute and the inclusion of Muslim groups on the U.S. Treasury Department's Office of Foreign Asset Control (OFAC) Terrorist List, such as Hamas and Hezbollah, which did not present an immediate threat to U.S. interests. The most that U.S. policy makers could hope for was the *enactment* (not enforcement) of anti-money laundering and counter-terrorist financing legislation.[15]

LEGISLATIVE RESPONSES

Throughout all these early difficulties and tensions, the United States had one steadfast ally in the region—Bahrain. As the site of the only permanent U.S. naval base in the Gulf (euphemistically referred to as an "administrative support unit"), Bahrain has always had a special relationship with the United States. For years Bahrain had been trying to maintain its image as the premier offshore banking center for the Middle East. Its main competitor was and remains Dubai. In order to distinguish itself from nearby Dubai, Bahrain's strategy was to portray its financial regulatory environment as unassailable in the hopes of attracting discriminating investors.[16] It was one of the first Arab countries to enact anti-money laundering legislation, which went into effect in January 2001. (See table 9.1.) At that time, terrorist financing was on few policy makers' minds. Bahrain's new legislation did not touch upon this topic, although at the time it was praised as a model for the rest of the region to follow. Perhaps following Bahrain's lead—and also in consideration of the Gulf Cooperation Council's (GCC's) membership in the Financial Action Task Force (FATF)—most of the other GCC states began drafting and reviewing anti-money laundering legislation in early 2001.

After September 11th, terrorist financing, and the related topic of money laundering, moved to the top of the agenda. Within a month of the attacks, the six member countries of the GCC (Bahrain, Kuwait, Oman, Qatar, Saudi Arabia, and the UAE) pledged to have a unified GCC law on money laundering enacted by the end of 2001 and in place at the start of 2002. It soon became clear that the different institutional climates in each of the six countries precluded a unified law and that each member state would need to pass its own piece of legislation. Bahrain's money laundering law did not cover terrorist finances and just needed updating. At least two of the other GCC states[17] had draft laws under review at the time of the attacks, so they were more or less ready to speed up deliberations and enact legislation quickly. Saudi Arabia, known for its snail-paced bureaucracy, was one of the last Gulf states to have rigorous laws enacted, and only after much stalling and outside pressure.

Unfortunately, the initial drafts of many of these new laws did not clarify the problem and nature of terrorist financing. The draft laws were anti-money laundering laws first and foremost, and as such defined money laundering as the movement and concealment of funds *derived* from criminal activities. Terrorism was sometimes included in the list of predicate offenses, but rarely was there any stipulation that funds *destined* for the commission of terrorist acts, or funds belonging to designated terrorist organizations, should be frozen or confiscated. There was and continues to be a prevailing view among policy makers and bank compliance officers in the region that it is virtually impossible to know whether funds are being moved with the intention of committing future terrorist acts.[18]

The first major row that erupted had to do with Egypt's draft anti-money laundering law. Egyptian legislators were already bristling from the perception that the United States was "foisting" this new law and others like it only on Arab and Islamic countries.[19] So they insisted that the law cover only drug trafficking crimes and not allow the freezing of accounts or disclosure of account information for entities that other countries choose to designate as sponsors of terrorism. Egyptian bankers also voiced their opposition to the proposed law, arguing that it would jeopardize their clients' privacy and possibly deter investment. The former chairman of the Egyptian Banking Federation publicly declared that "terrorists hold no bank accounts in Egypt, and there are no known cases of money laundering in Egyptian banks."[20]

Some of this resistance could be construed as mere posturing, as Egypt had already been designated as a Non-Cooperative Country on Money Laundering by FATF before September 11th. The designation, and the threatened sanctions that went along with it, no doubt played a role in speeding up the drafting of a law, but it also generated much anger and resentment and accusations of double standards. The debate in parliament grew very heated. The liberal Wafd Party and the Muslim Brotherhood MPs voiced strong objections, warning that the new law would put Egypt at the mercy of "the U.S. approach to squeezing terrorist funds." Another independent MP warned, "We must not be committed to implementing U.S. verdicts that consider freedom fighters such as Hizbullah in Lebanon and Hamas in Palestine as terrorists."[21] Ultimately, however, the first draft of the law was approved by nearly all the MPs with only three abstentions.

Thinking that the preparation and approval of a draft bill would be sufficient to remove them from the Non-Cooperative Countries list, many Egyptian policy makers were stunned when the United States publicly rejected the draft bill as unacceptable two weeks later. The initial draft did not adequately allow for the freezing and seizing of suspect funds, nor did it clearly criminalize terrorist financing. When it became clear that removal from the blacklist would not happen without new revisions, the law was revised and approved several months later, albeit with much grumbling.

Meanwhile, U.S. policy makers were also putting pressure on Saudi Arabia. This pressure was met with resistance because of perceived U.S. self-righteousness and double standards. All fingers were pointing to Saudi Arabia immediately after 9/11, when it was discovered that 15 of the 19 hijackers were Saudi. But there were even more fingers pointed following damning accusations in published reports by international experts suggesting that Saudi Arabia was the main source for terrorist finance, largely by way of poorly regulated Islamic charities. Since charitable giving, or *zakat*, is a religious obligation taken quite seriously by all devout Muslims, the repeated attacks on Saudi charities by Western policy makers and Western media outlets were seen as an attack on Islam. And since the Saudi royal family's tenuous hold on power depends on an implicit understanding they have with the

TABLE 9.1 *Legislative Responses*

COUNTRY	MONEY LAUNDERING OR ANTI-TERRORISM LAW ENACTED	PROVISIONS ON TERRORIST FINANCING AND OTHER COMMENTS
Algeria*	January 2005	Terrorist financing covered by law. Requires reporting of suspicious transactions when funds "seem destined to finance terrorism."[22]
Bahrain**	January 2001 (Decree Law no. 4) 2002–04 (Ministerial Orders 7, 18, & 23)	Subsequent revisions address terrorist financing and extend coverage to securities dealers and insurance brokers. Additional counter-terrorism financing provisions of an anti-terror law are due to be voted on in fall 2006.
Egypt**	May 2002 Law no. 80/2002 (Enacted March 2003)	The Law only covers proceeds of terrorist crimes. But in January 2005, a National Committee for Combating Money Laundering and Terrorism Financing was created.
Iraq	CPA Order No. 93 Anti-Money Laundering Act of 2004	Law criminalizes money laundering and terrorism finance.
Jordan*	Regulations on currency transaction reporting, August 2001, amended in 2003	Draft law presented in March 2005, but not given urgency. As of July 2006, the law had not yet been passed.[23] Bank secrecy can be waived in suspected terrorist financing cases.
Kuwait	March 2002 Law no. 35	Financing of terrorism *not* criminalized as of 2004.[24] Nor are provisions in place for freezing suspected terrorist assets. But Ministerial Decision No. 11 (11/224) sets up a committee to draft further anti-money laundering and counter-terrorism–financing legislation.
Lebanon	July 2001 (Law no. 318) October 2003 (Laws no. 547, 553)	Law no. 553 details penalties for persons who financially support terrorist acts or organizations.
Libya	Draft law	Terrorist financing is not specifically mentioned, but the penal code is open to wide interpretation.

Morocco	June 2003 (Anti-terrorism bill)	Allows for "freezing of suspect accounts and prosecution of terrorist finance related crimes."[25] Anti-money laundering law still pending as of December 2005.
Oman	March 2002 Royal Decree 34	In July 2003, Oman issued a supplemental report to the UN stating that "the legal ML [money-laundering] freezing measures designated by the Act are applied to both residents and nonresidents holding funds . . . linked to terrorist-related activities."[26]
Qatar	September 2002, August 2003, February 2004	2003 amendment broadens definition of money laundering to include terrorist financing. 2004 Combating Terrorism Law covers terrorist financing. Regulations issued in 2005.
Saudi Arabia*[27]	2003 Royal Decree no. M/39	Anyone who finances "terrorism, terrorist acts and terrorist organizations . . . shall be deemed a perpetrator of a money laundering crime."[28]
Syria	December 2003, May 2005, Leg. Decree No. 33	Penal code treats financers of terrorism as accessories to the crime.
Tunisia	December 2003	Criminalizes "support and financing to individuals, organizations or activities related to terrorism."[29]
U.A.E.	January 2002, Federal Law No. 4, July 2004, Law 1/2004	Covers assets *derived* from criminal acts such as terrorism. Imprisonment of 7 years, fines up to Dh300,000 for individuals, Dh1 million for institutions. Law 1/2004 criminalizes terrorist financing.
Yemen	April 2003, Republican Law 35	Covers money laundering only, but other pieces of legislation allegedly "treat terrorism and its financing as serious crimes."[d]

* Ratified the UN Convention on Combating Terrorist Financing
** Signatory only to the UN Convention on Combating Terrorist Financing

country's religious authorities, there was very little the Saudi government could or would do in the months after 9/11 to curtail the activities of suspect charities. At the same time, Arab cultural conventions would not allow the Saudis to treat visiting American officials and investigators rudely by refusing to cooperate. Instead, they played a stalling game. Whenever American officials would impatiently inquire as to the progress of legislative reforms and measures to monitor charities, they were assured that the proper authorities were working on it. Unfortunately, there was little leverage the United States could apply. Unlike Egypt, Saudi Arabia was not dependent on billions of dollars of annual U.S. assistance.

This stalling game continued for some time, and would have continued much longer were it not for a number of events in 2003 that shocked the Kingdom out of its complacency. In May a series of bombings in Riyadh was a wake-up call to the Saudi authorities, who until then were largely denying the existence of Islamic militants in the Kingdom. In November 2003, a bloody attack on an expatriate residential compound added further urgency to the need to stem the flow of funds to terrorist groups. The Financial Action Task Force and International Monetary Fund (FATF-IMF) evaluation was also an incentive to speed up anti-money laundering and counter-terrorism financing (AML-CTF) reforms.[30] Because the FATF-IMF evaluation report was given far more weight and legitimacy than U.S. recommendations in the Arab world, the Saudis were eager to comply with the recommendations. Moreover, non-compliance would have been embarrassing in light of Saudi Arabia's membership in the GCC, which is a member organization of FATF.[31] For example, the Saudis were quick to ratify the UN Convention on the Prevention of Terrorist Financing, after their failure to ratify it was cited more than once in the evaluation report.

IMPLEMENTATION

Once all of these laws were in place, the next step was implementation: issuance of specific regulations and guidelines, training of compliance officers, and holding of conferences and workshops to apprise all financial sector employees of the new requirements. The UAE Central Bank in Abu Dhabi took the lead in this effort, hosting more workshops and conferences than any other Arab country, often inviting regulatory officials from other parts of the world who had not yet implemented AML-CTF legislation to come for training. By October 2005, the UAE had hosted 240 training programs, seminars, and workshops on money laundering and/or terrorist financing. (See table 9.2 for a sample of some of these conferences.) Some of these workshops and conferences were government-sponsored, others were conducted by private financial institutions, and still others were jointly sponsored between governments or between government and the private sector. Perhaps the most important one of all was a series of seminars for ministers of finance and central bank governors from all over the Arab world that was organized alongside the annual meetings of the World Bank and the IMF held in Dubai in September 2003. While the seminars' themes (Economic Policy, Investment Opportunities, and Regulations in the Arab Region) were broad, at least one day was spent on the topic of fighting money laundering.

While most of the countries in the region with large banking sectors have the means to implement new AML-CTF regulations, many Arab countries are too poor to pay for training workshops to bring both the public and private sectors into compliance. Recognizing this, the United States Agency for International Development (USAID) provided Egypt with $150 million in July 2002 specifically to help the Egyptian government combat money laundering. The UAE also made a pledge in 2003 to help emerging market countries set up their legal and regulatory structures for fighting money laundering and terrorism financing.[32] One area that could use subsidized assistance in the future is technology. Financial institutions need to rely on specialized software to help them detect suspicious accounts or transactions, or to screen the many lists of designated suspects. While most large Western banks have adopted such technology, according to a survey conducted in October 2004, fewer than 5 percent of Arab banks and financial institutions have anti-money laundering software.[33]

ENFORCEMENT

The theory is nice: if you mandate banks to report all significant or suspicious financial transactions, you can track funds used to finance terror organizations. If you can track those funds, you can also block them. If you can block those funds, then terrorism will stop because it will go bankrupt.

JOSH MARTIN, 2002

TABLE 9.2 *Selected Conferences and Seminars on AML–CTF*

TITLE AND TOPIC	LOCATION	DATE
Prevention & Detection of Money Laundering for Trade and Professional Service Organizations	Riyadh, Saudi Arabia	October 2001
Money Laundering Conference	Muscat, Oman	November 2001
Five-day Seminar for the Gulf Cooperation Council (GCC) State Audit Institutions on Fighting Financial Crimes	Dubai, UAE	December 2001
Conference on "Financial Issues in the Post-September 11th Era" (Topic: Money Laundering & Bank Vulnerability)	Manama, Bahrain	January 2002
Asian Regional Conference on Money Laundering	Riyadh, Saudi Arabia	January 2002
GCC Security Chiefs (Topic: Money Laundering and Crime)	Abu Dhabi, UAE	April 2002
Union of Arab Banks Workshop on Money Laundering	Amman, Jordan	April 2002
Money Laundering Workshop	Sana'a, Yemen	May 2002
Sixth GCC Banking Conference (Money Laundering and the Financing of Terrorism one of four topics)	Muscat, Oman	October 2002
Conference on Prevention and Detection of Fraud and Money Laundering	Doha, Qatar	October 2002
Forum on Money Laundering through Commercial Transactions	Abu Dhabi, UAE	October 2002
Anti-Money Laundering Conference	Dubai, UAE	November 2002

Arab Interior Ministers' Council Meeting (terrorism and crime the main topics)	Tunis, Tunisia	January 2003
Seminar on Combating Money Laundering and Terrorist Funding	Abu Dhabi, UAE	February 2003
Islamic Banking Conference: Adapting to a Rapidly Changing Regulatory and Financial Environment	Manama, Bahrain	March 2003
Three-day seminar on "The Fight against Money Laundering and Terrorist Financing"	Manama, Bahrain	June 2003
Seminar on Money Laundering for Arab Ministers of Finance and Central Bank Governors	Dubai, UAE	September 2003
Inaugural Meeting of the Middle East and North Africa Financial Action Task Force (MENAFATF)	Manama, Bahrain	November 2004
2nd Annual Conference of the UAE National Anti-Money Laundering Committee	Al-Ain, UAE	December 2004
International Conference to Combat Terrorism	Riyadh, Saudi Arabia	February 2005
Two-day joint GCC-EU seminar on combating terrorist financing	Abu Dhabi, UAE	March 2005
Conference on Anti-Money Laundering and Counter Terrorism Financing	Sharm El Sheik, Egypt	September 2005
Second plenary meeting of MENAFATF	Beirut, Lebanon	September 2005
Seminar on the "Legal and Regulatory Framework Implementing Anti-Money Laundering and Combating of Terrorist Financing"	UAE	October 2005
Conference on "Developing the Ability to Combat Money Laundering and Terrorist Financing"	Central Bank of Syria	December 2005
Conference on Confronting Money Laundering Operations and Financing Terrorism	Kuwait	January 2006

Mandating banks to report all suspicious activity unfortunately does not necessarily lead to compliance. Laws and regulations must be seriously enforced
for compliance to occur. Even when the state lacks the resources to investigate a majority of suspicious cases, a high degree of compliance can nevertheless be achieved with a few highly publicized, successful prosecutions.

In the Arab world, the earliest cases of recognizable enforcement arose in
Lebanon, primarily because Lebanon was one of the first countries in the
region, after Bahrain, to have an anti-money laundering law enacted.
Although the law was not specific about funds *intended* for the financing of
terrorism, nonetheless, Lebanese banks complied in the months following
9/11 with several requests to freeze suspected terrorist accounts. One of
these suspect accounts allegedly had $2.19 million. Of 29 investigations
launched by the Lebanese Financial Intelligence Unit and referred to the
prosecutor's office between May 2001 and May 2002, 9 involved alleged terrorist financing. A skeptic might argue that this level of cooperation more
likely came about because of Lebanon's eagerness to be removed from
FATF's blacklist of Non-Cooperative Countries and Territories (NCCT).
But prosecutions have continued since then, although not at the same pace,
with names and entities of accounts to be frozen published in the press.

The process of evaluation and peer pressure applied by FATF, now in
conjunction with the IMF, does seem to work. Lebanon worked hard to
speed up financial sector reforms after it was placed on the blacklist, as did
Egypt. And Lebanon worked hard to demonstrate that its new law was being
enforced. It is no coincidence that Lebanon and Egypt, the only Arab countries to be blacklisted by FATF, have a better track record on enforcement.
That is *not* to say that *all* blacklists work. But FATF's NCCT blacklist was
more widely recognized than the U.S. Office of Foreign Assets Control
(OFAC) list, which is considered far more biased in the eyes of Arab institutions. The FATF list also names countries, not individuals, so there was more
incentive for governments to do what needed to be done to meet FATF's
standard of compliance. Since 2003, the FATF blacklist has largely been
shelved and countries instead are evaluated by teams of representatives from
FATF, the IMF, and/or the World Bank.

Saudi Arabia, which is a member of the FATF by way of the GCC, was the
next country to be evaluated by FATF. When the first IMF evaluation was
scheduled in 2003, the Saudis postponed it until 2004 to give them more
time to achieve compliance. By the time the evaluation team finally arrived,

the Saudis had not only put into place their new regulations but had also prepared a full report to demonstrate all that they had done since September 2001, including freezing 42 accounts belonging to 8 account holders.[34] More than 150 accounts were investigated in the four months following 9/11. What is not clear is whether there have been any successful prosecutions thus far. One criticism that has been voiced repeatedly is that many wealthy financiers with alleged ties to terrorist finances have close connections to the royal family and are therefore immune from prosecution.

Another area of frequent criticism is the oversight, or lack thereof, of charities in the Kingdom. As indicated earlier, charitable giving is an obligation for all practicing Muslims. Since none of the contributions are tax deductible, there was never any need to record donations. Many donations were made in the form of cash. What happened to that cash once it was donated was not always clear. Western officials still believe that many of the donations made to Saudi-based charities find their way into the hands of terrorist organizations.

The first indication that the Kingdom was ready to address this issue was the announcement in 2003 that donation boxes would be removed from public places and mosques. More restrictions followed. Now all charities in Saudi Arabia must obtain a license from the Ministry of Labor and Social Affairs or the Ministry of Islamic Affairs. They need permission from the Saudi Arabian Monetary Agency to open a bank account and may only use one account. Charities also face tough restrictions on cash transactions and overseas transfers. Whether they are allowed to deposit cash donations is unclear, as an official report suggests that no "cash transactions" are permitted.[35] Moreover, all donors, no matter how small or large, must provide identification information. A new Public High Commission is also supposed to be set up, which will oversee charitable activities that take place outside of the country.[36]

Enforcement in the neighboring UAE was more immediate and forthcoming, in spite of the irritation voiced by many UAE officials at American pressure. In the first few months after 9/11, the government froze 14 bank accounts and had an additional 128 accounts under investigation.

The real challenge for regulatory authorities in the UAE was not the formal banking system but rather how to monitor the more than $5 billion in worker remittances and other transactions transferred through small money exchange houses and *hawaladar*s.[37] The first step was to require licensing of all money exchange houses and to impose strict reporting requirements on these exchange houses. Beginning in October 2001, all exchange houses were to record customer identification information on all transactions above Dh2000 (US$544). Many money changers were dubious about whether this would catch any criminals or terrorists, but they were nonetheless compelled to comply.[38] Within one month of the new regulations, at least one money exchange house was closed down and nine other exchange houses investigated for "lapses."[39]

Bringing informal *hawala* operators into compliance presented yet another challenge. After consultations with the Pakistani government and other countries with *hawala* activities, a conference was held in Abu Dhabi in May 2002 to discuss whether *hawala* transactions should be legalized so that they might be more easily monitored. Out of that conference came the Abu Dhabi Declaration on Hawala. The Declaration formally legitimized *hawala* activities, but it required that *hawaladars* register with the regulatory authorities and report all suspicious transactions, as well as transactions above a certain threshold. The Declaration was endorsed by all the individual participants at the conference. However, not all the *countries* represented at the conference endorsed the Declaration. For example, in Saudi Arabia *hawala* transactions remain illegal, with strict penalties for violators.[40]

The issues of implementation and enforcement of anti-money laundering and counter-terrorist financing laws and regulations will remain at center stage for some time to come. One positive development has taken place that specifically addresses the long-standing complaint that enforcement is being rudely forced by the West, with insufficient Arab involvement. The tiny kingdom of Bahrain has stepped forward to assume the leadership of a FATF-style regional body for the Middle East. The Middle East and North African Financial Action Task Force (MENAFATF), headquartered in Manama, Bahrain, held its inaugural meeting in late November 2004. The membership includes 14 Arab countries.[41] A few of its stated objectives include:

> To build effective arrangements throughout the region to combat effectively money laundering and terrorist financings in accordance with the particular cultural values, constitutional framework and legal systems in the member countries; To adopt and implement the 40 Recommendations of FATF against money laundering; To adopt and implement the Special Recommen-

dations on the FATF against terrorist financings . . . To work together to identify money laundering and terrorist financing issues of a regional nature, to share experiences of these problems and to develop regional solutions for dealing with them.[42]

Although the first objective seems to leave open loopholes, most observers see the establishment of this FATF-style regional body as an extremely positive development. Bahrain takes its leadership role in this effort very seriously. As the Bahrainis see it, strengthening financial regulations in the Arab world will only attract *more* investment to the region, something most of these countries dearly depend on.

"The World List Order"

Cooperation in the effort to track down and seize terrorist funds assumes, of course, that all parties adhere to similar criteria for what constitutes "terrorist funds."[43] After September 11th, there was no need for debate over whether Osama bin Laden and al Qaeda were terrorists. But there was much political pressure in the United States to add more organizations and individuals to the OFAC list of designated individuals and entities supporting terrorism in order to provide governments with more means to dismantle such organizations. Suddenly, in addition to al Qaeda, other Middle Eastern groups were added to the U.S. list, including Hamas and Hezbollah. In a sarcastic response to the ever lengthening OFAC list, an Egyptian columnist for a state-owned magazine suggested that the U.S.-dominated "new world order" should instead be called "the world list order," suggesting that "the United States is using lists to manipulate the world."[44] It did not escape the notice of Arab commentators that neither Hamas nor Hezbollah presented an immediate threat to the United States. Hamas and Hezbollah did, however, present a threat to Israel, and they were both Islamic. This was subsequently interpreted as a joint U.S.-Israeli attack on Islam, and was met with much outrage throughout the region, both publicly and privately.

In due course, other non-Islamic groups were added to the OFAC list, such as the FARC, Ejército de Liberación Nacional (ELN) and Autodefensas Unidas de Colombia (AUC) in Colombia, the Basque separatist group ETA, the International Sikh Youth Federation, and Aum Shinrikyo. But a highly publicized report on terrorist financing by the Council on Foreign Relations (CFR) in October 2002[45] put to rest any doubt in the minds of the Arab world that the United States was limiting its offensive to Islamic groups. The CFR report was purported to be about terrorist financing in general, but the only groups mentioned in the report were al Qaeda, Hamas, and Hezbollah. Arab readers found the tone of the report hostile and prejudiced towards Islam in general, adding fuel to well-worn conspiracy theories about Israel's influence on U.S. foreign policy.

Citing the old adage that one group's terrorist is another group's freedom fighter, Arab leaders strongly resisted pressure from U.S. officials to go after funds belonging to Hamas and Hezbollah. While many concurred that the killing of women and children by Hamas suicide bombers was unconscionable—and as some pointed out, contrary to Islam—they also insisted that the majority of Hamas' funds were spent on much-needed social services for Palestinians in the Occupied Territories.

Hezbollah, meanwhile, is a recognized political party in Lebanon. It gained notoriety by fighting Israeli occupation of southern Lebanon in the 1980s and 1990s, and most recently by withstanding the Israeli assault on Lebanon following the kidnapping by Hezbollah of two Israeli soldiers in July 2006. Perceived efforts on the part of U.S. politicians to demonize Hezbollah after 9/11 led to a backlash in Lebanon and throughout the Arab world. Senator Bob Graham, chairman of the U.S. Senate Intelligence Committee, was quoted in the Lebanese press saying, "Hizbullah, of course, is the A-team of terrorism. Hizbullah has killed hundreds of Americans over its history. It's the most vicious and effective terrorist organization in the world."[46] What Senator Graham was referring to was the bombing of the U.S. embassy and U.S. Marine barracks in Beirut in 1984, acts that were carried out by Amal, a predecessor of Hezbollah. That it was not actually Hezbollah that carried out those acts was a point repeatedly made by Arab commentators, but the argument fell on deaf ears. Even more upsetting were suggestions in the U.S. press that Hezbollah and al Qaeda were working together,[47] a claim Arab governments, investigators, and journalists vehemently denied. They were also upset that Hezbollah could even be compared to a group like al Qaeda, let alone be designated as a terrorist organization. In the words of one Lebanese journalist, "Beirut is not prepared even to contemplate naming Hizbullah as a terrorist organization. This position, moreover, is supported by the majority of Lebanese as well as by many Arab countries."[48]

The argument over whether Hamas should be designated a terrorist organization is more complicated, with most Arab countries, and initially many European countries as well, making a distinction between the organization's military and political branches. But as many U.S. officials were quick to point out, whether the money goes into one pocket or another, it is still the same pair of pants. However, the Palestinian-Israeli conflict is something most Arabs feel passionate about. Indeed, most see all Palestinian groups as part of a legitimate resistance force fighting Israeli occupation, a view that is reinforced by a barrage of sensational reporting from the front lines of the conflict.

These definitional discrepancies have presented a major stumbling block to further cooperation from Arab governments on the terrorism financing front. It could even be argued that U.S. insistence on pushing Arab governments to freeze and seize Hamas- and Hezbollah-related funds was undermining Arab willingness to go after al Qaeda funds in the first few years after 9/11.[49] Only by 2004 did the United States appear to back off. Even the follow-up report on terrorist financing from the Council on Foreign Relations was careful not to mention Hezbollah.[50] U.S. government officials also seem to have stepped back from pushing for a crackdown on Hezbollah. But U.S. efforts to stop Hamas have not subsided, and this still remains a major point of conflict with the Arab world, with oblique references made on many official occasions. In the closing session of the Arab League meeting in Tunis in May 2004, for example, the League's Secretary General presented a number of statements and resolutions, two of which highlight this tension:

[We will] continue to work within the framework of international legitimacy, and cooperation between the Arab states and the international community, to fight terrorism in all its forms in order to uproot it, dismantle its networks, address its causes and fight money laundering, drug trafficking and organized crime *whilst distinguishing between terrorism that we reject and the right of peoples to resist occupation.* [Emphasis added]

The Arab countries are committed to continue to contribute to the international efforts exerted to combat and confront the phenomenon of terrorism in all its forms, *not to confuse between Islam and terrorism, and to distinguish between legitimate resistance and terrorism.*[51] [Emphasis added]

Conclusions

Two conclusions emerge from this overview of Arab government responses to the problem of terrorist financing. The first conclusion is that the U.S. government must carefully pick its battles. As U.S. insistence on going after the funding of other Arab groups besides al Qaeda engenders more anger and resistance, it is clear that if the United States truly wishes to have the full support of the Arab world in freezing and seizing al Qaeda–related assets, it must back off from its offensive against groups like Hezbollah and Hamas. This may be difficult in light of the long-standing U.S. commitment to Israel's security, but the trade-off is clear. Perhaps one possible way around the prickly issue of defining terrorist financing is to encourage and assist the passage, implementation, and enforcement of stricter anti-*money laundering* legislation (as long as terrorist financing is a designated predicate offense).

A second conclusion or observation that arises from a review of legislative responses in the region is the lack of uniformity in AML-CTF compliance in the region. To date, the countries that have received the most attention—Bahrain, Egypt, Lebanon, UAE, and Saudi Arabia—are also the countries with some of the strictest legislation currently in place. Of these countries, Bahrain and the UAE have an exemplary record of enforcement. The enforcement records of Saudi Arabia, Egypt, and Lebanon are still spotty but nonetheless significant compared to other Arab states. But there are other countries in the region that have been slow to enact legislation (Morocco, Tunisia,[52] and Libya) or have not adequately implemented their new laws (Kuwait). It would seem very easy, therefore, if a terrorist organization wanted to move money out of the region, to transmit funds from one of these jurisdictions, none of which is on FATF's list of Non-Cooperative Countries.

To close the net around those countries lacking adequate controls, it becomes all the more important for the international community to support regional initiatives such as MENAFATF. One way the West can unobtrusively assist in the effort to strengthen AML-CTF efforts would be to subsidize capacity building in the area of compliance. Already the U.S. government has helped Egypt in this way, but there are many other candidate countries that will need assistance to enforce and implement new legal regimes. It is an expensive proposition, as such capacity building would include not just the cost of compliance training, but also the acquisition of compliance software and other related technology. But of all the strategies at our disposal, this appears to be one of the most cost-effective.

CHAPTER TEN

Terrorism Financing in Europe

LORETTA NAPOLEONI

Is the West winning the war on terror? Five years into this new type of conflict the results are discouraging. On the one hand, counter-terrorism financing strategies have been weakened by the enemy's ability to exploit globalization to its own advantage; on the other hand, governments have failed to implement a multilateral policy under the umbrella of an international organization to fight terrorism financing. The consequences of the U.S.-led war in Iraq have dramatically altered Islamist terror's financial landscape, often making policies obsolete before they are implemented.

Since September 2001, some countries, in particular the United States, have single-handedly introduced tough anti-terrorism policies and regulations. However, these measures have not prompted similar legislation in other global financial centers such as Europe. Compared to the American response, Europe's policy has been fragmented and reactive. The responses to the attacks in Madrid in March 2003 and in London in July 2005 confirm that European states continue to develop an incremental law enforcement–centered approach to countering terrorism financing. Within this framework, the European Union has failed to achieve a high degree of integration in counter-terrorism policies.[1]

In a globalized world, the absence of a coordinated international framework to combat terrorist finances allowed terrorists' financiers to shift their activities towards jurisdictions with the laxest regulatory framework. Implemented outside an international framework, a tough U.S. policy had a limited impact, if any, on the global funding of Islamist terrorist organizations because terror financiers simply moved their assets out of the United States and into the less regulated European financial markets. The consequences of a unilateral approach to terrorist financing go well beyond the failure to stop terror financing. U.S. counter-terrorism policies also encouraged the displacement of terrorists' operational activities and, by doing so, turned Europe into one of the main fronts for jihadi terrorism today.

The U.S.-led war in Iraq triggered major metamorphoses in the structure and financing of the jihadist movement in Europe and the Mideast. Far from curbing the growth of Islamist terror, the personnel and financial requirements of the Iraqi insurgency activated a new network of loosely connected, homegrown, and self-funded jihadist cells. Their inspirational leader was Abu Musab al Zarqawi, who first drew widespread public attention on February 5, 2003, when Secretary of State Colin Powell identified him as the link between Saddam Hussein and al Qaeda in a presentation to the UN Security Council. Far from being a bridge between the two, al Zarqawi was not even a member of al Qaeda.[2] However, he was able to skillfully transform the international attention garnered by his actions in Iraq to turn the battered al Qaeda organization into a global anti-imperialist ideology able to inspire self-organizing jihadi cells in Europe and elsewhere.[3]

The European Islamist Terror Network

Since the attacks of September 11, 2001, the structure of Islamist armed organizations and their global web has evolved. Before these attacks, the network was small and highly integrated, but today it resembles a cluster of decentralized, loosely connected, and often self-financing networks, as investigations into the Madrid and London bombings suggest. It is now apparent that it was September 2001 that prompted a major metamorphosis inside the jihadist movement.

The desire of radical Islamist groups to emulate the September 2001 attacks, coupled with counter-terror measures such as the war in Iraq, fueled the network's transformation. This is especially true since counter-terror measures have been perceived by Muslims, including those born in Europe, as hegemonic and anti-Muslim. Europe has also seen the spontaneous emergence of homegrown jihadist groups whose members have not been trained in Islamist camps in Afghanistan or Sudan. This was the case, for example, with the cells that carried out the Madrid and London attacks. These groups do not have official links with al Qaeda or Osama bin Laden but operate under the ideological umbrella of al Qaedism.[4]

Up until the September 2001 attacks, the main task of the European terror web was to supply funds and recruits for Islamist armed groups operating outside of Europe. French-born Zacarias Moussaoui, the convicted co-conspirator in the September 2001 attacks, reached London penniless and in search of his own identity as a Muslim. The mosque network provided him with both financial and emotional support. Once ready, he was sent to Afghanistan, where al Qaeda put him through extensive training and eventually deployed him to attack the United States.

After September 2001 the European terror network continued to supply recruits to carry out attacks outside Europe. In April 2003 two British suicide bombers staged suicide attacks in Tel Aviv. In 2004 Jean-Louis Bruguiere, the French anti-terrorism investigative magistrate, admitted that since the summer of 2003 dozens of new European recruits had reached Iraq.[5] Italian magistrates concluded that most of them were recruited through the European mosque network and used as suicide bombers.[6] The major departure from pre-September 2001 recruitment methodology has been the inclusion of women among suicide bombers. In the fall 2005, a Belgian woman who had converted to Islam carried out a suicide mission in Baghdad. She was deployed by al Zarqawi's jihadist group, which confirmed that the Jordanian-born terror leader has access to the European jihadist network.

The impact of the war in Iraq on European public opinion turned this region into a rich recruiting ground for al Zarqawi, whose network was only loosely connected to al Qaeda prior to November 2004, when Osama bin Laden acknowledged his leadership of al Qaeda in Iraq. In the Mediterranean, al Zarqawi's high media profile facilitated the recruiting work of a handful of close lieutenants responsible for supplying European suicide bombers to Iraq.[7]

Since September 2001, the European Islamist terror network has also been able to take advantage of Central European countries as locations for their activities. The lack of effective counter-terrorist controls, coupled with porous borders, has made it less difficult for members of Islamist terror organizations to travel. Operating on the eastern fringes of the European Union has also allowed Islamist cells to establish contacts with the Balkan mafia to purchase arms and explosives.[8] The bulk of the trade in arms and explosives transits via southern Italy, principally through the port of Gioia Tauro in Calabria, and it is managed through joint ventures with local organized crime. As the investigation into the Madrid bombing documented, acquiring explosives in Western Europe presents terrorists with serious difficulties due to tight police controls. The explosives utilized in the Madrid bombing were collected over a period of a year by a worker in a coal mine in the Spanish region of Asturias; the worker then bartered the explosives for drugs provided by the Madrid bombing cell.[9] The lax rule of law in some Central European states facilitates terrorists' acquisition of false identities. As documented by *Sunday Times* correspondent Nick Fielding, these false identities are mass-produced in Central Europe, are extremely authentic looking, and are very cheap. They cost as little as £600 each, while on the European black market forged passports cost £7,000.[10]

Europe: Islamist Terror's New Front

Cities are undoubtedly primary targets of the Islamic jihadi groups in Europe. This has been proven by the Madrid and London attacks, and the strategy has been openly acknowledged by the Islamist jihadi leadership in public statements. "Strikes within cities are a type of military diplomacy," stated the *Al Battar*, al Qaeda's virtual magazine issued after the attack in Madrid.

> This type of attack is often written with blood, embellished with body parts and perfumed with gunpowder. . . . Strikes bear a political meaning related to the conflict in ideology. They are considered a message sent to multiple parties, thus choosing the targets is done with extreme precision. Those bombings—such as the CIA building bombing, the East Riyadh operation— were well executed and were the sparks to awaken the struggling youth.[11]

Most European intelligence services expect further attacks on cities, and after the Madrid attack even European politicians admitted that the danger was very serious. The London attacks in July 2005 demonstrated that existing counter-terrorism measures were not sufficient to prevent repeated attacks on mass transit targets.

The European terror campaign has completely different aims from the attacks against the United States carried out before September 2001. Al Qaeda and Osama bin Laden are not directly involved in the European campaign, which is instead led by new leaders, the most prominent of whom was al Zarqawi before his death in June 2006. These leaders hope to terrorize European populations and force them to put pressure upon the politicians to abandon an increasingly unpopular war in Iraq. The outcome of the Spanish elections in the immediate aftermath of the 2003 Madrid bombing suggests that the strategy may be working in some cases. Public reaction to the bombings, and the perceived manipulation by Prime Minister Aznar's government of information about the attacks, may have provided the margin of victory for the Partido Socialista Obrero Español (PSOE) and its policy of disengagement from Iraq. The November 2003 car bomb attacks in Istanbul similarly reinforced Turkey's reluctance to back the war in Iraq.

Paradoxically, attacks in Europe and those against European interests in the Middle East, as well as kidnappings and beheadings of European nationals, strengthen a growing anti-American sentiment among the population. People see these actions as a confirmation that Europe should not be involved in what is perceived as an American crusade. This perception was fueled by the unwillingness of the Bush administration to carry on the fight against terror under the umbrella of the UN and by its determination to go to war with Iraq, a country with no direct link to al Qaeda or the Islamist terror system.[12] Al Qaeda and Osama bin Laden clearly intend to exploit this sentiment, as suggested by bin Laden's surprising three-month truce offered to induce European leaders to leave Iraq, an offer made just a few weeks after the Madrid bombing.[13]

Funding the European Terror Network

Governmental and societal responses to the attacks of September 2001 prompted the transfer of large sums of Saudi money from the United States to Europe. In August 2002 the filing of a lawsuit by the relatives of the victims of September 2001 against several members of the Saudi elite, the country of Sudan, and a number of Persian Gulf banks and charities led Saudis to withdraw $200 billion worth of assets held in the United States. The bulk of the money was reinvested in Europe in equities, bonds, and real estate. Overall, Saudi financiers are believed to have had about $750 billion invested in the United States.[14] According to the United Nations, Saudi funds still find their way to support Islamist terror groups in the Muslim world and in Europe.[15]

European counter-intelligence believes that a network of mosques continues to be a powerful instrument for recruiting, funding, and coordinating the activity of cells and armed groups linked to Islamist terror in Europe and abroad. Italian authorities are adamant that since September 2001 Arab terror sponsors have provided funds for the recruitment and indoctrination of potential suicide bombers living in Europe. An intercepted conversation inside the Milan mosque of Via Quaranta confirmed the identity of some of the sponsors. "The thread begins in Saudi Arabia," said an unidentified Arab visitor to the Imam of the mosque. "Do not even worry about money because Saudi Arabia's money is your money."[16] Spanish counter-terrorism officers have claimed that some European mosques are "havens for al Qaeda planning and fund-raising."[17] In the spring of 2004, Spanish magistrates discovered that a Spanish cell, Soldiers of Allah, which started in Madrid's Abu Baker mosque in 1994, provided support and money to the Hamburg cell that participated in the September 11, attack.[18] Until the Madrid bombing, counter-terrorism intelligence services underestimated the role played by the mosque network.

The funding network for terrorist groups in Europe continues to evolve. It is widely believed that al Zarqawi's European network benefited directly from funds originating in Saudi Arabia, but there is no evidence that al Qaeda played an intermediary or coordinating role. Furthermore, funding from outside the region is less relevant today than before the attacks of September 2001. Groups have been encouraged to become (or have spontaneously become) self-funded, and both the Madrid bombing and the Casablanca attacks in 2003 were self-funded. European intelligence agencies admit that an emulation factor among those eager to support al Qaeda has encouraged self-funding. As an Italian magistrate argued, "For people who have no link with al Qaeda, people who never travelled to the camps, and that after September 2001 felt compelled to join in the fight, it is easier to fund themselves with criminal activities than to get in touch with al Qaeda and ask for money."[19]

The financial role played by al Qaeda has changed since September 2001. These were the last attacks fully planned, funded, and executed under the direct supervision of al Qaeda's leadership. In the Bali bombing, al Qaeda played the role of terror venture capitalist rather than that of organizer. The most recent attacks in Europe, including the brutal killing of Theo Van Gogh in Amsterdam, are the work of individuals and groups whose only link to al Qaeda is ideological. European Islamist armed groups, although inspired by bin Laden and the September 2001 attacks, are not directly tied to the man or his organization. These groups use both legitimate and illegitimate activities to raise money within Europe rather than receiving it from the al Qaeda organization. Sponsorship by groups within Arab countries and funds gathered by the mosque network provide a source of legitimate funds that can be diverted to fund terror groups without the need for money laundering. Funding can be stretched by requiring members of Islamist armed organizations to have legitimate jobs, and in Spain and Italy, several worked as mechanics and waiters to support themselves.

Nevertheless, illegitimate activities provide the bulk of the funding for European jihadi terrorism. An estimated two-thirds of terror financing originates from criminal and illegal activities, which range from large fraud to petty crime.[20] As a case in point, Farid Belaribi, an Algerian immigrant jailed in England in the summer of 2003, helped raise $250,000 through an international fraud network that targeted banks and credit card companies in Europe and in Dubai.[21] In 2002 inside the EU, credit card losses due to fraud amounted to $424 million, and experts suggest that this money bankrolls crime and terrorism.[22] In addition, some cells in the European network fund themselves by trafficking drugs, as the Madrid bombing investigation revealed.[23] While the London bombings of July 2005 were also self-financed, the money was raised "by methods that would be extremely difficult to identify as related to terrorism or other serious criminality."[24] The bulk of the funding came from one bomber, who defaulted on a £10,000 personal loan and was overdrawn on his credit cards, while another bomber bounced a number of personal checks in order to make purchases in the weeks before the bombing.[25]

The primary channels that terror sponsors use to move money within

Europe are shell banks and offshore facilities. The USA Patriot Act enacted after the September 2001 attacks, prohibited U.S. banks and U.S.-registered foreign banks from doing business with shell banks, but there are no such restrictions in Europe. Italian magistrates investigating the Milan mosque in Via Quaranta discovered that the cell received funds, denominated in euros, from Arab countries via British offshore accounts.[26] Once money has successfully entered the European banking system, it can be wired and withdrawn anywhere. Members of terror groups operating in Europe use ATM machines, as the September 2001 hijackers did, to access the cash made available by their sponsors. Those who participated in the Bali, Istanbul, and Madrid attacks also used ATM machines.[27] Islamist groups also rely on couriers and *hawaladars* to transfer money and gold to Europe. A courier delivered $50,000 of the $150,000 used to fund the November 2003 bombing in Istanbul; the balance of the funds was already in Turkey.[28]

Globalization and the Ineffectiveness of Counter-Terrorism Measures

Western democracies, particularly in Europe, have been unable to track the profits of legitimate businesses diverted to terror groups. Such difficulties derive from the nature of the globalized financial market, which allows investments—especially those funds generated by legitimate businesses managed by sympathizers—to be easily converted and geographically relocated to serve the objectives of terrorist organizations. The case of Youssef Nada, an Egyptian designated as a terror financier by the United Nations, illustrates the difficulty that even highly capable European states face in targeting terrorist finances.[29] Until December 2003, Nada, whose UN designation made him subject to sanctions (including a travel ban), moved freely across borders in Europe and thus had easy access to most of his wealth.[30] Clearly the UN sanctions against Nada were not enforced by the authorities of the countries he visited. Admittedly, the geography of Europe and its political integration make it hard to implement travel bans, but borders exist even inside the European Union and we would expect Nada to face obstacles to his freedom of movement. Yet in 2003 and 2004 Nada was able to liquidate several of his enterprises and relocate the funds out of reach of government authorities, an activity that took him across the Swiss border multiple times, always undetected by border authorities.

The Financial Action Task Force (FATF), an international organization promoting anti-money laundering practices worldwide, blames a lack of cooperation and poor information-sharing practices among countries for the failure to cut off terrorist finances from the Western financial system.[31] In all fairness, counter-terrorism agencies often have little information to share anyway, especially once funding enters the offshore banking system.

The FATF also concurs with the United Nations that the targeting of Islamist charities has been of questionable effectiveness. Charities closed in one country often reappear after a few months somewhere else under a new name. The Al Haramain charity, which had been designated in 2002 as a front for al Qaeda in Bosnia and Sudan, opened an Islamist school in Jakarta in December 2003.[32] Since its closure, it had also resurfaced in Bosnia twice under a different name. A FATF officer admitted that charities can be relocated as quickly as money can be wired from one place to the next. The speed at which offices move from country to country remains a by-product of globalization and the deregulation of financial markets.

Similarly, the global financial system enables terrorist financiers to store and route their funds around the most restrictive jurisdictions, such as the United States following the enactment of the USA Patriot Act in 2001. As Anne Clunan documents in chapter 15, this legislation greatly increased the reporting requirements for financial transactions in the United States. The immediate beneficiaries of such legislation have been the euro currency and European banks. As the euro has increasingly become a parallel reserve currency for the world, private foreign investment has gravitated towards Europe to avoid the oversight and regulation found in the United States. In December 2003, a British banker admitted that several merchant banks operating in Asia and Africa detected a tendency for legitimate investors to shift away from the dollar and towards the euro. Amid the uncertainty of the war on terror, the euro seemed a more secure reserve currency in which to "park" capital.

Evidence of the relative attractiveness of Europe as a locus for illegal financial transactions is confirmed by the behavior of organized crime. Traditional organizations such as the Sicilian Cosa Nostra and the Calabrian 'Ndrangheta are taking increasing advantage of the European Union's legal loopholes on money laundering. According to Italian intelligence services, the money laundering activities of Italian organized crime increased by 64 percent from the end of 2001 to the end of 2003, garnering hundreds of million euros.[33] There is also evidence that weak border controls allow the movement of bulk currency and commodities by criminal organizations. The failure of European states and institutions to control illegal financial movements by organized crime is a likely indicator that terrorist organizations have access to similar channels.

European Responses to Terrorism Financing

Europe has offered terror financiers an attractive opportunity by failing to enact homogenous and comprehensive legislation similar to the USA Patriot Act. The European Union (EU) has fostered significant political and economic integration, yet its power to counter-terrorist financing is limited to issuing directives and guidelines. While the European Union has worked collectively to develop legal responses to terrorism financing, these regulations may or may not be implemented or enforced by the individual member states.

Acting quickly, by September 21, 2001, the European Council had already identified a series of counter-terrorism measures that created the following: joint investigation teams of police and magistrates from throughout the EU to target terrorists; a common list of terrorist organizations; apparatas for routine information exchanges about terrorism between the member states; a specialist anti-terrorist team within Europol; a cooperation agreement on terrorism between Europol and the relevant U.S. authorities; and Euro-just, a coordination body composed of magistrates, prosecutors, and police officers.[34] Soon after, the European Union ratified the United Nations Convention for the Suppression of the Financing of Terrorism. The European Union also agreed to implement in full UN Security Council Resolution 1373 on the fight against terrorism, and it cooperated with the FATF to develop new guidelines on money laundering that targeted terrorist finances.

Similar to the strategy pursued by Washington, Europe's strategy also focused on freezing terrorist financial assets. On December 27, 2001, the Council of the European Union approved a regulation for the freezing of funds and passed a prohibition against providing funds, assets, economic resources, or financial services to individuals, groups, or entities with proven links to terrorist organizations. Under this regulation, over € 100 million of assets belonging to persons, entities, and states sponsoring terrorist acts have been frozen throughout the EU. In June 2003, at the U.S.-EU Summit in Washington, extradition and mutual legal assistance agreements were signed, expanding law enforcement and judicial cooperation.

After the 2003 Madrid attack, the EU issued an action paper that called for better implementation of the existing legislation against terrorism.[35] On March 25, 2004, the 25 current and future EU member states agreed to a comprehensive package of anti-terrorism measures that will increase data sharing and speed up the deployment of biometric identification in Europe.[36] In March 2004 the EU also appointed a czar for anti-terrorism. In April 2004, the EU and the U.S. Department of Homeland Security signed an agreement calling for the prompt expansion of the Container Security Initiative (CSI) throughout Europe, thus enhancing efforts to prevent terrorists from exploiting the international trading system to conduct bulk movements of currency and commodities. On June 10, 2004, the European Commission announced "the creation of an electronic database aimed at preventing the financing of terrorism and of certain foreign regimes. The database, established in partnership with four European credit sector federations, lists persons, groups, and entities that are subject to EU financial sanctions."[37]

Nevertheless, despite all these measures, the European Union did not go as far as the United States in closing loopholes in its financial system to bar its use by terror financiers. Although European countries have battled terror for decades, they have never considered it a global phenomenon. European armed organizations, either right-wing or left-wing, were localized, and they exclusively operated within the borders of each nation. Thus terrorism was considered a domestic phenomenon, and it is still addressed as such. A major obstacle to comprehensive anti-terrorist legislation in Europe remains the lack of a proper definition of terrorism accepted by all the EU members. For example, Italy does not consider terrorism a crime but rather an objective that demands an additional punishment. By contrast, terrorism is designated a crime in the United Kingdom. Even after the Madrid attack, which should have been Europe's wake-up call, the differences among domestic legislation continue to be a major obstacle to the creation of a common and successful anti-terrorist framework. The EU's so-called Third Money Laundering Directive was controversial enough to delay its passage until late 2005.

In addition, the lack of homogeneity of terrorism legislation among national jurisdictions enables members of armed organizations to exploit loopholes that allow them to seek and obtain political asylum in contiguous European countries. During the 1970s and 1980s, several members of the Italian Red Brigade, for example, took refuge in France, where legislation did not recognize "political crime" or allow the preventive incarceration common to Italian anti-terrorist legislation. During a special meeting on September 13, 2004, the European Commission attempted to remedy this gap by proposing a European arrest warrant to supplant the current system of extradition treaties between member states. This new proposal included a common definition of terrorism and its related penalties.[38] However, the definition of terrorism still varies in the domestic legislation of each member state, and the legality of the European arrest warrant is still being challenged in some jurisdictions. The case of Hamdi Isaac, arrested in Rome on suspicion of participating in the July 21, 2005, failed bombings in London, suggests that the European arrest warrant still needs further institutionalization and operationalization. Given the different national jurisdictions involved, Italy and the United Kingdom required several weeks to agree on where Hamdi Isaac should be initially prosecuted and when he would be extradited.[39]

Despite decades of economic and political integration in the context of the European Union, there is also a lack of trust among European security services. According to Spain's Baltasar Garzon, who is one of the most prominent anti-terrorism magistrates in Europe, there is a lack of solidarity and a continued prevalence of national self-interest among the European state security services. Concerns over national sovereignty and interests have delayed formal cooperation, and security services instead rely on personal contacts and informal associations to implement collective responses.[40]

Popular opinion within Europe also leads European politicians to be hesitant about cooperating fully in international counter-terrorism efforts. In some countries, public resentment of United States foreign policy, particularly in the Middle East, is pervasive, and politicians therefore avoid taking stands that might lead them to be perceived as too supportive of U.S. interests. Several European states disagree with the way the United States is holding suspects without trial in Guantanamo Bay. They also question the validity of the information collected from such prisoners. Significant political parties and non-governmental organizations in many European countries fear that anti-terrorist policies could pose a threat to human rights and democracy. When the British Home secretary introduced tough new anti-terrorist laws after the Madrid bombing, several human rights groups criticized the laws as threats to democracy. In addition, since many European countries have substantial non-integrated Moslem populations, politicians are very careful about embarking on any legislation that could be perceived as racist or targeting Islam.

Conclusion

In the aftermath of September 2001, the United States took the lead on counter-terrorism policies, often unilaterally bypassing most of the international community, including the UN. The USA Patriot Act succeeded in curbing terror financing in the United States but did little to reduce terror financing globally. Terror financiers and money launderers simply moved their businesses across the Atlantic to Europe. The result was an increase in both terrorist operations and terrorist financing in the European Union. Responding to the USA Patriot Act and the monitoring of funds flowing through the U.S. financial system, terror money traveled elsewhere to be laundered, often landing in Europe. With a new common currency, porous borders, declining economic and financial barriers, and lax legislation governing offshore banking, Europe became and remains the ideal terrain for money laundering, currency smuggling, and other forms of illegal financial activity conducive to financing terror.

Lack of agreement between EU member states, combined with the new problems posed by European Union enlargement, slowed the development of effective counter-terrorist measures. Counter-terrorism policy lies at the intersection of criminal law and national security, two areas where EU member states have jealously preserved their national prerogatives. Similarly, the strong feeling among the European population that the "war on terror" was an American–Middle Eastern problem undermined the political will to develop effective responses. The Madrid and London bombing attacks did bring global terror home to the Europeans; however, the bombings were also perceived as tied to the unpopular U.S.-led war in Iraq. While the Madrid attack led to a more coordinated effort within the EU, the fear of discriminating against European Muslim populations remains the main obstacle to a tough U.S.-style counter-terror policy.

The lesson to be learned from the Madrid and London bombings is that terrorist financing is still evolving. Homegrown, self-funded jihadist groups in Europe are inspired by Iraq and are operating under the umbrella of a new anti-imperialist ideology: al Qaedism. Unlike al Qaeda, their primary target is not the United States but Europe. After September 2001, these groups used terror financiers' seed-money, which migrated to Europe after the introduction of the USA Patriot Act in the United States, to galvanize their operations. Today, these groups need very little money to carry out attacks inside European cities, so little that they can easily self-fund their activity. It is this new scenario that European counter-terrorism financing efforts should begin to address.

CHAPTER ELEVEN

Terrorist Financing and Government Responses in East Africa

JESSICA PIOMBO

This chapter analyzes the nature of transnational terrorist financing in East Africa and the responses of area governments to combat terrorist finance. I make the argument that patterns of terrorist finance in East Africa may have been less affected by the post- 9/11 global war on terror than those in other areas of the world. In the wake of the 9/11 strikes, the global emphasis on combating terrorism by "following the money trail" meant the large-scale adaptation of existing anti-money laundering (AML) regimes to serve as counter-terrorist finance (CTF) weapons. This adaptation forced groups to shift out of formal and into informal sectors of finance. Efforts to combat terrorist finance in East Africa followed a similar trajectory, but much earlier than in the rest of the world. Following the 1998 embassy bombings in Kenya and Tanzania, the United States stepped up efforts to reduce the Sudanese government's support for bin Laden and encouraged area governments to implement AML regimes. Post 9/11, the region is slowly adapting these AML measures into CTF regimes, yet the transformation is far from complete, and implementation remains a problem.

Unlike terrorist organizations in the other regions examined in this volume, transnational and local terrorist organizations in East Africa had concentrated most of their financial activities in informal sectors long before 2001. Local groups had always relied on informal mechanisms, based on the culture and economies of the region in which they operated. When the 1998 embassy bombings focused U.S. attention on al Qaeda's regional activities, the organization was forced to shift its resources out of the formal sector long before it followed suit in other areas of the world. By September 2001, radical Islamist and terrorist organizations operating in East Africa had already taken advantage of the region's porous borders and large unregulated areas to smuggle people, arms, and illicit goods to finance their operations. Prior to 2001, support from official sponsors such as Saudi Arabia, the Islamic government in Sudan, and other benefactors supplemented the financial base of the organizations in this region. By the time the U.S. government began its international drive after September 2001 to develop an international counter-terrorism finance regime based on anti-money laundering policies, terrorist finance networks operating in East Africa had already achieved some insulation from these measures.

Given the nature of the terrorist organizations in East Africa, their sources of funding, and available financial channels, CTF measures that focus on formal and informal banking institutions will not have much effect on terrorist financing in East Africa. A broader range of counter-terrorism activities, such as capacity building for local police and security forces, are the ones that will more effectively combat terrorist finance in East Africa. Policy makers and analysts should recognize that funding mechanisms used by terrorists in the East African region had already become decentralized, and the use of informal transfer mechanisms was already common practice among such organizations before 9/11. There are also compelling reasons why governments in the region are reluctant to create strong AML and CTF regimes and are unwilling to devote scarce resources to efforts to combat terrorist finance explicitly.

The real fight against terrorist finance in the region needs to center on capacity building for police and security forces that will allow them to effectively police borders and control illicit activities such as smuggling, arms transfers, and human trafficking. These are exactly the areas that are currently prioritized in U.S. government activities in the region, which is a positive development. Not only will such efforts yield more concrete results against terrorist finances, but governments in the region may cooperate more readily in the implementation of the policies since the benefits will extend beyond addressing the threat of terrorism.

Background: Rising Concern for Terrorism in Africa

Over the course of the past decade, international concern for Sub-Saharan Africa has steadily increased, and for the United States, the region has achieved an unprecedented degree of strategic importance. The principal factors explaining this trend are the strategic location of the continent for U.S. counter-terrorism efforts; issues of piracy and the increasing influence of Islamic militias in Somalia; the growing importance of Africa as a source of natural resources, especially oil; and the growing demand for peacekeeping forces and humanitarian resources from the international community generated by persistent political instability in the region. In Sub-Saharan Africa, East Africa has been the site of the most long-standing terrorist organizations and operations, and the region serves as the hub of U.S. antiterror activities. Regional patterns to the nature of Islamic groups, their organization and recruitment patterns, and their scope of operations and goals, influence the way that they finance themselves. Conditions of statelessness, porous borders, and large Muslim communities further render this region critically important when studying terrorist finance in Africa.

Transnational terrorist organizations exist in other parts of Africa, yet East Africa has attracted special interest from the United States and the international community because of its early links to transnational Islamic terrorism. In 1998, United States embassies in Dar es Salaam, Tanzania, and Nairobi, Kenya, were bombed, killing a handful of U.S. citizens and hundreds of Kenyans and Tanzanians. In 2002, a popular tourist destination in Kenya, Mombasa, witnessed two further terrorist strikes, this time in the form of coordinated and simultaneous attacks on an Israeli-owned hotel popular with Western tourists and on an Israeli-chartered aircraft departing from the Mombasa airport.

The region has also been a home for the al Qaeda organization and its leader, Osama bin Laden. Sudan provided both training camps and a source of financial support for his organization during the early 1990s. Sudan and Somalia have both served as training grounds and transit routes for al Qaeda, and the agents who attacked the embassies in Kenya and Tanzania were closely linked to cells in Sudan and Somalia. In the wake of the embassy bombings, an organized al Qaeda cell was uncovered in Nairobi, Kenya. The evidence of al Qaeda activities in the region was strong enough for President Bill Clinton to order strikes against a Sudanese chemical factory owned by an associate of bin Laden, thought to be producing the precursors to chemical weapons.[1] The challenge to Somalia's transitional government by the Islamic Courts in Mogadishu puts that country once again at the forefront of U.S. concern. The region keeps reappearing as a focus of U.S. counter-terrorism efforts.

Terrorist Finance in East Africa: The Nature of the Threat

Before turning explicitly to terrorist finance, we need to understand the terrain that is being covered. "East Africa" spans Sudan, Ethiopia, Eritrea, Djibouti, Somalia, Kenya, Tanzania, and Uganda. The Horn of Africa, a subregion of East Africa, encompasses Eritrea, Djibouti, Ethiopia, Sudan, and Somalia. The entire eastern seaboard of the continental United States, from Maine to the top of Florida, could fit within the territory of Somalia alone. Not only are the distances vast, but they have historically been populated by nomadic peoples. Distances and shifting populations make ruling difficult for regional governments.

In addition to a complicated geography, governance is complicated by a history of decentralization in most of the region. State borders, artificially layered onto the area by colonial rulers, are almost impossible to enforce. Trading and smuggling routes are centuries old, whether they involved the *khat* (*qhat*) trade in northern Sudan and Somalia or the spice trade along the coast from Zanzibar to Yemen. The porous borders and migrant groups therefore facilitate the transport of goods and commodities such as weapons and people (i.e., slaves) that can be traded for revenue. Along the coast of the Horn and down into East and Central Africa, small trading boat (*dhow*) traffic is virtually impossible to monitor, adding a maritime dimension to the difficulties in tracking terrorist activities and financial patterns. In addition, the near statelessness of Somalia and the ongoing conflicts in Sudan provide added vulnerabilities and areas in which terrorists can operate and Islamists can gain supporters.

Despite this permissive environment, the indigenous terrorist threat in the area has not been considered a major threat by the U.S. government, which has focused almost exclusively on the threat posed by transnational jihadi organizations originating outside of East Africa. Even though there are at least 10 radical Islamist groups operating in the region (a conservative estimate), none of these groups has been added to the U.S. State Department's list of "designated foreign terrorist organizations" (FTOs). The groups originating and operating in Sub-Saharan Africa that have thus far been the focus of State Department attention are neither Islamic nor designated as FTOs, but are instead on the terrorist exclusion lists used to deny visas for travel to the United States.[2] These groups hail from a variety of countries, and only one of the groups so designated, the now-defunct Al Ittihad al-Islamiyya (AIAI), originated in an East African country (Somalia). This reflects the narrow concern of the U.S. government with the threat posed by al Qaeda in the region.

ORGANIZED TERRORISM IN EAST AFRICA

Al Qaeda and Lebanese Hezbollah are the primary transnational terrorist organizations that operate in Sub-Saharan Africa. Hezbollah's activities are confined mostly to West Africa, which falls outside the scope of this chapter. Al Qaeda first established itself in East Africa, and from there has attempted to spread into West, Central, and Southern Africa. Al Qaeda's presence in the eastern region is both direct, with agents operating in several countries, and indirect, through the creation of satellite organizations and the recruitment of existing organizations to al Qaeda's cause. In 1991 the leader of Sudan's National Islamic Front (NIF) government, Hassan al Turabi, invited Osama bin Laden to live in Sudan. During that time, bin Laden established multiple businesses in Sudan, and he set up al Qaeda training camps in the more remote areas.[3] With the support of the NIF, bin Laden created the Islamic Army Shura, which he intended to function as a coordinating body for a consortium of terrorist groups allied with him.[4] In East Africa, groups from Somalia and Eritrea were formally associated with Islamic Army Shura, and informal associations were established with groups in Uganda and several West African states. Al Qaeda has increased its direct presence in much of East Africa during recent years, extending its reach from Sudan in the north to Tanzania and perhaps even into Malawi in the south, which is why the region increasingly figures in U.S. counter-terrorism efforts.[5]

Al Qaeda operates directly in the region alongside a pervasive network of local groups, some of which are affiliated with this transnational organization and many of which are not. In fact, the bulk of Islamist "terrorist" organizations in East Africa are those that originated in the area and operate with a regional agenda. Many of these groups existed before al Qaeda attempted to organize them into a loose hierarchy, and so far these local groups have not become deeply entrenched in the al Qaeda network. The most important obstacle to a closer alliance has been that local Islamist groups have a primary loyalty to their clans and ethnic tribes, a loyalty that has not always been compatible with al Qaeda's transnational agenda.[6] Local Islamist groups are primarily concerned with the overthrow of their governments, and they focus on destabilizing neighboring governments in order to assist their ethnic compatriots who were stranded across the state borders established by colonial powers. With such locally delimited agendas, these groups are of only limited concern to the international community. The one exception here is the international concern at the emergence in Somalia of the Islamic Court militias, which, while Islamist, also provide the first measure of security to the Somali people in almost 15 years.[7]

Across Africa, extremist organizations have operated successfully both in unstable countries, such as Somalia and Liberia, and in some of the most stable governments, such as South Africa and Kenya. The conventional wisdom that failed states are breeding grounds for terrorism is belied by the experience of African countries: most groups can be found in states with at least a modicum of law and order, such as Kenya and South Africa. Terrorist groups tend to use the failed states (such as Somalia) as staging grounds and transit points rather than as sites for sheltering long-term organizational and financial networks. Al Qaeda operatives actually stand out too much in Somalia to stay there for long periods of time, and the transnational groups find the clan-based warfare and seeming anarchy of acephalous societies difficult terrain in which to recruit and prosper.[8] Without a reliable and secure commercial infrastructure, it becomes difficult to move commodities and illicit goods to fund terrorist activities. The only proven al Qaeda cells in East Africa have been uncovered in Kenya, one of the most politically stable and developed countries in the region. Even in West Africa, where Hezbollah obtains diamonds from conflict zones and stateless areas, terrorists find it necessary to transport them via the Lebanese diaspora community that lives in the more politically stable countries.

Given these organizational patterns, terrorist financing mechanisms operate at several levels and are shaped by both group agendas and the uncertain environments in which they operate. For groups operating in Sub-Saharan Africa, and especially in East Africa, the transition in the organization of terrorist finance dates from the 1998 embassy bombings rather than from the 2001 attacks on the Pentagon and the World Trade Center. These shifts should be considered in context, since most of these organizations already relied on informal avenues even before 1998, particularly human couriers, *hawaladars*, and other alternative remittance systems,

In the past, funding for local terrorist organizations and al Qaeda has derived both from operations within the region, such as trade in illicit goods, and from direct cash transfers from Yemen, Saudi Arabia, Iran, and the Sudanese government.[9] The flow of money often comes through the embassies themselves:

> The leader of one 10-member Islamist cell claims his group receives funding from contacts in Yemen and Saudi Arabia. "The money comes through their embassies in Dar es Salaam. . . . The money is officially used to buy medicine, but in reality the money is given to us to support our work and buy guns."[10]

During the 1990s, Saudi financiers and the NIF government of Sudan were prolific benefactors of both al Qaeda in East Africa and local groups. The NIF was linked to the funding of terrorist organizations throughout the Horn of Africa, particularly the Eritrean Islamic Jihad and the Eritrean Liberation Front. From 1993 to 2004, Sudan was on the State Department's list of states supporting terrorism. Since 1996, in the wake of a failed assassination attempt on Egyptian President Hosni Mubarak by al Qaeda agents based in Sudan, the Sudanese leadership has backed away from patronage activities and has moved away from its extreme radical agenda. By 2001, all extremist Islamist elements had been completely pushed out of the government, prompting the creation of a new political party, led by Islamist Hassan al Turabi, that now competes with the government.

Financial flows in the region move between terrorist organizations, but rarely does the region serve as a source of funding for the larger transnational al Qaeda network. The one exception that we know about is bin

Laden's use of the businesses he started in Sudan in the early 1990s to raise funds to distribute to affiliated organizations worldwide, but that is unlikely to have continued beyond his departure in 1996.[11]

Al Qaeda does provide direct support to affiliate groups in the region, logistically supporting groups in Somalia (the now-defunct AIAI and a shadowy network of loosely linked jihadists who are slowly replacing it), Ethiopia (Union of the Mujahidin of Ogaden and the Oromo-Somali-Afar Liberation Alliance, or OSALA), and Eritrea (Eritrean Islamic Jihad Movement, also known as Jamal Jihad).[12] Most support from al Qaeda to local East African organizations constitutes weapons or trainers, rather than direct financial resources.[13] Al Qaeda has also helped to facilitate cooperation between local groups.

SELF-FUNDING LOCAL TERRORIST ORGANIZATIONS

If local groups are not obtaining most of their financing from al Qaeda, then how do they support themselves? There are three primary sources: trade and smuggling, alternative remittance systems, and foreign patrons.[14] It is virtually impossible to rank these in order of importance, as the unclassified sources on the subject do not provide figures or other metrics. East Africa shares connections with the Middle East that do not exist in West, Central, or Southern Africa, and these connections underlie most of the financing mechanisms.

Many of the people who inhabit the region are descendants of migrants who traveled into the area from the Middle East, who retain the nomadic traditions of their ancestors, and who still identify themselves as Arabs. Trade in spices, commodities and agricultural products, animals, slaves, and other goods, whether conducted via overland or sea routes, has long connected the areas. Today, a primary source of funding comes from the profits of smuggling and arms transfers that follow these old trade routes.

A second major source for funding East African terrorist organizations is financial assistance from Islamic charities and alternative remittance systems. Several charities were identified as financing the terrorists who bombed the U.S. embassies in 1998, and Mercy International Relief Organization was publicly named as a sponsor of this incident.[15] Large portions of the citizens in East African countries are Muslim, and therefore the Islamic charity network has substantial roots. There are large diaspora communities of East

Africans spread throughout the world, and many of the expatriates send funds home to their relatives through the informal banking system of *hawala*. Both the charities and the *hawala* networks have served as entry points for terrorist financiers in the past.

When money is generated through illegal activities, it often gets laundered through investments, foreign exchange scams, import-export businesses, casinos, and real estate deals.[16] This is only a partial list; the varieties of money-laundering activities "are only limited by opportunity and human imagination."[17] Distribution then occurs through cells and groups, often established according to networks of personal ties and family/ethnic relationships.[18] Resources are often transported by human couriers or through *hawaladars*, rather than through the formal banking system.

The informal and personal nature of financial flows in the region is facilitated by porous borders and by poor control over foreign exchange (particularly in Eritrea, Kenya, Zanzibar, and Uganda). Area governments do not have the capacity to patrol borders, and in some cases, governments tacitly have agreed not to even try to enforce the state delimitations (as with the southern boundary between Ethiopia and Somalia, for example). The large areas of uncontrolled or conflict-prone territories provide cover for smuggling, arms dealing, and people trafficking, and those activities serve both as revenue sources and as channels by which to transport al Qaeda operatives and materials.

Unlike organizations in many areas of the world, radical jihadi organizations in East Africa do not stage large-scale attacks in order to attract increased financial support from local residents. Instead, the large-scale attacks are used to send messages overseas. For example, one assessment of the 2002 Mombasa attacks argued:

> The Mombasa attacks . . . serve two purposes. One is specifically to draw the Israelis further into a regional war on terror. The other is to demonstrate, by attempting to shoot down an airliner, that the reach of al Qaeda and its associates is potentially worldwide.[19]

Similarly, kidnappings for money are not widespread, and the involvement in the narcotics trade is minimal.

Many factors in East Africa work to make the region less conducive to more formal and institutionalized forms of terrorist finance. Large-scale money transfers are constrained by strict controls on foreign exchange. In Ethiopia's government-controlled banking system, strict controls limit the possession of foreign currency and push money laundering practices outside the formal banking system.[20] Also, most countries in the area have cash-based economies and antiquated banking systems, or in the case of Somalia, no centralized banking system at all. Computerization of the banking industry, outside of Kenya, tends to be minimal. The only offshore bank is located in Djibouti, and according to the State Department's International Narcotics Control Strategy Report (INCSR) assessments it is not a site of significant money laundering.[21] As the computerization and formalization of the banking system improves, the attractiveness of the area for more sophisticated methods of money laundering (such as currency conversion, speculation, transfers, as well as offshore banking) will increase. The capacity for surveillance will likely lag behind technological innovation, which could provide an opportunity for terrorist financiers to exploit.

Finally, many of the countries in the Horn of Africa have been devastated by civil wars, further limiting the attractiveness of these areas for transferring and storing terrorist financing. The area's risky financial climate limits the cash flow generated through investments such as businesses and construction projects, providing less cover to mask terrorist funding within the financial system. This reinforces an intra-regional trend towards using the states outside the Horn region, such as Kenya and Tanzania, with more formal financial systems and larger economies.

Government Responses

Counter-terrorism measures in East Africa fall into three categories: military responses to terrorist organizations; programs designed to reduce the supply of terrorists and their supporters, such as poverty alleviation and economic development activities; and counter-terrorist finance policies. In East Africa, as in the Tri-Border Area of Latin America, issues of border control, security, and the general ability to enforce law and order should be considered a central part of the regional response to combat terrorist finance.

Despite the location of terrorist finance in the informal economy, international efforts to counter-terrorist finance tend to focus on the formal economy: monitoring of cash flows and large foreign exchange transactions, banking regulations and reporting requirements, legislation and enforcement of provisions for asset forfeiture, and penalties for providing material support to known terrorist organizations. These measures are not the most appropriate ones to target terrorist finance in the conflict-prone or informal economies that characterize many East African states, particularly Somalia and Sudan. Somalia, which has no effective government, cannot implement AML or CTF regimes, and it lacks all enforcement capacity to prevent the flow of terrorists and terrorist finance through the region. Sudan, divided by a decade of war into multiple regions, can hardly maintain a consistent national policy. For the most part, therefore, Somalia and Sudan are not included in discussions on government response, nor are they included in many of the data sources relied upon in this section.

LEGISLATIVE RESPONSES IN EAST AFRICA

Several of the East African countries have had anti-money laundering legislation on the books since the early 1990s, when legislation was first passed to target narcotics trafficking. Even after more than a decade, however, these AML regimes remain far from comprehensive, though since September 2001 there have been attempts to strengthen these legislative arrangements and transform them into counter-terrorism instruments. Three countries have criminalized terrorist financing since September 2001, but other regional governments have preferred to extend their AML regimes rather than create legislation specifically to deal with terrorist finance.

From table 11.1, it is obvious that the countries with the most comprehensive AML regimes are Tanzania, Djibouti, and Kenya, followed far behind by Uganda, Ethiopia, and Eritrea. The countries with AML legislation mandate that banks record large financial transactions, maintain the records over time, and require banks to cooperate with international law enforcement agencies. Governments also pledge to provide mutual assistance to one another's AML efforts, and they have a system in place to identify and seize assets derived from illegal activities. Tanzania's laws are the oldest; in 1991 the government passed AML legislation, and it is working to draft new legislation oriented towards comprehensive sanctions on terrorist financing. Kenya originally enacted narcotics-related AML legislation in 1994, and post-9/11 it has been working with the U.S. Treasury to strengthen those provisions. In response to U.S. pressure and activities

TABLE 11.1 *Anti-Money Laundering Regimes in East Africa*

	DJIBOUTI	ERITREA	ETHIOPIA	KENYA	TANZANIA	UGANDA
Criminalized Drug Money Laundering	Y	N	N	Y	Y	Y
Criminalized Beyond Drugs	Y	N	N	N	N	N
Criminalized Financing of Terrorism	Y	N	N	N	Y	Y
Record Large Transactions	Y	Y	Y	Y	Y	N
Maintain Records over Time	Y	Y	Y	Y	Y	N
Reporting of Suspicious Transactions	M	N	M	P	P	N
Financial Intelligence Unit	N	N	N	N	N	N
System for Identifying/Forfeiting Assets	N	N	N	Y	Y	N
Arrangements for Asset Sharing	N	N	N	N	N	N
Cooperation with International Law Enforcement	Y	Y	N	Y	Y	Y
International Transportation of Currency	N	N	N	Y	N	N
Mutual Legal Assistance	Y	N	N	Y	Y	N
Non-bank Financial Institutions	Y	N	N	N	N	N
Disclosure Protection "Safe Harbor"	Y	N	N	N	Y	Y
Party to 1988 UN Drug Convention	Y	Y	Y	Y	Y	Y
Party to UN Terrorism Financing Convention	N	N	N	Y	Y	Y

Note: Y = Yes, N = No, M = Mandatory reporting, P = Permissible reporting
SOURCE: United States Department of State, Bureau for International Narcotics and Law Enforcement Affairs, *International Narcotics Control Strategy Report (INCSR), Volume II: Money Laundering and Financial Crimes*, March 2006, table on pages 50–58, available at http://www.state.gov/p/inl/rls/nrcrpt/2006/vol2/html/62141.htm. The 2006 report provides data collected through December 31, 2005, with the exception of countries that have ratified the UN International Convention for the Suppression of the Financing of Terrorism. INCSR 2006 only provides information accurate as of December 31, 2003. This table provides information on parties to the Convention as of March 2006.

post-9/11, Uganda and Djibouti have begun to create AML legislation (through working with the Financial Action Task Force [FATF] and the FATF-Style Regional Bureaus). Djibouti passed a comprehensive AML law in December 2002 that included the criminalization of terrorism financing. In contrast, as of June 2006, the Ugandan Parliament had not passed AML legislation drafted in 2003. The AML regimes that exist are of limited effectiveness because formal foreign exchange mechanisms are virtually unregulated: Kenya's laws are not enforced in practice, while Ethiopia only informally monitors foreign currency exchange by virtue of the limits it sets on the amount of foreign currency that can be brought into the country.

The informal systems, where most of the currency exchanges and money transfers actually take place, are by their nature also unregulated. Kenya has a large cash economy and large flows of remittances repatriated by the Kenyan diaspora. Tanzania's Zanzibar island is mostly Muslim and is integrated into trade with the Middle East, much of which takes place through traditional informal arrangements. The inability to regulate the informal financial system is particularly glaring and represents a major gap in the AML regimes of Kenya and Tanzania, the two most economically developed states in the region. Ethiopia's and Eritrea's banking systems are only now being computerized at an extremely slow pace. In Djibouti, only 6 percent of the population utilizes the formal banking system. Without some effective system to monitor *hawala* networks and other informal value transfer systems (IVTS), the standard package of CTF measures, even if legislated, will miss most terrorist financial flows.

MOVING FROM AML TO CTF

Contemporary measures to counter-terrorist finance have grown out of existing anti-money laundering regimes. The U.S. Treasury and other international organizations that support such efforts have concentrated on helping countries to establish viable AML mechanisms with the hope of then building on these to add a CTF capability. In some respects, the East African countries are following this trend, but progress is patchy. Of all the regional countries, only Tanzania, Uganda, and Djibouti have specifically criminalized terrorist finance, in bills passed in 2002 and 2004. Eritrea has had a bill to criminalize terrorist financing under review in parliament since 2003, yet as of September 2006, it had not legislated any CTF measures.

In terms of the FATF-Style Regional Bureaus (FSRBs), Tanzania and Kenya play leading roles in the East and Southern African Anti-Money Laundering Group (ESAAMLG), which attempts to coordinate the creation of AML and CTF regimes in the region. ESAAMLG predates the war on terror, as it was founded in Tanzania in 1999. ESAAMLG is slowly beginning to tackle terrorist finance, though since only two East African countries are members, its impact in the region is likely to be limited. The organization tends to focus on the Southern African states.

Compliance with international conventions to suppress terrorist finance is uneven in the region. Only two countries, Sudan and Kenya, have signed all 12 international counter-terrorism conventions sponsored by the United Nations.[22] Six have signed the UN Convention for the Suppression of the Financing of Terrorism: Djibouti (signed but not ratified), Kenya, Somalia (signed only), Sudan, Tanzania, and Uganda. Ethiopia and Eritrea have signed only the 1988 UN Drug Convention (which calls for legislation against money laundering), while Djibouti has signed both the 1988 Drug Convention and the Convention for the Suppression of the Financing of Terrorism. Tanzania and Uganda have signed the drug and terrorist financing suppression conventions, as well as the 2002 UN Convention against Terrorism and Organized Crime.

BUILDING CAPACITY AND IMPLEMENTATION RESPONSES IN EAST AFRICA

The record for enforcing the AML legislation that does exist is poor, and for CTF measures, it is nonexistent. Few of the East African governments have implemented even their basic AML regimes in a comprehensive or effective manner. Only Tanzania has actually prosecuted cases of money laundering, and these have only been related to corruption. None of the area countries have prosecuted a single case of money laundering related to terrorist finance. No state has created a Financial Intelligence Unit (FIU) to direct investigations into terrorist financing and related activities, though there is some progress on this front: Djibouti is in the process of establishing an FIU within the Central Bank, while Ethiopia's new criminal code (adopted in 2005) mandates the establishment of an FIU (Article 684[1]).[23]

Since the U.S. war on terror began in late 2001, rather than moving off of the State Department's list of major money laundering countries, several

East African countries have graduated from countries that the United States "monitors" to a more serious list of countries about which the United States is "concerned." In a 2004 INCSR report Kenya and Tanzania moved from the list of monitored countries to those of "concern," while Djibouti appeared on the list of monitored countries for the first time, taking its place alongside Uganda and Ethiopia. Eritrea, in response to improvements in both terrorist financing and money laundering efforts, initially moved off the lists altogether in 2004, but it reappeared as a country of concern in 2005. All remain in these positions as of December 2005.[24] That most of the East African countries analyzed in the INCSR have become of increasing concern to the United States attests to the problems in the level of state commitment and capacity to combat money laundering and terrorist finance in East Africa.

EXPLAINING THE INEFFECTIVENESS OF AML AND CTF REGIMES
IN EAST AFRICA

Why has there been so little movement in the East African region on combating terrorist finance? There are a number of disincentives for implementation of the legislation that does exist. These include capacity constraints and issues of political will that are tied to the political and economic realities that affect the survival and prosperity of key interest groups in the region.

Capacity constraints are a basic factor undermining the fight against terrorist finance in East Africa. According to INCSR, virtually none of the financial systems in East Africa have effective regulation. Law enforcement capabilities are considered too basic, financial institutions are not sophisticated enough to track most money laundering transactions, and officials in both arenas are often corruptible. Moreover, law enforcement agencies and political agents in the region are widely considered among the most corrupt elements of society, further undermining their credibility to combat terrorist finance.

The political will to fight terrorism is also lacking in East Africa. First, most area governments do not see the war on terror as a major priority. U.S. officials report that most African leaders consider the war on terror an American concern, rather than their own. Most of the countries in East Africa are experiencing severe humanitarian and/or economic crises, and these are much higher on the priority action list for local political elites.

Accordingly, governments aim scarce resources at improving living standards and basic services, rather than supporting U.S. government initiatives.

Given this reality, only U.S. pressure can improve the participation and performance of East African governments in the fight against terrorist finance. However, CTF measures rank relatively low on the U.S. government's foreign policy agenda for the war on terror in Africa. For example, in June 2003 the U.S. government established the $100 million East Africa Counterterrorism Initiative (EACTI), which operates to strengthen the capacity of area security forces, provide education and training, and help combat terrorist finance.[25] Despite official rhetoric that the program will help to target financial sources, EACTI funding focuses on strengthening coastal, border, customs, airport, and seaport security and on training law enforcement officials.[26] Combating terrorist finance does not even register in this list of priorities. The exceptions to this trend are Kenya and Tanzania, whose tourist industries have yet to fully recover from the 1998 attacks. One would expect these two countries to rank among the most active in the war to combat terrorist finance. Yet while Tanzania has become an active member in ESAAMLG and has initiated CTF legislation, Kenya has not.

Second, the political will is undermined by the basis for political power for these regimes. Even if the governments had the capacity to crack down on smuggling rings that finance terrorists, they have strong political reasons for failing to create and enforce effective AML or CTF regimes. Implementing effective measures would threaten how these governments hold onto power. For Kenya, by far the most corrupt country in the region, even if local leaders considered that the war on terror was as important as did the United States, the measures that restrict the flow of terrorist finance would most likely harm their own survival.[27] Consider the analysis of George Kegoro, who wrote that

> the Kenyan state is perceived as an active participant in criminal activities that generate money that may need to be laundered. It is, therefore, not expected that the state would be effective in fighting crime or in carrying out anti-money laundering measures.[28]

When rulers survive through patronage networks and kleptocracy, they will resist creating comprehensive AML and CTF regimes because doing so would only hurt their political survival.

This insight helps to explain why Tanzania has shown more progress than Kenya in this arena. In Kenya, for instance, one of the major avenues of money laundering is through the sale of stolen motor vehicles. Police and politicians will be slow to crack down on these activities because they are often tied into the process of money laundering of the proceeds.[29] Tanzania and Kenya are both relatively corrupt, but Kenya ranks as more corrupt on the scale kept by Transparency International than does Tanzania: in the 2005 corruption perceptions index, Kenya ranked 144 out of 158 countries surveyed (in the same cohort as Sudan and Somalia), as opposed to Tanzania's ranking of 88.[30] Therefore, Kenyan rulers should be more vulnerable to anti-corruption measures than Tanzanian, which could help to explain why two countries, both affected by terrorist incidents, would diverge in the creation of CTF legislation. Tanzanian officials, however, are not completely insulated from this pressure: while they have created the legislation, they have yet to vigorously enforce it.

Finally, governments are also reluctant to crack down on informal money exchange systems and smuggling because there simply are no substitutes in these cash-based economies. The archaic nature of formal banking systems reinforces the reliance on alternative remittance systems. Even when they are relatively well developed, formal banking systems are used by only a fraction of each country's populace. For example, in Djibouti only 6 percent of the population uses the formal banking system.[31] In Sudan, Ethiopia, and northern Somalia, the same planes utilized in the (illegal) *khat* trade are also used to smuggle other things, such as money, arms, and people. If governments cracked down on the *khat* trade in order to get at the terrorist finance routes, they would face mass protest.[32] Therefore, tough regulation of informal banking systems and smuggling routes would result in sharp resistance to the governments of the region, potentially leading to political upheaval. The prospect of inciting mass riots and unrest makes governments even more reluctant to do what they need to in order to stop the financial flows that terrorist organizations can manipulate.

Conclusion

Beyond paying lip-service and accepting foreign aid, East African governments will not cooperate with U.S. priorities on counter-terrorism financing until some of their other pressing concerns (such as poverty, economic development, and corruption) are addressed. Classic development aid, therefore, should not be sacrificed to the current obsession with the war on terror. African governments, which from the end of the Cold War to the initiation of the war on terror had been relatively neglected by U.S. assistance, are basking in the new attention and will accept whatever assistance the U.S. government will supply, but that is unlikely to translate into effective implementation of CTF policies.

Given that the most common forms of generating funds in East Africa do not rely on financial institutions of any kind but involve smuggling, arms transfers, and people trafficking, methods such as better surveillance of coastal traffic, increased customs efficiency, and improved border and seaport security could all work to reduce the non-traditional methods of terrorist financing that exist throughout the region. Strengthening law enforcement capacities may help area governments uncover and stop the sources of terrorist finance in the region. Such measures would also slow or reverse the increase in money-laundering activities that has caused several countries to move up on the INCSR table of monitored countries.

In turn, law enforcement officials need to have the incentives to achieve a level of professionalism that dissuades them from engaging in illegal activities. Without this, local law enforcement will never hunt down those who are involved in the criminal activities that terrorists use to generate funds because they would be targeting the very same activities in which so many of them currently engage. Therefore, U.S. counter-terrorism assistance designed to strengthen local security institutions may indirectly work to the benefit of the war on terrorist finance.

Ultimately, explicitly anti-terrorist financing measures, whether they involve combating the corruption and criminal activities that generate many of the financial flows in the region or whether they focus on tracing the money once it is generated and distributed, will come to fruition only when rulers no longer rely on patronage bases that could be harmed if strong AML and CTF regimes are implemented. This means that the traditional concerns of democracy and development, such as transparency, good government, and the rule of law, are still important in the war against terror and terrorist financing in East Africa.

CHAPTER TWELVE

Terrorist Financing and Government Responses in Southeast Asia

AUREL CROISSANT AND DANIEL BARLOW

Introduction

In the wake of the events of 9/11, Southeast Asia has achieved a dubious reputation as a major hotspot of transnational Islamist terrorism.[1] Terrorist activities in Southeast Asia, however, vary greatly between countries and even between regions within countries. The landscape of terrorist groups is very heterogeneous with reference to the nature of the groups, their origins and patterns of organization, their political agendas and tactics, and, last but not least, their financing methods.

One can distinguish three different sources of funding for terrorist groups in the region: criminal activities, charities, and commercial activities. While most local groups depend on the first and second sources, access to the third source is easier for transnational groups. Because of the heterogeneous nature of terrorist groups in the region and the fact that the nature of a terrorist group and its operational environment affects its capacity to acquire funding, a variety of government responses is needed for successful counter-terrorist financing in Southeast Asia. Accordingly, we examine the degree of compliance with, and implementation of, international norms of counter-terrorism finance (CTF) in the ten area countries along four aspects of CTF policies. It is important to note, however, that we evaluate the countries not in absolute terms but relative to each other. In other words, our findings say more about intra-regional trends and differences than about the status of individual countries compared to nations in other regions outside of Southeast Asia. Furthermore, this analysis uses information solely from publicly available and unclassified sources. While this approach increases the transparency of the findings and allows other scholars to review and control the findings, it does so at the cost of additional evidence available from classified material and confidential sources.

The comparative study in this chapter proceeds in five steps. Section one provides a brief overview about the nature of terrorism and recent trends in terrorist activities in the region. The following section analyzes local and transnational sources and patterns of terrorism financing in Southeast Asia. The third part of the chapter investigates the Southeast Asian government responses on the terrorist finance front, looking at both legislative and policy responses, and the extent to which those laws and policies have been implemented and enforced in recent years. Section four examines the reasons for the different degrees of compliance with, and implementation of, anti-money laundering (AML) and counter-terrorist financing (CTF) measures. The final section summarizes the findings and presents some tentative conclusions.

Nature and Extent of the Terrorist Threat in the Region

Before turning to terrorist finance, we must understand the terrain that is being covered. Recent terrorist events in the region, such as the Bali bombing on October 12, 2002, the Davao City Airport bombing in the southern Philippines in March 2003, and the attack on the Australian Embassy in Jakarta on September 10, 2004, have attracted international coverage. However, it is important to note that large areas of the region were hotspots of terrorism or other forms of insurgency long defore 2001.[2] While most groups involved in the numerous ethno-nationalist or ideology-driven conflicts in Southeast Asia do not meet the standard definitions of terrorism, these violent conflicts have contributed to the rise of terrorist groups in

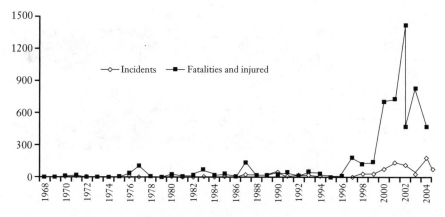

FIGURE 12.1 Terrorism Trends in Southeast Asia (January 1, 1968–May 31, 2005)

recent years in two ways. First, some Islamist terrorist organizations, such as the Philippine Abu Sayyaf Group, evolved out of an ongoing armed conflict. Second, and more frequently, the shifting kaleidoscope of conflicts and their socioeconomic and political consequences create the appropriate operational environment for local and transnational terrorist groups.

Recent studies paint a bleak picture of the dynamics of Islamist terrorism in the region.[3] However, not everyone agrees with the view that the region is a "second front" in the war on terrorism. At a first glance, one must admit that the figures from the RAND and Oklahoma City National Memorial Institute for the Prevention of Terrorism (MIPT) database, the preferred source of quantitative data about terrorism, suggest that the overall number of terrorist attacks in the region of Southeast Asia has dramatically increased in recent years, as shown in figure 12.1.

A leading terrorism specialist, Rohan Gunaratna, argues that since the 1990s, the center of gravity of terrorism has shifted from the Middle East to the Asia-Pacific region.[4] According to this view, Southeast Asia has become the southern extension of a crisis zone reaching from Central Asia through South Asia to its most southern tail, Indonesia and the Philippines.[5]

The actual realities in the region are more complex than the "second front" catchphrase suggests. Although Southeast Asia is home to a number of al Qaeda cadres, and it is beyond doubt that some groups are linked to al Qaeda or are inspired by the radical ideas and the spirit of international jihadism, most Islamic groups in the region are in fact non-violent. So far,

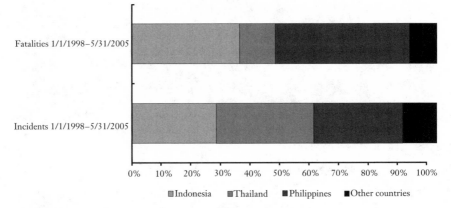

FIGURE 12.2 Hotspots of Terrorism in Southeast Asia

only a small number of indigenous terrorist groups have been involved in transnational terror. Often, controversial and far-reaching conclusions are based on anecdotal evidence that has been taken out of context or is derived from unverifiable, anonymous, or highly partisan sources.[6]

Upon further analysis, the data show that terrorism is concentrated in a small number of Southeast Asian nations. As shown in figure 12.2, the main problem countries are now Indonesia, the Philippines, and Thailand.

In accounting for the recent increase in terrorism in these countries, it is crucial to understand that terrorism or insurgency in all three countries predates the seminal events of September 11, 2001, and is very much mixed with ethno-religious separatism. Muslim insurgency in the Philippines, for example, is an old conflict, and the Moro militant groups emerged long before 2001. In addition, contrary to popular reporting by the international media, one of the most potent militant groups militarily and politically in the region is not one of the Muslim insurgencies or Islamist terrorist organizations, but rather the armed movement of the Communist Party of the Philippines that emerged in the 1960s.[7] In Indonesia, two of the major violent conflicts are the insurgencies in Aceh and Irian Jaya, both of which originated in the 1950s and 1960s.[8] The recent unrest in southern Thailand is also accurately understood as the resurrection of a prolonged cycle of conflict rather than a new phenomenon.[9]

One must also recognize that most of the terrorist organizations currently operating in the Southeast Asian theater are local in nature and are well-entrenched in their social, political, and economic environments. The major Islamist terrorist organizations are currently the Abu Sayyaf Group (ASG), the Moro Islamic Liberation Front (MILF), Jemaah Islamiyah (JI), and al Qaeda. It is widely accepted that al Qaeda has strong links with JI, which in turn is linked to the MILF, Abu Sayyaf, and other groups. Gunaratna estimates that before 9/11 about 20 percent of al Qaeda's organizational strength was in Asia, concentrated in the Philippines, Malaysia, Singapore, and Indonesia. Others argue that beginning in the late 1990s, al Qaeda, through JI, established an informal regional jihadi coalition called the Rabitatul Mujahidin, a suspected collection of groups and individuals who share a common experience of jihad either in Afghanistan or the Maluku archipelago.[10]

In the past, the MILF has consistently denied any connections with al Qaeda. Although the organization has not been declared a terrorist organization by the U.S. government, there is some evidence that MILF was forging ties with the ASG and evolving into an international terrorist organization.[11] Intelligence sources also point to MILF's links to al Qaeda and Middle Eastern and South Asian groups. A recent report by Philippine intelligence details the seven-year history of MILF cooperation with numerous Islamic terrorist organizations from Indonesia and Malaysia.

There are several smaller local groups that are suspected to be linked in one form or the other to the JI network. In addition, several terrorist organizations from outside the region, such as the Liberation Tigers of Tamil Eelam (LTTE) and pro–al Qaeda groups from Bangladesh and Pakistan are said to have a presence in the region, mostly through involvement in the regional arms trade, money laundering, and other criminal activities.[12]

Sources and Patterns of Terrorism Financing

As a result of their different nature, organization, motivations, and opportunities, terrorist organizations in the region differ somewhat in the combination of ways they raise and transfer funds for specific operations. Although terrorist funding in Southeast Asia stems from many different sources, there are three major local and international sources of terror finance: (1) criminal activity; (2) charities; and (3) front companies and investments.

The general pattern is that localized and well-established terrorist organizations such as ASG or MILF rely more heavily on criminal activity or local donations to sustain themselves financially, while receiving more logistical and organizational support from outside sources such as al Qaeda. In contrast, regional groups that are localized to Southeast Asia but are transnational in nature, such as JI, rely both on localized criminal activity and donations but also receive greater funding from international sources using a sophisticated network of charities and businesses. Once a group generates funds, it distributes them across international boundaries using various methods that include bulk cash transfers, informal value transfer systems (IVTS), and front companies in various countries in the region. Al Qaeda has relied on a complex network of front companies and charities in place in the region since the late 1980s to generate and launder funds to support both their regional and international agendas.

THE ROLE OF CRIMINAL ACTIVITY IN FUNDING TERRORISM

Most terrorist organizations in the region have a strong tradition utilizing the same techniques as organized crime. Decades-old insurgent groups, ethnic armies, and organized crime have long used the region as a center for laundering and generating illegitimate funds from criminal activities such as illicit drug production and the small arms trade.[13] Particularly in the 1990s, in response to the erosion of state support after the end of the Cold War, criminality became the most pragmatic avenue to secure finances for future operations. Factors that have contributed to this development by allowing for a booming regional money laundering system are weak regulatory financial systems, porous borders, and a thriving underground remittance system, particularly in Cambodia, the Philippines, Vietnam, and Thailand. The passive compliance by government officials in various countries and the co-optation of corrupt political and judicial authorities have also been conducive to the diversification of terrorist groups into a wide variety of criminal activities and the rapid and covert movement of funds derived from those activities.[14]

ASG revenues come from a variety of sources, including taxation, extortion, and smuggling. There is little evidence to suggest that the group receives voluntary contributions from NGOs or commercial companies.[15] In addition, kidnapping for ransom is another tactic often used to raise money and force political concessions. The UN reported that Abu Sayaaf funds its operations in the southern Philippines through this technique and was paid millions of dollars in 2000 for the release of hostages seized in Malaysia.[16]

Drawing on the strong Moro maritime heritage, ASG is also involved in piracy in Philippine coastal waters and sometimes farther from home.[17]

ASG also collects money from drug smugglers by acting as a protector for foreign trafficking syndicates. Whether ASG is directly involved in drug production remains unclear. Although the U.S. Bureau for International Narcotics and Law Enforcement Affairs in a recent report states the group is operating a "thriving marijuana production site in Basilan,"[18] the authors interviewed officers and personnel of the armed forces of the Philippines who were deployed in Jolo and Basilan. These officers and personnel report that they have not observed any ASG involvement in drug trade, but they have seen members of MILF and the Moro National Liberation Front (MNLF) who were under the influence of drugs. There were also some Filipino Muslims arrested in Manila involved in drug activities who were allegedly linked to ASG, but these accusations proved to be unfounded. We also have testimony from ASG hostages stating that they did not observe their captors to be involved in drug-related activities.

Intelligence sources indicate that MILF received financial help from al Qaeda as early as 1988, after bin Laden sent his brother-in-law, Mohammed Jamal Khalifa, to the Philippines to establish a financial infrastructure for his terrorist network. Khalifa began to covertly channel money to the MILF. Both Al Haj Murad, the MILF vice chairman for military affairs, and MILF founder Salamat Hashim repeatedly admitted that the MILF received money from Khalifa and bin Laden, but they said the funds were used for humanitarian aid. In fact, MILF seems to acquire most of its funds not from external sources (i.e., state support, charities, wealthy individuals from other Muslim countries, or the Moro diaspora outside of the Philippines) but from illegal logging, local drug production and trafficking, arms trafficking, and the institution of *zakat*, which takes the character of a compulsory "jihad tax" in those areas under de facto control of the MILF.[19] According to the Philippine authorities, there are extensive links between drug trafficking activities and the MILF. The U.S. government concurs, "In the Central and Western Mindanao areas controlled by MILF, mounting evidence indicates the presence of several clandestine methamphetamine laboratories. The drugs produced by these labs are distributed within the Philippines and possibly exported to other countries."[20] MILF is also widely believed to be at the forefront of the illicit arms trade importing weapons from South Asia and reselling them throughout Southeast Asia.[21]

Although JI is supported through a network of international charities, and funding was received directly from al Qaeda for the Bali and Jakarta Marriott bombings, it also generated funds itself through criminal activities such as the robbery of a gold shop in Serang.[22] This technique, known as *fa'i*, plays an integral part in the JI fund-raising technique. *Fa'i* is the robbing of non-believers as a way of raising funds for jihad. The practice was first used by Darul Islam (DI) and was later utilized by most DI factions, including JI. According to the International Crisis Group, "The reliance on *fa'i* meant that from the beginning in Indonesia there has been a symbiotic relationship between petty criminals and thugs on the one hand, and *mujahidin* on the other."[23]

THE ROLE OF CHARITIES IN FUNDING TERRORISM

Charities are a second source of funds for terrorist organizations in the region. These are particularly relevant for groups such as JI. Specifically, Saudi charities have been used to support JI and al Qaeda cells operating in the region. The expanding network of Islamic charities has its social and cultural foundation in the centuries-old tradition of charitable giving, or *zakat*. *Zakat* is a pillar of the Islamic faith and a religious obligation taken quite seriously by Muslims.[24] As a result, many Muslims feel an obligation to donate money to Islamic charities for the purpose of *khairat* (the giving of charity for charity's sake) and education. Particularly in poorer regions such as Mindanao, many people rely on these charities to provide basic assistance and access to education, and governments are reluctant to interfere with the charities' operations.[25] However, terrorist organizations in the region have taken advantage of these charities to fund their activities.

According to a UN report, al Qaeda has provided substantial financial resources for radical extremist groups in Southeast Asia, including JI and al Qaeda cells in Manila and Singapore, through Islamic charities. These relationships emerged in the late 1980s and early 1990s, when Mohammed Jamal Khalifa first traveled to the southern Philippines and later returned to establish a logistical support base in the Philippines.[26] Khalifa directed a Saudi Arabian charity known as International Islamic Relief Organization (IIRO). Intelligence reports indicate that IIRO was used to support local terrorist operations throughout Southeast Asia.[27] Khalifa also established a charity known as the International Relations and Information Center

(IRIC).[28] IRIC was responsible for numerous charitable activities in the Philippines. However, IRIC bank accounts were also tied to the plan by Khalid Sheik Mohammed, Ramzi Yousef, and Wali Khan Amin Shah to blow up 11 American jetliners in early 1995, in what was known as the "Oplan Bojinka plot."[29]

Komite Penanggulangan Krisis (KOMPAK) in Indonesia is another Islamic charity that has close ties to terror in Southeast Asia. Aris Munandar, one of the founders of KOMPAK, is closely related to Abu Bakar Ba'asyir, the spiritual leader of JI, who was convicted for his knowledge of the Bali and Jakarta Marriot bombings. KOMPAK has several regional offices and has employed persons closely associated with terrorist activities throughout Southeast Asia. These include Imam Hanafi, who bought weapons in Mindanao in March 2000 for fighters in Ambon; Suryadi Mas'uf, who is alleged to have traveled to the southern Philippines with KOMPAK money to buy weapons; Agus Dwikarna, who was arrested at Manila's International Airport in March 2002 carrying C-4 explosives in his suitcase; and Tamsil Linrung, who was identified by Omar al-Faruq, a top al Qaeda financier, as a member of JI who participated in three terrorism planning meetings held in Malaysia in 1999 and 2000.[30]

FORMAL AND INFORMAL ENTERPRISES AS A SOURCE OF TERRORISM FUNDING

Southeast Asia's friendly business environment and tremendous economic growth in the early 1990s made it an attractive location for transnational terrorist groups to establish front companies capable of generating profits for terrorist operations. According to information from the Thai financial investigative unit, three Middle Eastern general trading companies, Al Jallil Trading Co. Ltd., Al Amanah Enterprise Co. Ltd., and Sidco Co. Ltd. were shut down for their role in the financing of al Qaeda.[31] A white paper released by the Singapore Ministry of Home Affairs cast light on the operations of JI and its economic wing, which was tasked to generate long-term sources of funds and income to finance JI activities and operations. According to the white paper, "All JI-run businesses had to contribute 10% of their total earnings to the group."[32] JI leadership controlled these funds and used them to procure weapons, fund operations, and support jihadi training camps in the Philippines and Afghanistan.

By using front companies, terrorist organizations are able to generate and hide funds in the legitimate economy, thereby making the process of laundering funds unnecessary. This modus operandi is more likely to be used by al Qaeda than by local groups such as ASG or MILF because it requires large amounts of capital and skills to found front companies that are capable of generating funds to sustain themselves and the organization. According to the FBI, Zacarias Moussaoui received a $2,500 monthly stipend as a "marketing consultant" for a Malaysian computer technology firm, Infocus Tech, while the Kuala Lumpur–based firm, Konsojaya Trading Company, financed the Bojinka plot and the Ramzi Yousef 1993 World Trade Center bombing.[33]

Terrorists in the region have also relied on bulk cash transfers to provide payments to operatives. Riduan Isamuddin, better known as Hambali, responsible for operations of JI in Southeast Asia, has taken advantage of the loose border controls to transfer large amounts of money throughout Southeast Asia. A 2005 UN report gives an example of how Hambali was able to use bulk cash transfers to pass funds to various sources to support Jemaah Islamiyah operations in Indonesia:

> Hambali passed funds to Wan Min Wan Mat (a financier for Jemaah Islamiyah) who transferred approximately US$30,000, including some Thai currency, to Ali Ghufron, alias Mukhlas (head of one of Jemaah Islamiyah's operational units and older brother of two of the Bali bombers, Amrozi and Ali Imron). The funds were moved in two installments between July and September 2002 by Indonesian laborers working in Malaysia and were delivered to Mukhlas at his home in Lamongan, Indonesia.[34]

Hambali also sent $30,000 of al Qaeda money to Indonesia in April 2003 through cash couriers to finance the bombing of the Marriott Hotel.[35] Finally, as Nikos Passas discusses in chapter 2, terrorists in the region have relied on the *hawala* system to transfer funds.

Describing State Responses to Terrorism Financing

Since terrorist organizations in Southeast Asia rely on different means to raise and transfer funds, a variety of responses will be needed to counter-terrorist financing in the region.

The extent to which countries in the region comply with and implement international standards to counter the financing of terrorism can be examined along four different dimensions: (1) legal frameworks; (2) regulatory measures covering both the formal sector (e.g., banking) and the informal (e.g., IVTS, charities); (3) the level of sophistication of their administrative infrastructure for addressing terrorist financing; and (4) evidence of enforcement.[36] While the items in the legal and regulatory frameworks may be viewed as measures of norm compliance, administrative and enforcement measures are proxies for the extent to which the norms have actually been implemented.

COMPARING THE LEGAL FRAMEWORKS

In terms of legal frameworks, most countries in the region have taken basic steps to transfer international norms into national law. With the exception of Cambodia and Laos, each country in the region has criminalized money laundering for illicit activities beyond those related to drug profits and has systems in place to freeze and forfeit assets that are tied to money laundering. Overall, as table 12.1 shows, the countries with the most comprehensive frameworks are Brunei and Singapore, followed by Indonesia, Malaysia, and Thailand. Cambodia, Laos, and Burma have the weakest legislation.

There are some weaknesses to the system. For example, under Bank of Indonesia regulations, law enforcement officials may order the seizure of assets of individuals or entities that have been either declared suspects or indicted for a crime, but in practice to identify such assets they must have the cooperation of the banks. In Malaysia, the Anti-Money Laundering Act of 2001 covers fairly comprehensively all aspects of criminal proceedings related to money laundering, but "reporting institutions complain of their ignorance with respect to reporting requirements on currency transactions, monetary instruments and foreign accounts."[37] As a result, law enforcement agencies do not have the information needed to quickly freeze the assets of criminals or terrorists. In addition, only Brunei, Indonesia, Singapore, Thailand, and (most recently) Malaysia have criminalized the financing of terrorism.

Southeast Asia developed the majority of its AML legislation only after the events of 2001. The more developed economies of Singapore, Malaysia, and Thailand were the first to institute laws to combat money laundering and began the process in the late 1990s. Indonesia and the Philippines only

TABLE 12.1 *Legal Framework*

	BRUNEI	BURMA	CAMBODIA	INDONESIA	LAOS	MALAYSIA	PHILIPPINES	SINGAPORE	THAILAND	VIETNAM
Criminalized Drug Money Laundering	1	1	1	1	0	1	1	1	1	1
Criminalized Beyond Drugs	1	1	0	1	0	1	1	1	1	1
System for Identifying/Forfeiting Assets	1	1	0	1	0	1	1	1	1	1
Criminalized Financing of Terrorism	1	0	0	1	0	1	0	1	1	0
Party to the International Terrorism Financing Convention	1	0	0	0	0	0	1	1	1	1
Member of APG	1	0	1	1	0	1	1	1	1	0
Total	6	3	2	5	0	5	5	6	6	4

Note: The value 1 indicates that there is some legal framework in place; the value 0 indicates its absence.
Source: United States Department of State, Bureau for International Narcotics and Law Enforcement Affairs, *International Narcotics Control Strategy Report (INCSR), Volume II: Money Laundering and Financial Crimes*, March 2005, table on pages 56–64; and website of the Asia Pacific Group.

did so under extreme pressure from the international community and were only removed from the Financial Action Task Force's (FATF's) Non-Cooperative Countries and Territories list in February 2005. Recently enacted legislation in the Philippines and Indonesia has been praised by the United States, the United Kingdom, and FATF, and both the Philippines and Indonesia are making progress in developing a sound strategy to stop money laundering and terror financing from taking place in their economies. Much of the original legislation addressed only the formal financial sectors, as legislation did around the world. This focus created problems for effective CTF in Southeast Asia, since many countries have susceptible informal economies.[38] Recently, some nations in Southeast Asia have begun to address informal financial institutions.

In addition to the aforementioned weaknesses, international cooperation is also underdeveloped. Brunei, Cambodia, the Philippines, Singapore, and Vietnam are the only parties to the UN Convention for the Suppression of the Financing of Terrorism. Other governments in the region, like Indonesia, have signed the convention but have failed to ratify it. The Asia Pacific Group on Money Laundering (APG) is a regional FATF-style body. With the exception of Laos, Burma, and Vietnam, which maintain observer status, all Southeast Asian nations are full members of the APG.[39] The APG is working with its members to facilitate the adoption, implementation, and enforcement of internationally accepted standards against money laundering and the financing of terrorism.

REGULATING THE FORMAL AND INFORMAL FINANCIAL SECTORS

An assessment of government responses to terrorist financing must also take into account if, and to what extent, governments have put in place a variety of different regulatory measures to prevent terrorist financing from simply shifting from one sector to another. Specifically, governments must ensure banking compliance through continuous reporting and must regulate the informal sector, including IVTS, money changers, casinos, and charities. As shown in table 12.2, thus far only Burma, Singapore, and Thailand have employed a comprehensive approach to counter-terrorism financing. While most nations in Southeast Asia (with the exception of Laos) require suspicious transaction reporting and maintain records of financial transactions, only about half monitor large transactions. With the exception of Cambodia,

TABLE 12.2 *Variety of Approaches*

APPROACH	BRUNEI	BURMA	CAMBODIA	INDONESIA	LAOS	MALAYSIA	PHILIPPINES	SINGAPORE	THAILAND	VIETNAM
Regulation of Non-financial Institutions	1	1	0	1	0	1	0	1	1	1
Recording of Large Transactions	0	1	1	0	0	0	1	1	1	0
Maintenance of Records over Time	1	1	1	1	0	1	1	1	1	1
Reporting of Suspicious Transactions	1	1	1	1	0	1	1	1	1	1
Total	3	4	3	3	0	3	3	4	4	3

Note: The value 1 indicates that an approach has been used; the value 0 indicates that it has not.

Source: United States Department of State, Bureau for International Narcotics and Law Enforcement Affairs, *International Narcotics Control Strategy Report (INCSR, 2005), Volume II: Money Laundering and Financial Crimes*, March 2005, table on pages 56–64.

Laos, and the Philippines, each country now has some controls in place to regulate the informal financial sector. Malaysia is a prime example of the extensive efforts made to regulate charities. The Registrar of Societies in Malaysia supervises and controls charitable organizations and mandates that every registered society of a charitable nature submits its annual returns. This ensures that financial transactions are recorded and reviewed. Activities that are deemed suspicious are reported to Malaysia's financial intelligence unit (FIU). In addition, tax laws encourage reporting of contributions by making them tax deductible.

However, the strengths of each of the regulations and the extent to which they are implemented and effective in individual countries remain a matter of concern. Most of the institutions that regulate the informal financial sector are newly instituted and will need to be strengthened over the coming years.

COMPARING STATE ADMINISTRATIVE CAPACITY

Legal and regulatory frameworks are only part of the picture; states must also have a strong and diverse administrative structure to implement CTF and AML measures. Table 12.3 indicates the vast differences among the countries along this dimension.

Six countries in Southeast Asia have Financial Intelligence Units (FIUs). Four of those are members of the Egmont Group, the premier international organization of FIUs. By participating in the Egmont Group, the FIUs are under obligation to assist other members with their investigations and with the tracking and freezing of funds worldwide. There is also evidence of international cooperation and additional resources being committed to CTF and AML initiatives. For example, the Asia Development Bank has taken steps to assist Thailand, the Philippines, and Vietnam with improving AML and CTF strategies and cooperation. There is also cooperation between enforcement agencies in the region through information sharing, tracking, and freezing of assets through Mutual Legal Assistance (MLA) treaties.

There is an effort in countries such as Cambodia, Laos, and Vietnam to establish FIUs and to improve the infrastructure; however, with such large informal sector economies and limited financial institutions, AML and CTF reforms are unlikely to be very effective. While Singapore, Thailand, and Malaysia score high with regard to their administrative capacity, the Philippines and Indonesia are often cited as the two most troublesome coun-

TABLE 12.3 *Administrative Framework*

	BRUNEI	BURMA	CAMBODIA	INDONESIA	LAOS	MALAYSIA	PHILIPPINES	SINGAPORE	THAILAND	VIETNAM
FIU	0	1	0	1	0	1	1	1	1	0
Additional Resources Committed or Further Assistance Sought	1	0	0	1	0	1	1	1	1	1
Cooperation with International Law Enforcement	1	1	1	1	0	1	1	1	1	0
Mutual Legal Assistance	1	1	0	1	0	1	1	1	1	1
Member of Egmont Group	0	0	0	1	0	1	0	1	1	0
Total	3	3	1	5	0	5	4	5	5	2

Note: The value 1 indicates that there is some administrative framework in place; the value 0 indicates its absence.
Source: United States Department of State, Bureau for International Narcotics and Law Enforcement Affairs, *International Narcotics Control Strategy Report (INCSR, 2005), Volume II: Money Laundering and Financial Crimes*, March 2005, table on pages 56–64; Egmont Group website.

TABLE 12.4. *Evidence of Enforcement*

	BRUNEI	BURMA	CAMBODIA	INDONESIA	LAOS	MALAYSIA	PHILIPPINES	SINGAPORE	THAILAND	VIETNAM
Arrests Relating to Terrorist Financing	0	0	0	1	0	0	1	0	0	0
Assets Frozen	0	0	0	1	0	0	1	1	1	0
Total	0	0	0	2	0	0	2	1	1	0

Note: Countries not reporting or reporting that no actions took place are scored 0.
Source: Country reports to the UN Counter-Terrorism Committee.

tries when it comes to the administrative means for effective CTF. While this is certainly true, both countries have at least begun to seek international cooperation to develop stronger institutions—although these may ultimately be weakened by corruption and a lack of resources.

ENFORCING COUNTER-TERRORISM FINANCE POLICIES

Enforcement of the legal framework, international obligations, and administrative measures is the most critical element in CTF in Southeast Asia. As table 12.4 shows, only a minority of governments in Southeast Asia are either able or willing to demonstrate that the measures discussed so far are more than window dressing for Western governments.

Of the countries surveyed, only Indonesia, the Philippines, Thailand, and Singapore provide evidence of credible efforts to enforce their CTF regimes. Each of these countries has demonstrated arrests, prosecutions, and seizures, or freezing assets relating to terror finance. In the Republic of the Philippines and Indonesia, prosecutions have taken place only since 2004. It should be noted, however, that Indonesia has gone beyond the requirements of UN Resolution 1267 and frozen bank accounts of individuals not on the Consolidated List but who held assets on behalf of listed persons. In contrast, the governments of Burma and Vietnam have stated that they have examined their financial records but found no assets of UN-designated terrorists or terrorist organizations, and Brunei, Malaysia, Cambodia, and Laos have failed to report any seizures or arrests. However, one must keep in mind that the lack of reports on actions taken may also be a consequence of the fact that there are no bank accounts to freeze or people to arrest. While this certainly is a possibility, doubts remain that this is major cause for the lack of any report on seizures and arrests, at least in Malaysia where substantial evidence of terrorist financing activity exists.

Overall, as the preceding discussion shows, countries converge on norm compliance—measured as the spread of the international norms and practices that make up the new CTF and the transformation of these rules into national laws and regulations—but this does not lead automatically to implementation. Rather, states in the region diverge regarding the extent to which they implement the norms of the new CTF regimes. This pattern is summarized in table 12.5.

Within each row of table 12.5 countries that achieve full compliance with

TABLE 12.5 *Relative Degree of Norm Acceptance and Compliance*

	RELATIVE DEGREE OF ACCEPTANCE AND COMPLIANCE					
	WEAKEST ←				→ STRONGEST	
Legal Framework	Laos	Cambodia	Burma	Vietnam	Indonesia Malaysia Philippines	Brunei Singapore Thailand
Multidimensional Approach	Laos		Cambodia Philippines		Indonesia Malaysia Vietnam Brunei	Burma Singapore Thailand
Administrative Framework	Laos	Cambodia Vietnam	Brunei Burma Philippines			Indonesia Malaysia Singapore Thailand
Enforcement	Brunei Burma Cambodia Laos Malaysia Vietnam				Thailand Singapore	Indonesia Philippines

all of the criteria are rated strongest, and states that are non-compliant on all measures are rated weakest. Cambodia and the Philippines are scored lower in the multidimensional approach because they do not regulate the informal financial sector. They do, however, have comprehensive legislation for ensuring banking compliance. Overall, Singapore shows the strongest degree of compliance and implementation, followed by Thailand and Indonesia. They are followed, albeit after a considerable gap, by Malaysia, the Philippines, and, even further behind, Brunei. Burma, Cambodia, Laos, and Vietnam have the least developed AML-CTF regimes.

Explaining Variations in Government Responses

What factors account for the discrepancy between norm compliance and norm implementation and for the differences between individual countries in the region? From the general literature on compliance and implementation, we find that no single dominant factor can be singled out as the primary cause.[40] Regardless of their theoretical approach, most scholars would agree that the panoply of possible factors that explain why states do or do not comply with international rules and implement national regulations and laws is broad, ranging from general factors such as international vulnerability, the definition of national identities and interests, political institutions, and administrative and state capabilities to policy-field specific factors such as, in the case of CTF, the operational environment in which terror financiers operate, including the characteristics of formal and informal financial systems.

Regarding the regional convergence on legal frameworks, the most important factor is certainly external pressure. Given the dynamics of the international war on terrorism and the current zeitgeist in counter-terrorism among Western governments and international organizations such as the UN, the Organization for Economic Cooperation and Development (OECD), and the Asian Development Bank (ADB), there is enormous pressure on Asian governments to show at least a minimum level of norm acceptance. Most area governments, which are externally vulnerable and which have a high interest in foreign aid, have realized that the costs of legislative activism are considerably lower than the costs of blatant disregard of international norms and rules. In other words, governments may accept the international standards formulated by Western governments and establish legal frameworks for an AML and CTF regime because re-writing legal textbooks is an inexpensive means for avoiding the high costs related to deviant behavior. This calculus of legal window-dressing helps to explain why even countries like Cambodia, Vietnam, and especially Burma have introduced some legislative measures and seem to follow a multidimensional approach.

In this regard, the timing of legislative activism is telling. As table 12.6 shows, with the exception of Brunei, Singapore, and Thailand, no Southeast Asian country had started major policy activities before 2001.

Whereas the Philippines and Indonesia enacted anti-money laundering laws in 2001 and 2002 respectively, both had to amend the legislation to be more in line with international standards after FATF deemed the original laws inadequate. Singapore, Thailand, and Brunei, together with Malaysia, have strong anti-money laundering regimes, partially because these countries have developed formal financial sectors and offshore financial centers

TABLE 12.6 *Timeline for the Introduction of Selective Measures of AML and CTF*

	1999	2000	2001	2002	2003	2004	2005
Criminalized Money Laundering	Singapore Thailand	Brunei	Malaysia Philippines	Indonesia Burma			Vietnam
Criminalized Terror Financing			Brunei	Indonesia Singapore	Thailand		Malaysia
FIU	Singapore Thailand			Malaysia Philippines	Indonesia	Burma	
Recording of Large Transactions	Singapore Thailand	Brunei	Philippines	Cambodia		Burma	
Report of Suspicious Transactions	Singapore Thailand	Brunei Vietnam	Indonesia	Malaysia	Cambodia Burma Philippines		

Source: United States Department of State, Bureau for International Narcotics and Law Enforcement Affairs, *International Narcotics Control Strategy Report (INCSR), Volume II: Money Laundering and Financial Crimes,* various editions; reports by the UN Monitoring Group; and newspaper accounts.

(OFCs). OFCs like Labuan in Malaysia and the Brunei International Off-shore Financial Centre (IOFC) are particularly vulnerable to money laundering (and terrorism financing) because they use anonymity as a major selling point.[41] Therefore, these states have a strong interest in protecting their formal financial sectors, not from terrorism in particular but from ill-gotten funds in general. At the same time, however, countries may refuse to govern *too* extensively their financial sectors for fear of disrupting their economies. A dilemma is thereby formed that may be described as follows: The need to protect financial sectors from illicit money and to preserve trust of external actors helps to explain why governments with developed OFCs and formal financial sectors have an interest in institutionalizing AML regimes. The fear of disrupting the flow of finances, on the other hand, may contribute to the reluctance of governments in regard to comprehensive or effective implementation of these rules.

There is also a close relationship between the development of the formal financial sector and the rate at which governments act to inhibit money laundering. In other words, countries that rely on largely underdeveloped formal financial sectors are less likely to be quick to respond with formal legislation and efforts to stamp out terror financing because formal regulation is necessarily less effective. Countries that rely on remittances from overseas and IVTS are less likely to interfere with terror finance for fear of disrupting their economies. Thus, the extent of regulatory problems posed by informal money transfer and alternative remittance systems—such as *hawala*, the Chinese *fei ch'ien*, or the Thai *poey kuan*—is directly related to the degree of maturity of the national banking sector. Almost by definition, any exact assessment of the size of IVTS is almost impossible. Those informal systems share a common set of operational characteristics that make them highly exploitable for various forms of crime, including terrorism.[42]

Domestic factors may be more important for explaining variation in compliance and implementation than the pressure and enforcement capacity of international actors. From the perspective of compliance and implementation research, non-compliance with international norms and practices is the consequence of a misfit between international rules and national context. Following the misfit hypothesis, non-compliance is common when rules are inconvenient for governments because they create costs that governments do not want to afford or cannot afford.[43] In this regard, states' definitions of their national interests and their institutional capacities are the core variables.

Furthermore, the ultimate effectiveness of CTF also depends on the nature and scope of the problem.

In addition to factors such as international vulnerability and the operational environment of terror finance, including aspects of the formal and informal financial sectors, administrative and governmental effectiveness also affect compliance levels. For several reasons, states in the region span a wide range in terms of the degree of government effectiveness, especially the quality, competence, and independence from political pressure of bureaucracies. In addition, the effectiveness and predictability of the judiciary and the law enforcement apparatus, and the extent to which public power is exercised for private gain, varies considerably, ranging from high-quality bureaucracies and relatively low levels of corruption (at least compared to other countries in the region) in Singapore and Malaysia to disorganized bureaucracies and hyper-corruption in countries such as Burma, Cambodia, Indonesia, and the Philippines. In countries characterized by highly ineffective governments, rudimentary rule of law, and high levels of political corruption, it is highly implausible to expect effective AML and CTF regimes. Corrupt legislators are less likely to pass CTF laws, and corruption undermines the implementation of regulations by individuals in the financial sectors and the public administration (see table 12.7).

Two examples illustrate the relationship between the variables in table 12.7. First, leaving aside the anomaly of Burma (with a relatively high degree of norm compliance but low implementation), evidence from the other nine Southeast Asian countries suggests that one of the issues that particularly bedevil the anti-money laundering efforts in the region is the high level of corruption. While Asia-Pacific is less prone to the problem of corruption than many regions in the world, the available corruption data indicate a broad range of experiences across the region. Some jurisdictions fare extremely well in independent assessments of corruption (Singapore), others exhibit moderate levels (Malaysia, Brunei, and Thailand), while Cambodia, Burma, Indonesia, Laos, the Philippines, and Vietnam have major problems in this area, according to various sources.[44]

The deeper the swamp of political corruption, the shallower is the personal interest of politicians—either cabinet members or members of the parliament—in the passage of an effective money laundering statute. Corruption and money laundering are in fact inseparable. In countries with high levels of political corruption such as the Philippines and Indonesia, law-

TABLE 12.7 *Government Effectiveness and Control of Corruption in Southeast Asia*

	BRUNEI	BURMA	CAMBODIA	INDONESIA	LAOS	MALAYSIA	PHILIPPINES	SINGAPORE	THAILAND	VIETNAM
Government Effectiveness	0.96	−1.29	−0.56	−0.56	−0.80	0.92	−0.06	2.26	0.28	−0.27
Control of Corruption	0.32	−1.37	−0.90	−1.16	−1.25	0.38	−0.52	2.30	−0.15	−0.68

Note: Scores are between −2.5 and 2.5, with higher values indicating higher levels of effectiveness and control of corruption. Government Effectiveness combines perceptions of the quality of public service provisions, the quality of bureaucracy, the competence of civil servants, the independence of the civil service from political pressures, and the credibility of the government's commitment to policies. Control of Corruption indicators measure perceptions of corruption.

Source: World Bank Governance Indicators, taken from Daniel Kaufmann, Aart Kraay, and Massimo Mastruzzi, *Governance Matters III: Governance Indicators for 1996–2002*, the World Bank, June 30, 2003 (http://www.worldbank.org/wbi/governance/pdf/govmatters3.pdf).

makers may delay and dilute legislation that changes the policy status quo towards internationally accepted standards of AML and CTF, since they seek to ensure that the laws they draft will not be used against them at a later stage.[45] There is also justified concern in the financial sector that information provided to law enforcement agencies will be passed to the criminals who will target officials and their families in a calculated attempt to prevent the further reporting of suspicious activities. Effective AML and restricting the flow of terrorist finance may not only have a low priority here but may even be harmful for the political and economic survival of elites.

Second, some aspects of implementation, such as comprehensive and well-informed compliance with record-keeping and auditing rules or fully staffing new organizations, may take time. Other aspects of implementation, such as standing up and funding new organizations and oversight bodies, may be accomplished more readily. However, in many parts of the region, states simply lack the resources to improve administrative capabilities in order to regulate financial activities of terrorist organizations through these new organizations. In the Philippines, Indonesia, Burma, and Cambodia, where over-politicized and under-equipped administrations and the erosion of the government's monopoly on the use of force constitute a fundamental problem of good governance, the lack of compliance with international norms can hardly be blamed solely on the lack of political will of governments.

Despite all of the policy talk and legislative activity in recent years, the international community has only recently begun to make practical assistance available for capacity-building in Southeast Asia. The European Union is funding the implementation of UN Security Council Resolution 1373 among a number of regional governments such as the Philippines and Indonesia, although the effectiveness of these efforts is questioned. At the Asia-Pacific Economic Cooperation (APEC) Leaders Forum 2003, agreement was reached to establish a regional security fund, to be administered by the Asian Development Bank. It will assist the Philippines and Indonesia in enhancing their border protection capacity; some of this additional funding will be made available for anti-money laundering purposes. However, given the chronic disorganization in the Indonesian and Philippine bureaucracies and the endemic corruption in the judiciary and security apparatus in both countries, it seems unlikely that these measures will have a strong impact.

Finally, one factor that is mostly overlooked in the scholarly debate on compliance with international norms in Southeast Asia, and especially in the literature on CTF, is the institutional framework of governments, specifically the distribution of veto authority, which shapes the overall character of the policy environment in which executives and legislators operate. As the imaginative work of George Tsebelis and others on decision-making processes in different institutional settings and their effect on the capacity of political systems to alter the policy status quo shows, policy stability is correlated with the number of institutional and partisan veto players, the ideological distance between them, and the internal coherence of each actor.[46] Democratic systems with many partisan and institutional veto players and strict political constraints on the executive will have difficulties in adopting international norms of CTF because their capacity to produce policy changes is low. More authoritarian regimes with strong and cohesive executives that dominate the policy-making process should exhibit a higher capacity to reform their legal and regulatory framework, *if* the policy preferences of executives and political elites favor such a policy change.

A quick glance at the overview of institutional characteristics of the political systems in Southeast Asia in table 12.8 supports this overall assumption. Although the variation in government CTF policies in Southeast Asia has many sources, one important explanation is that altering policies is easier in some countries than in others. While governments in semi-democratic Singapore and Malaysia face only weak institutional constraints and, through their dominant and cohesive political parties, have absolute control over policy making, governments in the new democracies in the region have to deal with large numbers of veto players. This was the case for Thailand before 2001 but is especially true for the Philippines and Indonesia.[47] In these two nations, strict constitutional constraints, a fragmented political party system, and uncohesive political parties inhibit compliance with the international norms and principles of CTF. The executives in both the Philippines and Indonesia presumably had the political will to adapt their policies to international CTF standards—given pressure from external actors and the occurrence of transnationally linked terrorist bombings in their countries. Despite this, both countries remained on FATF's list of Non-Cooperative Countries until 2005.

The fact that the authoritarian governments in the region do not coalesce around a single pattern of compliance and implementation does not contradict the expectation concerning the relevance of institutional factors but rather supports the argument that other factors are also relevant.

TABLE 12.8 *Regime Characteristics in Southeast Asia*

	BRUNEI	BURMA	CAMBODIA	INDONESIA	LAOS	MALAYSIA	PHILIPPINES	SINGAPORE	THAILAND	VIETNAM
Regime Type*	A	A	A	D	A	SD	D	SD	D	A
Constraints on Executive	NA	3	4	6	3	4	6	3	7	3
Party System Fragmentation	NA	NA	2.3	7.1	NA	1.2	3.5	1.04	1.6	NA

*A = Autocracy; D = Democracy; SD = Semi-democracy

Notes: The Polity IV Project's data set has annually coded ratings on the qualities of political institutions: competitiveness of executive recruitment, extent of executive constraints, and openness of political competition. These ratings have been combined into a single measure of **Regime Type**: the Polity score, ranges from -10 (fully institutionalized autocracy) to +10 (fully institutionalized democracy). Countries with Polity scores from 6 to 10 are counted as democracies, and countries with Polity scores of -10 to -6 are considered autocracies. **Constraints on Executive** refers to the de facto independence of the chief executive according to Polity IV. Scores for the year 2003 are between 1 and 10; the higher the score, the weaker the independence of the head of government. **Party System Fragmentation** refers to the effective number of parties in parliament at the most recent election.

Sources: Polity IV data are available at http://www.cidcm.umd.edu/inscr/polity/report.htm. Data are taken from Aurel Croissant, "Asien und Pazifik," Bertelsmann *Transformation Index 2006* (Guetersloh, Germany: Bertelsmann, forthcoming).

Conclusion

This comparative study of terrorist financing and government responses in Southeast Asia examines how terrorist groups in the region finance their activities; what measures, legislative and otherwise, have been employed by the governments in the region to combat terrorism financing; and what factors account for the discrepancy of norm compliance and implementation in the region. Our analysis of sources and patterns of terrorism finance in the region shows that terrorist organizations employ various means to generate and channel funds.

The analysis detected two major trends in AML-CTF in the region. While countries converge on the transformation of international rules into national law, they diverge in terms of rules implementation. Singapore shows the strongest degree of compliance and implementation, followed by Thailand and Indonesia. They are followed, albeit after a considerable gap, by Malaysia, the Philippines, and, even further behind, Brunei. Although laws may be on the books, they are not *effectively* implemented. The relevant governmental institutions are not well developed, and international law enforcement cooperation is slow. Furthermore, despite all of this policy and legislative activity, little practical assistance is available to financial institutions that are supposed to identify terrorist financing. Islamic charities and the informal value transfer systems such as *hawala* are still largely unregulated, and evidence for enforcement of existing rules is often lacking. The Philippines, partly due to the well-developed legal framework and evidence of enforcement, does better than is often portrayed. However, corruption and lack of an effective bureaucracy remain the Achilles' heel of CTF in that nation.

While to some extent it is certainly correct that, as one observer has criticized recently, "Southeast Asia hasn't stopped the terror funding," our analysis shows that this sweeping criticism fails to account for nuanced differences in the regional trends and the nature of the problem.[48] Rather, our analysis shows that considerable differences in scope, pace, and success of compliance and implementation between countries are related to several factors: the preferences and calculations of rational political actors; the institutional capacity of political systems to produce policy changes; administrative and law enforcement capacities, especially in those countries that are the major theatres of terrorism financing; and characteristics of the financial systems.

Finally, we also find a general relationship between the development of the formal financial sector and the rate at which governments act to inhibit money laundering. Countries that rely on remittances from overseas and funding from charities are less likely to interfere with terror finance for fear of disrupting their economies. In addition, CTF measures that focus on formal banking institutions are of only limited effectiveness, given the high relevance of the informal financial sectors. Even CTF measures that focus on informal banking institutions will be of only limited effectiveness in raising terrorists' transaction costs and disrupting terrorists' financial networks because local terrorist groups are often entrenched in a network of decades-old insurgencies and organized crime and have learned to take advantage of the region's porous borders and large unregulated areas to rely on smuggling of people, arms, drugs, and other forms of illicit crime such as piracy and kidnapping for ransom. In this context, an additional challenge in suppressing fund-raising efforts of terrorist groups is the problem of separating funding for terrorist actions and for non-terrorist activities such as other forms of armed struggle or social work by the same organization, especially in those cases of terrorism that are related to protracted separatist conflicts (e.g., the southern Philippines).

CHAPTER 13

Terrorist Financing and the Tri-Border Area of South America

*The Challenge of Effective Governmental Response
in a Permissive Environment*

JOHN L. LOMBARDI AND DAVID J. SANCHEZ

Although there are many centers of terrorist financing throughout the world, a considerable amount of money flows through Latin America—partly because of its well-developed financial institutions, partly because of the instability and ineffectiveness of its legal and governmental institutions, and partly because of the close nexus between terrorist financing and the global drug trade. Within this hemispheric context, the region where Argentina, Brazil, and Paraguay meet has drawn considerable attention and provides an opportunity to get as good a glimpse of the global terrorist financial network as is available. This area known as the Triple Frontier or, more commonly, the Tri-Border Area (TBA), is a haven for terrorists, arms and drug smugglers, money launderers, tax evaders, document forgers, as well as legitimate or semi-legitimate commercial and financial operatives.[1]

Sufficient evidence suggests that the TBA is a strategically important area in the global war on terrorism precisely because it is a *permissive environment* providing safe haven for Islamic extremist terrorist networks and their activities.[2] Hezbollah, the Islamic Resistance Movement (Hamas), Islamic Jihad, al Muqawamah, Egyptian Islamic Group, and possibly al Qaeda, in a much more limited fashion, reportedly have extensive financial and logistical operations in the area raising, laundering, and transferring money; recruiting operatives; and, in the case of Hezbollah, directly supporting terrorist activities.[3] The rise of the TBA's profile as a major nexus of financial and logistical operations for terrorists and drug cartels has inevitably drawn the attention of the three host nations, the United States, and international law enforcement and counter-terrorist organizations. This chapter critically examines the potential regional and international security threat resident in this permissive environment and, more specifically, the general effectiveness of the collective governmental response to counter-terrorist financing in the TBA after 9/11.

Permissive Environment

The three primary cities of the TBA are Ciudad del Este, Paraguay; Foz do Iguaçu, Brazil; and Puerto Iguazú, Argentina. All three cities are plagued with pervasive official corruption, weak legislation, poor law enforcement, non-transparent financial institutions, poor economic conditions, a general lack of respect for the rule of law, and poorly monitored borders—characteristics that permit and facilitate terrorist financial and logistical operations.[4]

The intersection of these three countries with competing economic interests reduces the effectiveness of law enforcement in the region. As a free trade zone and major center of legal and illegal commerce, local officials struggle with the task of physically inspecting the daily traffic. Because the flow of people and commerce between the three cities is so large and the economic value of moving this business is so high, security issues usually fall victim to the need to move the traffic through expeditiously. Argentine intelligence, for example, estimates that "seventy million dollars of uncontrolled cross-border transactions occur every day" in the region.[5] Despite national efforts to implement more stringent laws regarding the amount of goods that can cross borders,[6] the estimated flow of between 30,000 and 40,000 people per day[7] prevents any serious effort to enforce existing customs or immigration laws.[8] Additionally, violent crime is reportedly on the rise in the TBA, and interviews with customs officials highlight the extremely dangerous nature of evening interdiction operations against smugglers utilizing the

Iguazú and Paraná rivers.[9] Finally, poor and slow international law enforcement coordination, which must occur between bureaucracies in capitals hundreds, even thousands, of miles apart inhibits the joint action required to successfully disrupt illegal traffic and carry out effective operations against resident terrorist and criminal networks.

FUND-RAISING ACTIVITIES

Terrorist fund-raising activities in the TBA include both licit (e.g., donations) and illicit (e.g., smuggling, money laundering, extortion, counterfeiting) activities. There is little current information regarding the sums of money raised by Islamic extremists in the region, and the available evidence derives primarily from a few individual cases. Most of the current knowledge regarding terrorist financing methods in the TBA comes from the Assad Ahmad Barakat legal case. Barakat operated primarily out of the Galería Page shopping center in Ciudad del Este, described by Argentine police as the regional command post for Hezbollah.[10] Barakat's direct links to Hezbollah reportedly came to the attention of local law enforcement and intelligence officials as early as 1999. A Brazilian Federal Police intelligence report sent by the Brazilian government to Paraguayan authorities between late 1999 and early 2000 mentioned three confirmed Hezbollah leaders with whom Barakat had met annually during trips to Lebanon.[11] Additionally, Brazilian Federal Police intelligence affirmed that "Barakat, the businessman, is thought to be one of the Hezbollah leaders in the region, where he arrived in 1987."[12] In December 2001, Asunción's *Ultima Hora* newspaper reported that local intelligence services, which were collecting information on the activities of Lebanese citizens in the TBA, had found evidence regarding Barakat's fund-raising activities for Hezbollah in the region.[13]

The Barakat legal case, which concluded with his prosecution and sentencing to six and one-half years in prison for tax evasion in May 2004, was significant because it effectively highlighted Hezbollah's financial and logistical modus operandi in the TBA. According to the head of the Paraguayan National Police (PNP) anti-terrorism unit, the Secretariat for the Prevention and Investigation of Terrorism, Barakat utilized counterfeiting, money laundering, blackmail, and death threats to send at least $50 million to Hezbollah from 1995 until his arrest in June 2002.[14]

DRUG AND ARMS SMUGGLING

In 2003, Brazilian authorities estimated that the Lebanese mafia and Hezbollah moved approximately 400 to 1,000 kilograms of Colombian cocaine through the TBA to São Paulo, Brazil.[15] Lebanese citizen Ali Assi and Lebanese businessmen Bassam Naboulsi and Hassan Abdallah Dayoub were all arrested on drug trafficking charges between May 2002 and May 2003. All three were TBA residents associated with Hezbollah financier Assad Ahmad Barakat.[16]

The Lebanese mafia and Hezbollah associates also reportedly facilitate arms smuggling in the TBA.[17] A Paraguayan raid on Rajkumar Naraindas Sabnani's house in July 2002 uncovered orders for weapons and an authorization to use $30 million for arms deals. Sabnani, an East Indian merchant, was also linked to Assad Ahmad Barakat and allegedly served as his liaison to the Hong Kong mafia.[18]

COUNTERFEITING AND MONEY LAUNDERING

Counterfeiting cash and official government documents is among the many facilitating activities in the TBA that support terrorist and criminal networks. Assad Ahmad Barakat is thought to have distributed at least a portion of $60 million in counterfeit bills originating from Colombia.[19] Terrorist operatives can use falsified documents to facilitate travel to and from targets without scrutiny from government security personnel. Falsified documents can also be sold to raise cash or, more significantly, be used to establish fake identities and companies, validate false invoices, and create other important papers needed to establish money laundering fronts or process drug or other illicit proceeds. Pirated software is also a major source of revenue for Islamic extremist groups in the TBA. In 2001, Paraguayan authorities seized 5,000 pirated Nintendo compact discs worth approximately $160,000. The seizure uncovered a new route for pirated video games used by Barakat. Additionally, Paraguayan authorities charged Ali Khalil Mehri with pirating computer software worth millions of dollars, some of which was allegedly transferred to Hezbollah.[20]

Money laundering also generates revenue for terrorist networks operating in the TBA. Money from drug smuggling, extortion, and intellectual property theft must often be passed through legitimate businesses before it can be used. Terrorists and their associates use money exchange houses and front companies to clean this illicitly gained cash. In Ciudad del Este, there are reportedly 400 such money exchange houses, only 11 of which are actually legal.[21] Brazilian authorities estimate that as much as $10 million could flow through Brazilian money exchange houses or front companies each day, and that as much as $6–10 billion could flow through the TBA each year.[22] Additionally, charitable donations can easily be intermingled with criminally generated revenue, providing a relatively secure method of laundering illegally obtained money.

DONATIONS, EXTORTION, AND REMITTANCES

Charitable donations represent a major source of revenue for extremist organizations in general. These gifts have proven effective for terrorists because governments find it very difficult to differentiate between legitimate charitable giving and support for terrorist organizations. Islamic extremists in the TBA have utilized charitable donations in this context. When Paraguayan authorities raided Assad Ahmad Barakat's business, Casa Apolo, for example, they found a certificate thanking him for a $3,353,149 donation to the Martyrs Social Beneficent Organization.[23]

Traditional extortion is another method used in the TBA for terrorist financing. Hezbollah associates in the TBA extorted Lebanese businesspeople, both Muslims and Christians, to donate funds to Hezbollah. More specifically, Assad Ahmad Barakat associate Sobhi Mahmoud Fayad placed thank-you certificates in the windows of business owners in return for their donations. Fayad also reportedly threatened to spread rumors in the TBA that these business owners and their respective family members were spies for the Israeli government if they did not donate funds to Hezbollah.[24]

Revenue generated by Islamic extremists in the TBA must ultimately be transferred to the extremists' parent terrorist organizations. Methods utilized for such transfers include simple individual remittances, legal donations to charitable organizations, and bank transfers between legitimate or semi-legitimate financial organizations. Paraguay's Secretariat for the Prevention of Money Laundering, for example, identified 45 people who made individual transactions of over $100,000 from the TBA to the Middle East between 1998 and 2001.[25] Ali Nizar Dahroug, an alleged al Qaeda point man in the

TBA, reportedly wired approximately $80,000 a day to banks in the United States and the Middle East.[26] The existence of non-transparent financial institutions in the TBA provides terrorist financiers with relatively secure, less scrutinized official systems through which they can transfer large sums of money. Additionally, the strong privacy protections existing in most banking laws and traditions facilitate money laundering by reducing the risk of discovery. Private money transfers, derivatives trading, commodities trades, real estate purchases, and smuggling (e.g., of drugs and arms) are also common methods of terrorist financing in the region.[27]

THE CHANGING ENVIRONMENT

Some scholars have recently suggested that the TBA is no longer the lucrative source of terrorist financing that it once was.[28] Possible reasons given for the region's alleged decline in this context include (1) increased security pressure by local law enforcement and intelligence officials after the Hezbollah-linked terrorist attacks in Buenos Aires (1992 and 1994); (2) increased public attention regarding terrorist financing activities in general after 9/11; and (3) fear of prosecution of resident Islamic extremists, especially after the successful prosecution and sentencing of Assad Ahmad Barakat. According to this argument, a substantial number of terrorist financiers have fled the TBA to find safe haven in seemingly more permissive environments, including São Paulo, Brazil; Iquique, Chile; Maicao, Colombia; Margarita Island, Venezuela; and Colón, Panama.[29] In sum, whereas the TBA used to be *the* critical node for terrorist financing in Latin America, it is quickly becoming just one of several key nodes in the hemisphere.

Governmental Responses

Numerous multilateral, sub-regional, and national governmental organizations, agreements, and policies formally constitute the counter-terrorist financing regime in the TBA.[30] The scope of this section will include a critical examination of the following in this context: the Organization of American States (OAS) and the Inter-American Convention against Terrorism; the Tripartite Commission of the Triple Frontier ("Three Plus One"); the Financial Action Task Force of South America against Money

Laundering; and Argentina, Brazil, and Paraguay's respective national-level governmental efforts to strengthen their legal, financial, and regulatory infrastructures to more effectively combat money laundering and terrorist financing.

THE OAS AND THE INTER-AMERICAN CONVENTION
AGAINST TERRORISM

In June 2003, the OAS sponsored the Inter-American Convention against Terrorism. The stated purposes of this convention are to "prevent, punish, and eliminate terrorism."[31] The Inter-American Convention against Terrorism is arguably the most significant counter-terrorism milestone passed by the OAS because it incorporates the major United Nations anti-terrorism conventions, including the International Convention for the Suppression of the Financing of Terrorism. The convention advocates the institution of legal and regulatory regimes to combat terrorist financing throughout the Western Hemisphere. More specifically, Article 4 of the convention outlines the following: (1) a comprehensive domestic regulatory and supervisory regime for banks, other financial institutions, and other entities deemed particularly susceptible to use for the financing of terrorist activities; (2) measures to detect and monitor movements across borders of cash, bearer negotiable instruments, and other appropriate movements of value; and (3) measures to establish and maintain financial intelligence units to serve as national centers for the collection, analysis, and dissemination of pertinent money laundering and terrorist financing information.[32]

According to Ambassador Cofer Black, the U.S. Department of State Coordinator for Counter-terrorism, the OAS's Inter-American Committee against Terrorism (CICTE) is leading the hemisphere's collective response to marshal resources and expertise to combat terrorism and terrorist financing.[33] The basic objectives of CICTE are to (1) enhance the exchange of information via the competent national authorities, including the establishment of an inter-American database on terrorism issues; (2) formulate a proposal to assist member states in drafting appropriate counter-terrorism legislation in all states; (3) compile the bilateral, sub-regional, regional, and multilateral treaties and agreements signed by member states and promote universal adherence to international counter-terrorism conventions; (4) enhance border cooperation and travel documentation security measures;

and (5) develop activities for training and crisis management.[34] CICTE also actively supports projects in financing counter-terrorism, strengthening border controls, developing effective counter-terrorism legislation, enhancing cyber security, and protecting critical infrastructure.[35]

One potential limitation of the CICTE, however, is suggested by the empirical evidence: multilateral agreements tend to be less effective than sub-regional or bilateral ones because they often result in "watered down" products in order to reach consensus.[36] Like other multilateral organizations, CICTE is also limited by a lack of legal authority to ensure implementation of its recommendations and compliance with multilateral agreements.

THE TRIPARTITE COMMISSION OF THE TRIPLE FRONTIER (THREE PLUS ONE)

The Tripartite Commission of the Triple Frontier, a sub-regional-level counter-terrorism security mechanism, was established by the three TBA countries in 1998. In 2002, the governments of the three TBA countries invited the government of the United States to join them in a "Three Plus One" meeting. Three Plus One meetings serve as a continuing forum for counter-terrorism cooperation and prevention among all four countries.[37] At the December 2003 Three Plus One meeting, high-level governmental delegations from each country met in Asunción, Paraguay, to exchange views on terrorism prevention in the region and on measures to enhance cooperation. These measures included proposals to establish a joint regional intelligence center, convene a conference of Three Plus One–partner financial intelligence units in the first half of 2004, deepen border security cooperation, and increase dialogue among national prosecutors responsible for counter-terrorism cases.[38] The parties concluded that intelligence reporting indicating possible operational activities by terrorist groups in the TBA remained uncorroborated by intelligence and law enforcement officials, and they identified money laundering and terrorist financing in the region as their primary concerns.[39]

The Three Plus One, like the CICTE, does not have the legal authority to ensure compliance with its agreements or implementation of its recommendations. More significantly, the primary limitation of the Three Plus One is the fundamentally differing national security perceptions exhibited by all four countries regarding terrorism and terrorist financing. In short, a collective sense of urgency regarding these potential threats in the TBA does not currently exist.[40]

The Financial Action Task Force of South America against Money Laundering (GAFISUD) was created in December 2000, and its membership includes nine South American countries, including Argentina, Brazil, and Paraguay. Its purpose is "to work toward developing and implementing a comprehensive global strategy to combat money laundering and terrorist financing as set out in the FATF Forty Recommendations and Nine Special Recommendations."[41] GAFISUD has also developed a Plan of Action against Terrorist Financing aimed at strengthening the national anti-money laundering and counter-terrorist financing policies of its member states.[42] This includes (1) encouragement of the creation of the offense of money laundering in relation to serious crimes; (2) the development of legal systems to investigate and prosecute these offenses; (3) the establishment of systems for reporting suspicious transactions; (4) the promotion of mutual legal assistance; (5) support for the training of persons involved in anti-money laundering efforts; and (6) provision for regional factors to be taken into account in the implementation of anti-money laundering measures.[43]

GAFISUD's primary limitation is that, although it was created on the original FATF model, not all of its member states are FATF members.[44] Argentina and Brazil, for example, are FATF members, and the FATF considers them to have relatively effective systems in place to combat money laundering. At the same time, however, Paraguay is not a FATF member and the FATF describes its legal, operative, and financial system as "underdeveloped."[45] Consequently, GAFISUD has not yet achieved parity in the effectiveness of all of its member states' national and collective capabilities to combat money laundering and terrorist financing.

NATIONAL GOVERNMENTAL EFFORTS

The special relationship between money laundering and terrorist financing has compelled the national governments of Argentina, Brazil, and Paraguay to institute and implement several legislative changes intended to strengthen their respective anti-money laundering and counter-terrorist financing regimes. The government of Argentina adopted the Bill on Money Laundering on April 13, 2000. This legislation became Law 25.246 on May 5, 2000. According to the U.S. State Department, "Law 25.246 expands the predicate offenses for money laundering to include all crimes listed in the Penal Code, sets a stricter regulatory framework for the financial sectors, and creates a financial intelligence unit (FIU), the Unidad de Información Financiera (UIF), under the Ministry of Justice and Human Rights."[46] On October 21, 2003, draft legislation to criminalize terrorist financing was introduced to the Argentine Chamber of Deputies. It was stalled there for nearly two and a half years, only attaining passage on March 30, 2006, during a visit by the FATF President and Executive Secretary.[47] Despite all of the above measures to combat money laundering and terrorist financing, the government of Argentina has failed to take a single investigated case to trial.

Brazil's national anti-money laundering regime is based on Law 9.613, which was implemented on March 3, 1998. Law 9.613 criminalizes money laundering related to drug trafficking, terrorism, arms trafficking, extortion, and organized crime, and penalizes offenders with a maximum of 16 years in prison.[48] This law also created a financial intelligence unit, the Council for the Control of Financial Activities (COAF), under Brazil's Ministry of Finance. In January 2001, the government of Brazil enacted Complementary Law 105 and its implementing Decree 3,724 to amend bank secrecy regulations prohibiting the dissemination of bank, account number, and financial transaction details to national governmental entities other than the Central Bank and congressional investigative committees. On July 9, 2003, the government of Brazil implemented Law 10.701 to modify Law 9.613. Law 10.701 specifically criminalizes terrorist financing and makes it a predicate offense for money laundering. "The law also establishes crimes against foreign governments as predicate offenses, requires the Central Bank to create and maintain a registry of information on all bank account holders, and enables the COAF to request from all government entities financial information on any subject suspected of involvement in criminal activity."[49]

Paraguay is the only TBA country that has not yet implemented specific counter-terrorist financing legislation. In November 2003, the government of Paraguay drafted new anti-money laundering legislation that was still under review as of April 2006 by the Paraguayan Congress. More specifically, the draft legislation identifies the Secretariat for the Prevention of Money

Laundering as Paraguay's sole financial intelligence unit and establishes it as an independent agency that reports directly to the Office of the President. The draft legislation also establishes money laundering as an autonomous crime punishable by a prison term of 5 to 20 years, establishes predicate offenses as any crime that is punishable by a prison term exceeding 6 months, and specifically criminalizes money laundering tied to the financing of terrorist groups or acts.[50] The government of Paraguay is also currently drafting a specific counter-terrorist financing bill; however, given the length of time the Paraguayan Congress has taken to review the anti-money laundering legislation, passing either piece of legislation anytime soon seems unlikely.

Despite the lack of specific anti-terrorist statutes, the government of Paraguay has been notably successful in temporarily disrupting some key terrorist financing networks in the TBA through its successful prosecution, conviction, and sentencing of three alleged Islamic extremist financiers: Sobhi Mahmoud Fayad in November 2002, Ali Nizar Dahroug in August 2003, and Assad Ahmad Barakat in May 2004.[51] Barakat represents the most significant conviction to date. Subsequent to his sentencing, the U.S. Department of the Treasury designated him a "key terrorist financier" pursuant to Executive Order 13224. According to Juan Carlos Zarate, the Assistant Secretary of the Treasury for Terrorist Financing, "from counterfeiting to extortion, this Hezbollah sympathizer committed financial crimes and utilized front companies to underwrite terror."[52]

GOVERNMENTAL RESPONSES BEFORE AND AFTER 9/11

Before 9/11, the only notable arrest of a terrorist financier in the TBA was Ali Khalil Merhi in February 2000.[53] Within 10 days of 9/11, however, Paraguayan law enforcement officials, reportedly under intense pressure from the U.S. government, arrested 16 Lebanese nationals who had illegally entered Ciudad del Este.[54] By early October 2001, shortly after he was added to the Bush administration's terrorist list, Paraguayan law enforcement officials executed the first of several raids against Assad Ahmad Barakat.[55] On November 8, 2001, Paraguayan law enforcement officials arrested Sobhi Mahmoud Fayad. Increased U.S. government pressure after 9/11 thus served as a necessary catalyst to motivate Paraguay's governmental response to combat terrorist financing in the TBA. The attacks of 9/11, however, did not have a similar effect regarding Brazil's governmental response. More specifically, despite compelling evidence of money being illicitly transferred through Foz do Iguaçu, the Brazilian government continues to vehemently deny that any terrorist financing activities take place on its side of the border.[56] One possible explanation for Brazil's denial in this context is that the Iguaçu Falls, located near the TBA, is a very popular tourist destination. Consequently, admitting that terrorism or terrorist financing activities occur in Brazil could adversely affect the substantial revenue generated by the Brazilian tourism industry in the region.

Given the numerous multilateral, sub-regional, and national governmental organizations, agreements, and policies that have been initiated and implemented to combat terrorist financing in the TBA, a fundamental question suggests itself: *How effective has the governmental response been to combat terrorist financing in the region, specifically after 9/11?* In short, the governmental response has not been particularly effective, and the region consequently remains a permissive environment threatening regional and international security. The ongoing Kassem Mohamad Hijazi legal investigation in Ciudad del Este is an illustrative case in point. Paraguayan prosecutors indicted Brazilian resident Kassem Hijazi on February 8, 2005, for illicitly transferring approximately $80–100 million to multiple foreign countries from October 2001 to October 2003.[57] During this two-year period, Hijazi allegedly utilized his business, Telefax Sociedad Anónima, six small money exchange houses, and 113 local businesses to execute approximately 1,800 illegal money transfers, including at least one documented individual transfer of $150,000 to Lebanon.[58] According to Paraguayan prosecutors, Hijazi illicitly transferred money to Chile, China, Iran, Kuwait, Lebanon, Palestine, Panama, Spain, Taiwan, Thailand, and the United States.[59] More significantly, Paraguayan authorities suspect that a portion of the money transferred to the Middle East was intended to fund Islamic terrorist groups, specifically Hezbollah.[60]

Although the Paraguayan government continues to investigate Hijazi, the damage in this case has been done. Hijazi successfully transferred exceptionally large sums of money to the Middle East with unacceptable ease. In fact, when press reporters asked a Central Bank of Paraguay representative how this was possible, the representative responded: "We are not police officers."[61] Although certainly not police officers, the Central Bank is charged with investigating individual money transfers of over $10,000. The Central

Bank and Paraguay's financial intelligence unit allegedly failed to investigate any of Hijazi's money transfers or those of the six small money exchange houses with which he operated.[62]

BARRIERS TO FURTHER STRENGTHENING THE COUNTER-TERRORIST FINANCING REGIME

The multilateral, sub-regional, and national governmental efforts to combat money laundering and terrorist financing in the TBA represent critical steps in the right direction towards strengthening the region's counter-terrorist financing regime. The path to further strengthening this regime, as demonstrated in the Hijazi case, is obstructed by several major barriers. The first barrier is the differing national security perceptions exhibited by the United States, Argentina, Brazil, and Paraguay regarding terrorism and terrorist financing. The government of Brazil is the biggest obstacle in this regard due to its refusal to concede that terrorism and terrorist financing exist within its borders and its relative hegemonic position vis-à-vis Argentina and Paraguay in the region. Moreover, Latin American countries simply do not consider terrorism the most important problem in the TBA—or in the hemisphere, for that matter.[63] Reducing poverty and hunger, bolstering civil society, empowering women, promoting development, deepening democracy, freeing trade in agriculture, and strengthening ties to the European Union are generally considered more pressing issues for Latin American countries.[64]

A second major barrier is corruption in the region. All three TBA countries have exhibited levels of governmental corruption that are of concern. More specifically, "governmental, political, financial, and diplomatic corruption in Paraguay and the TBA allows individuals associated with organized crime and terrorist groups to bribe judges, purchase entry visas, and engage in any number of other criminal activities that might overlap with legitimate economic activities."[65] The marketability and profitability of corruption in the TBA leaves very little incentive for government officials to enforce existing laws or to institute and implement legislative changes to further strengthen the region's counter-terrorist financing regime.

A third major barrier is the lack of human and economic resources to combat money laundering and terrorist financing in the TBA. National governmental efforts to counter organized crime and terrorist groups in the region have been hindered by inadequate funding and investigative capabilities, poor training, and a lack of demonstrated motivation by law enforcement personnel.[66] The most dramatic example of this challenge is evident in Paraguay, where there are only about 200 prosecutors nationwide for a population of approximately 5.5 million, and only 10 of them are specifically dedicated to financial crimes.[67] Given the inadequate number, training, and funding of prosecutors specializing in financial crimes, in confluence with the inherent difficulty of prosecuting money laundering and related terrorist financing legal cases, progress regarding the successful prosecution of these cases will inevitably remain very slow.[68]

Political constituents in each of the three TBA countries represent a fourth major barrier to further strengthening the region's counter-terrorist financing regime. In Argentina, "proposed antiterrorism legislation has long provoked an active debate over the balance between civil rights and the need to address potential terrorism."[69] After suffering through decades of military dictatorship under General Alfredo Stroessner, from 1954–1989, some Paraguayan citizens are understandably ambivalent and even apprehensive about possible anti-terrorism legislation. Moreover, all three TBA countries have productive and influential Muslim populations that would probably oppose any new legislation inhibiting their ability to remit funds to the Middle East or that would, in their perception, increase the probabilities of anti-Muslim profiling or police harassment. Notable populations of Middle Eastern immigrants also make extremists hard to distinguish among the general Muslim population.

The final, and arguably most significant, barrier to further strengthening the region's counter-terrorist financing regime is the challenge of effective governmental response within the context of globalization. "Globalization requires openness and the unfettered ability to move about, and terrorists find openness conducive to carrying out their nefarious actions."[70] Further complicating matters is that all three TBA countries are members of the South American Common Market (MERCOSUR), an economic integration agreement formally launched in 1991 between Argentina, Brazil, Paraguay, and Uruguay that aims to improve the efficiency of the four member economies through the process of opening markets and accelerating economic development.[71] Citizens in the region enjoy relative freedom of movement among MERCOSUR countries, but combating terrorism and terrorist financing suggests closure and restriction of movement.[72] In short, the strategies for strengthening the region's counter-terrorist financing regime and promoting economic development and growth through global-ization cannot be mutually exclusive. This dilemma must be adequately rec-onciled to garner full cooperation by the governments of Argentina, Brazil, and Paraguay in the combating of terrorism and terrorist financing in the TBA.

Overall Assessment

The TBA is a critical, strategic node in the global war on terrorism because it remains a permissive environment for Islamic extremist networks to gen-erate and transfer immeasurable quantities of revenue for their respective parent terrorist organizations; it is also a possible false document facilitation point for subsequent terrorist travel throughout MERCOSUR and else-where, including the United States. There is no credible evidence, however, confirming the participation of TBA Islamic extremists in higher echelon organizational decision-making regarding terrorist operations.

The TBA, however, is not the only such critical node in Latin America. Scholarly research suggests the existence of "several free-trade areas in Latin America with large Middle Eastern populations that allow Islamic ter-rorist groups, organized crime mafias, and corrupt officials to thrive in a mutually beneficial, symbiotic relationship."[73] The inherent difficulty of combating terrorist financing in the TBA highlights the challenge this threat poses to regional and international security. Consequently, the existence of terrorist safe havens is just as important, if not more important, than the actual amount of revenue generated in the TBA or other similar permissive environments. The potential consequence of safe havens warrants closer scrutiny.

The governments of Argentina, Brazil, and Paraguay have instituted and implemented several multilateral, sub-regional, and national governmental initiatives to combat terrorist financing in the TBA. However, these efforts alone do not necessarily translate into significant achievement. Increased U.S. government pressure on the TBA governments after 9/11, specifically on Paraguay, seemingly had the greatest impact on the temporary disruption of suspected terrorist financing networks in the region. Although the Paraguayan government has not yet demonstrated the political will to increase its institutional capacity to combat terrorist financing, it has

effectively used its existing powers to address the issue through the investigation of suspected terrorist financiers for various crimes, including tax evasion, perjury, and the production and use of false documents. The efficacy of
this counter-terrorist financing strategy was the primary lesson learned from
the Fayad, Dahrough, and Barakat legal cases. Consequently, the Paraguayan
government indicted Kassem Hijazi for tax evasion, making false declara-
tions, and maintaining false bookkeeping records in March 2004.[74] Hatem
Ahmad Barakat, Assad Ahmad Barakat's brother, was indicted, prosecuted,
and subsequently sentenced to six years in prison in April 2006 in Ciudad del
Este for the aggravated production and use of false documents.[75] Hatem, like
his brother Assad, is a suspected Hezbollah financier.[76]

Although the law enforcement–based approach has temporarily disrupted
some key terrorist financial networks in the TBA, suspected terrorist
financiers usually are not prosecuted and sentenced until well after the
raised funds have been transferred to their respective parent terrorist organizations. Consequently, increased and aggressive U.S. bilateral assistance for
appropriate Argentine, Brazilian, and especially Paraguayan law enforcement and counter-terrorist intelligence officials is recommended to address
the challenges in the TBA that threaten regional and international security.
Building the capacity of partner-nation law enforcement and counter-
terrorism intelligence officials would serve as a force multiplier to more
effectively combat terrorism and terrorist financing in the region.

This chapter demonstrates the potential regional and international security threat resident in the TBA and similar permissive environments in the
Western Hemisphere. The significant barriers to effectively combating terrorism and terrorist financing in the region, however, cannot be effectively
overcome until the United States fully engages itself in Latin America to
develop a comprehensive hemispheric security strategy and genuinely balances its national security priorities with those of the governments of Latin
America. Better governance, free markets, a modern strategy to improve
regional security, and clear communication of U.S. and Latin American
interests are fundamental to combating terrorism and securing peace and
prosperity in the hemisphere.[77]

CHAPTER FOURTEEN

Anti-Terror Strategy, The 9/11 Commission Report, and Terrorism Financing

Implications for U.S. Policy Makers

RAPHAEL PERL

Throughout the course of history, few, if any, wars against groups using terrorist-type tactics have been won by defensive operations. Accordingly, United States anti-terrorism strategy relies heavily on the doctrine of preemption. As a subset of this framework of preemption, U.S. strategy targets the financing of terrorism.

The 9/11 Commission Report's recommendations include two overarching policy questions related to the sponsorship of terror: (1) what strategy—or mix of strategies—best addresses the issue of terrorist financing; and (2) to what degree are the goals and objectives of such a strategy realistically achievable, cost effective, and in tandem with other counterterrorism, foreign, and domestic policy objectives? Central to the policy debate is deciding on and prioritizing strategic goals; then a framework can be created to measure the effectiveness of efforts designed to address terror finance.

This paper provides an overview of United States anti-terrorism strategy and the overall role of terror financing within the framework of current policy. It then looks at The 9/11 Commission Report's approach to terror-finance strategy and identifies issues and challenges facing decision makers. It argues that U.S. policy should shift away from a focus on seizing terrorist assets and towards an intelligence-based approach to countering terrorism financing.

U.S. Anti-Terror Strategy

U.S. anti-terrorism strategy is governed by the National Strategy for Combating Terrorism, an interagency document released by the White House on February 14, 2003.[1] This framework is designed to complement other elements of the National Security Strategy,[2] including sub-strategies for homeland security, weapons of mass destruction, cyberspace, critical infrastructure protection, and drug control. Whereas the National Strategy for Homeland Security focuses on preventing terrorist attacks *within* the United States, the National Strategy for Combating Terrorism focuses on identifying and defusing threats *before* they reach U.S. borders.[3] Incorporated in the National Strategy for Combating Terrorism are a strong preemptive component, a strong focus on reducing proliferation of weapons of mass destruction, and a defense-in-depth framework.[4]

The intent of the strategy is to stop terrorist attacks against the United States, its citizens, its interests, and its friends and allies around the world, as well as to create an international environment inhospitable to terrorists and their supporters. All instruments of U.S. power—diplomacy, economic policy, law enforcement, financial policy, information dissemination, intelligence, and the military—are to be called upon to combat international terrorism. The plan fits into the wider strategic concept of "defense-in-depth," which projects four concentric rings of defense against terrorist attacks against the United States.[5]

The Bush Administration's 2003 National Strategy for Combating Terrorism is founded on four pillars—defeat, deny, diminish, and defend.

- Together with U.S. allies, *defeat* terrorists by attacking their sanctuaries; leadership; command, control, and communications; material support; and finances. Components include (1) identifying and locating terrorists by making optimal use of all intelligence sources, both foreign and domestic; and (2) destroying terrorists and their organizations by capture, detention, prosecution using special forces and other military power and specialized intelligence resources, and through international cooperation to curb terrorist funding.

- *Deny* terrorists state sponsorship, support, and sanctuary/safe havens. A central strategy objective is to ensure that other sovereign states take similar actions within their sovereign territories and areas in neighboring countries that they may control. Elements include (1) tailoring strategies to induce individual state sponsors of terrorism to change policies; (2) promoting international standards for combating terrorism; (3) eliminating sanctuaries; and (4) interrupting terrorist ground, air, maritime, and cyber traffic in order to deny terrorists access to arms, funding, information, weapons of mass destruction (WMD) materials, sensitive technology, recruits, and funding from illicit drug activities.

- *Diminish* underlying conditions that terrorists exploit by fostering economic, social, and political development, market-based economies, good governance, and the rule of law. Partner with the international community to alleviate conditions leading to failed states that breed terrorism; and use public information initiatives to de-legitimize terrorism.

- *Defend* U.S. citizens and interests at home and abroad to include protection of physical and cyber infrastructures.

Central to the National Strategy for Combating Terrorism is law enforcement cooperation, an increasingly important component of which involves curbing terrorist financing.[6] Viewed primarily within the context of a law enforcement framework centered on international cooperation, the National Strategy for Combating Terrorism places a moderate to strong priority on combating terrorist financing.

Under the strategy, the raison d'être for a policy focus on terrorism financing is to deny funding to terrorist groups—to disrupt and destabilize their operations by causing them to expend added effort to secure funding at the expense of other operational activities. Although the use of covert activity as a means of disrupting money flows is not specifically addressed, arguably it should be contemplated as part of a comprehensive preemptive, network-destabilizing approach.

The 9/11 Commission Report

On July 22, 2004, the National Commission on Terrorist Attacks upon the United States (the 9/11 Commission) issued its final report.[7] Included in it are 41 recommendations for changing the way the government is organized to combat terrorism and how it prioritizes its efforts. Many of the Commission's recommendations are consistent with elements of the administration's February 14, 2003, National Strategy for Combating Terrorism.[8] Both address diplomacy and counter-proliferation efforts, preemption, intelligence and information fusion, winning hearts and minds (not only by public diplomacy, but also with policies that encourage development and more open societies), law enforcement cooperation, combat of terrorist financing, and defense of the homeland.[9]

The 9/11 Commission's recommendations fall into the following categories: (1) preemption (attacking terrorists and preventing the growth of Islamic terrorism by methods that include targeting financial facilitators and funds); (2) protection against, and preparation for, attacks; (3) coordination and unity of operational planning, intelligence, and sharing of information; (4) enhancement, through centralization, of congressional intelligence effectiveness, as well as counter-terrorism oversight, authorization, and appropriations; (5) centralization of congressional oversight and review of homeland security activities; and (6) an increase in Federal Bureau of Investigation, Department of Defense, and Department of Homeland Security capacities to assess terrorist threats and concomitant response strategies and capabilities. The report specifically recommends openly confronting two issues: problems in the U.S.-Saudi relationship (terrorist patronage, the billions of dollars in support of fundamentalist *madrasah* schools,[10] often breeding grounds for Islamist fundamentalists susceptible to terrorist recruiters), and the issue of ideological incitement. The report also recommends sustaining aid to Pakistan and Afghanistan, perceived to be vital geo-strategic allies in the global war on terror.[11]

The topic of terror funding is further addressed in an in-depth supplemental report released by the Commission in August of 2004.[12] The Commission specifically recommended in its main report that

> Vigorous efforts to track terrorist financing must remain front and center in U.S. counter terrorism efforts. The government has recognized that infor-

mation about terrorist money helps us to understand their networks, search them out, and disrupt their operations. Intelligence and law enforcement have targeted the relatively small number of financial facilitators—individuals al Qaeda relied on for their ability to raise and deliver money—at the core of al Qaeda's revenue stream. These efforts have worked. The death or capture of several important facilitators has decreased the amount of money available to al Qaeda and has increased its costs and difficulty in raising and moving the money. Captures have additionally provided a windfall of intelligence that can be used to continue the cycle of disruption.[13]

In the text of the report, the Commission points out that targeting terror financing helps gather information on terror networks and coalitions and increases the costs to al Qaeda and other groups of raising money, both in terms of financial expenditures and organizational energy. Moreover, if al Qaeda is replaced by smaller, decentralized groups, the assumption that terrorists need a financial support network may become outdated.[14] In what some see as a contradictory viewpoint, the supplemental staff report from the Commission on terror financing emphasizes that the U.S. government has made little leeway in deciphering al Qaeda funding channels and that the organization adapts quickly and effectively to financial obstacles posed by government activity.[15]

In effect, the Commission calls for redefining terrorist financing strategy goals away from a focus on seizing assets and towards a focus on gathering intelligence.[16] Three factors are cited in support of such a shift in policy focus. First, there is the realization that it may not be achievable or cost effective to deny terrorists funding in any meaningful sense, that is, "that trying to starve the terrorists of money is like trying to catch one kind of fish by draining the ocean."[17] Second, it is acknowledged that terrorists increasingly seek more informal methods of moving, obtaining, and storing funds, thus making it more difficult for authorities to seize amounts of significance. Third, a concern is expressed that as terrorist networks become increasingly decentralized, they may become financially self-supporting, making it even harder to track or capture their funds. Similar conclusions were previously reached by many in the war-on-drugs policy community concerning efforts to interrupt finances of the drug trade.

There are, however, some problems with, and omissions from, the report. One potential shortcoming with the Commission's reasoning is that although dollar amounts seized may be small and statistically insignificant, such funding may also be critical to the execution of terrorist operations and thus the ultimate impact of such seizures on thwarting imminent terrorist activity may be quite high.

Another prickly problem not dealt with in the report—and arguably beyond the primary scope of the Committee's mandate—is the subject of centralization and/or coordination of United States federal efforts designed to track terrorist financing.[18] Likewise, coordination with the United Nations Counter Terrorism Committee (under the rubric of UN Security Council Resolution 1373) in order to maximize the use of relatively scarce manpower resources is not addressed in the Commission report.[19]

The report does not address two additional benefits of targeting financing: that such measures (1) may prove useful as a coalition-building tool, and (2) may have a chilling effect on donations to terrorist groups, thereby reducing the potential of these groups to recruit new donors from among sympathizers or "sideline/fringe" supporters. Additionally, the report omits the need to train other countries to improve their laws, regulations, and manpower resources, enabling them to curb terrorism fund-raising and transfers of funds.

Subsequent to the release of the Commission report, Congress passed the Intelligence Reform and Terrorism Prevention Act of 2004.[20] The law (Sec. 7118) states that "efforts to track terrorist financing must be paramount in United States counterterrorism efforts" and requires that within 270 days (Sec. 6303) the Secretary of the Treasury submit a report to Congress evaluating and making recommendations on (1) the effectiveness of current efforts to curtail terrorist financing; (2) the relationship between terrorist financing and money laundering, including the illicit drug trade and political corruption; (3) the effectiveness of efforts to protect critical financial infrastructure; and (4) ways to improve international cooperation on terrorist financing.

Issues for U.S. Decision Makers

Despite its overt praise for United States' efforts aimed at combating terror finance—which have resulted in intelligence windfalls, closing of charities, and arrest of key benefactors—the underlying message sent by the

Commission report about the focus and effectiveness of the strategy amounts to nothing less than a policy bombshell. Implied in the report is the notion that previous policy mindsets that placed a strong emphasis on seizing terrorist assets hold little or no promise of success in combating the financial support of Islamist terrorism. This in turn raises questions. In what areas, if any, are chances for success promising? What strategy—or strategy mix—is appropriate to address the problem of terrorist financing? How much policy focus should it be given? What should the rationale for that policy focus be? And, finally, how does one get the most bang for the buck?

At least four issues are central to the policy debate emerging in the wake of The 9/11 Commission Report. They include:

1. On what assumptions should policy be based?
2. What should the goals and objectives of policy be?
3. How does one measure success or failure of policy implementation?
4. What specific policy options may hold promise of success?

POLICY ASSUMPTIONS

In the past, core beliefs underlying U.S. policy were that significantly diminishing the financing of terrorist causes was achievable and that decreasing funding would reduce terrorist activity. The 9/11 Commission Report's comparison of attempts to dry up terrorism finance with "draining the ocean" challenges the assumption that financing of terror can be reduced on a grand scale.[21] A likely result is a shift away from a focus on seizing money to a more multifaceted approach, within which viewing money trails as sources of intelligence is central. Arguably, such a policy shift is well underway.

While recognizing that the goals of seizing assets and tracking them are not mutually exclusive, The 9/11 Commission Report emphasizes that the United States must expect "less from trying to dry up terrorist money and more from following the money for intelligence, as a tool to hunt terrorists, understand their networks, and disrupt their operations."[22] In the words of Commission Chairman Thomas Kean, "we have been spending a lot of energy in the government trying to dry up sources of funding. . . . Obviously if you can dry up money, you dry it up, but we believe one thing we didn't do effectively is follow the money. That's what we have to do."[23]

Further challenging a policy focus on seizing funds, the report suggests that given the increasingly decentralized structure of terrorist groups, the assumption that terrorists need a financial support network may become out-dated.[24] A related concern is the degree to which the United States and the international community have the infrastructure in place to effectively detect and monitor transactions associated with terrorist activity.

ESTABLISHING GOALS AND OBJECTIVES

Setting goals is central to policy formulation and implementation. In a past era of state-sponsored terrorism, where denying terrorist support was seen as realistically achievable, policy goals centered on drying up financial support from state actors, and where this failed, on seizing and impounding assets. Many investigators migrated to the financial tracking component of the counter-terrorism community from the counter-drug community, where attempting to seize assets was a high-profile, widely-accepted, and entrenched practice. This further reinforced a mind-set focused on interdicting funds.

The 9/11 Commission Report opens the door to a more holistic approach in which financing is seen within the broader policy objectives of a strategy that goes beyond seizing assets. Under such a plan, money is viewed as a facilitator—only one of many tools at the terrorists' disposal. Confiscating sums of money is a priority, not because the amounts are large, but because the intended uses of the funds are crucial to an imminent attack. Since current anti-terror policy places a high value on denying terrorists access to weapons of mass destruction, a core objective of post-9/11 policy is to deny them critical-mass funding that could be used for WMD purchases.

MEASURING SUCCESS

Indicators of the success or failure of policies serve as important tools in better enabling decision makers to fund policies that work and revise or abandon those that do not. The challenge facing policy makers is *how* to measure successes, or failures, of policies. Signs of effectiveness cannot be measured in a vacuum; they must be measured in the context of policy goals and objectives.

Moreover, since terrorists and those charged with combating terrorism have differing goals and objectives, the definitions of success differ for each group. For example, success for those charged with securing an airport may be claimed by citing the absence of attacks and the high-profile presence of security personnel and detection technology. In the same situation, victory for the terrorist network may be claimed because the enemy has expended unnecessary resources protecting a facility that was never targeted, resulting in fewer available resources to devote to other counter-terror goals, such as combating terrorist financing. One potential pitfall plaguing measurements of success is an over-reliance on quantitative data at the expense of its qualitative significance.

Candidates for a multi-dimensional metric to analyze qualitative strategy victories include: (1) assets and money confiscated; (2) lessened desire of people to give money to terrorist causes; (3) money not given, i.e., the chilling effect of policies on contributions; (4) changes in levels of terrorist recruitment; (5) numbers of terrorist operatives apprehended or killed; (6) the public relations impact on a society of government policies that target terrorist financing; (7) the disruptive effects on terrorist activities and organizational infrastructures, including deterring or slowing down potential attacks; (8) the impact on coalition building; and (9) the curbing of other criminal activities—especially activity linked to terrorist groups—such as the illicit drug and arms trades and piracy of intellectual property.

Finally, there remains the intelligence value of policies employed. Clearly, here, an important measure would be the finding that intelligence directly prevented catastrophic terrorist events.

POLICY OPTIONS

Increasingly, analysts compare terrorist financing to a hydra—if one head gets cut off, two more appear—leaving policy implementers always behind the power curve. To counter this phenomenon, some propose that a viable strategy should focus not only on money but on the demand driving the money. Within such an expanded policy framework, funding for terror is viewed as a product of an ideology that must be countered.

Inherent in this view is the assumption that as long as there is a desire for people to donate to radical Islamist causes, they will find a way to do so, even if under the guise of charitable contributions. In this line of reasoning, the struggle over terrorism finance boils down to a struggle of ideology, and an increasing number of analysts advise that until nations recognize and come to terms with this, they will not substantially affect terrorist financing and will not win the war on terror.

Undermining the effectiveness of U.S. policies designed to combat terror financing is a perception that they are contrary or hostile to a central tenet of Islam, *zakat*, which requires financial contribution to Islamic causes.[25] To counter this problem, some advocate that policy needs to facilitate channeling of charitable donations to non-jihadist causes; this tactic would necessitate the identification of organizations and charities that *are* terrorist connected or terrorist fronts. On the other hand, donors need to be able to identify legitimate charities without terrorist connections.[26] Central to such efforts are better communication and greater government understanding of the cultural basis and operational dynamics of Islamic charities. For example, under a recently created Treasury Department–FBI joint outreach program, agency representatives are conducting seminars in the Arab-American community to increase awareness of agency concerns and of potential pitfalls with regard to charitable donations. There is a similar need internationally.

An array of policy options exists for decision makers in devising more effective strategies to deal with the phenomenon of terrorist financing. I list nine notable examples here:

1. Rethinking assumptions and expanding policy to include a demand-supply framework aimed at reducing the pool of potential contributors to terrorist causes, including working with those who offer alternatives to radical Islam and those who seek to discredit the ideology of radical Islamists.

2. Adopting a mind-set that increasingly views money as a tool of terrorism and as a source of information to be studied, not merely as a product to be seized.

3. Placing more emphasis on international coalition building with much of the focus on diplomacy rather than on seizing assets or monitoring financial flows. Once built and solid, a coalition of this nature could be expanded into other areas of mutual interest and concern. This approach would likely require additional funding both for diplomacy and for training U.S. and foreign specialists in detecting and countering terrorist fund-raising and money transfers.

4. Initiating a concerted effort—starting from scratch and mindful of the protection of civil liberties—to determine what data is currently available on terrorist financial flows, how to obtain more of it, and how to apply state-of-the-art technology to analyze the data with the objective of identifying sinister patterns of activity.

5. Concentrating on high-value targets: significant money, suspicious transactions, key financiers, and charities and front groups.

6. Giving the matter of state sponsorship of terror an invigorated priority. To what degree is the current policy focus on al Qaeda-type networks drawing attention away from the reported role of states such as Saudi Arabia, Iran, and Syria in funding, facilitating, or countenancing the financing of terror? What enticements and sanctions can the United States and the international community bring to bear on so-called "rogue nations"?

7. Developing and implementing more proactive policies. For example, how might we maximize the legal right of contributors worldwide to demand an accounting of how charitable donations are used? How might the funding of militant *madrasahs* throughout the world better be discouraged? How will a terrorist organization respond to the shutting down of a particular source of funding, and how does one stay ahead of the curve? (Staying ahead may include utilizing sting operations, covert actions, and other means against terrorist financial centers, businesses, and individuals engaged in facilitating terrorism through funding.)

8. Devoting more policy focus to combating criminal activities—such as piracy of intellectual property rights, narcotics and human trafficking, counterfeiting—that are being used as sources of funding by terrorists.

9. Committing adequate funding to implement policy. In the past there have been numerous charges of insufficient funding to combat terrorism finance.[27]

Conclusion

Arguably, in the global war on terror, the man with the money is as dangerous as the man with the gun. Despite the difficulties of interrupting terrorist financing, policies that ignore or downplay the importance of money appear to be unwise, since successful confiscation of funds can derail terrorist operations. Moreover, detecting and tracking illicit transactions can yield valuable intelligence that may be unavailable from other sources. Since Islam and other world religions require charitable contributions from adherents—implying unstoppable cash flows—it is imperative that donations be channeled away from terrorist causes towards legitimate charities.

As The 9/11 Commission Report indicates, in the financial war on terror success should be measured not only quantitatively in terms of dollars seized but also by more subjective criteria, such as making financial transfers more labor-intensive for terrorists, thereby cutting into their time for actual operations.

It is important to recognize that fighting terrorism is often a matter of quietly making gains a yard or two at a time, not necessarily of spectacular interceptions of specific operations. Given the increasing financial and technological sophistication of our adversaries and the multiplicity of fund transfer methods, from money laundering to *hawala*, one should expect to interdict only a modest percentage of terrorist financing, and arguably should refrain from over-committing efforts to areas with diminishing returns. It is important to recognize the limits of policies designed to restrict financing of terrorism; although capturing funds can lessen the ability of terrorist organizations to recruit and conduct operations, such seizures will do little to deter individual suicidal fanatics. However, impounding funds intended as compensation to relatives of suicide bombers may indeed have a chilling effect on terrorist recruitment.

Preemptive action has been shown to be extremely effective from a public relations standpoint. When the finances of illicit charities are attacked globally, other charities, and even uncooperative governments, often take positive steps to avoid further "loss of face." It is vitally important for policy formulators to understand in depth the social and cultural values of other countries that may be very different from their own in order to maximize the positive influence of anti-terror and anti-terror finance strategies worldwide.

Educational systems imbued with hatred and bigotry, whether parochial or secular, furnish an unending supply of future contributors to terrorist causes. It should be a policy priority to reduce the fomenting of terrorism brought about by extreme bias, hyperbole, lies, and calls to violence in educational materials. In concrete terms, this means addressing head-on the serious problem of militant Islamist *madrasahs* by helping host countries channel funds towards those schools that teach mainstream "peace-based" interpretations of Islam. Benign religious schools form an intrinsic and valuable educational element of many societies, including those in the West, and funding for Islamic schools with positive social curricula should be encouraged. Moreover, efforts to reduce funding to *madrasahs* would likely encounter resistance and lead to conflict—although monitoring funding sources could be helpful in ensuring that donations do not come with strings attached to teach militancy and violence.

Increasingly, analysts urge that within the financial arena, as well as in other aspects of terrorism, a balance must be struck between the vigorous pursuit of anti-terrorism policies and the protection of civil liberties. Some contend that individual rights have already been eroded to a dangerous extent in pursuit of homeland security. Admittedly, enhancing security requires an increased degree of government intervention. But clearly the avowed intent of United States policy makers is not to defend freedom abroad while compromising it at home.

Formulation of policy in the complex constellation of trade-offs associated with counter-terrorism in general, and combating terrorist financing in particular, would be facilitated by the constructive involvement of academicians and scholars, religious and community leaders, diplomats, military commanders, politicians, and others. An interdisciplinary task force that merges government expertise with that of the private sector, the scientific community, and academia might well make important inroads towards understanding the multifaceted nature of the problem. Discussions could also include the best ways to work with the United Nations and willing partner countries.

The 9/11 Commission Report has created an environment that fosters open and creative dialogue about the goals and objectives of terror finance policy and the best ways to implement them. Subsequently, Congress passed the Intelligence Reform and Terrorism Prevention Act of 2004, which requires the administration to prepare and submit a report evaluating the current state of U.S. efforts to combat and curtail terrorist financing. This report might well form the basis for ongoing executive and congressional endeavors to reevaluate where the effort against terrorism financing has been going, where it should be going, and how best to define and achieve success.

CHAPTER FIFTEEN

U.S. and International Responses to Terrorist Financing

ANNE L. CLUNAN

According to one well-informed observer, the U.S. effort to combat terrorists' access to financial resources is the most successful part of the global community's counter-terrorism strategy since the al Qaeda September 11, 2001, attacks on the United States.[1] The international norms and practices that make up the new counter-terrorist financing (CTF) frame have spread rapidly in the past three years. However, the ultimate effectiveness, measured in terms of implementation and enforcement, of the new CTF regime depends on states' redefinition of their national interests to include combating terrorist finance and a new understanding of the collective responses necessary to manage the non-state actors involved.

Combating Terrorist Financing: A Collective Action Problem

Terrorist financing incorporates two distinct activities: transferring funds for specific terrorist attacks, and ongoing fund-raising to support terrorist organizations. Operatives use transferred funds to finance mundane items such as food, lodging, and transportation; they also make purchases of legal precursors for bomb making (the 2004 Madrid bombings relied on cell phones for detonation triggers). Such transactions are mainly pre-crime; they are perfectly legal until they can be linked to support for a criminal act.[2] They are also minute in monetary value and therefore extremely hard to detect in the absence of other indicators. Tracking such transactions raises a number of legal and civil liberties issues.[3] Difficulties in detection are immeasurably increased if cash is used and the formal financial system is avoided.

The second set of terrorist financial activities involves raising funds to support ongoing terrorist operations, training, and propaganda, often through illicit means that are more susceptible to traditional anti-money laundering (AML) or general crime-fighting tools. Terrorists also receive money from legitimate humanitarian and business organizations that may or may not know that their funds are going to terrorism. Legitimate funds are commingled with those destined for terrorists, making it extremely difficult for governments to track terrorist assets in the formal financial system. Yet tracking is even more difficult in the largely unregulated informal systems— such as those operated by money remitters and *hawaladars*—which may engage in trade-based money laundering.[4]

A truly effective international effort to combat terrorist financing requires well-functioning, transparent, and non-corrupt economies with appropriate anti-money laundering legal frameworks regulating both the formal and informal financial/trade services. It demands an ability to enforce laws and collect and share real-time intelligence and documentary evidence using properly trained financial intelligence experts, criminal investigators, prosecutors, regulators, customs agents, and bank employees.[5]

Building the institutional capacity to combat money laundering is the key component of fighting terrorist financing. Without developing such a capacity, states are unable to pursue law enforcement-based approaches to combating terrorism financing. Sustained political will is necessary to ensure that the power granted by legislation is matched with the capacity to implement it both within and across national jurisdictions. Complexity arises from the political problems of achieving and sustaining cooperation among diverse public and private actors, especially national economic institutions and security agencies.

From a theoretical perspective, countering terrorist financing is a classic collective action problem. The majority of states would benefit from limiting the ability of non-state terrorist groups to finance violent challenges to state authority and control. It is in states' best interests to ensure that terrorist penetration and exploitation do not disrupt domestic economies and the international financial system. On the other hand, each state has an incentive to pass the costs of constraining terrorist financing to others, as long as the costs of doing so are less than the benefits. By passing on the costs, a state may attract financial clients craving secrecy and appease domestic actors who oppose government scrutiny, including charities, casinos, banks, money services, and civil liberties advocates. In such cases, the collective action required is likely to be undermined by free riders.

Although there has been a rapid adoption of international CTF norms in the wake of the September 11, 2001, attacks on the United States, there has been only episodic success in their implementation. This pattern is not surprising. Formal adoption of legislation or regulation is a common way for states to avoid the penalties of non-adherence without having to pay the political—and other—costs of implementation. Domestically, many states—even the most developed—lack the institutional capacity to successfully implement and enforce the CTF regime's norms and practices.[6] Competing interests among those within and outside of government make compliance politically difficult.[7]

The analysis of U.S. efforts to combat terrorist financing is illustrative. The United States should have the will to develop a robust CTF regime after the terrorist attacks of September 2001. It has the expertise and resources to tackle the problem domestically and internationally. Yet the tremendous complexities of the issue and the competing interests at play have undermined the United States' CTF efforts. If the United States is unable or unwilling to combat the problem, there is little reason to expect other countries with less motivation and ability to do so on their own.

In many countries, the political pain brought on by efforts to comply with an international regime is deemed avoidable. States are much more likely to adopt, but not enforce, institutional changes unless their calculation of the costs of non-enforcement changes. This may occur for two reasons. States independently redefine their national interest to prioritize terrorist financing. Or the United States and other external actors promote change through the use of carrots and sticks. International regime theory is clear in this regard. The existence of a hegemon or a small group of powerful states (a k-group) that is both willing and able to promote and underwrite an international counter-terrorist finance regime is essential. A hegemon or k-group sets and imposes the rules of the game on free riders through the manipulation of transaction costs and incentives. As one of the centers of the international financial system, the United States is a necessary participant in the creation of a CTF regime, whether as the hegemon or as a member of the k-group.[8]

This chapter argues that the United States has been unwilling to underwrite a CTF regime. The main impetus for states to implement CTF norms has not been U.S. pressure but the exogenous shock of terrorist attacks. While Western efforts have been instrumental in the formal adoption of the international regime, implementation has most often been the product of individual states redefining their interests in the wake of terrorist attacks.

International Efforts to Combat Terrorist Financing before September 11, 2001

Prior to the terrorist bombings of the U.S. embassies in Tanzania and Kenya in 1998, the issue of terrorist financing had been handled in the context of state sponsors of terrorism. After 1998 the focus expanded to non-state actors' activities in money-laundering and criminal finance. Efforts to curtail the flow of funds to terrorists therefore took different approaches: either pressuring states to curb their support for terrorism or ensuring that states had the domestic capacity and incentives to suppress transnational criminal networks.

TARGETING THE CHANGING SOURCES OF TERRORIST FUNDS

Countries have long been divided ideologically over the political motivations of violent organizations—such as the Contras, the Palestinian Liberation Organization, the Irish Republican Army, Hamas, and Hezbollah—and therefore have been unwilling to uniformly define terrorism and terrorists. This lack of consensus has resulted in the proliferation of UN treaties dealing with particular terrorist acts (such as hijackings and political assassinations) rather than terrorism in general.[9] The focus has been on pressuring states directing or materially supporting such organizations. UN Security Council resolutions and treaties authorizing economic sanctions (and unilateral U.S. military strikes) were used to persuade state sponsors such as Libya and Sudan to stop their support for terrorism.[10]

Even after the 1998 embassy bombings, the UN Security Council emphasized the duty of states to suppress terrorism without re-framing the problem in terms of non-state-sponsored terrorism.[11] The 1999 UN Convention for the Suppression of the Financing of Terrorism highlighted state responsibility for the actions of private actors operating within their jurisdiction. UN Security Council Resolution 1269 (1999) was the first to use the term *terrorist financing*. It made clear that states harboring, funding, aiding, or failing to adopt measures to suppress terrorism would be held accountable for acts committed by the terrorists they sponsored. In conjunction with the demise of their Cold War sponsors, Sudan and Libya were effectively persuaded to suppress terrorism through the sanctions approach, but Afghanistan's Taliban was not.[12]

The state sponsorship of terrorism declined after the end of the Cold War as outcasts such as Libya, Iran, Syria, and Sudan sought to reduce their international isolation. Terrorist organizations increasingly relied on other means to fund their activities.[13] Although terrorists had long been involved in drug trafficking and organized crime, the international community had not explicitly linked the two. Drug traffickers and organized crime were dealt with under separate international agreements and agencies, such as the UN Office for Drug Control and Crime Prevention; disagreement over the definition of terrorism prevented the international community from including terrorist acts in many of these efforts.[14] No consensus on a definition appears likely.[15]

After the bombings of the U.S. embassies in Kenya and Tanzania, the United States and other Western countries pushed for international recognition that non-state actors were as complicit as states in supporting terrorism. Led by the United States, the Security Council passed Resolution 1267 in 1999 requiring sanctions on, and freezing of, the assets of the Taliban because of its support for al Qaeda. While this resolution reflected the traditional emphasis on targeting state sponsors (the Taliban), it was the first time the Council had recognized that a transnational terrorist group was a threat to international peace and security.[16]

Also in 1999, France led the UN in adopting the UN Convention on the Suppression of Terrorist Financing, recognizing that states had to work with one another and with private financial institutions to block the flow of terrorist funds. They were required to establish domestic legislation that criminalized terrorist financing and regulated financial industries within their jurisdiction.[17]

In 2000, the Security Council passed Resolution 1333, which imposed an arms embargo and travel ban on the Taliban. For the first time, it took on the non-state actor al Qaeda by freezing the financial assets of Osama bin Laden and those designated as his associates on a list maintained by the 1267 Committee.[18] Resolution 1333 began the transformation from the state-sponsor approach to a transnational, criminal finance approach.

INTERNATIONAL EFFORTS AGAINST CRIMINAL FINANCE

The creation of the Financial Action Task Force (FATF) on money laundering in 1989 marked the first in a series of efforts to establish informal inter- and transgovernmental bodies to handle the problem of criminal finance. FATF set and promoted best practices in combating transnational financial crimes and monitored the status of countries' legislative and regulatory conformity with these standards. In essence, it promoted the anti-money laundering standards put forward by the United States and the United Kingdom and universalized them.[19] It published a set of 40 recommendations in 1990 (revised in 1996) that laid out the basic framework in establishing comprehensive anti-criminal finance systems. In 2000 FATF began a campaign of "naming and shaming." It created a Non-Cooperative Countries and Territories (NCCTs) list that prompted many of those named to alter their domestic legislation in order to be removed. It further suggested a set of counter-measures that states could take against the NCCT countries to prod them into compliance.[20] A number of regional FATF-style organizations were established between 1999 and 2000.[21]

In 1995, the financial intelligence units (FIUs) of 20 states (led by the United States and Belgium) established an informal transgovernmental network for sharing information concerning money laundering. Dubbed the Egmont Group, it grew rapidly to 58 members by June 2001 and 101 by 2006.[22] It has been useful in improving information sharing, analysis, and training to combat money laundering.

The 2000 UN Convention against Transnational Organized Crime required member states to enact comprehensive domestic banking laws and regulations to deter and detect money laundering.[23] Major Western powers took the lead in developing a soft law regime to combat transnational criminal finance. The strategic emphasis was on ensuring that states had the domestic capacity to combat organized criminal finance by enacting and enforcing banking and anti-corruption legislation.

International Efforts to Combat Terrorist Financing after September 11th

On September 28, 2001, the UN Security Council passed a U.S.-sponsored resolution that obligated all members of the United Nations to act to suppress terrorism and terrorist financing.[24] Resolution 1373 is in effect a "mini treaty."[25] It requires the same changes to domestic legislation, denial of safe haven, and criminalization of terrorism as the 1997 Convention on the Suppression of Terrorist Bombing and the 1999 Convention on the Suppression of Terrorist Financing. Since these treaties were not yet in force on September 11, 2001, the Security Council used its Chapter VII authority in Resolution 1373 to obligate *all* members to implement their provisions.

Resolution 1373 went beyond Resolution 1267 in requiring states to act against all terrorist organizations and their associates, not merely al Qaeda and the Taliban. This broad language reflected the United States' determination to take advantage of the sympathetic post-9/11 environment in passing much tougher measures than states otherwise would have accepted.[26] Resolution 1373 established the Counter-Terrorism Committee (CTC) to monitor implementation and increase the capability of UN members to fight terrorism through the promotion and targeting of technical assistance.[27] Unlike the 1267 Committee, the CTC does not maintain a designated terrorist list (the United Kingdom would not support such a proposal),[28] and the CTC adopted a neutral profile to generate as much responsiveness from UN members as possible.[29]

The international response appears remarkable on its surface—over 100 nations drafted and passed laws addressing money laundering or terrorist financing shortly after 9/11. After the 9/11 attacks, the number of ratifications of UN conventions regarding terrorism soared, with 153 ratifying the 1999 Convention on the Suppression of Terrorist Financing and 146 ratifying the 1997 Convention on the Suppression of Terrorist Bombings.[30] A total of $136 million in assets was frozen ($36 million of which was in the United States).[31] Approximately 188 countries have the ability to freeze assets associated with al Qaeda and the Taliban and 170, against terrorist groups more generally.[32]

In October 2001, the FATF expanded its anti-money laundering mission to include terrorist financing and issued "Nine Special Recommendations." The Egmont Group also took terrorist financing under its purview. The widespread acceptance of multilateral norms to prevent terrorist use of the formal financial system led states to seek membership in the Egmont Group and ensure their removal from the FATF Non-Cooperative Countries and Territories list.[33] The International Monetary Fund (IMF) and World Bank agreed to provide technical assistance toward compliance with FATF's recommendations and to include AML considerations in their evaluations.[34]

The international effort on terrorist financing, while impressive, has been largely superficial. States have taken steps they otherwise would have resisted by passing domestic legislation and ratifying the UN's various conventions. The shock of the 9/11 terrorist attacks on the United States, combined with Western pressure, made the costs of non-adoption higher.

But the only carrot offered by Resolution 1373 was technical assistance in combating terrorist financing, for which a meager $20 million has been spent by the United States since 9/11.[35] The United States is not very active in the work of the UN's CTC and devotes much more attention to the 1267 Committee. It prefers expanding the al Qaeda and Taliban list to sanction governments, groups, and individuals. It uses bilateral and regional organizations to monitor and encourage compliance rather than develop a global multilateral regime focusing on technical assistance.[36] Of the $2.2 million given to the UN to implement technical assistance in CTF, the United States contributed less than 10 percent, while Austria alone made up over half of the contributions.[37] Indeed it appears that there is agreement at the political level in the United States that working through multilateral fora is "a waste of time."[38]

The sticks involve designations and sanctions (under Resolutions 1373, 1333, and 1267) and international pressure (FATF's list of NCCTs). States initially followed the United States' lead and designated individuals and entities that the United States had named under Executive Order 13224. But because of early U.S. errors and the widespread perception that designations were made for domestic political consumption, states—including almost all European states—now prefer to follow the UN's lead.[39] Some U.S. officials indicate that the Abu Ghraib scandal and the war in Iraq have lessened Middle Eastern countries' interest in working with the United States.[40]

U.S. threats of financial sanctions have produced some important changes in state behavior regarding freezing of assets and compliance with FATF standards. But in the cases of most concern to the United States, particularly Saudi Arabia, Indonesia, and the Philippines, U.S. officials indicate that it was the domestic experience of terrorism that has sparked real action on counter-terrorist financing. As one official commented, it was only after al Qaeda "fouled its own nest" that these states began to take action. Even then, the bulk of cooperation has not been in designations or bolstering implementation of the CTF regime, but in capturing and eliminating terrorist financiers.[41] U.S. officials have repeatedly stated that foreign governments do not see the institutional structures that facilitate terrorist financing as their problem, and that they do little to enforce anti-money laundering and terrorist financing measures.[42]

The prospects for sustaining international collaboration and solidifying a global CTF regime are mixed. On the one hand, ongoing terrorist attacks are continual reminders of the danger of allowing penetration of national and international financial systems. On the other, the major actors interested in, and necessary for, creating a CTF regime have different priorities, as exemplified by the manner in which the European Union has responded.[43]

At a basic level, the original EU members are vitally concerned with ensuring that new and old members improve their counter-terrorism laws. For them, 9/11, the 2004 Madrid bombings, and the 2005 London bombings demonstrate that Islamic radicalism is a homegrown threat not only to the United States but to Europe as well. Internationally, the Europeans emphasize a global, multilateral approach to AML-CTF standard-setting and technical assistance and downplay the utility of designations and asset freezes. They favor using the UN system to create a global counter-terrorist regime and address the root causes of terrorism. In cooperation with the United States, Europeans took measures to counter-terrorist financing after 9/11 and to improve their compliance with FATF standards.[44] However, they seem to have moved away from a willingness to focus on high-profile designations and toward an intelligence-based approach that emphasizes European and G8 information sharing.[45]

While formally supportive of the work of the UN, the United States has chosen to use UN instruments for the narrow purpose of targeting Islamist groups rather than combating terrorism more broadly, and has favored bilateral and regional information sharing and technical assistance in its list of "countries of concern" over global, multilateral efforts.[46] There is not the fundamental rift with Europe that exists on the broader U.S. willingness to unilaterally use force in waging its war on terror, yet the differences are significant enough to impede collective action to create a robust counter-terrorist financing regime. The United States seems to prefer the current patchwork approach of utilizing the multiple international frameworks (IMF–World Bank, FATF, 1267 Committee). The Europeans' interests are broader, seeking to create rule-of-law economies and attack the root causes of terrorism through multilateral best practices and technical assistance. Without U.S. interest in promoting and underwriting the costs of such a global regime, it is likely that collective action will fail to produce the public good of a global financial system that is less penetrable by terrorists.

U.S. Efforts to Combat Terrorist Financing Prior to September 11th

Prior to the 2001 attacks, there was no sustained, concerted effort by the United States to counter-terrorist financing. The 9/11 Commission Report and the 9/11 Commission Staff Monograph on Terrorist Financing paint a picture of disaggregated data collection, mistaken understandings regarding information sharing, conflicted organizational cultures, and interrupted attention spans that impeded the government and Congress from focusing on the issue of terrorism and how it was funded. The only governmental body consistently focused on the issue was the White House, particularly the National Security Council (NSC), which since 1985 has coordinated government efforts to counter terrorism.[47]

Terrorism was one of the first national security issues facing the new Clinton administration. In January 1993, two CIA employees were assassinated outside CIA headquarters in Virginia, and the next month, the World Trade Center was bombed.[48] In 1995, Clinton issued classified Presidential Decision Directive (PDD) 39, making detection and prevention of weapons of mass destruction (WMD) terrorism the highest priority for his staff and all agencies. In 1998, he gave NSC Counterterrorism Security Group (CSG) Director Richard Clarke direct access to cabinet level officials. He also issued two PDDs outlining 10 counter-terrorism programs and agency responsibilities. The Department of Justice and the FBI took the lead on the domestic front, while the CIA, the State Department, and others were responsible for the foreign front.[49]

Despite high-level attention and support from the President, the NSC was incapable of systematically engaging and directing a host of sub-units within various government agencies to address the problem of terrorism.[50] Because of the Attorney General's concerns, the CSG director was only authorized to give advice regarding budgets and to coordinate interagency guidelines for action, not direct agencies to take action.[51] One former NSC official suggested that this was the fundamental problem that prevented successful interagency coordination and action.[52] Ironically, the successful prosecution of the 1993 World Trade Center terrorists undermined the White House's efforts to reframe its approach to terrorism and terrorist financing.[53]

Throughout this period, knowledge specific to how terrorism finances worked was scarce and poorly sourced.[54] The CIA was aware that bin Laden had provided funds to several terrorist organizations but not that he was at the heart of a terrorist network. As late as 1997 it identified him merely as an extremist financier.[55] Because the National Security Advisor had expressed a personal interest in terrorist financing, the chief of the CIA's Directorate of Operations was able to set up a unit to track terrorist financial links in 1996. It focused solely on bin Laden, however, and quickly moved away from a focus on financial links to operational planning.[56]

The issue of terrorist financing gained more attention after the bombings of the U.S. embassies in Nairobi and Dar es Salaam in early August 1998. NSC Senior Director Clarke established an NSC-led interagency group on terrorist financing which also included the Treasury Department, CIA, FBI, and State Department. Although the CIA cooperated in this group, the FBI would not meaningfully participate.[57] The NSC alone maintained pressure on the Saudis for access to a suspected al Qaeda financial officer.[58] The President and the State Department, again after NSC urging, began to pressure Pakistan about its support for jihadists in Kashmir and for the Taliban. The President issued Executive Order 13099 freezing all financial holdings that could be associated with bin Laden.[59]

Despite the increased focus on CTF from the White House, there was little change in the behavior of federal agencies. The FBI was gathering intelligence against organizations suspected of raising funds for terrorists on a field-office level, with no centralized collection or sharing system in place.[60] In

March 2000, at Richard Clarke's urging, the Treasury Department became the home for a new Foreign Terrorist Asset Tracking Center (FTATC), a recommendation seconded by the independent Bremer Commission on Terrorism. President Clinton authorized its creation as part of a $300 million counter-terrorism initiative in May 2000, with $100 million designated for countering terrorist financing. Congress authorized FTATC's funding in October of that year. Yet neither Treasury nor the CIA was willing to commit resources for building the center. In spring 2001, National Security Advisor Condoleeza Rice approved the establishment of the office, but again the Treasury Department failed to follow through. After 9/11, the FTATC was hastily staffed in only three days.[61]

Despite the lack of coordinated effort within the executive branch prior to 9/11, there was an ad hoc system of laws, authorities, and regulations in place that addressed terrorist finances. These rules both criminalized the provision of funds to terrorists and provided the government the means to collect information with which to detect the flow of such funds. The 1990 Anti-Terrorism Act made the provision of material support, funding, and financial services for foreign terrorist organizations illegal. In 1995 the Clinton administration pushed for increased federal criminal laws, making it easier to deport terrorists and act against their fund-raisers. After the Aum Shinrikyo chemical weapons attack on the Tokyo subway and the Oklahoma City bombing, Clinton proposed increased wiretapping and electronic surveillance authority for the FBI and new funding for the FBI, CIA, and local police.[62] The 1996 Anti-Terrorism and Effective Death Penalty Act made the provision of support of terrorism a criminal act. It also allowed civil suits against any foreign state, state agency, or instrumentality that committed or aided in the commission of a terrorist act.[63] A series of anti-money laundering statutes made conducting financial transactions to further or to conceal criminal acts illegal.[64]

FINANCIAL INDUSTRY OBJECTIONS
AND EXECUTIVE DISCRETION

Despite these advances in CTF legislation, the financial industry blocked most efforts in the 1990s to strengthen the AML regime. The 1970 Bank Secrecy Act was the basis for an anti-money laundering legal framework, requiring banks to create audit trails of large transactions and to allow law enforcement access to the information or face criminal penalties. In 1985 the Federal Reserve and the Office of the Comptroller of the Currency began requiring financial institutions to submit suspicious activity reports (SARs). Determination of what constituted suspicious activity, however, fell to the discretion of bank employees. The Annunzio-Wylie Anti-Money Laundering Act of 1992 added Treasury to the list of agencies able to require SARs and, for the first time, required banks to keep records of wire transfers.[65]

However, the banking industry successfully defeated Treasury's initial attempts to specify exactly what information was to be collected on wire transfers. By preventing the creation of standardized records, the efficiency and speed with which law enforcement could access such information was significantly impaired.[66]

The Treasury Department lobbied for controls on foreign banks with U.S. accounts in 1999 and 2000, but despite bipartisan support in the House, the effort stalled in the Senate Banking Committee when the chair rejected further banking regulations.

In 1999 Treasury and federal regulators proposed know-your-customer requirements to ensure that banks would take reasonable steps to know the beneficial owner of an account and the sources of funds flowing through accounts. The result was a firestorm of controversy and resistance from the banking industry. Not only did the efforts fail, but Congress even considered weakening the existing money-laundering controls then in place.[67]

Opponents of these AML regulations argued that the requirements would do little to aid in the detection of terrorist funds, since they were designed to detect cash flows exceeding $10,000 and terrorist funds increasingly flow outside the formal financial system. Proponents replied that increased requirements, attention to suspicious activity reports, and standardized information retrieval were critical in identifying patterns of activity associated with terrorist financing and generating evidentiary trails for tracking terrorists.

The informal financial system—e.g., money remitters and other money services businesses—became increasingly important as money launderers and terrorists shifted their operations outside the formal financial system. Congress had authorized Treasury in 1994 to draw up regulations governing the informal sector. But additional efforts to regulate it were also thwarted. These regulations were not issued until 1999 with an implementation date of December 2001. In yet another delay, the Treasury Department announced in the summer of 2001 that implementation would take place in 2002.[68]

The most powerful legal tool in the counter-terrorist financing effort prior to 9/11 was the 1977 International Emergency Economic Powers Act (IEEPA). In times of national emergency derived from "unusual or extraordinary" foreign threats, the President could use PDDs to block U.S. imports from, and exports to, those individuals or organizations associated with that threat. Once the Office of Foreign Assets Control (OFAC) in the Department of the Treasury identified the designated individuals or entities, their U.S. bank accounts were frozen.

The courts have given the President wide latitude in using this authority since IEEPA is a law regarding foreign policy and national security and, therefore, a political rather than legal issue.[69] The United States had long used this tool to freeze the U.S. assets of states sponsoring terrorism, such as Iran, Libya, and Sudan. According to the 9/11 Commission staff, "in the 1990s the government began to use these powers in a different, more innovative way, to go after non-state actors."[70]

In 1995, President Clinton used his authority under IEEPA to freeze the U.S. assets of Colombian drug trafficking organizations and bar U.S. businesses from dealing with the traffickers or their front companies. The same year, President Clinton used it to sanction terrorists seeking to disrupt the Middle East Peace Process.[71]

OFAC had hoped to target bin Laden in this way but did not have access to the intelligence required to make the case until after the 1998 embassy bombings. At that time, the president formally designated bin Laden and al Qaeda. This had little practical effect, however, since bin Laden had moved most of his assets out of the formal financial system. When the president designated the Taliban in 1999 for harboring bin Laden and al Qaeda, Taliban assets worth over $34 million held in private U.S. banks and $217 million in gold and deposits held at the Federal Reserve were blocked.[72]

By the end of the Clinton presidency, non-state terrorists and their finances were recognized as serious threats to U.S. national security.[73] But this shift occurred only as a consequence of the terrorist attacks on the United States in 1993, 1998, and 2000.[74] Moreover, the White House was incapable of translating this recognition into a coordinated and effective domestic and international counter-terrorist effort.[75] Congress did not make this shift and continued to use sanctions against states as its principal tool.[76] This hindered the United States' ability to work with critical states such as Pakistan on suppressing al Qaeda and pressuring the Taliban.[77] Domestic ideological battles often interfered with serious attention to the issue,[78] and Congress reacted only in a minimal fashion to the attacks of the 1990s. According to the 9/11 Commission, "terrorism was a second- or third-order priority within the committees of Congress responsible for national security."[79] The new Bush administration did not begin its term with the understanding of non-state threats that the Clinton administration had acquired, and foreign policy priorities—such as national missile defense—were driven by the familiar paradigm that states posed the most serious threats facing the United States.[80]

U.S. Efforts to Combat Terrorist Financing after September 11th

The shock of the September 11, 2001, attacks caused radical changes in the way the United States framed and managed the issue of terrorist financing. Within days, federal bureaucracies came together in an effort to understand the financial basis of the attacks. Agencies immediately established new units to work on the problem and agreed to interagency cooperation.

The FBI, which was harshly criticized in the 9/11 Commission Staff Monograph for its failures prior to 9/11, established an interagency Financial Review Group—later known as the Terrorist Financing Operations Section (TFOS)—within days of the attacks. Its focus was on ensuring that the United States develop a real-time tracking capability for urgent financial investigations and that each terrorism investigation have a financial component. Most importantly, for the first time it coordinated the FBI's counterterrorist financing efforts in a single office.[81]

Other agencies followed the example. The U.S. Customs Service established Operation Green Quest to investigate terrorist financing. The Justice Department reallocated resources to create a unit devoted to pursuing and coordinating terrorist financing criminal investigations nationwide.[82] The CIA created a new interagency section to develop long-term intelligence on terrorist financing, to track terrorists, and to disrupt their operations. In 2003, the Joint Terrorism Task Force combined the investigative efforts of the FBI, Justice Department, Customs (now under the Department of Homeland Security), and the Internal Revenue Service.

After the attacks, the NSC immediately set up an ad hoc structure, which was replaced by a Policy Coordinating Committee (PCC) on Terrorist

Financing in March 2002.[83] An Independent Task Force on Terrorist Financing of the Council on Foreign Relations recommended that the NSC take the lead on the PCC because of the diplomatic and intelligence aspects of counter-terrorist financing. It also recommended that the administration designate a single point person for terrorist financing in the NSC to ensure the requisite level of priority and integration with the government's broader counter-terrorism strategy,[84] particularly with regard to Saudi Arabia.[85] As of late 2006, these recommendations have not been followed.

INTERAGENCY DISCORD

A number of bureaucratic battles developed in the aftermath of the September 11th attacks. The Treasury Department was at the center of most of them. Within the Treasury Department, the Office of Foreign Asset Control (OFAC) was hastily made the home of the Foreign Terrorist Assets Tracking Center (FTATC). Initially made up of the same agencies as Customs' Operation Green Quest, FTATC never fully functioned at Treasury. The CIA took over the operation, and in November 2002, the officially renamed Foreign Terrorist Asset Tracking Group (FTATG) was an independent entity administered by the CIA. Neither the Treasury Department nor its Financial Crimes Enforcement Center (FinCEN) detailed analysts to FTATG.

A second bureaucratic battle took place between the FBI's TFOS and the Customs Service's Operation Green Quest, overlapping interagency groups investigating terrorist financing. The formation of an FBI-led Joint Terrorism Task Force in 2003 resolved the problem by ensuring the continued participation of experts at Customs (now the Immigration and Customs Enforcement [ICE] branch of the Department of Homeland Security).[86]

A third bureaucratic battle between the State and Treasury Departments developed over which agency should lead the international effort to implement CTF measures via technical assistance.[87] After 9/11, an interagency Terrorist Finance Working Group (TFWG) was established. Co-chaired by the State Department's Office of the Coordinator for Counter Terrorism and the Bureau for International Narcotics and Law Enforcement Affairs, it reports to the NSC's Policy Coordinating Committee. The TFWG assists important countries in identifying weaknesses in financial systems and making them less vulnerable to terrorist manipulation. It provides technical assistance and training on establishing and implementing legal and regulatory frameworks that comply with UN Resolution 1373; creating financial intelligence and financial crimes units; and prosecuting and adjudicating terrorism finance crimes.[88]

At the same time, the Treasury Department's Office of Technical Assistance secured $2.2 million from Congress for counter-terrorism financing training. Not cooperating in the TFWG, Treasury has worked through Congress to take control in the PCC away from the NSC. It seeks to gain authority to lead in the TFWG in intelligence and operations, and in producing a counter-terrorist financing strategy report that emulates the State Department's *International Narcotics Control Strategy Report.*[89]

The State Department has resisted Treasury's efforts.[90] Officials at the State Department, FinCEN, and OFAC suggest that cooperation in providing technical assistance on counter-terrorist financing may be eroding because of problems with personalities, particularly in the Office of Technical Assistance. One FinCEN official called the TFWG "dysfunctional."[91] High-level Treasury officials continue to stress designations and freezing as key tools in the CTF fight. But working-level officials at the State Department and FinCEN point out that designations are largely ineffective, since funds move into alternative financial systems. Instead, they emphasize the importance of extending anti-money laundering efforts to these systems and using intelligence gathered from AML measures to track and to disrupt terrorist activities.[92]

Beneath these battles is a fundamental policy debate over which one of two strategies is most appropriate and effective in suppressing terrorist financing. The first approach focuses on designating and detaining terrorists and their associates, freezing their assets, and passing the necessary legislation to make such designations and freezes legal. The second, follow-the-money, strategy focuses on improving regulation of formal and informal financial systems and on enhanced intelligence collection, analysis, and sharing to track and disrupt terrorist operations.

One would expect from a bureaucratic politics model that different government actors would express distinct preferences regarding these strategies. Agencies with financial regulatory, anti-money laundering, and law enforcement powers—such as the Departments of Treasury and Justice—prefer the designation and asset freezing strategy. The White House, feeling pressure to demonstrate results, also prefers this approach, since designations are highly public and visible as those suspected of financing terrorists are rounded-up in sweeps as the designations are unsealed. The freezing of assets is quantifiable; it provides an easily-communicated measure of the government's success in vigorously suppressing terrorism.

In contrast, the intelligence community prefers the follow-the-money approach. This strategy offers greater potential for tracking and killing or capturing terrorists, as well as for providing the data necessary to build terrorist profiles. For the foreign affairs agencies, the covert nature of this intelligence strategy increases the government's flexibility in working with foreign countries, as secret assistance may be more forthcoming than a public show of support. For the financial services industry, the intelligence strategy means that tighter government regulations are less likely, or, at a minimum, that publicity regarding their cooperation with government authorities regarding client information is less prominent.

Although the strategies are not mutually exclusive, single-minded reliance on one can seriously impede the effectiveness of the other. Resources are not infinite. The bureaucratic interests within each strategy create a tendency among agencies to withhold information and guard organizational prerogatives. The 9/11 Commission reported that bureaucratic compartmentalization and turf battles that existed prior to 9/11 represented massive failures in detecting and preventing terrorist attacks.[93]

Early in the Bush administration, the designation-freeze approach to combating terrorist financing dominated, though both strategies were pursued.[94] Under his IEEPA authority, President Bush issued Executive Order 13224 designating bin Laden and al Qaeda and authorizing the freezing of assets of entities associated with them, calling it the "first strike in the war on terror." This order affirmed OFAC's authority, derived from Clinton-era executive orders, to go after bin Laden's and al Qaeda's assets.

In October 2001, President Bush signed the Patriot Act into law. It significantly expanded the government's regulatory authority, especially within the Treasury Department, regarding money laundering and criminal finance. The know-your-customer and wire transfer requirements, which had been defeated by the banking industry in 2000, went into effect. Giving power to the Department of the Treasury to designate countries or business sectors that fail to meet minimum anti-money laundering standards, it can impose sanctions and other special measures—such as restricting countries' or financial institutions' access to the U.S. financial system.[95] In addition, the

Patriot Act empowered the Director of Treasury's OFAC to freeze assets before legally sufficient evidence had been collected.[96] After the attacks, OFAC used names provided by the CIA to add feverishly to the designations list and to make high-level, public announcements on the freezing of terrorist assets. As the 9/11 Report put it:

> The goal set at the policy levels of the White House and Treasury was to conduct a public and aggressive series of designations to show the world community and our allies that we were serious about pursuing the financial targets. It entailed a major designation every four weeks. . . . Treasury officials acknowledged that the evidentiary foundations for the early designations were quite weak. . . . The rush to designate came primarily from the NSC.[97]

The White House, the Secretary of the Treasury, and the Attorney General all trumpeted these actions. The intelligence supporting some of the highest-profile designations was seriously flawed from a legal perspective, and the volume of money disrupted was significantly overstated.[98] In August 2002, under pressure from allies and some U.S. citizens, the United States was forced into the embarrassing position of removing some foreigners from the lists.[99] It was also unable to attain a conviction on a terrorism charge for a leader of an Illinois charity.[100] One State Department official described the initial post-9/11 designations as a political process driven by "the need for public action and the availability of a hammer."[101] The CIA reasoned that the designations would have little or no effect on terrorists, who would simply move their funds to other non-designated institutions. It reportedly successfully pressed for more attention to the follow-the-money strategy.[102]

The debate over strategies in turn depends on how closely one identifies the problem of terrorist financing with that of state responsibility and control. The powers granted to regulators and the Treasury under the Patriot Act are anti-money laundering tools, designed for tracking large sums of money.[103] But these sums are tiny when placed in the context of a global financial system through which many billions of dollars move every day. The Clinton Treasury Department learned this when it sought to freeze bin Laden's assets. Unable to gain sufficient information on these assets—in large measure because the fund-raising for al Qaeda was dispersed and commingled with legitimate humanitarian donations[104]—it sought anti-money laundering tools from Congress more appropriate to finding terrorist finances, but to no avail.

After its early missteps in pursuing the designations strategy, the Bush administration began emphasizing the intelligence strategy.[105] In June 2006 the *New York Times* reported that secret monitoring of the SWIFT financial database—the central hub for global banking transactions—led to the arrest of the alleged mastermind of the 2002 Bali nightclub bombings.[106] Designations have declined, as have the amounts of frozen assets.[107] The change in emphasis suggests that the Bush administration is beginning to reach conclusions similar to the Clinton administration regarding states' capabilities in controlling non-state terrorists, at least in the area of counter-terrorism finance. Rather than emphasizing a state's power and responsibility to shut down terrorists' access to finances, a gradual understanding of the need for comprehensive financial regulation and information is developing— though its robustness is subject to the turf battles discussed above. However, no comprehensive anti-terrorist financing policy exists in the United States, and resources have not been dedicated to the government's broad goals.[108]

Conclusion

What does the U.S. effort to counter-terrorist financing augur for the global effort? By all accounts, the horror of the September 11th attacks galvanized government bureaucracies and broke down interagency walls that had withstood lesser challenges.[109] Interagency cooperation, as well as the banking industry's cooperation with the government, was unprecedented in the immediate aftermath of the attacks. This cooperation remains a marked improvement over the pre-9/11 situation.

But there are strong indicators that the passage of time may erode the political will to put the national interest ahead of private and bureaucratic ones. Working-level officials repeat that "we're not going to be the reason 9/11 happens again," and this makes them willing to encourage the interagency process.[110] But they worry that the issue of counter-terrorist financing has slipped in the hierarchy of priorities at higher levels of government.[111] This concern is echoed in high-profile criticism from outside of government.[112] Interagency cooperation that was unprecedented immediately after 9/11 has eroded. The U.S. effort to counter-terrorist financing is being funded largely through reallocations from other budget lines rather than through a significant new budgetary commitment.[113] Banks are reportedly experiencing "blocking fatigue." The international community is willing to act only under UN designations, and U.S. actions in Iraq have made some states reluctant to follow the U.S. lead in implementing and enforcing legislative changes.[114] U.S. willingness to underwrite technical assistance to enforce the CTF regime has been minimal ($20–30 million since 2001) in comparison with funding for the broader U.S. war on terrorism.

However, the United States and its European allies have succeeded in globalizing the anti-money laundering framework and re-casting it as a regime to combat terrorist financing. But the U.S. domestic approach to the problem of terrorist financing has changed in the period since 2001, and its international efforts reflect this shift. Its international efforts now focus more on sharing intelligence with other states to track, capture, or kill important terrorist finance figures using bilateral pressure on a small number of countries rather than underwriting a global multilateral regime.[115] While there has been substantial and important movement through informal international bodies such as FATF and the Egmont Group, the United States has not supported the work of the UN's Counter-Terrorism Committee. Unwilling to underwrite a formal counter-terrorist financing regime under Resolution 1373, the United States has focused on the narrower issue of al Qaeda under Resolution 1267.

Fundamentally, the United States has devoted the majority of its attention internationally to the global war on terror, which it defines to include the war in Iraq. The United States' international efforts on terrorist financing illustrate that the war on terror is not really global for the United States but is focused on 20 states where al Qaeda and other Islamic terrorists operate. The United States has committed the bulk of its counter-terrorist financing efforts on targeted groups and individuals, rather than on building a robust international regime. The prospect for successful global development of national institutional capacities, therefore, seems to depend on states' recognition that terrorist financing is their problem, too, not just a United States problem.

The developed countries, with the most domestic capacity to combat terrorist financing, recognize this threat. Even they, however, have been inconsistent in their willingness to enforce counter-terrorist finance laws and engage in international cooperation. Less-developed countries without this capacity often do not even see the threat. Redefining the national interest to include countering terrorist finance unfortunately appears to rise and fall with states' experience of terrorist attacks.[116] Without such attacks, and without Western pressure and incentives to do so, it is unlikely that states will take the requisite steps to build and enforce an effective global counter-terrorist financing regime.

CHAPTER SIXTEEN

Terrorist Financing

Explaining Government Responses

JEANNE K. GIRALDO AND HAROLD A. TRINKUNAS

Tougher norms against terrorism and terrorism financing have propagated rapidly since the September 11, 2001, attacks in New York and Washington. UN and U.S. actions have greatly strengthened the international regime against terrorism financing. Most UN member states have become parties to the International Convention for the Suppression of the Financing of Terrorism and many have passed legislation criminalizing terrorism financing. Since the attacks, terrorism finance has also moved high on the agenda of key financial institutions, such as the G-8's Financial Action Task Force (FATF) and, increasingly, the World Bank and International Monetary Fund (IMF). Yet despite this increased agreement on the need to attack terrorist finances, the evidence reviewed in this volume suggests that there are still significant shortfalls in the implementation and execution of counter-terrorism finance (CTF) policies. At the same time, there is a growing debate over the effectiveness of CTF measures, which contributes to the increasing unwillingness of key governmental and private sector actors to cooperate.

While there are some shortcomings in the promotion of the new CTF regime by the U.S. and international actors, we argue that the most important source of divergence in government responses is domestic factors: variations in government perception of the effectiveness of counter-terrorism financing policies, variations in resistance to CTF policies by domestic constituencies, and variations in state capacity to implement and execute the prevailing counter-terrorism finance strategy. Essentially, we argue that while the emerging international regime pushes all member states to at least address the issue of countering terrorism financing, this result is filtered by domestic factors that determine whether a country actively and effectively addresses this threat.

This chapter reviews the evolution of counter-terrorism finance policies, comparing the periods before and after the September 11, 2001, terrorist attacks to highlight the development of a common international response to the threat. The chapter will then examine the obstacles to crafting sustained international cooperation in this arena, including the domestic sources of variation in terrorism finance policies around the globe. Finally, we identify the emerging debates over the adequacy of the prevailing post-9/11 policies and raise the question of whether it is possible to measure the effectiveness of these policies.

The Evolution of Government Responses to Terrorism Financing

Countering terrorism financing was a low priority for the United States, most of its allies, and international institutions prior to the 9/11 terrorist attacks. To the extent financing was addressed, the focus was on drying up the sources of terrorists' money rather than identifying and dismantling the financial networks themselves. Governments worked to pressure the states or groups that sponsored terrorism rather than to find the money as it moved through offshore accounts and underground financial channels. Diplomatic pressure and the blocking of state sponsors' assets under the International Emergency Economic Powers Act of 1977 were the earliest tools used to fight terrorist finances. As it became evident that states were not the only sponsors of terrorism, governments began to take a somewhat broader view of the problem, targeting the criminal activities and individuals that financed terrorism.

The United Kingdom was one of the first to realize the importance of focusing on the criminal activities that provided financial support for terrorist organizations. As the Irish Republican Army switched from high-risk bank robberies to extortion, fraud, and tax evasion to fund their operations in the early 1980s, the British created a Terrorist Financing Unit that employed individuals well versed in financial investigative techniques.[1] The United States was much slower to acknowledge the link between criminal activities and terrorist financing; even though the Reagan administration linked the drug trade to "terrorists" in Colombia in the 1980s, this recognition served mainly to delegitimize the rebels rather than to signal a new counter-terrorist strategy.

By the end of the 1990s, governments were increasingly focused on individual sponsors of terrorism and terrorist organizations themselves. In 1996, the United States passed the Law on Material Support to Terrorist Organizations, which criminalized terrorist financing and, after the 1998 African embassy bombings, used Executive Orders to freeze assets linked to Osama bin Laden. In 1999 the UN began to specifically establish a legal framework to counter-terrorist financing through the establishment the UN Convention against Terrorist Finances and through Security Council action (UNSC 1267) against al Qaeda and the Taliban regime in Afghanistan, as Victor Comras discusses in chapter 7 in this volume.

U.S. implementation and enforcement of terrorist financing provisions lagged substantially throughout the period as these efforts ran into opposition from civil liberties organizations, the financial sector, and political actors. FBI investigations into terrorist financing were hampered by a lack of international cooperation, the perceived inability to commingle information produced by intelligence operations and criminal investigations, and sensitivity to charges of profiling if it singled out Islamic organizations and charities for investigation. Furthermore, FBI headquarters did not systematically track and analyze information provided by field offices in counter-terrorist financing investigations, as the 9/11 Commission later discovered, and the Department of Justice also had no national program for using such information as was available to successfully prosecute terrorism financing cases.[2] At the same time, U.S. intelligence agencies—which did not share the FBI's focus on traditional investigative techniques—failed even to undertake the necessary initial investigations into terrorist finances. As early as 1995, the CIA was tasked by the National Security Council to track the finances of al Qaeda, but the mission was deemed to be "too hard."[3] Instead, the working group that was supposed to track al Qaeda's finances defaulted to a task that fell more comfortably within the intelligence agency's "comfort zone"—tracking Osama bin Laden.

Following the 9/11 terrorist attacks on the United States, restricting terrorist access to resources became a priority for many governments and international organizations. In fact, targeting terrorist finance was the first response to the attacks by the Bush administration. Seizing terrorist assets and publicly designating terrorism supporters was meant to signal to both terrorists and the public that the United States was determined to respond quickly.

These measures represented a continued reliance on basic anti-money laundering tools that had been adapted for counter-terrorism purposes in the late 1990s, as Anne Clunan details in chapter 15 of this volume. By the end of September 2001, the Bush administration had issued Presidential Order 13224, which expanded government powers to freeze terrorist assets and established a list of organizations and persons to be targeted. The USA Patriot Act Title III enhanced regulatory oversight of financial institutions, increased identification requirements for users, closed loopholes that previously existed for foreign correspondent bank accounts, and generally required greater record keeping. A number of U.S. government agencies activated task forces to deal with the problem of terrorist financing; these included the FBI's Terrorism Financing Operations Section (TFOS); the long delayed interagency Foreign Terrorist Assets Tracking Group (FTATG) all-source intelligence center; and Operation Green Quest that brought together Customs and Treasury officials.

Other priority targets of the U.S. government after the September 2001 attacks were Islamic charities and *hawala*s suspected of serving as funding sources and financial channels for moving terrorist money. The FBI had begun investigating a number of individual charities and *hawaldars* during the 1990s (often in response to suspicious activity reports filed by financial institutions), but its investigations did not gain urgency until the attacks occurred. The immediate result was the closure of some significant charities and the prosecution of their leadership, although questions were later raised about the accuracy of the investigations.[4] The more important long-term result was that the U.S. government and international organizations began to devise and promote regulatory frameworks that would prevent the abuse of charities and *hawala*s by terrorist financiers (and other criminals).

Internationally, the United Nations Security Council, which had been monitoring al Qaeda activities since 1999, adopted a similar strategy in its early response to the 9/11 attacks by mandating worldwide criminalization of terrorist financing activities through its resolutions 1373 and 1390. By

September 11, 2004, nearly $142 million in terrorist assets had been seized by governments worldwide.[5] FATF joined in this strategy by issuing nine special recommendations on terrorist financing to reinforce its pre-existing list of 40 anti-money laundering "best practices."[6] Police and intelligence efforts in Spain, France, Germany, and the United Kingdom have identified and broken up significant al Qaeda support cells and prosecuted their membership, in part by following the money trail generated by the attacks.

The attacks of September 11, 2001, galvanized international action against terrorism. Although the General Assembly had passed the Convention for the Suppression of the Financing of Terrorism in December of 1999, only four countries had become parties to the Convention prior to September 11, 2001.[7] By December of 2003, that number had increased to 106 and, two years later, to 149 countries. Of the 200 countries and territories monitored by the U.S. State Department for money laundering and terrorist financing activities, 65 percent (130 of 200) had ratified the Convention by the end of 2004 (a total that increased to 73 percent by the end of 2005).[8] In addition, 61 percent of the countries and territories monitored by the United States (123 of 203) had passed laws criminalizing terrorist financing by the end of 2005.[9]

Despite this impressive adherence to international treaties and norms, more costly implementation efforts lag behind. A significant number of states have yet to develop the complicated and expensive enforcement apparatus required for effectively tracking terrorist finances. We see evidence of this dynamic confirmed in the regional case studies in this volume on East Africa, South America, and Southeast Asia.[10] Although significant strides have been made in building administrative capacity since 2001 (the number of Financial Intelligence Units worldwide increased from 55 to 101 in only four years), only two-fifths of the countries monitored by the United States have both criminalized terrorist financing and created the Financial Intelligence Units (FIUs) that might contribute to enforcing this legislation.[11] Even where FIUs exist, their capacity to enforce CTF norms has been called into question.

Explaining Government Responses to Terrorism Financing

At the most basic level, whether or not a government complies with a set of international prescriptions for addressing a problem will depend on how governing elites perceive the costs and benefits associated with the policies.

External factors, in particular the ability of international institutions and the United States to provide incentives for cooperation with suggested norms and to monitor compliance, affect the costs and benefits associated with CTF policies. At one level, external capacity to influence counter-terrorist financing policies is fairly well developed, given the relative newness of activity in this area. The United States and international institutions have been able to build on an anti-money laundering apparatus that had been in place for more than a decade prior to the 2001 terrorist attacks to promote CTF policies, though their efforts have been slowed by missteps and infighting.

The more significant challenge for advocates of an international regime is that CTF policies seem to provoke somewhat greater levels of domestic resistance than do other counter-terrorism policies. Even though the 9/11 attacks had a galvanizing effect on U.S. leaders and attracted widespread sympathy for the United States from the world community, the consequence has not been the development of a consensus on the desirability of adopting counter-terrorism finance policies. Countries such as the Philippines and Indonesia that have been willing to cooperate with the United States in the investigation and arrest of suspected terrorists have been reluctant to implement tougher counter-terrorism financing legislation. John Lombardi and David Sanchez note in chapter 13 that Paraguayan officials were willing to investigate and arrest terrorist financiers, yet the country has been slow to adopt CTF legislation such as the criminalization of terrorist financing or to create a system for asset forfeiture. As is detailed below, this reluctance can be explained by the perceived weakness of the link between certain assets and terrorist attacks, the power of well-placed groups that oppose such legislation, and the complexity of monitoring terrorist finances that overwhelms the bureaucratic capacity of most states.

EXTERNAL FACTORS

The flurry of CTF activities in the period since the end of 2001 can be attributed in large part to the importance the United States and international organizations have assigned to terrorist financing. The G-8's Financial Action Task Force (FATF) and the Egmont Group, an umbrella group for financial intelligence units created in 1989 for anti-money laundering purposes, have been successful at promulgating minimum common standards for AML and CTF, but they lack enforcement powers beyond a "name and shame" strategy. The reduction of the FATF list of Non-Cooperative Countries and Territories from 23 to 1 since 2001 (only Myanmar is still on the list as of September 2006) suggests some success using this strategy. For example, this approach was significant in gaining compliance from Egypt and Lebanon, as Moyara Ruehsen shows in chapter 9, and from Indonesia and the Philippines. The International Monetary Fund and the World Bank have since entered the picture, replacing FATF's blacklist with their own efforts to assess compliance with the FATF's 40 recommendations on anti-money laundering and the 9 recommendations for combating the financing of terrorism. The UN Security Council has had some success in making information about individual state compliance with international CTF requirements more readily available than in the past, but it has made little headway in enforcing compliance.[12]

Despite these advances, there have also been some shortcomings. There is evidence that the U.S. emphasis on freezing assets, and the way in which this policy has been implemented, initially undermined cooperation in the broader fight against terrorist finances. For example, U.S. efforts to extend the list of targets beyond al Qaeda to include groups such as Hezbollah and Hamas, which commingle an apparatus of violence aimed at Israel with charitable and social service enterprises, quickly provoked both government and popular suspicion in the Middle East, as Ruehsen argues in chapter 9. Hasty and sometimes erroneous designations by the United States of certain Islamic charities, organizations, and individuals as supporters of terrorism contributed to creating public sentiment against the policy and made U.S. partners more cautious about sharing information and coordinating responses.[13] Furthermore, the United States has placed a premium on actionable intelligence leading to the removal of assets from the hands of terrorists rather than meeting the legal requirements that might generate successful prosecutions. This may be inhibiting intelligence and security cooperation with U.S. partners, particularly when evidence produced by U.S. CTF policies is considered classified and cannot be used to support legal prosecutions in foreign courts.[14]

Finally, it is not clear that U.S. efforts to support other countries in their crafting and implementation of CTF policies have been as coordinated and well-funded as possible. The State Department and Treasury continue to squabble for control over these support activities, and it is difficult to know how much money is devoted to these efforts, since budgets are either classified or not broken down into appropriate categories, but recent reports suggest that there are not enough qualified personnel to meet the overseas training needs.[15]

DOMESTIC FACTORS

The cases analyzed in this volume suggest that there are three domestic factors that influence the development and implementation of CTF policy: (1) the perceptions held by domestic political leaders of the costs and benefits of CTF policies; (2) the role of domestic political and social constituencies in influencing the formulation and implementation of CTF policies; and (3) the capacity of states to implement and enforce counter-terrorism finance prescriptions.

First, governing elites vary greatly in the extent to which they perceive CTF polices as beneficial. As chapter 10 by Loretta Napoleoni and chapter 15 by Clunan highlight, there is considerable disagreement between the United States and Europe. Lombardi and Sanchez in chapter 13 report difficulties with developing a policy consensus within and among democratic states in their case study of the South American Tri-Border region. Some countries are unwilling to admit that terrorist financing is a problem within their borders. Brazil, for example, dismisses notions that the Tri-Border Area is a "haven" for terrorist financiers, in part out of a desire to protect the tourist industry in the area. Similarly, Malaysia denies charges that front companies have operated in its territory and has refused to take action against them.

Other elites may be willing to address terrorism within their countries but do not see CTF policies as a cost-effective means to do so, and they may even fear that such policies would undermine their own power bases. Kenya, Indonesia, and the Philippines have all suffered from terrorist attacks, but they still lag in addressing terrorism financing due to domestic concerns over the broader impact of CTF measures on the less savory aspects of their political financing arrangements. Even countries such as Paraguay that have not experienced terrorist attacks but cooperate with the United States to combat the threat exhibit a reluctance to pursue CTF due to such concerns. Ruehsen's chapter 9 on Mideast government responses and Aurel Croissant and Daniel Barlow's analysis in chapter 12 of Southeast Asian responses also reveal political elites that are reluctant to become closely identified with the very broad scope of U.S. counter-terrorism finance policies or simply consider efforts in this area to be unrewarding. In the absence of political leadership, it is difficult to imagine that any country would develop an effective counter-terrorism finance strategy, particularly if we consider the next two domestic obstacles to policy formulation.

Second, the presence and strength of political and social actors who oppose CTF policies varies by country and region, ranging from radical movements in Muslim-majority states in the Middle East and Southeast Asia, to minority Muslim communities in Brazil and the United Kingdom, to human rights organizations and leading financial institutions in Europe and the United States that oppose the policies on privacy and civil liberty grounds. The institutional setting for policy making shapes which actors will have a veto over terrorism financing policy. For example, the analysis of CTF policies in Southeast Asia suggests that part of the variation can be explained by the contrast between the simplified decision-making processes of relatively authoritarian states, such as Singapore, with that of more democratic states where a much wider array of constitutional and political constraints slows the development of policy responses, as was initially the case in Indonesia and the Philippines. Croissant and Barlow's analysis in chapter 12 also suggests that party politicians may be opposed to the anti-money laundering content of contemporary CTF policy, since it would tend to reveal the questionable aspects of their own sources of financing. The role of regime type and the influence of domestic politics are supported by evidence from the other cases in this volume. The preferences and proclivities for action by veto players are therefore an important part of the cost-benefit calculation made by every state in developing its response to terrorism financing.

Finally, differences in state capacity across countries shape the effectiveness of CTF regimes. Implementing CTF policies, particularly those based on anti-money laundering techniques, requires providing additional resources, analytical systems, and trained personnel to relevant bureaucratic agencies, particularly financial intelligence units and banking regulators. For some of the cases surveyed in this volume, this level of state capacity is not available. States as diverse as Afghanistan, Cambodia, Kenya, and Paraguay simply lack the resources to dedicate to counter-terrorist financing activities, even if they had the political will to implement an aggressive policy. Even if the resources were available, it is not clear that political elites would prioritize expenditures on CTF policies over health care, education, and social welfare.

This is not to say that high-capacity advanced industrialized democracies do not also face their own seemingly intractable obstacles to generating a coherent and effective response. It is unclear what additional resources the United States has devoted to CTF, since it expects agencies to allocate personnel and funding to the effort within the scope of their existing budgets. In addition, organizational theory clearly predicts that government agencies should compete for resources and policy control at the expense of coordinated government action. Credit for successful interagency efforts is either shared with other agencies or monopolized by the agency housing the coordinating task force, thus discouraging real cooperation. One example of this is the Foreign Terrorist Asset Targeting Group (FTATG), which had been funded by Congress to function as lead intelligence group on terrorism financing yet lacked both a director and deputy director until November 2004 and relied on five temporary personnel seconded from other agencies to carry out its function.[16] As already mentioned, the departments of State and Treasury have been unable to cooperate on international support efforts. There is no reason to expect that other states would not also experience similar interagency and bureaucratic conflicts over policy implementation.

Evaluating the Effectiveness of CTF Policies after 9/11

Although there has been a great deal of activity on the CTF front since the end of 2001, it is not clear how effective these measures have been in disrupting terrorist activities. Much of the initial policy debate focused on the U.S. emphasis on freezing assets, an effort that quickly stalled. The much-touted $142 million in frozen terrorist assets has not changed very much since the end of 2002, and as of September 11, 2004, the United States had frozen only $4.5 million in al Qaeda–related funds, while other governments had frozen less than $72 million in suspected al Qaeda assets.[17] Yet, this represents a small portion of the reputed hundreds of millions of dollars raised yearly by groups such as al Qaeda, Hezbollah, Salafist Group for Prayer and

Combat (SGPC), Jemaah Islamiyah (JI) and other transnational jihadi organizations. Either terrorist financial assets have been grossly overstated in available open-source reports, or government efforts are missing their targets. It is likely that the truth lies somewhere in the middle.

As Raphael Perl notes in chapter 14, a policy of freezing terrorist assets has a number of useful features, which include denying terrorists access to assets needed to conduct further attacks, chilling the inclination of private individuals or organizations to donate funds to questionable (possibly terrorist-supporting) organizations, and raising public morale. However, the relative paucity of new freezing actions against terrorist assets and the need to gather actionable intelligence by tracking rather than seizing funds suggests that the U.S. government should complement the asset-freezing strategy with an intelligence-based approach—a shift recommended by Phil Williams in chapter 5 and by the 9/11 Commission. By all indications, such a shift has occurred, although—given the secrecy of intelligence operations—the benefits of such an approach are likely to be even more difficult to measure than those associated with asset-freezing and AML approaches.

The other major policy debate since the September 11 attacks has focused on whether anti-money laundering regulations are useful in attacking terrorist financial structures. Although the anti-money laundering effort has been notably useful in the forensic stage of reconstructing the money trail leading to terrorist attacks in New York, Nairobi, and Madrid, some have begun to question how much emphasis should be placed on this dimension of government policy. The anti-money laundering effort, which includes the FATF special recommendations on terrorist finances at the international level and the USA Patriot Act's tougher reporting requirements, has generated an unmanageable flood of data for government agencies. Even in the United States, the Financial Crimes Enforcement Network (FinCEN) and the Internal Revenue Service (IRS) report difficulties in handling the increased workload generated by new regulations. This problem is compounded by the tendency of private institutions to report all suspicious activity, no matter how trivial, to avoid blame for future intelligence failures. The growing costs and workload have not been matched by increased appropriations, in the case of government entities, or increased profits in the private sector.[18] Increased data collection in the absence of increased capability to process it makes it very difficult to produce useful and proactive intelligence based on anti-money laundering techniques.

The difficulty of using an anti-money laundering approach is increased by the fact that terrorist attacks tend to cost relatively small amounts of money, and most of these funds are not necessarily in need of laundering. It cost less than a half million dollars to conduct the 9/11 attacks and perhaps a tenth as much for the Madrid train attacks. In the case of Madrid, the operation was partially supported by the proceeds of local drug trafficking activities that were never laundered.[19] Most of the funding for the 9/11 attacks also does not appear to have required much in the way of money laundering services. Terrorists can relatively easily structure their financial movements to evade triggering suspicious activity reports, particularly since the triggers are relatively well-known. Detecting terrorist money in the midst of the vast daily flows of legitimate and criminal international financial transactions is thus a daunting task for which anti-money laundering techniques are not necessarily appropriate.

Others believe that asset seizures and AML-based measures can be effective but acknowledge that these efforts have been undermined by inconsistent implementation. As Napoleoni notes in chapter 10, individuals blacklisted as terrorist financiers by the United Nations have been permitted to travel freely and conduct business in Western Europe. She also suggests that increased regulations in the United States has merely led terrorist financiers to shift their operations to Europe.

The official U.S. government position is that terrorist financing has become "riskier, more costly, and more time-consuming" as a result of CTF efforts, and it is difficult to disagree with this assessment. *Inter alia*, assets have been frozen, financial intermediaries captured, and charities shut down, thus increasing the losses compared to the past and forcing efforts to circumvent these measures (e.g., reconstituting charities under new names). However, the real question is one of measuring the *degree* of effectiveness. Both critics and proponents of current counter-terrorist financing efforts assume that terrorists have responded rationally to increased government regulations and enforcement by shifting to activities and areas of the world that are relatively less regulated. Many argue that terrorists in general and al Qaeda in particular have come to rely increasingly on crime and cash couriers in the post-9/11 era as other means of financing and funds transfer are targeted. Some have argued that the al Qaeda network, to the extent that it still exists, relies less on Middle East sources of funding—which have come under increased scrutiny—and more on fund-raising in the relatively more lenient environs of

Southeast Asia.[20] It is important to note that, despite the plausibility of these arguments, there is little hard evidence to support them—or any other argument that terrorists have lessened their reliance on any one set of activities in favor of another. Critics cite the terrorists' ability to adapt as a sign of the futility of CTF efforts; proponents cite it as evidence of the effectiveness of existing policies and the need for additional measures.

It is difficult to determine which of these two positions is correct. The available evidence indicates that terrorists are adaptable and tend to have a variety of funding sources at their disposal. However, as chapter 2 by Nikos Passas makes clear, the overall revenues or relative importance of different types of financing for any one terrorist group cannot be determined with any certainty. Without this information, it is difficult to know where to focus CTF activities and whether or not they will have any impact on terrorist operations. More generally, analysts have been unable to devise useful "measures of effectiveness" in the fight against terrorist finances.[21] CTF policies are said to deter individuals from supporting terrorists, but deterrence is notoriously difficult to measure. As with other illicit activities such as money laundering, the secrecy of terrorist financing activities means that the evidence available about effectiveness is only fragmentary and inconclusive.

While the benefits of CTF policies are uncertain, the costs of poorly implemented or conceived efforts are often easier to measure in terms of the eroding public support for these policies. To the extent that the operation of charities and non-profit organizations is made more difficult by CTF measures, the provision of social services in poor regions can be gravely affected. Individual rights are easily undermined by administrative measures for seizing assets that require lower standards of proof than legal procedures and that often offer little recourse to their targets. The costs of implementing CTF measures in financial institutions are easily measured in dollar terms, but the private sector is given little feedback on the usefulness of this information. In contrast, reports are frequent comparing the mountains of information collected and the lack of leads developed.

Conclusion

This volume identifies the nature of the debates surrounding terrorism financing and government response, and we see a clear pattern of trends that date from well before the September 2001 attacks: terrorist organizations have been diversifying their funding sources for some time now, and this has meant that some have managed to evade the constraints imposed by external sponsorship and are thus able to generate more frequent and deadlier attacks. We also see evidence that terrorist organizations have managed to adapt, at least partially, to government policies, evidence that provides at least one measure of the impact of counter-terrorism efforts. We also note throughout this volume that governments, regardless of variations in the availability of resources and their willingness to combat terrorism, continue to face problems of international and interagency coordination and cooperation.

There are a number of possible solutions to the problems identified in this chapter. The first is to improve the cost-benefit ratio for states for participating in the CTF regime. This could be done through a structure of incentives (policies and resources) that provides benefits to states for cooperating with international counter-terrorism norms, allows them to pay off domestic veto players, and increases the costs of non-compliance. The international community would need to pay greater attention to funding regional CTF enforcement mechanisms, and it would also lead us to recommend that the United States assume more of the burden of supporting such multilateral cooperation. However, given the recent focus within the U.S. government on burden sharing with international partners, as evidenced by the 2005 report by the Government Accountability Office[22] and the reluctance among foreign governments to appear to cooperate too closely with the United States on unpopular aspects of the war on terrorism, this seems unlikely.

The second set of solutions is more nuanced and involves understanding the nature of the veto players in key countries and finding policy approaches that are good fits with their preferences on CTF policies, although this may prevent developing a coordinated global policy that would mitigate terrorist jurisdiction shopping. One example would be to build a stronger public-private partnership and consensus on terrorism financing policy, which might ameliorate the regulatory burden on financial institutions and reduce their defensive oversupply of information to government regulators. Another example would be to work closely with other countries to establish acceptable policies to regulate the financial transactions of *hawaladars* or charitable organizations in ways that accommodate local veto players and allow innocent participants to continue to reap the social benefits provided by these groups. These types of activities would reduce the political costs to government leaders of cooperating with the international CTF regime.

A third set of solutions would look at alternatives to the current CTF policies, particularly the intelligence-centered approach recommended by Phil Williams in chapter 5. Although this approach does have some disadvantages, it may provide governments with greater insights into the nature of the current terrorism networks, aid intelligence agencies in uncovering the scope and breadth of financial infrastructure, and, paradoxically, avoid many of the constraints imposed by local veto players due to its covert nature. However, it is clear that special attention would have to be paid to measuring the effectiveness of such a policy shift and addressing oversight requirements by participating governments and agencies. Such questions have already been raised in the media following the revelation in 2006 of U.S. government monitoring of international financial transactions using the SWIFT network, based in Belgium, as Phil Williams points out.

Notes

1. See, for example, Bruce Hoffman, *Inside Terrorism* (New York: Columbia University Press, 1999); and Ian Lesser, Bruce Hoffman, John Arquilla, David Ronfeldt, and Michele Zanini, *Countering the New Terrorism* (Santa Monica, CA: RAND, 1999).

2. The overview of terrorism financing by Nikos Passas in this volume is representative of this approach.

3. See, for example, U.S. Department of State, *Patterns of Global Terrorism 1996*, April 1997, available at http://www.fas.org/irp/threat/terror_96/index.html; Deborah McCarthy, "Narco-Terrorism: International Drug Trafficking and Terrorism: A Dangerous Mix," testimony of the Deputy Assistant Secretary for International Narcotics and Law Enforcement Affairs, U.S. Department of State, before the U.S. Senate Judiciary Committee, May 20, 2003; Thomas M. Sanderson, "Transnational Terror and Organized Crime: Blurring the Lines," *SAIS Review* 24, no. 1 (Winter/Spring 2004), 49–61; and "Countering the Terror-Crime Nexus," *Jane's Intelligence Review*, April 1, 2002, reporting on findings of a conference hosted by the Asia-Pacific Center for Security Studies. ("It was unanimously agreed that the end of the Cold War directly resulted in the decline of state sponsorship for terrorist groups, which led to a search for alternative financial sources.")

4. The discussion of state sponsorship throughout this section, as in the terrorism financing literature, is focused on state funding for terrorist groups and does not include (unless otherwise noted) direct logistical support for terrorist groups or passive state sponsorship. A recent book by Daniel Byman on state sponsorship discusses these issues and others, filling a significant void in the literature. See Daniel Byman, *Deadly Connections: States That Sponsor Terrorism* (New York: Cambridge University Press, 2005).

5. At any rate, state funding is still relatively plentiful in the post–Cold War era. In a survey of 74 insurgencies active since 1991, Byman et al. found that 44 received state support that was "significant or critical" to the survival and success of the movement. Other outside supporters were also important, but state sponsorship remained the most frequent source of outside support in the post–Cold War era: 21 move-

ments received significant support from refugees, 19 from diasporas, and 25 from other actors, such as Islamic organizations or relief agencies. See Daniel L. Byman, Peter Chalk, Bruce Hoffman, William Rosenau, and David Brannan, *Trends in Outside Support for Insurgent Movements* (Santa Monica: RAND, 2001), 2. Relatedly, Paul Collier and Anke Hoeffler found that the end of the Cold War (used as a proxy for the importance of state funding of insurgents) had little impact on the incidence of civil war. See Collier and Hoeffler, "Greed and Grievance in Civil War," World Bank working paper, October 21, 2001, http://www.worldbank.org/research/conflict/papers/greedandgrievance.htm.

6. On the "new terrorism," see Steven Simon and Daniel Benjamin, "America and the New Terrorism," *Survival* 42, no. 1 (2000): 59–75. For a contrary view, see David Tucker, "What Is New about the New Terrorism and How Dangerous Is It?" *Terrorism and Political Violence* 13, no. 3 (Autumn 2001): 1–14.

7. Byman et al.'s (*Trends in Outside Support for Insurgent Movements*, 23) review of 77 insurgencies active since 1991 concludes that geopolitical concerns are the most important factor motivating state support for insurgents.

8. See Stéphane Courtois, Nicolas Werth, Jean-Louis Panné, Andrzej Paczkowski, Karel Bartosek, and Jean-Louis Margolin, *The Black Book of Communism: Crimes, Terror, Repression*, translated by Jonathan Murphy and Mark Kramer, consulting editor Mark Kramer (Cambridge, MA: Harvard University Press, 1999), 358–59.

9. James Adams, *The Financing of Terror* (New York: Simon & Schuster, 1986); and Byman, *Deadly Connections*.

10. Andrew Silke argues that extortion against larger companies is more difficult because it is harder for paramilitaries to gain access to the leadership of the business and to hold one individual responsible. Large contractors have also been able to resist extortion by walking off their building sites. The unfinished construction projects anger the local community and threaten to turn them against the paramilitaries. See Andrew Silke, "In Defense of the Realm: Financing Loyalist Terrorism in Northern Ireland—Part One: Extortion and Blackmail," *Studies in Conflict & Terrorism* 21 (1998), 331–61.

11. Vanda Felbab-Brown notes that the notoriously ruthless Sendero Luminoso in Peru used much less violence against peasants in coca-producing areas than in other areas, presumably because there was a greater coincidence of interests between the guerrillas and peasants. Sendero also did not want to endanger their drug income by alienating the peasant growers. See Vanda Felbab-Brown, "The Coca Connection: The Impacts of Illicit Substances on Militarized Conflicts," unpublished manuscript, Department of Political Science, Massachusetts Institute of Technology, April 2004.

12. This information can also be used to intimidate givers, as references to relatives in the home country can be construed as a veiled threat.

13. Although fluctuations in diaspora giving can also work to the benefit of the organization, as demonstrated by a dramatic upswing in donations following a successful Tiger offensive in 2000, the LTTE has demonstrated a preference for a steady stream of income. As a result, by the mid-1990s, legitimate investments represented

half of the group's international revenue. See Rohan Gunaratna, "Sri Lanka: Feeding the Tamil Tigers," in Karen Ballentine and Jake Sherman, eds., *The Political Economy of Armed Conflict: Beyond Greed and Grievance*, (Boulder, CO: Lynne Rienner Publishers, 2003), 197–223.

14. See Karen Ballentine, "Beyond Greed and Grievance: Reconsidering the Economic Dynamics of Armed Conflict," in Ballentine and Sherman, eds., *The Political Economy of Armed Conflict*, 271.

15. Guerrilla competition with paramilitary groups for control over coca-growing lands and trafficking routes led to a situation where peasants were routinely abused by both sides to terrorize them into not supporting the "opponent." The result has been a displaced population of millions.

16. Mia Bloom, *Dying to Kill: The Allure of Suicide Terror* (New York: Columbia University Press, 2005).

17. Collier and Hoeffler, "Greed and Grievance in Civil War."

18. The long-standing argument that terrorist-criminal collaboration is merely tactical is still often rightly made. However, there is a growing recognition, even by many of the authors who used to deny its significance, that there may be a qualitative shift in the nature of terrorist involvement in crime.

19. Paul Watson and Sidhartha Barua, "Response to Terror; Worlds of Extremism and Crime Collide in Indian Jail," *Los Angeles Times*, February 8, 2002. On Madrid, Phil Williams, personal communication with the authors, November 2004.

20. One of the first to stress the multiple means of raising and transferring funds was William Wechsler in his aptly titled "Strangling the Hydra: Targeting Al Qaeda's Finances," in James F. Hoge, Jr., and Gideon Rose, eds., *How Did This Happen? Terrorism and the New War* (New York: Public Affairs Publishing, 2001). For a fairly neutral description of al Qaeda's financial network, see Rohan Gunaratna, *Inside Al Qaeda: Global Network of Terror* (New York: The Berkeley Publishing Group, 2003). On operational efficiencies of this network, see, for example, Mark Basile, "Going to the Source: Why Al Qaeda's Financial Network Is Likely to Withstand the Current War on Terrorist Financing," *Studies in Conflict and Terrorism* 27: 169–85; and Russ Marion and Mary Uhl-Bien, "Complexity Theory and Al-Qaeda: Examining Complex Leadership," paper presented at Managing the Complex IV: A Conference on Complex Systems and the Management of Organizations, Fort Meyers, FL, December 2002. Available at http://isce.edu/ISCE_Group_Site/web-content/ISCE%20Events/Naples_2002/Naples_2002_Papers/Marion_Uhl-Bien.pdf (accessed August 28, 2005).

21. For an example of network theory applied to al Qaeda, see Lesser et al., *Countering the New Terrorism*. For an example of complexity theory applied to al Qaeda, see Marion and Uhl-Bien, "Complexity Theory and Al-Qaeda." Both theoretical approaches tend to be biased towards stressing the efficiency of the resulting organizational forms. As Marion and Uhl-Bien note, for example, "Complexity Theory is primarily about the dynamics of networks: it is the study of self-reinforcing interdependent interactions and how such interactions create evolution, fitness and surprise."

22. Chris Strohm, "Federal Commission Outlines Sept. 11 Plot," *GovExec.com Daily Briefing*, June 16, 2004.

23. Cited in Nimrod Raphaeli, "Financing of Terrorism: Sources, Methods, and Channels," *Terrorism and Political Violence* 15 (Winter 2003).

24. For instances from the 1990s in which al Qaeda financing of external operations was "inadequate," see Gunaratna, *Inside Al* Qaeda, 86. Although the author stresses that "Al Qaeda did not compromise its operational effectiveness by penny-pinching" in the case of the 9/11 attacks, he does not reconcile this with the many occasions in which al Qaeda has been willing to sacrifice operational effectiveness. RAND analyst Bruce Hoffman goes further than most in suggesting a typology of groups (professional cadres, trained amateurs, local walk-ins, and like-minded guerrillas and terrorists) that receive different levels of funding from al Qaeda, but since the main point of his article is to highlight Osama bin Laden's leadership skills, Hoffman does not consider the possibly negative implications of this financing system for terrorist effectiveness. See Bruce Hoffman, "The Leadership Secrets of Osama bin Laden: The Terrorist as CEO," *Atlantic Monthly*, April 2003.

25. However, at least some of the instances of underfunding occurred during periods when al Qaeda was thought to be awash in funds.

26. Rohan Gunaratna, "The Evolution of Al Qaeda and Its Financial Infrastructure," Workshop on Combating the Financing of Terrorism, December 5–6, 2005, available at http://pforum.isn.ethz.ch/docs/6BFAACE9-65B0-58E9-237336310B11 DD9F.pdf (accessed January 30, 2006).

27. See, for example, Chris Dishman, "Terrorism, Crime, and Transformation," *Studies in Conflict and Terrorism* 24 (2001): 43–58.

28. In their pioneering work on terrorism financing in Northern Ireland, John Horgan, Max Taylor, and Andrew Silke have argued that the political costs associated with some fund-raising methods have created tensions between the post-ceasefire political leadership and the financing units within Protestant paramilitary groups and the Provisional Irish Republican Army. See Silke, "In Defense of the Realm"; John Horgan and Max Taylor, "Playing the 'Green Card'—Financing the Provisional IRA: Part 1," *Terrorism and Political Violence* 11, no. 2 (Summer 1999): 1–38; and Horgan and Taylor, "Playing the 'Green Card'—Financing the Provisional IRA: Part 2," *Terrorism and Political Violence* 15, no. 2 (Summer 2003): 1–60. There are also indications that similar splits may be nascent within the FARC in Colombia.

CHAPTER 2

1. For a complete description of these efforts, see chapter 15, by Anne Clunan.

2. Some analysts, for example, question the extent to which terrorist organizations exploit charities, noting that only a few cases have held up in court in Europe. See Jeroen Gunning, "Terrorism, Charities and Diasporas," in *Financing Global Terrorism*, edited by Thomas J. Biersteker and Sue E. Eckert (Oxford: Routledge: forthcoming in 2007).

3. For an unrealistic view, see the statement of U.S. Treasury Under Secretary for International Affairs John B. Taylor in 2005: "Hatred fuels terrorism, but money makes their lethal schemes achievable. By breaking the financial backbone of terrorist groups and insurgents, we can encumber and thwart their short-term ambitions while rupturing and dismantling their long-term agendas. Choking off funds that aid terrorist efforts can lead to the ultimate ruin of terrorist organizations." John Taylor, "Under Secretary Taylor's Remarks on Combating Terrorist Financing at the G-7 Meeting of Finance Ministers and Central Bank Governors," February 5, 2005, JS-2231, Office of Public Affairs, Dept. of the Treasury, available at http://www .ustreas.gov/press/releases/js2231.htm, accessed June 23, 2005. Beyond such statements, lofty expectations underlie current recommendations (see UN Monitoring Team, "Second Report of the Analytical Support and Sanctions Monitoring Team Appointed Pursuant to Resolution 1526 [2004] Concerning Al-Qaida and the Taliban and Associated Individuals and Entities," 2005, available at http://daccessdds.un.org/ doc/UNDOC/GEN/N05/240/73/PDF/N0524073.pdf?OpenElement) and practice (e.g., strong actions by Immigration and Customs Enforcement against unlicensed money remitters in the United States).

4. For example, a report on the Saudis by French author Jean-Charles Brisard has been self-labeled and cited as a "Report prepared for the President of UN Security Council of the United Nations," but it was neither solicited nor endorsed by the UN. Jean-Charles Brisard, *Terrorism Financing: Roots and Trends of Saudi Terrorism Financing*, cited in "Saudi Arabia: Terrorist Financing Issues," Congressional Research Service Reports, October 3, 2004, available at http://fpc.state.gov/fpc/37089.htm, accessed June 24, 2005.

5. National Commission on Terrorist Attacks upon the United States, *The 9/11 Commission Report*, Washington D.C., 2004, pp. 13, 20 (hereafter referred to as the "*The 9/11 Commission Report*"). *The 9/11 Staff Monograph on Terrorist Financing* also dispelled many popular myths, including the notion that al Qaeda profited from speculating on fluctuations in the stock market after the September 11, 2001, attacks. See National Commission on Terrorist Attacks upon the United States, "Monograph on Terrorist Financing," Washington, D.C., 2004; hereafter referred to as *The 9/11 Staff Monograph*.

6. *The 9/11 Staff Monograph*, p. 13.

7. See State Department global terrorism annual reports at www.state.gov/s/ct/ rls/pgtrpt/2003/.

8. See R. Thomas Naylor, "The Insurgent Economy: Black Market Operations of Guerilla Organizations," *Crime, Law and Social Change* 20 (1993): 13–51.

9. See *The 9/11 Commission Report*. Also see Maurice R. Greenberg, chair, *Terrorist Financing: Report of an Independent Task Force* (New York: Council on Foreign Relations, 2003); Matthew A. Levitt, "The Political Economy of Middle East Terrorism," *Middle East Review of International Affairs* 6 no. 4: 49–65; and Levitt, "Combating Terrorist Financing, Despite the Saudis," *Policywatch* 673, available at http://64.233.187 .104/search?q=cache:BKQyUelGXj4J:washingtoninstitute.org/watch/Policywatch/

policywatch2002/673.htm+POLICYWATCH+Combating+Terrorist+Financing, +Despite +the+Saudis+673&hl=en.

10. "USA vs. Usama bin Laden Trial Transcripts: Digital transcripts from the Court Reporter's Office," available at http://cryptome.org/usa-v-ubl-dt.htm, accessed June 24, 2005.

11. UN Monitoring Team, "Second Report," para. 65, 94 ff.

12. Personal interviews in August and November 2004 with Jean-Luis Brouguières, the lead prosecutor of terrorism cases in France for the last 25 years, and with members of the British Terrorist Finance Intelligence Unit, August 2004.

13. See Y. Dandurand and V. Chin, *Links between Terrorism and Other Forms of Crime*, Report to Foreign Affairs Canada and the United Nations Office on Drugs and Crime (Vancouver, 2004). See also chapter 3, by John Picarelli and Louise Shelley, in this volume.

14. Dandurand and Chin, *Links between Terrorism*. See also the Library of Congress' May 2002 report, *A Global Overview of Narcotics-Funded Terrorist and Other Extremist Groups*, Library of Congress, Washington, D.C., accessed at http://www .loc.gov/rr/frd/pdf-files/NarcsFundedTerrs_Extrems.pdf.

15. Thomas R. Naylor, *Wages of Crime: Black Markets, Illegal Finance, and the Underground Economy* (Ithaca, NY, and London: Cornell University Press, 2002); Dandurand and Chin, *Links between Terrorism*.

16. Alliances between traffickers and terrorists are unlikely to last very long, because the two types of groups have fundamentally different objectives in their relations with the government and the general population. Militants desire a change of the status quo, whereas criminal enterprises are politically conservative and simply wish to manipulate or partially neutralize political systems. In addition, any open association with drug trafficking or other serious crimes would be politically damaging to many militant groups and could antagonize those upon whom they rely for recruitment and material support.

17. Passas, *The Trade in Diamonds: Vulnerabilities for Financial Crime and Terrorist Finance* (Vienna, Virginia: FinCEN, U.S. Treasury Department, 2004). *The 9/11 Commission Report*, 2004. *The 9/11 Staff Monograph*, p. 23, clarifies that "Allegations that al Qaeda has used the trade in conflict diamonds to fund itself similarly have not been substantiated."

18. See Doug Farah's series of articles in the *Washington Post*: "Al Qaeda Cash Ties to Diamond Trade," November 2, 2001, p. A01; "Digging Up Congo's Dirty Gems," December 30, 2001, p. A01; "Al Qaeda's Road Paved with Gold; Secret System Traced through a Lax System in United Arab Emirates," February 17, 2002, A01; "Report Says Africans Harbored Al Qaeda; Terror Assets Hidden in Gem-Buying Spree," December 29, 2002, A01; "Liberian Is Accused of Harboring Al Qaeda," May 15, 2003, A18; "Al Qaeda's Finances Ample, Say Probers," December 14, 2003; and his book, *Blood from Stones: The Secret Financial Network of Terror* (New York: Broadway Press, 2004). The other four sources are: the *Wall Street Journal* (Robert Block, "Liberia Cooperates in Study of Terrorist in Diamond Trade"; *Wall Street*

Journal, November 21, 2001, p. A11; Robert Block, "Spreading Influence: In South Africa, Mounting Evidence of al Qaeda Links—Officials Cite Smuggling Cases and a Deadly Bombing," *Wall Street Journal*, December 10, 2002, p. A1); a BBC documentary, *Blood Diamonds*, October 21, 2001, available at http://news.bbc.co.uk/1/hi/programmes/correspondent/1604165.stm; a report by the non-governmental organization Global Witness, "For a Few Dollars More: How Al Qaeda Moved into the Diamond Trade," April 2003, 1–97; and leaked reports or public statements from the Special Court for Sierra Leone—established by an Agreement between the United Nations and the Government of Sierra Leone pursuant to Security Council resolution 1315 (2000) of August 14, 2000 (for example: Rod MacJohnson, "'Blood Diamonds' Initiative a Mixed Success in War-Scarred Sierra Leone," *Agence France Presse*, May 18, 2003; Doug Farah, "Liberian Is Accused of Harboring Al Qaeda," *Washington Post*, May 15, 2003, p. A18).

19. My research over the last nine months has revealed numerous gaps in the evidence, erroneous statements, exaggerations, and implausible assumptions. My sources include interviews with intelligence personnel and investigators from the UN, the United States, and Europe; NGO officials; reporters; industry participants; and academics who studied the diamond industry in the past five years. I also reviewed the transcripts and the evidence from the trial for the West African embassy bombings, literature on the subject, and public and confidential reports. Finally, I used NIPS/Leadminer program analysis of import data over the last 15 years for supplementary analysis. See Passas, *The Trade in Diamonds: Vulnerabilities for Financial Crime and Terrorist Finance* (Vienna, Virginia: FinCEN, U.S. Treasury Department, 2004).

20. *The 9/11 Commission Report*, 2004, p. 171.

21. Christian Dietrich, Audition de M. Christian Dietrich (IPIS), diamond analyst, paper presented at the Commission d'Enquete Parlementaire, Belgique, available at http://www.senat.be/crv/GR/gr-06.html; Royal Canadian Mounted Police, "Link between Al Qaeda and the Diamond Industry," 2004, available at http://www.rcmp.ca/crimint/diamond_e.htm, accessed June 26, 2005.

22. *United States of America v. Usama Bin Laden et al.*, S(7) 98 Cr. 1023, transcripts available at http://cryptome.org/usa-v-ubl-dt.htm.

23. Christian Dietrich and Peter Danssaert, "Antwerp Blamed, Again," IPIS (International Peace Information Service) and Diamondstudies.com, November 16, 2001, available at http://ossaily.bravehost.com//antwerpblamedagain.htm.

24. See Passas, *Informal Value Transfer Systems and Criminal Organizations: A Study into So-Called Underground Banking Networks* (The Hague: Ministry of Justice, The Netherlands, 1999); Passas, "Financial Controls of Terrorism and Informal Value Transfer Methods," in *Transnational Organized Crime: Current Developments*, Henk van de Bunt, Dina Siegel, and Damian Zaitch, eds. (Dordrecht, Netherlands: Kluwer, 2003); Passas, "Hawala and Other Informal Value Transfer Systems: How to Regulate Them?" *Journal of Risk Management* 5, no. 5 (2003): 39–49; Passas, "Informal Value Transfer Systems, Terrorism, and Money Laundering," report prepared for the

National Institute of Justice and Financial Crimes Enforcement Network, January 2005, available at http://www.ncjrs.org/pdffiles1/nij/grants/208301.pdf; Passas, "Indicators of Hawala Operations and Criminal Abuse," *Journal of Money Laundering Control* 8, no. 2: 168–72; Passas, *Informal Value Transfer Systems and Criminal Activities* (The Hague: Ministry of Justice, The Netherlands, 2005); Mohammed el Qorchi, Samuel M. Maimbo, and John F. Wilson, "Informal Funds Transfer Systems: An Analysis of the Informal Hawala System," International Monetary Fund, Occasional Paper No. 222, 2003; Rensselaer Lee, "Terrorist Financing: The U.S. and International Response," Congressional Research Service, Doc. RL31658, 2002; Samuel. M. Maimbo, *The Money Exchange Dealers of Kabul: A Study of the Informal Funds Transfer Market in Afghanistan*, World Bank Working Paper No. 13 (Washington: World Bank, 2003). See also Financial Action Task Force (FATF), *2000–2001 Report on Money Laundering Typologies* (Paris: Financial Action Task Force, OECD, 2001); FATF, *Combating the Abuse of Alternative Remittance Systems: International Best Practices* (Paris: Financial Action Task Force, OECD, 2003); and Christine Howlett, *Investigation and Control of Money Laundering via Alternative Remittance and Underground Banking Systems* (Sydney: Churchill Fellowship, 2001).

25. See especially Passas, "Informal Value Transfer Systems, Terrorism and Money Laundering"; Passas, *Informal Value Transfer Systems and Criminal Activities*; Passas, *The Trade in Diamonds: Vulnerabilities for Financial Crime and Terrorist Finance* (Vienna, Virginia: FinCEN, U.S. Treasury Department, 2004).

26. Confidential, personal interviews with the UK Charity Commission, London, England, August 2004.

27. The settlement process is the most vulnerable to abuse and least visible part of the *hawala* business (see Passas, "Hawala and Other Informal Value Transfer Systems"; Passas, "Indicators of Hawala Operations and Criminal Abuse"; Passas, "Informal Value Transfer Systems and Criminal Activities"; Passas, "Informal Value Transfer Systems, Terrorism, and Money Laundering"; and Passas, Law Enforcement Challenges in Hawala-Related Investigations," *Journal of Financial Crime* 12, no. 2 (2004): 112–19).

28. *The 9/11 Staff Monograph*.

29. U.S. Department of State, "International Narcotics Control Strategy Report 2003," available at http://www.state.gov/g/inl/rls/nrcrpt/2003/vol2/html/29843.htm.

30. *The 9/11 Commission Report*, pp. 254 and 545.

31. Lee, "Terrorist Financing," and "International Narcotics Control Strategy Report 2003."

32. See Martin A. Weiss, "Terrorist Financing: The 9/11 Commission Recommendation," CRS Report for Congress, February 2005, available at http://www.fas.org/sgp/crs/terror/RS21902.pdf; and Juan Carlos Zarate, Assistant Secretary Terrorist Financing and Financial Crimes, U.S. Department of the Treasury, testimony before the House Financial Services Committee, Subcommittee on Oversight and Investigations, February 16, 2005, available at http://www.ustreas.gov/press/releases/js2256.htm.

33. Passas, *Informal Value Transfer Systems and Criminal Organizations*; and Passas, "Informal Value Transfer Systems, Terrorism, and Money Laundering."

34. Alexei Vassiliev, "Financing Terror: From Bogus Banks to Honey Bees," *Terrorism Monitor* 1, no. 4, October 10, 2003, available at http://www.jamestown.org/terrorism/news/article.php?issue_id=2873, accessed June 27, 2005.

35. *The 9/11 Staff Monograph*; and Judith Miller and Jeff Gerth, "Al Qaeda—Trade in Honey Is Said to Provide Money and Cover for bin Laden," *New York Times*, October 11, 2001, p. A1.

36. UN Monitoring Team, "Second Report," p. 12.

37. See testimony of Louis J. Freeh, Director, Federal Bureau of Investigation (FBI), "President's Fiscal Year 2000 Budget," before the Senate Committee on Appropriations, Subcommittee for the Departments of Commerce, Justice, and State, the Judiciary, and Related Agencies, Washington, D.C., Feb. 4, 1999.

38. Contrast, for example, Rohan Gunaratna, *Inside Al Qaeda: Global Network of Terror* (New York: Columbia University Press, 2002); and Jason Burke, *Al-Qaeda: Casting a Shadow of Terror* (London, New York: I.B. Tauris, 2003).

39. For a more detailed discussion, see chapter 15, by Anne Clunan, in this volume.

40. "Saudis Defend against Terrorism," *Deutsche Press-Agentur*, December 3, 2002; "Saudi Arabia: Saudi Arabia Combating Terror Financing," *Global News Wire—Asia Africa Intelligence Wire*, December 3, 2002.

41. "U.S. and Saudis Act to Freeze Charity's Assets," *New York Times*, January 23, 2004; Tom Godfrey, "Canadian Assets Frozen; RCMP Sweep in on $2 Million Thought Connected to al-Qaida Terrorist Network," *Ottawa Sun*, November 8, 2001.

42. FBIS Report, "Interfac Diplomatic Panorama for 07 Sep 04," *Moscow Interfax*, September 7, 2004.

43. Ibid.; "Frozen Assets Figure Doubles to $344,000," *Calgary Herald* (Alberta, Canada), November 17, 2001; Jason Bennetto, "U.K. Police Freeze $70m in Taliban Money," *Hamilton Spectator* (Ontario, Canada), October 4, 2001; Erika Kinetz, "Caribbean Weighs Costs; Offshore Centers Adjust to New OECD Rules," *International Herald Tribune*, May 16, 2002.

44. Government agencies still do not have clear guidelines on how they ought to interface with financial institutions regarding classified information. The 9/11 Commission rejected the idea of giving security clearances to bankers, while current technologies and infrastructure are not adequate to provide limited, ad hoc access to bank information for counter-terrorist finance purposes.

45. UN Monitoring Team, "Second Report."

46. See case studies on Barakaat and some charitable organizations in the 9/11 Staff Monograph," 67ff. See Lee, "Terrorist Financing"; and the UK Charity Commission website, http://www.charity-commission.gov.uk, where results of its investigations are reported. In the case of the Palestinians' Relief and Development Fund, known as Interpal—which was declared by U.S. presidential decree to be a "Specially Designated Global Terrorist" organization for allegedly supporting Hamas' political

or violent militant activities—the Commission reported that U.S. authorities could not provide evidence to support allegations made against Interpal within the agreed upon time frame. As a result, Interpal's bank accounts were unfrozen, and the inquiry was closed in September 2003. Charity Comission for England and Wales, "Palestinians' Relief and Development Fund," last updated October 4, 2004, available at http://www.charity-commission.gov.uk/investigations/inquiryreports/interpal.asp, accessed June 27, 2005.

47. Tom Godfrey, "Canadian Assets Frozen; RCMP Sweep in on $2 Million Thought Connected to al-Qaida Terrorist Network," *Ottawa Sun*, November 8, 2001; "Italy Seized al-Qaida funds," *Deutsche Press-Agentur*, August 29, 2002; "Frozen Assets Figure Doubles to $344,000," *Calgary Herald* (Alberta, Canada), November 17, 2001; Jason Bennetto, "U.K. Police Freeze $70m in Taliban Money," *Hamilton Spectator* (Ontario, Canada), October 4, 2001.

48. Although U.S. Treasury Secretary Paul O'Neill named Barakaat as the "money movers, the quartermasters of terror" and argued that it is "a principal source of funding, intelligence and money transfers for bin Laden," no terrorism charge was made against the defendants. While Mohamed Hussein was eventually convicted of operating a money transfer service without a state-required license, his Canada-based brother, Liban Hussein, was not extradited by the authorities despite a U.S. request. All charges against him were dropped and his assets unfrozen. Nonetheless, Liban Hussein's name remained on the UN blacklist, despite the statement of a Canadian Justice spokesperson: "We looked at the evidence, . . . and then it became clear there was no evidence." Rico Carisch, "How Have Networks Such as Al-Barakat and Al-Taqwa Been Used by Terrorists?" paper presented at the conference Financing Global Terrorism, at Brown University, May 2004, Providence, Rhode Island; and Douglas W. Cassell, "Patriotism and Due Process," *Chicago Daily Law Bulletin*, June 6, 2002, p. 6.

CHAPTER 3

A portion of the research supporting this chapter was supported by Grant No. 2003IJCX1019 awarded by the National Institute of Justice, Office of Justice Programs, U.S. Department of Justice. Points of view in this document are those of the authors and do not necessarily represent the official position or policies of the U.S. Department of Justice. The authors would like to thank Phil Williams, Doug Hart, Patti Craig-Hart, Steven Simon, Tamara Makarenko, Bartosz Stanislawski, Nabi Abdullaev, Keeli Nelson, and David Sklar for their generous assistance in the production of this work.

1. Robert M. Perito, "Afghanistan," testimony, U.S. Senate Foreign Relations Committee, May 12, 2004; Tamara Makarenko, "Crime, Terror and the Central Asian Drug Trade," *Harvard Asia Quarterly* 6, no. 3 (Summer 2002).

2. For more detailed analysis of the links between narcotics and terrorism, see LaVerle Berry et al., "A Global Overview of Narcotics-Funded Terrorist and Other Extremist Groups," U.S. Library of Congress Federal Research Division, May 2002, taken from the Library of Congress website: www.loc.gov/rr/frd/pdf-files/Narcs-FundedTerrs_Extrems.pdf, accessed October 13, 2004.

3. Greg Campbell, *Blood Diamonds: Tracing the Deadly Path of the World's Most Precious Stones* (Boulder, CO: Westview Press, 2002); Douglas Farah, *Blood from Stones: The Secret Financial Network of Terror* (New York: Broadway Books, 2004).

4. Douglas Farah, "Terrorist Responses to Improved U.S. Financial Defenses," testimony before the Subcommittee on Oversight and Investigations of the U.S. House of Representatives Committee on Financial Services, February 16, 2005, http://financialservices.house.gov/media/pdf/021605df.pdf.

5 Sari Horwitz, "Cigarette Smuggling Linked to Terrorism," *Washington Post*, June 8, 2004, A1.

6. See the website of this project at www.antimoneylaundering.ge.

7. "Supporting Hezbollah," *National Post*, February 15, 2002, A15.

8. Louise Shelley and John T. Picarelli, "Methods Not Motives: Implications of the Convergence of International Organized Crime and Terrorism," *Police Practice and Research* 3, no. 4 (2002): 313.

9. Interview with Nepalese general, National Defense University, Washington, D.C., March 2004.

10. Jonathan Winer, "Origins, Organization and Prevention of Terrorist Finance," testimony before the Senate Committee on Governmental Affairs, July 31, 2003. Also see the Council on Foreign Relations, *Terrorism Questions and Answers: Abu Sayyaf*, at http://cfrterrorism.org/groups/abusayyaf2.html.

11. Bartosz Stanislawski, "Cuidad del Este and the Nexus between Transnational Organized Crime and International Terrorist Groups: A Case Study," unpublished monograph, Transnational Crime and Corruption Center, American University, Washington D.C., 2004, 31–36.

12. Anna Repetskya, "The Classification of the Criminal Exploitation of People and Problems of Criminal Responsibility for It," in E. V. Tiuriukanova and L. D. Erokhina (eds.), *Trade in People: Socio-Criminological Analysis* [in Russian] (Moscow: Academia, 2002), 59–88; also Luz Estella Nagle, "The Situation within Colombia: A Pressure Cooker Spilling Over," American Bar Association's Standing Committee on Law and National Security, http://www.abanet.org/natsecurity/nagle.html, accessed October 13, 2004.

13. Justin Sparks, "'We All Thought They Were Going to Put a Bullet in Our Heads,'" *London Times*, May 18, 2003.

14. Stanislawski, "Cuidad del Este."

15. Ron Noble, "The Links between Intellectual Property Crime and Terrorist Financing," testimony before the House International Relations Committee, July 16, 2003.

16. Interview with UK Home Office official, UK Home Office Headquarters, London, March 30, 2004.

17. Paul Kaihla, "Forging Terror," *Business 2.0*, December 2002.

18. See the series entitled "The Terrorist Within: The Story of One Man's Holy War against America," *Seattle Times*, accessed at http://seattletimes.nwsource.com/news/nation-world/terroristwithin/.

19. Louise Shelley and John Picarelli et al., *Methods and Motives: Exploring Links between Transnational Organized Crime & International Terrorism* (Washington D.C.: TraCCC, 2005), available at: http://www.american.edu/traccc/resources/publications/picare01.pdf.

20. John Thompson and Joe Turlej, *Other People's Wars: A Review of Overseas Terrorism in Canada*, Mackenzie Institute Occasional Paper, June 2003, 99.

21. Elaine Sciolino and Jason Horowitz, "The Talkative Terrorist on Tape: Madrid Plot 'Was My Project,'" *New York Times*, July 12, 2004.

22. Martin Arostegui, "ETA Has Drugs for Weapons Deal with Mafia," *United Press International*, October 3, 2002.

23. Glenn Curtis, *The Nexus among Terrorists, Narcotics Traffickers, Weapons Proliferators and Organized Crime Networks in Western Europe*, U.S. Library of Congress Federal Research Division, December 2002, 11.

24. Rohan Gunaratna, "Al-Qaeda Finances," presentation to the University of Pittsburgh Workshop on Financial Dimensions of Terrorism, March 20, 2004.

25. Ian Cuthbertson, "Prisons and the Education of Terrorists," *World Policy Journal* 21 (Fall 2004), 15–22

26. John Horgan and Max Taylor, "Playing the Green Card: Financing the Provisional IRA—Part 2," *Terrorism and Political Violence* 15, no. 2 (Summer 2003), 11–17.

CHAPTER 4

The author thanks Marc Sageman for sharing his data on the global Salafi jihad. Ethan Bueno de Mesquita, James Fearon, Jeanne Giraldo, Kelly Greenhill, Stephen Krasner, Charles Perrow, Scott Sagan, Harold Trinkunas, and especially David Siegel provided tremendously helpful comments and criticisms on the underlying logic of the paper.

1. Alan Cullison, "Inside Al Qaeda's Hard Drive," *Atlantic Monthly*, September 2004.

2. William F. Weschler and Lee S. Wolosky, "Terrorist Financing: Report of an Independent Task Force Sponsored by the Council on Foreign Relations," Council on Foreign Relations, 2002, 6.

3. "Report on Money Laundering and Terrorist Financing Typologies," Financial Action Task Force, 2004, 6.

4. "APG Annual Typologies Report," Asia/Pacific Group on Money Laundering, 2004, 32, views terrorist organizations as able to agilely shift between multiple avenues to raise and use funds and to divert them from charitable uses with no mention of transaction costs or the organizational infrastructure requirements.

5. Jean-Charles Brisard, "Terrorism Financing: Roots and Trends of Saudi Terrorism Financing," JCB Consulting, 2002, 6. See also "The Jemaah Islamiyah Arrests and the Threat of Terrorism," in *White Paper* (Singapore: Ministry of Home Affairs, 2003), 6.

6. Although as the quote illustrates, some groups engage in auditing and do find problems.

7. Rohan Gunaratna, *Inside Al Qaeda* (New York: Columbia University Press, 2002) 61–65. See also Renesselaer Lee, *Report for Congress: Terrorist Financing: The U.S. and International Response* (Washington D.C.: Congressional Research Service, 2002), 8–11.

8. Jessica A. Stern, *Terror in the Name of God: Why Religious Militants Kill* (New York: Harper Collins, 2003), 213–16.

9. Rachel Ehrenfeld, *Funding Evil: How Terrorism Is Financed and How to Stop It* (Chicago: Bonus Books, 2004), 93.

10. Douglas Farah, *Blood from Stones: The Secret Financial Network of Terror* (New York: Broadway Books, 2004), 164.

11. "Indonesian Backgrounder: Jihad in Central Sulawesi," in *ICG Asia Report* (International Crisis Group, 2004), 9–10.

12. Ethan Bueno de Mesquita, "Conciliation, Counter-Terrorism, and Patterns of Terrorist Violence: A Comparative Study of Five Cases" (paper presented at the Annual Meeting of the Midwest Political Science Foundation, 2003), 6–7.

13. For example, Crenshaw and Bueno de Mesquita consider the problems created by differing levels of ideology for terrorist organizations trying to make peace. Martha Crenshaw, "How Terrorism Declines," *Terrorism and Political Violence* 3, no. 1 (1991); Ethan Bueno de Mesquita, "The Terrorist Endgame: A Model with Moral Hazard and Learning," *Journal of Conflict Resolution* 49, no. 2 (2005).

14. A more general problem is that most studies of terrorism fail to consider the great heterogeneity of terrorists. This problem is explored in Jeff Victoroff, "The Mind of the Terrorist: A Review and Critique of Psychological Approaches," *Journal of Conflict Resolution*, 49, no. 1 (2005).

15. Ibid., 15.

16. I thank Ethan Bueno de Mesquita for pointing this out.

17. Such delegation is risky. In 1995, Osama bin Laden reportedly had to rebuke the financiers of an aborted plot for their inadequate attention to security. Committee on Governmental Affairs, *Terrorism Financing: Origination, Organization, and Prevention: Saudi Arabia, Terrorist Financing, and the War on Terror*, July 31 2003, 42.

18. For example, the planning and bomb-making for the African embassy bombings were conducted by individuals who left the country shortly before the actual attacks.

19. Marc Sageman, private communication, January 8, 2005.

20. Disillusionment with the behavior of more senior members has led to compromise in the past. L'Houssaine Kherchtou testified for the prosecution in the Kenya embassy bombing case because he had seen senior members of the team embezzling funds. Marc Sageman, *Understanding Terror Networks* (Philadelphia: University of Pennsylvania Press, 2004), 180.

21. This analysis was developed independently from Frey and Luechinger, who present a similar argument using supply and demand curves. Their interest is in assessing deterrence strategies in the war on terror. Deterrence is understood as raising the demand curve. For many states, increased deterrence requires increased state centralization, which raises the supply curve because centralized states are more vulnerable. The change in the equilibrium level of terror from efforts to enhance deterrence is thus undetermined. Bruno S. Frey and Simon Luechinger, "Terrorism: Deterrence May Backfire," in *IEER Working Papers* (Zurich: 2002), 14–15.

22. For example, Palestinian terrorist groups that do not have access to Palestinian Authority funding compete for popular support by committing attacks and contesting responsibility for them. See, for example, Mia M. Bloom, "Palestinian Suicide Bombing: Public Support, Market Share, and Outbidding," *Political Science Quarterly* 119, no. 1 (2004): 72.

23. We lack evidence about the relative importance of different fund-raising sources for major terrorist groups.

24. Sageman uses data on 172 of these individuals in Sageman, *Understanding Terror Networks*. I conducted independent coding of operational roles for those participating between 1997 and 2003.

25. Maria A. Ressa, *Seeds of Terror* (New York: Free Press, 2003), 158–60.

26. All other things being equal, this means that recruitment and retention should be easier in economically disadvantaged areas.

27. This analysis does not deal with the possibility of disagreement over goals. Such disagreement is clearly a source of inefficiency, but it is not clear how disagreements over goals will affect terrorist financing.

28. Formally: $U(I,W|A_i) = p_{i,I}\alpha I + p_{i,w}(1-\alpha)W)$ and $\neg[p_{i,I} = p_{i,w} \forall A_i]$. Note that the probabilities of the payoffs need not sum to 1, formally: $p_{i,I} + p_{i,w} \in [0,2]$.

29. This progression need not happen within one organization. For example, many of the leaders in JI have been waging jihad together, at varying levels of intensity, since the mid-1980s. "Jemaah Islamiyah in South East Asia: Damaged but Still Dangerous," in *ICG Asia Report* (International Crisis Group, 2003), 7–9.

30. Anecdotal evidence from trial transcripts and other sources suggests that volunteerism is a primary method of selection with leaders choosing from among volunteers. See, for example, *The 9/11 Commission Report: Final Report of the National Commission on the Terrorist Attacks Upon the United States*, National Commission on the Terrorist Attacks upon the United States, 2004.

31. Jeremy Weinstein discusses a slightly different adverse selection problem in his work on rebel groups in Sierra Leone. He posits that a wage that brings high-

quality recruits will also bring in low-quality individuals. As leaders are unable to observe the recruits' type, they face an adverse selection problem. See Jeremy Weinstein, "Resources and the Information Problem in Rebel Recruitment," *Journal of Conflict Resolution* 49, no. 4 (2005), 603.

32. I thank Scott Sagan for pointing this out.

33. Groupe Salafiste pour la Prédication et le Combat (GSPC), an Algerian terrorist organization, uses just such a recruitment system in expatriate Algerian communities in France. See Sifaoui's journalistic account of his penetration of a GSPC fund-raising and recruiting cell in Paris. Mohamed Sifaoui, *Inside Al Qaeda: How I Infiltrated the World's Deadliest Terrorist Organization* (New York: Thunder's Mouth Press, 2003).

34. I thank Charles Perrow for pointing out this objection.

35. Alan B. Krueger and Jitka Maleckova, "Education, Poverty, and Terrorism: Is There a Causal Connection?" *Journal of Economic Perspectives* 17, no. 4 (2003): 141–42. Sageman, *Understanding Terror Networks*, 77. Claude Berrebi, "Evidence about the Link between Education, Poverty, and Terrorism among Palestinians," *Princeton University Industrial Relations Sections Working Paper* 477 (2003): 38.

36. In 2002, one PLO planner was paid $17,500 for a series of attacks, according to captured PLO documents. Families of PLO employees who die conducting attacks receive $2,000. Ehrenfeld, *Funding Evil*, 93. On Kashmiri middlemen see Stern, *Terror in the Name of God*, 235.

37. For the general development of this problem see David M. Kreps, *A Course in Microeconomic Theory* (Princeton, NJ: Princeton University Press, 1990), chaps. 16 and 17.

38. Relaxing this assumption would make it easier for the agent to skim money, as the agents could effectively con the principals. Assuming that the cost/success-probability ratio is shared information is thus a harder case for the idea that agency problems can plague terrorist groups. If the logic holds here, it will hold when the cost/success-probability ratio is private information.

39. Relaxing this assumption entails a security cost; we discuss this in the next section.

40. The existence of such a market is not so far-fetched. During the 1970s there were two markets for terrorist expertise. In one market, terrorist groups, especially Palestinian groups, competed for state support. In the other market, groups shared resources and technical expertise. James Adams, *The Financing of Terror* (London: New English Library, 1986), 42–43, 51–52. More recently, JI reportedly paid the Moro Islamic Liberation Front (MILF) for the use of training facilities. "Southern Philippines Backgrounder: Terrorism and the Peace Process," in *ICG Asia Report* (International Crisis Group, 2004), 15, 22.

41. Donald Masciandaro, *Global Financial Crime: Terrorism, Money Laundering and Offshore Centres* (Hampshire, UK: Ashgate, 2004).

42. One consequence of this argument, considered with the selection argument, is that financial networks should prefer using illicit channels to raise funds.

43. When support network members set the number and cost of attacks, they choose the most efficient funding level given the funding-success relationship, as this is the cheapest way to achieve the threshold level of impact.

44. Al Qaeda reportedly followed a pattern similar to this through the September 11 attacks. See "Staff Statement No. 15: Overview of the Enemy," National Commission on the Terrorist Attacks upon the United States, 2004, 11.

45. By the selection argument, the individual's weight on wages is likely to be larger than his weight on impact. Even if that condition does not hold, all that is required is that the marginal increase in impact times the weight and probability on impact is less than the marginal increase in wages times the weight and probability on wages.

46. This is where it becomes important that fund-raising related to impact is not the sole source of money to many groups of concern.

47. We explore this equilibrium fully in Jacob N. Shapiro and David A. Siegel, "Underfunding in Terrorist Operations," unpublished manuscript, Stanford University.

48. Many observers argue that al Qaeda no longer exercises the centralized control over finances indicated by the al Zawahiri quotation. Since al Qaeda is widely considered to be resource-rich, this change dovetails nicely with the analysis.

49. More opportunities for Bayesian updating. The more such opportunities leaders have, the closer their beliefs come to the true relationship.

50. Cullison, "Inside Al Qaeda's Hard Drive."

51. For example, JI recruits within existing social networks and encourages intermarriage among members' families. "Al-Qaeda in Southeast Asia: The Case of the Ngruki Network in Indonesia," in *Indonesia Briefing* (International Crisis Group, 2002). See also "Jemaah Islamiyah in South East Asia: Damaged but Still Dangerous."

52. Lisa C. Caroll, "Alternative Remittance Systems Distinguishing Sub-Systems of Ethnic Money Laundering in Interpol Member Countries on the Asian Continent," Interpol, 2004, 9.

53. Even Osama bin Laden's family has not been aggressively tracked or pursued since 9/11.

54. An example of this dynamic is how the IRA suffered a substantial loss in popularity after the Omagh bombings. Bueno de Mesquita, "Conciliation, Counter-Terrorism, and Patterns of Terrorist Violence," 22.

55. This scenario matches the Palestinian case where the Israeli public has become accustomed to terror attacks. Consistent with this theory, I have been unable to find evidence that Palestinian groups rely on trust-inducing relationships.

56. Al-Aksa Martyr's Brigades, for example, make payments to planners and bomb-makers after attacks. Ehrenfeld, *Funding Evil*, 92–93.

57. "Testimony of FBI Agent John Anticev on Odeh," United States of America v. Usama bin Laden, et. al., 5 (7) 98 Cr. 1023, February 27, 2001, 1630–38. See also Brian Michael Jenkins, *Countering Al Qaeda* (Santa Monica: RAND, 2002), 5. Groups

may also require recruits to demonstrate their commitment by participating in violent actions before they join. See Sun-Ki Chai, "An Organizational Economics Theory of Antigovernment Violence," *Comparative Politics* 26, no. 1 (1993): 103.

58. News accounts of al Qaeda's greater decentralization since the United States began an aggressive worldwide campaign may indicate a choice to trade efficiency for security.

CHAPTER 5

The author would like to thank John Picarelli for his assistance in the preparation of this paper, and Paul N. Woessner and Shannon Horihan for their comments on an earlier draft. He also benefited from discussing some of the issues raised here with Professor Davis Bobrow and Dennis Gormley. The author alone is responsible for the arguments and conclusions.

1. See David Snowden, "Complex Acts of Knowing: Paradox and Descriptive Self-Awareness," *Journal of Knowledge Management* 6, no. 2 (May 2002).

2. For the distinction between signals and noise, see the classic study by Roberta Wohlstetter, *Pearl Harbor: Warning and Decision* (Stanford, CA: Stanford University Press, 1962).

3. The $147 million figure is provided at the U.S. Department of the Treasury web page on Terrorism and Financial Intelligence, the section on Recent Accomplishments. See www.treas.gov/offices/enforcement/.

4. UN Monitoring Group, *Second Report of the Monitoring Group Established Pursuant to Resolution 1363 (2001) and Extended by Resolutions 1390 (2002) and 1455 (2003), on Sanctions against Al-Qaeda, the Taliban and Individuals and Entities Associated with Them*, S/2003/1070, December 2, 2003, 13.

5. Ibid., 25.

6. Ibid., 39.

7. Ibid., 40.

8. See John Arquilla and David Ronfeldt, *Networks and Netwars* (Santa Monica, CA: RAND, 2001).

9. UN Monitoring Group, *Second Report of the Monitoring Group*, 4.

10. Ibid., 15.

11. See Matthew Levitt, "Charitable Organizations and Terrorist Financing: A War on Terror Status-Check," draft paper presented at the University of Pittsburgh Workshop on the Dimensions of Terrorist Financing, March 19–20, 2004.

12. See UN Monitoring Group, "Letter dated 31 July 2004 from the Coordinator of the Analytical Support and Sanctions Monitoring Team established pursuant to resolution 1526 (2004) addressed to the Chairman of the Security Council Committee established pursuant to resolution 1267 (1999) concerning Al-Qaeda and the Taliban and associated individuals and entities." Details of the costs of the attacks are

also quoted in "Al Qaeda Does Terror on a Budget: UN Report," Associated Press, August 27, 2004. See the summary at http://www.ctv.ca/servlet/ArticleNews/story/CTVNews/20040827/alqaeda_costs_040826?s_name=election2005&no_ads=.

13. Moreover, in this case drug traffickers had joined the terrorist network. See Sebastian Rotella, "Jihad's Unlikely Alliance," *Los Angeles Times*, May 23, 2004.

14. Steven Erlanger and Chris Hedges, "Missed Signals: Terror Cells Slip through Europe's Grasp," *New York Times*, December 28, 2001, available at www.pulitzer.org/year/2002/explanatory-reporting/works/122801.html.

15. Paul Harris, Burhan Wazir, and Kate Connolly, "Al-Qaeda's Bombers Used Britain to Plot Slaughter," *The Observer*, April 21, 2002.

16. Ibid.

17. Ibid. An alternative or additional possibility is that French intelligence informed the German authorities of what was going on. See "Ten Islamic Militants Jailed over French Bomb Plot," *Reuters*, December 16, 2004.

18. James A. Damask, "Cigarette Smuggling: Financing Terrorism?" Mackinac Center for Public Policy, July 1, 2002, available at www.mackinac.org/article.asp?ID=4461; and Manuel Roig-Franzia, "Man Convicted of Using Smuggling to Fund Hezbollah," *Washington Post*, June 23, 2002.

19. *Funding Terror: The Liberation Tigers of Tamil Eelam and Their Criminal Activities in Canada and the Western World* (Toronto: Mackenzie Institute, 1996).

20. See "Attack on Terrorism—Inside al-Qaeda," *Financial Times*, November 28, 2001.

21. "Spanish Police Identify Financial Mastermind of Madrid Bombings," *El Pais* (Madrid), May 17, 2005.

22. Ibid.

23. The National Commission on Terrorist Attacks upon the United States, "Monograph on Terrorist Financing: Staff Report to the Commission," which is available at http://www.9-11commission.gov/staff_statements/index.htm, concludes that no SARS were filed relating to financial transactions involving the hijackers. A SunTrust Bank SAR was widely reported at the time, however, by media including the *Financial Times*. Interestingly, many references to it seem to have disappeared from the internet.

24. Global Futures Partnership, Central Intelligence Agency, *The Ecology of Warning: How the Organizational Environment Affects Strategic Intelligence* (June 2002).

25. The National Commission on Terrorist Attacks on the United States, "Monograph on Terrorist Financing: Staff Report to the Commission."

26. For an excellent introduction to this controversy, see the entry on Society for Worldwide Interbank Financial Telecommunication on Wikipedia, at http://en.wikipedia.org/wiki/SWIFT.

CHAPTER 6

1. Steve Coll, *Ghost Wars: The Secret History of the CIA, Afghanistan, and bin Laden, from the Soviet Invasion to September 10, 2001* (New York: Penguin Books, 2004), 238.

2. Council on Foreign Relations, *Terrorist Financing*, Report of an Independent Task Force, October 2002, 1.

3. Kenneth Katzman, "Afghanistan: Post-Governance, Security, and U.S. Policy," *CRS Report for Congress*, Congressional Research Service, December 28, 2004 (Update), 23.

4. Office of the Secretary of State, Office of the Coordinator for Counterterrorism, *Patterns of Global Terrorism: 1996 — Asia Overview*, April 1977.

5. Chalmers Johnson, *Blowback: The Costs and Consequences of American Empire* (New York: Metropolitan Books, 2000).

6. Reported Soviet deaths are usually suggested to be significantly less than these statistics, which come from official Soviet documents. See Lester W. Grau and Michael A. Gress, eds., *The Soviet-Afghan War: How a Superpower Fought and Lost* (Lawrence: University of Kansas, 2002).

7. *Mujahidin* refers to an Islamic guerrilla, literally "one who fights in the cause of Islam."

8. See Coll, *Ghost Wars*.

9. Ahmed Rashid, *Taliban: Militant Islam, Oil and Fundamentalism in Central Asia* (New Haven, CT: Yale University Press, 2001), 186.

10. Ibid., 184.

11. Ibid.

12. Anthony Davis, "How the Taliban Became a Military Force," in William Maley, *Fundamentalism Reborn? Afghanistan and the Taliban* (Lahore, Pakistan: Vanguard Books, 1998), 45.

13. Ahmed Rashid, "Pakistan and the Taliban," in William Maley, *Fundamentalism Reborn? Afghanistan and the Taliban* (Lahore, Pakistan: Vanguard Books, 1998), 78.

14. Davis, "How the Taliban Became a Military Force," 69.

15. Ibid., 70.

16. Ibid., 183.

17. Rashid, "Pakistan and the Taliban," 72.

18. Ibid., 72.

19. Ibid., 73.

20. Ibid., 81.

21. "Afghanistan, Crisis of Impunity: The Role of Pakistan, Russia, and Iran in Fueling the Civil War," *Human Rights Watch* 13, no. 3 (July 2001), 25.

22. Ahmed Rashid, *Jihad: The Rise of Militant Islam in Central Asia*, (New Haven, CT: Yale University Press, 2002), 217.

23. Rashid, "Pakistan and the Taliban," 84.

24. Ibid., 77.

25. Ibid., 78.

26. For a discussion of how opium production and transport help sustain the Taliban, see Mark A. R. Kleiman, "Illicit Drugs and the Terrorist Threat: Causal Links and Implications for Domestic Drug Control Policy," *CRS Report for Congress*, Congressional Research Service, June 22, 2004.

27. Jonathan Goodhand, *Frontiers and Wars: A Study of the Opium Economy in Afghanistan* (London: University of London, January 2003), 4.

28. United Nations, Office on Drugs and Crime, *Afghanistan Opium Survey 2004*, November 2004.

29. Rashid, *Taliban*, 120.

30. Rashid, *Taliban*, 118.

31. Ibid.

32. Barbara Crossette, "Taliban Seem to Be Making Good on Opium Ban, U.N. Says," *New York Times*, February 7, 2001.

33. United Nations, *Afghanistan Opium Survey 2004*.

34. Anthony Davis, "Afghan Drug Output Wanes—But Only under Taliban," *Jane's Intelligence Review*, October 22, 2001, available at http://www.janes.com/security/internationalsecurity/news/jir/jir001022_3_n.shtml. United Nations, *Afghanistan Opium Survey 2004*.

35. Goodhand, *Frontiers and Wars*, 6.

36. National Commission on Terrorist Attacks upon the United States, *The 9/11 Commission Report*, Washington D.C., 2004, 483.

37. *The 9/11 Commission Report*, 372.

38. Febe Armanios, "Islamic Religious Schools, Madrasas: Background," *CRS Report for Congress*, Congressional Research Service, October 29, 2003.

39. Ibid., 55.

40. *The 9/11 Commission Report*, 55.

41. Simon Reeve, *The New Jackals: Ramzi Yousef, Osama bin Laden and the Future of Terrorism* (Boston: Northeastern University Press, 1999).

42. Coll, *Ghost Wars*, 155.

43. Michael Rubin, "Who Is Responsible for the Taliban," *Middle East Review of International Affairs* 6, no. 1 (March 2002): 8.

44. Interview with Peter Jouvenal, veteran British cameraman and journalist and long-time Afghan observer. Jouvenal orchestrated the first-ever interview with Osama bin Laden with Peter Arnett and Peter Bergen. Also see Milton Bearden, "Afghanistan, Graveyard of Empires," *Foreign Affairs*, November/December 2001.

45. Rashid, *Taliban*, 130.

46. Those who did return home became popularly known throughout the Arab world as "Afghanis." In their home countries they built a formidable constituency.

47. Rashid, *Taliban*, 130.

48. Alfred B. Prados and Christopher M. Blanchard, "Saudi Arabia: Terrorist Financing Issues," *CRS Report for Congress*, Congressional Research Service, December 8, 2004, 2–3.

49. "Overview of the Enemy," 9/11 Staff Statement Number 15, June 16, 2004, available at http://ctstudies.com/Document/911_Commission_Overview_of_Enemy .html. See also Matthew Levitt, "Tackling the Financing of Terrorism in Saudi Arabia," *PolicyWatch*, no. 609, The Washington Institute for Near East Policy, March 11, 2002.

50. *The 9/11 Commission Report*, 55.

51. James Bruce, "Arab Veterans of the Afghan War," *Jane's Intelligence Review* 7, no. 4 (April 1, 1995) 175.

52. See U.S. Department of the Treasury, "Treasury Secretary Paul O'Neill Remarks on New Terrorist Financing Designations," December 20, 2001, http://www.treas.gov/press/releases/po885.htm; "Remarks by Treasury Secretary Paul O'Neill on New U.S.-Saudi Arabia Terrorist Financing Designations," March 11, 2002, http://www.treasury.gov/press/releases/po1086.htm; "Designation of 10 Terrorist Financiers Fact Sheet," April 19, 2002, http://www.treas.gov/press/ releases/po3014.htm; "Additional Al-Haramain Branches, Former Leader Designated by Treasury as Al Qaida Supporters," June 2, 2004, http://www.treas.gov/ press/releases/js1703.htm.

53. "It is unlikely that bin Laden could have returned to Afghanistan had Pakistan disapproved. The Pakistani military intelligence service probably had advance knowledge of his coming, and its officers may have facilitated his travel." *The 9/11 Commission Report*, 63.

54. Peter Bergen, "He Is Back . . . Osama bin Laden Makes His Return," *Washington Times*, October 26, 2000.

55. Anonymous, *Imperial Hubris: Why the West Is Losing the War on Terrorism* (Washington, D.C.: Brassey's, Inc., 2004), 140–41. We now know that "Anonymous" is Michael Scheuer, a 22-year veteran of the CIA and once head of the agency's Osama bin Laden unit.

56. Ibid., 66.

57. All six of the Yemeni suspects in the bombing of the USS Cole shared a background as Afghan Arab veterans of the anti-Soviet Afghan jihad.

58. *The 9/11 Commission Report*, 58.

59. Ibid., 66.

60. *The 9/11 Commission Report*, 66.

61. Jean-Charles Brisard, *Zarqawi: The New Face of Al-Qaeda* (New York: Other Press, 2005), 16.

62. Brisard, *Zarqawi*, 67, testimony of Shadi Abdallah, Germany judiciary proceedings in the case of Al-Tawhid 2002.

63. Ibid., 71–72.

64. Ibid., 72.

65. Ibid., 120.

66. Ibid., 150–51.

67. U.S. Department of State, "Designation of Gulbuddin Hekmatyar as a Ter-

rorist," Press Statement, February 19, 2003, www.state.gov/r/pa/prs/ps/2003/17799.htm.

68. Carlotta Gall, "11 Chinese Workers Killed in Rebel Attack in Afghanistan," *New York Times*, June 10, 2004.

69. For example see: "Statement of Gulbuddin Hekmatyar of 25 April 2003," posted on the Commonwealth Institute website, http://www.comw.org/warreport/fulltext/0304hekmatyar.pdf.

70. Coll, *Ghost Wars*, 211.

71. Ibid., 292.

72. Ibid., 238.

73. Ibid., 190.

74. Ibid., 213.

75. Ibid., 154.

76. Jonathan Marshall, *Drug Wars: Corruption, Counterinsurgency and Covert Operations in the Third World* (Forestville, CA: Cohan and Cohen, 1991), 51.

77. Barnett R. Rubin, *The Fragmentation of Afghanistan*, 2nd ed. (New Haven, CT: Yale University Press, 2002), 257.

78. *Washington Post*, May 13, 1990. Also see Cynthia Cotts, "Opium for the Masses," *Village Voice*, 2004, www.villagevoice.com/news/0143,cotts,29356,6.html.

79. Veronique Maurus and Marc Rock, "The Most Dreaded Man of the United States, Controlled a Long Time by the CIA," *Le Monde*, September 14, 2001.

80. Rashid, *Taliban*, 85.

81. Katzman, "Afghanistan," 7.

82. Roahn Gunaratna, *Inside Al-Qaeda: Global Network of Terror* (New York: Columbia University Press, 2002), 17.

83. Anonymous, *Through Our Enemies' Eyes: Osama bin Laden, Radical Islam, and the Future of America* (Washington, D.C.: Brassey's Inc., 2003), 275.

84. Jean-Charles Brisard, *Zarqawi*, 25.

85. Robert Baer, *Sleeping with the Devil: How Washington Sold Our Soul for Saudi Crude* (New York: Crown, 2003), 100.

86. Ibid.

87. Anonymous, *Imperial Hubris*, 34; Jon Lee Anderson, *The Lion's Grave: Dispatches from Afghanistan* (New York: Grove Press, 2002), 192.

88. *The 9/11 Commission Report*, 252.

89. John Cooley, *Unholy Wars: Afghanistan, America and International Terrorism* (London: Pluto Press, 2002), 212; and Office of the Secretary of State, *Patterns of Global Terrorism: 1996—Asia Overview*.

90. Cooley, *Unholy Wars*.

91. *The 9/11 Commission Report*, 58; Coll, *Ghost Wars*, 275.

92. Coll, *Ghost Wars*, 275.

93. *The 9/11 Commission Report*, 146.

94. Rashid, *Taliban*, 263.

95. Rashid, *Taliban*, 176.

96. Rashid, *Taliban*, 198.

97. Coll, *Ghost Wars*, 83.

98. Anonymous, *Through Our Enemies' Eyes*, 92.

99. For example, see Chalmers Johnson, "Blowback," *The Nation*, October 15, 2001.

100. Coll, *Ghost Wars*, 277.

101. United Nations Office on Drugs and Crime and the Government of Afghanistan's Counter Narcotics Directorate, "Afghanistan Opium Survey, 2005," November 2005.

102. Author's interview with U.S. military officers in Kabul, Afghanistan, September 2005.

CHAPTER 7

The views expressed in this article are based largely on my observations and experience as one of five international monitors charged by the UN Security Council to oversee the effectiveness of measures adopted against al Qaeda and the Taliban.

1. This is the finding of the 9/11 Commission. See The 9/11 Commission on Terrorist Attacks upon the United States, *Staff Monograph on Terrorist Financing*, 9 (hereafter referred to as *The 9/11 Staff Monograph*).

2. See Evan Kohlmann, *Al-Qaida's Jihad in Europe: The Afghan-Bosnian Network* (New York: Berg Publishers, 2004).

3. See *The 9/11 Staff Monograph*, 20–21.

4. See *The 9/11 Staff Monograph*, 22–24.

5. "The U.S. intelligence community largely failed to comprehend al Qaeda's methods of raising, moving, and storing money, because it devoted relatively few resources to collecting the strategic financial intelligence that policy makers were requesting or that would have informed the larger counterterrorism strategy." *The 9/11 Staff Monograph*, 5.

6. See the UN Monitoring Group, First and Second Reports of the Monitoring Group Established Pursuant to United Nations Security Council Resolution 1363 (2001) and Extended by Resolutions 1390 (2002) and 1455 (2003) on Sanctions against al Qaeda, the Taliban and Individuals and Entities Associated with Them" (hereafter referred to as "First Report of the UN Monitoring Group), S/2003/669 (July 8, 2003)" and "Second Report of the UN Monitoring Group, S/2003/1070 (December 3, 2003)." On al Qaeda's use of the drug trade, see Senate Caucus on International Narcotics Control, "Money Laundering: Current Status of Our Efforts to Coordinate and Combat Money Laundering and Terrorist Financing," Hearings, March 4, 2004; see also Pierre-Arnaud Chouvy, "Narco-Terrorism in Afghanistan,"

Terrorism Monitor 2, no. 6, March 25, 2004. On diamonds and other precious commodities, see Douglas Farah, *Blood from Stones: The Secret Financial Network of Terror* (New York: Random House, 2004).

7. See U.S. General Accounting Office, "Terrorism Financing: U.S. Agencies Should Systematically Assess Terrorists' Use of Alternative Financing Mechanisms," GAO-04-163, November 2003, 9; see also Second Report of the UN Monitoring Group, S/2003/1070 (December 3, 2003).

8. See *The 9/11 Staff Monograph*, 10.

9. See Victor Comras, "Following Terrorists' Money," *Washington Post*, June 4, 2005, p. A17.

10. See John Lumpkin, "Insurgents Infiltrating Iraq Have Cash," Associated Press, October 21, 2004.

11. See Kohlmann, *Al-Qaida's Jihad in Europe*.

12. See, for example, Raymond Bonner, "Philippine Camps Are Training Al Qaeda's Allies, Officials Say," *New York Times*, May 31, 2003.

13. See David Ottaway, "U.S. Eyes Money Trails of Saudi-Backed Charities," *Washington Post*, August 19, 2004.

14. See "Confessions of an al Qaeda Terrorist, American Interrogators Finally Got to Omar al-Faruq, Who Detailed Plans to Launch a New Terror Spree in Southeast Asia," Web Exclusive, *Time*, September 15, 2002, http://www.time.com/time/world/article/0,8599,351169,00.html. Ahmed Al-Fadl's testimony in the *United States v Usama Bin Laden et al.*, involving the embassy bombings can be found at http://news.findlaw.com/cnn/docs/binladen/binladen20601tt.pdf.

15. Despite reports that Khalifa is living in Saudi Arabia under house arrest, there are indications that he continues to conduct his business activities and to retain contacts with various radical Islamic groups. See Second Report of the UN Monitoring Group, S/2003/1070 (December 3, 2003).

16. Ibid.

17. See Michael Isikoff and Mark Hosenball, "Paying for Terror, Treasury Department Documents Detail the Murky World of Al Qaeda's Financing," Web Exclusive, *Newsweek*, May 12, 2004, at http://www.msnbc.msn.com/id/4963025/site/newsweek/.

18. See "Turkish Court Lifts Freeze on Yassin Al-Qadi's Assets," *Arab News* (Jeddah), August 8, 2006, at http://www.arabnews.com/?page=1&section=0&article=77594&d=9&m=8&y=2006.

19. See FATF, "Combating the Abuse of Non-Profit Organizations: International Best Practices," October 11, 2002, http://www.fatf-gafi.org/dataoecd/39/19/34033761.pdf.

20. See David D. Aufhauser, former U.S. Treasury Department General Counsel, "An Assessment of Current Efforts to Combat Terrorism Financing," statement before the Senate Committee on Governmental Affairs, June 15, 2004.

21. Second Report of the UN Monitoring Group, S/2003/1070 (December 3, 2003), paragraphs 40–43.

22. This CIA report was released under a Freedom of Information request. Extracts from the text of the report are available on the internet at www.centerforsecuritypolicy .org/cia96charities.pdf.

23. See *Minister of Citizenship and Immigration v. Mahmoud Jaballah*, Federal Court of Canada, Docket DES-6-99, November 2, 1999.

24. See UN Security Council, Philippine Country Report, UN Security Council Resolution 1267 and 1455, al Qaeda Sanctions Committee, S/AC.37/2003/(1455)/ 79, October 22, 2003.

25. U.S. Treasury Department, "Treasury Designates Director, Branches of Charity Bankrolling Al Qaida Network," Press Release HP-45, August 3, 2006, at http:// www.treas.gov/press/releases/hp45.htm.

26. See U.S. Treasury Department, "Treasury Designates Benevolence International Foundation and Related Entities as Financiers of Terrorism," Press Release PO-3632, November 19, 2002. In February 2003, Arnaout pleaded guilty to racketeering conspiracy, admitting to having fraudulently used charitable donations to provide assistance to fighters in Chechnya and Bosnia. Charges related to bin Laden and al Qaeda were dropped as part of the plea, and Arnaout agreed to cooperate with investigators.

27. Ibid.

28. See United Nations, Press Release SC/7331, March 15, 2002.

29. Second Report of the UN Monitoring Group, S/2003/1070 (December 3, 2003), paragraph 46.

30. See "Al-Haramain Shuts 3 Offices Abroad, 4 More to Close," *Arab News* (Jeddah), May 16, 2003.

31. See US Treasury Department," Press Release JS-1703, June 2, 2004.

32. See U.S. Treasury Department, "Treasury Department Releases List of 39 Additional Specially Designated Global Terrorists," Press Release PO-689, October 12, 2001.

33. See United Nations Security Council, "The New Consolidated List of Individuals and Entities Belonging to or Associated with the Taliban and Al-Qaida Organisation as Established and Maintained by the 1267 Committee," August 24, 2006, at http://www.un.org/Docs/sc/committees/1267/1267ListEng.htm.

34. See "Rabita Trust," *South Asia Terrorism Portal*, at www.satp.org/satporgtp/ countries/pakistan/terrorstoutfits/Rabita_trust.htm.

35. See U.S. Treasury Department, "Treasury Department Statement on the Designation of Wa'el Hamza Julidan," Press Release PO-3397, September 6, 2002.

36. "United Nations Security Council, "The New Consolidated List."

37. While LDI remains on the UN designated list, it is still believed to be active in Kuwait, Pakistan, and Afghanistan. See Second Report of the UN Monitoring Group, S/2003/1070 (December 3, 2003), paragraph 58.

38. See Victor Comras, "Pakistan Charity Jamaat-Ud-Dawa Added to Global Terrorist List, but Not Its Leaders," *The Counterterrorism Blog*, April 30, 2006, http://counterterrorismblog.org/2006/04/pakistan_charity_jamaatuddawa.php; Vic-

tor Comras, "Terrorism Tainted Lashkar-e-Taiba Continues as a Major Player in Kashmir Earthquake Relief Effort," *The Counterterrorism Blog*, November 22, 2005, http://counterterror.typepad.com/the_counterterrorism_blog/2005/11/terrorism_taint.html.

39. Kenneth Dam, "The Role of Charities and Non Profit Organizations in the Financing of Terrorism," testimony before the Senate Subcommittee on International Trade and Finance, August 1, 2002. Dam listed several charities formed with the principal intention of raising funds for al Qaeda. Two examples he cited were the Afghan Support Committee and the Revival of Islamic Heritage Society. Both defrauded donors by falsely publicizing the organizations' actual activities.

40. See U.S. Treasury Department, "Typologies and Open Source Reporting on Terrorist Abuse of Charitable Operations in Post-Earthquake Pakistan and India," at http://www.treas.gov/offices/enforcement/key-issues/protecting/docs/charities_post-earthquake.pdf.

41. See Dr. Quintan Wiktorowicz, Rhodes College, "The Role of Charities and Non Profit Organizations in the Financing of Terrorism," testimony before the Senate Subcommittee on International Trade and Finance, August 1, 2002.

42. See Victor Comras, "Abu Hamza al-Masri Conviction: An Important Step Forward in the UK's War on Terrorism," *The Counterterrorism Blog*, February 7, 2006.

43. Second Report of the UN Monitoring Group, S/2003/1070 (December 3, 2003), paragraph 68.

44. See UN Security Council, Philippine Country Report, UN Security Council Resolution 1267 and 1455, al Qaeda Sanctions Committee, October, 2004 S/AC.37/2003/(1455)/79, October 22, 2003.

45. Second Report of the UN Monitoring Group, S/2003/1070 (December 3, 2003), paragraph 55. See also Commonwealth of Australia, Parliamentary Debates, House of Representatives, Official Hansard, no.10, 2003 (May 14, 2003), Question No. 1645, Foreign Affairs, Southeast Asia.

46. See the 9/11 Commission on Terrorist Attacks upon the United States, *The 9/11 Commission Report*, footnote 14 to chapter 5, which reports information from an interrogation of Hambali, November 19, 2003.

47. UN Security Council Resolution 1390 (2002) directed that all countries shall "freeze without delay the funds and other financial assets or economic resources of . . . [designated individuals and entities] including funds derived from property owned or controlled, directly or indirectly, by them or by persons acting on their behalf or at their direction, and ensure that neither these nor any other funds, financial assets or economic resources are made available, directly or indirectly, for such person's benefit."

48. More recently Liechtenstein amended its company registration laws to require companies to provide a profile of their activities and assets. See also Second Report of the UN Monitoring Group, S/2003/1070 (December 3, 2003), paragraphs 70–81.

49. Lisa Myers and Aram Roston, "Alleged Terror Financier Operates in Plain

Sight," *NBC Nightly News*, June 30, 2005, at http://www.msnbc.msn.com/id/8421366/.

50. According to Matthew A. Levitt, "At the New York trial of four men convicted of involvement in the embassy attacks, a former al-Qaeda member named several charities as fronts for the terrorist group, including Mercy. Documents presented at the trial demonstrated that Mercy smuggled weapons from Somalia into Kenya, and Abdullah Mohammad, one of the Nairobi bombers, delivered eight boxes of convicted al-Qaeda operative Wadi el-Hage's belongings—including false documents and passports—to Mercy's Kenya office." House Subcommittee on International Trade and Finance, "The Role of Charities and NGOs in the Financing of Terrorist Activities," Hearings, August 1, 2002.

51. See David Kane, Affidavit in the Matter of Searches Involving 555 Grove Street, Herndon, Virginia, and Related Locations, U.S. District Court for the Eastern District of Virginia, Alexandria Division, October (2003).

52. Ibid.

53. See Steven W. Casteel, Assistant Administrator for Intelligence, Drug Enforcement Administration, "Narco-Terrorism: International Drug Trafficking and Terrorism—A Dangerous Mix," testimony before the United States Senate Committee on the Judiciary, May 20, 2003. See also "Terrorism's Harvest, How Al Qaeda Is Tapping into the Opium Trade to Finance Its Operations and Destabilize Afghanistan," *Time*, Asia Edition, August 9, 2004; Mark Schneider, "Colombia in Kabul," *Washington Times*, December 4, 2003; and Mark McDonald, "Tajikistan at Crossroads of the Drug Trade. Desperately Poor, It Fights a Losing Battle," *Detroit Free Press*, May 4, 2004.

54. See interview with Mirwais Yasini, head of the Counter Narcotics Directorate (CND) Kabul, IRIN News Service, Oct 19, 2004.

55. See Tamara Makarenko, "Crime, Terror and the Central Asian Drug Trade," *Harvard Asia Quarterly*, Spring 2002.

56. See Jeffrey Robinson, "How Petty Crime Funds Terror," *International Herald Tribune*, August 13, 2004.

57. See Todd M. Hinnen, "The Cyber-Front in the War on Terrorism: Curbing Terrorist Use of the Internet," *The Columbia Science and Technology Law Review*, 2004, at http://www.stlr.org/html/volume5/hinnen.pdf.

58. See Farah, *Blood from Stones*.

59. See, for example, "For a Few Dollars More: How al Qaeda Moved into the Diamond Trade," *Global Witness Report*, April 16, 2003; and Farah, *Blood from Stones*.

60. *The 9/11 Staff Monograph*, 4.

61. See, for example, the report by Glenn Simpson in the *Wall Street Journal*, dated June 28, 2004, which said that "United Nations war-crimes prosecutors have evidence that Aafia Siddiqui, believed to be al Qaeda's only female leader, visited Liberia in June 2001 to assist the terrorism group's alleged diamond-trading operations. . . . The dossier states that Sheik Ahmed Sahm Swedan, an al Qaeda leader who is on the FBI's Most Wanted Terrorist list, was visiting Monrovia, Liberia, at the

same time as Ms. Siddiqui." See also Bryan Bender, "Liberia's Taylor Gave Aid to Qaeda, UN Probe Finds," *Boston Globe*, August 4, 2004: "'Charles Taylor was in the back pocket of Al Qaeda,' said a US intelligence official. '... He was helping them launder money through the diamond mines.'" See also Douglas Farah and Richard Shultz, "Al Qaeda's Growing Sanctuary," *Washington Post*, July 14, 2004, 19.

62. Samih Ossaily and Aziz Nassour were convicted in December 2004 by an Antwerp, Belgium, court for illegally importing diamonds from Sierra Leone. Both had also been accused of money laundering and arms trading, and evidence was produced linking both to al Qaeda. However, both were acquitted of these charges on the basis of insufficient evidence.

63. As one account noted, "Weak and corrupt governments, vast, virtually stateless stretches awash in weapons, and impoverished Muslim populations make the region an ideal sanctuary." Douglas Farah and Richard Shultz, "Al Qaeda's Growing Sanctuary," *Washington Post*, July 14, 2004, 19.

64. Congress recently pressed the Treasury Department to issue final rules under Section 312 of the Patriot Act to impose greater monitoring over the use of correspondent accounts for money laundering and terrorism financing purposes. See Victor Comras, "Tightening Up on Correspondent Accounts for Non-US Persons," *The Counterrorism Blog*, September 21, 2005, http://counterterror.typepad.com/the _counterterrorism_blog/2005/09/tightening_up_0.html.

65. The Treasury Department claimed that "the principal owner of al Barakaat is a close personal friend and associate of Osama bin Laden. And we have compelling evidence that ... monies raised by al Barakaat are being used to support al Qaeda to fund terrorist training camps and to purchase arms for al Qaeda terrorists.... Al Barakaat was channeling as much as $15 to $20 million a year to al Qaeda." Press Briefing by Jimmy Gurule, then Under Secretary of Treasury for Enforcement, September 9, 2002. Treasury agents ended up shutting down eight al Barakaat offices in the United States. The 9/11 Commission staff, relying heavily on the research and testimony of an FBI agent looking into al Barakaat's role, expressed considerable doubt about the role al Barakaat has played in supporting al Qaeda (see *The 9/11 Staff Monograph*, 67ff). Treasury/OFAC based their designation of al Barakaat on intelligence information, which they still contend provides a reasonable basis to support the designation of al Barakaat as a terrorism-supporting entity.

66. According to the U.S. Treasury Department, "Bank Al Taqwa, for which Nasreddin is a director, was established in 1988 with significant backing from the Muslim Brotherhood. They have been involved in financing radical groups such as the Palestinian Hamas, Algeria's Islamic Salvation Front and Armed Islamic Group, Tunisia's An-Nahda, and Usama bin Laden and his Al Qaeda organization. Bank Al Taqwa was established in the Bahamas and is a close affiliate of the Al Taqwa Management Organization, which changed its name in the spring of 2000 to the Nada Management Organization. In 1997, it was reported that the $60 million collected annually for Hamas was moved to Bank Al Taqwa accounts. As of October 2000, Bank Al Taqwa appeared to be providing a clandestine line of credit to a close asso-

ciate of Usama bin Laden and as of late September 2001, Usama bin Laden and his Al Qaeda organization received financial assistance from Youssef M. Nada." U.S. Treasury Department, on the designation of Youssef Nada and Idris Nasreddin, Press Release PO-3380, August 29, 2002.

67. See Sam Vaknin, "Hawala, the Bank That Never Was," UPI International, 2001.

68. See Comras, "Tightening Up on Correspondent Accounts."

69. See Rohan Gunaratna, *Inside Al Qaeda: Global Network of Terror* (New York: Columbia University Press, 2002), 60–74.

70. See *The 9/11 Staff Monograph*, 29.

71. See Zachary Abuza, "Funding Terrorism in Southeast Asia: The Financial Network of Al Qaeda and Jemaah Islamiyah," *NBR Analysis* 14, no. 5, December 2003.

72. Ibid.

73. See Jonathan Schanzer, "Algeria's GSPC and America's 'War on Terror,'" Washington Institute Policy Paper 666, October 2002; and Council on Foreign Relations, "Africa Terror Havens," December 2003.

74. First Report of the UN Monitoring Group, S/2003/669 (July 8, 2003), paragraph 37.

75. The UN Security Council has passed a series of resolutions meant to strengthen the measures against al Qaeda and to encourage member countries to forward names of al Qaeda members and entities to the Al Qaeda and Taliban Sanctions Committee for listing. The resolutions include the following: 1267, 1390, 1455, 1456, 1526, 1617, and 1699.

76. First Report of the UN Monitoring Group, S/2003/669 (July 8, 2003).

77. See Victor Comras and Douglas Farah, "Tackling Al-Qaeda's Terror Network," *Financial Times*, February 5, 2004.

78. Second Report of the UN Monitoring Group, S/2003/1070 (December 3, 2003), paragraphs 80–83.

79. See Victor Comras, "Filling the Information Gaps on Al Qaeda," *Washington Post*, June 1, 2004.

80. Ibid.

CHAPTER 8

Matthew Levitt was a senior fellow and director of terrorism studies at the Washington Institute for Near East Policy at the time of his contribution to this volume. In November 2005, Dr. Levitt became the Deputy Assistant Secretary for Intelligence and Analysis at the Department of the Treasury. Previously, Levitt served as an FBI analyst providing tactical and strategic analysis in support of counter-terrorism operations. Levitt holds an MA and PhD in law and diplomacy from Tufts University's Fletcher School of Law and Diplomacy. The views in expressed in this chapter are those of the author and do not necessarily represent the views of the Department of the Treasury or the U.S. government. Julie Sawyer and Andrew Eastman, research assistants in the Washington Institute's terrorism studies program, assisted in the preparation of this chapter.

1. "US Deputy Secretary of State: Hizbalah A-Team of Terrorism," www.Albawaba .com, September 6, 2002; *Reuters*, "Hezbollah Says Will Defend Lebanon from U.S. Threats," September 6, 2002.

2. Matthew Levitt, "Hizbullah's African Activities Remain Undisrupted," *RUSI/ Jane's Homeland Security and Resilience Monitor*, March 1, 2004; Levitt, "Smeared in Blood, Hezbollah Fingerprints All Over Globe," *The Australian*, June 9, 2003; Ely Karmon, "Policy Focus No. 46, Fight on All Fronts: Hezballah, the War on Terror, and the War in Iraq," The Washington Institute for Near East Policy, December 2003.

3. U.S. Senate Select Committee on Intelligence, "Current and Projected National Security Threats to the United States," February 6, 2002, http:// intelligence.senate.gov/0202hrg/020206/witness.htm; see response #3 to "Question for the Record" on page 339 of GPO print edition.

4. U.S. Senate Select Committee on Armed Services, "Threats to National Security," February 12, 2003.

5. Levitt, "Hezbollah: A Case Study of Global Reach," International Policy Institute for Counter-Terrorism, September 8, 2003, http://www.washingtoninstitute .org/templateC07.php?CID=132.

6. U.S. Department of the Treasury, Office of Public Affairs, "Treasury Designates Six Al-Qaeda Terrorists," September 24, 2003, http://www.treas.gov/press/releases/ js757.htm.

7. National Commission on Terrorist Attacks upon the United States, "*The 9/11 Commission Report*," http://www.9-11commission.gov/report/index.htm.

8. Scott Wilson, "Lebanese Wary of a Rising Hezbollah," *Washington Post*, December 20, 2004, A17.

9. *Al-Watan*, "Iran Expands Its Palestinian Control; Offers al-Khadoumi Five Million Dollars," December 13, 2004.

10. *Susan Weinstein et al. v. the Islamic Republic of Iran et al.*, United States District Court for the District of Columbia, Civil Action No. 00-2601 (RCL), February 6, 2002.

11. Wilson, "Lebanese Wary of a Rising Hezbollah."

12. *United States of America v. Mohamad Youssef Hammoud et al.*, United States Court of Appeals for the Fourth District, No. 03-4253, September 8, 2004.

13. Filipino judicial and intelligence documents, author's personal files, including evidentiary material brought in *People of the Philippines v. Pandu Yudhawinata*, Crimi-

nal case No. 99-2013, Republic of the Philippines, Regional Trial Court, National Capital Judicial Region, Branch 117, Pasay City, November 1999.

14. Levitt, "Hezbollah: A Case Study of Global Reach."

15. Asociación Mutual Israelita Argentina (AMIA) Indictment, Expert Opinion of Bruce Hoffman. This indictment refers to the 1994 bombing of the Israel-Argentina friendship society building in Buenos Aires by individuals allegedly connected to Hezbollah.

16. AMIA Indictment, Expert Opinion of Ariel Merari.

17. Douglas Frantz and James Risen, "A Secret Iran-Arafat Connection Is Seen Fueling the Mideast Fire," *New York Times*, March 24, 2002.

18. Molly Moore and John Ward Anderson, "Suicide Bombers Change Mideast's Military Balance," *Washington Post*, August 17, 2002.

19. *Middle East Newsline*, "Iran Establishes Rocket Training Centers in Lebanon," August 8, 2002.

20. Nicholas Blanford, "Report Claims Iran Running Bekaa Training Camp," *Daily Star*, August 13, 2002 (the article also appeared in Arabic in the Beirut daily *An-Nahar*, August 13, 2002).

21. Avi Jorisch, *Beacon of Hatred: Inside Hezbollah's al-Manar Television* (Washington, DC: The Washington Institute for Near East Policy, 2004), 32.

22. Blanford, "Hezbullah Sharpens Its Weapons in Propaganda War," *Christian Science Monitor*, December 28, 2001; see also Jorisch, *Beacon of Hatred*, 32.

23. Robert Fisk, "Television News Is Secret Weapon of the Intifada," *The Independent*, December 2, 2000; see also Jorisch, *Beacon of Hatred*, 32; and Ali Nuri Zada, "Iran Raises Budget of 'Islamic Jihad' and Appropriates Funds to Fighters," *al-Sharq al-Awsat*, June 8, 2000; and *Al-Ra'y*, "Hizbollah Inaugurates Satellite Channel via ArabSat," May 29, 2000.

24. Zeev Schiff, "Don't Underestimate Assad Jr.," *Ha'aretz*, August 2, 2002.

25. Jack Katzenell, "Barak Signs Six Month Detention Order against Lebanese Suspect," *Associated Press Worldstream*, February 21, 2001.

26. *Ha'aretz*, "IDF Abducts Force 17 Member in Gaza, Arrests 4 Hamas Activists," January 2, 2002.

27. Lenny Ben-David, "Iran, Syria and Hezbollah: Threatening Israel's North," *Jerusalem Issue Brief* 2, no. 3 (2002).

28. Ben-David, "Iran, Syria and Hezbollah: Threatening Israel's North."

29. Blanford, "Emboldened by US Jibes, Hizbullah Prepares for War," *Christian Science Monitor*, February 8, 2002.

30. Daniel Sobelman, "Jordan to Indict 18 on Terror-Linked Charges," *Ha'aretz*, February 7, 2002.

31. Janine Zacharia, "Terrorist Camps in Lebanon, Syria Bigger Threat to U.S. Than Iraq," *Jerusalem Post*, July 8, 2002.

32. *Daily Star*, "Israel Arrests Arabs Spying for Lebanese Groups," August 6, 2002.

33. Dina Kraft, "Seven Israeli Arabs Charged with Spying for Lebanese Guerillas," *Associated Press Worldstream*, November 29, 2000.

34. *Al Sharq Al Awsat*, "Israel Announces the Arrest of Two Syrians in the Golan," August 8, 2002.

35. Levitt, "Hezbollah: A Case Study of Global Reach."

36. Independent Media Review Analysis, "Senior Fatah Militant in Lebanon Directed and Financed Serious Terror Attacks in Territories and Israel," May 26, 2002, http://www.imra.org.il/story.php3?id=12156.

37. Wilson, "Lebanese Wary of a Rising Hezbollah."

38. Hamid Ghiryafi, "Hizbullah Officials Carrying Donations Reportedly Killed in Lebanese Plane Crash," *al-Siyasah*, December 29, 2003.

39. Miriam Karouny, "Benin Plane Crash Deaths Rise to 111," *Reuters*, December 26, 2003.

40. Author interview with Israeli intelligence official, Tel Aviv, July 2003; see also Center for Special Studies (C.S.S.), "Hizbullah (Part I), Profile of the Lebanese Shiite Terrorist Organization of Global Reach Sponsored by Iran and Supported by Syria," Special Information Paper, June 2003, http://www.intelligence.org.il/eng/bu/hizbullah/hezbollah.htm.

41. *United States of America v. Mohamad Youssef Hammoud et al.*

42. *United States of America v. Mohammed Ali Hasan Al-Moayad*, Affidavit in Support of Arrest Warrant, Eastern District of New York, January 5, 2003; see also C.S.S., "Hizbullah (Part I)."

43. Mark S. Steinitz, "Middle East Terrorist Activity in Latin America," *Policy Papers on the Americas* 14, no. 7 (2003).

44. *Agence France-Presse*, "PLO Bids to Win Back Refugee Support," July 5, 1994; see also Muntasser Abdallah, "Iran Pours Thousands of Dollars in Lebanon's Palestinian Camps," *Agence France-Presse*, June 21, 2002.

45. Levitt, "Hezbollah: A Case Study of Global Reach."

46. Copy of receipt, included in evidentiary material brought in *U.S. v. Mohammed Hammoud et al.*, culled from author's personal files.

47. C.S.S., "Hizbullah (Part I)."

48. Wilson, "Lebanese Wary of a Rising Hezbollah."

49. E. Anthony Wayne, Assistant Secretary of State for Economic and Business Affairs, "The Hamas Asset Freeze and Other Government Efforts to Stop Terrorist Financing," Department of State testimony to the House of Representatives Committee on Financial Services, September 24, 2003, http://financialservices.house.gov/media/pdf/092403eaw.pdf.

50. Author interview with U.S. intelligence official, Washington, D.C., July 2003.

51. Maurice R. Greenberg, "Terrorist Financing: Report of an Independent Task Force Sponsored by the Council on Foreign Relations," The Council on Foreign Relations, October 2002.

52. John Mintz and Douglas Farah, "Small Scams Probed for Terror Ties: Muslim-Arab Stores Monitored as Part of Post-Sept. 11 Inquiry," *Washington Post*, August 12, 2002.

53. John Solomon, "U.S. Builds Terror Funding Cases," *Associated Press*, August 28, 2002.

54. *United States of America v. Mohamad Youssef Hammoud et al.*

55. Ibid.; see also Jeffrey Goldberg, "In the Party of God, Hizbullah Sets Up Operations in South America and the United States," *New Yorker*, October 28, 2002.

56. *United States of America v. Mohamad Youssef Hammoud et al.*

57. Ibid.

58. Jeffrey Goldberg, "The Party of God: Hezbollah Sets Up Operations in South America and the United States," *New Yorker*, October 28, 2002.

59. Paul D. Taylor, "Latin American Security Challenges: A Collaborative Inquiry from North and South," Newport Paper no. 21 (2004).

60. U.S. Department of Treasury, Office of Public Affairs, "Treasury Designates Islamic Extremist, Two Companies Supporting Hezbollah in Tri-border Area," June 10, 2004, http://www.treas.gov/press/releases/js1720.htm.

61. Steinitz, "Middle East Terrorist Activity in Latin America"; see also *United States v. Mohamad Youssef Hammoud et al.*

62. Taylor, "Latin American Security Challenges: A Collaborative Inquiry from North and South."

63. Kraft, "Seven Israeli Arabs Charged with Spying for Lebanese Guerillas"; see also James Bennet, "Israeli Bedouin Colonel Is Formally Charged with Spying," *New York Times*, October 25, 2002.

64. *New York Times*, "U.S. Drug Ring Tied to Aid for Hezbollah," September 3, 2002.

65. *Global Witness*, "For a Few Dollars More: How al Qaeda Moved into the Diamond Trade," April 2003, www.globalwitness.org/reports/show.php/en.00041.html.

66. Douglas Farah, "Liberian Is Accused of Harboring Al-Qaeda," *Washington Post*, May 15, 2003, A18.

67. *Algemene Dienst Inlichtingen En Veiligheid*, "Angolan Diamond Smuggling: The Part Played by Belgium," July 2000, included in *Global Witness*, "For a Few Dollars More: How Al-Qaeda Moved into the Diamond Trade."

68. Douglas Farah, "Digging Up Congo's Dirty Gems; Officials Say Diamond Trade Funds Radical Islamic Groups," *Washington Post*, December 30, 2001.

69. Ibid.

70. Glenn R. Simpson, "Expanding in an Age of Terror, Western Union Faces Scrutiny as Fund-Transfer System Grows in Risky Parts of the World," *Wall Street Journal*, October 20, 2004.

71. Author interview with Israeli officials, Tel Aviv, May 2004.

72. Ibid.

73. Cuba, Iran, Iraq, Libya, and Sudan are all subject to additional sanctions such as the Iran-Libya Sanctions Act (ILSA), the Helms-Burton Act, the Cuban Democracy Act, the Trade Sanctions and Export Enhancement Act, the Trading with the Enemy Act, the Arms Export Control Act, the International Emergency Economic Powers Act, and more. For a complete listing of the U.S. Treasury Department's

sanctions programs and country summaries, see http://www.treasury.gov/offices/enforcement/ofac/.

74. *United States of America v. Mohammed Ali Hasan Al-Moayad.*

75. *Agence France Presse*, "Lebanese Hezbollah official forced to leave Germany," January 5, 2005.

CHAPTER 9

1. The "Arab world" is taken to mean all Arabic-speaking countries in the Middle East. Thus, it covers all of the Middle East, with the exception of Turkey, Israel, and Iran.

2. Kawas, Nafez, "Hariri: Funds in Banks Too Small for Laundering," *Daily Star* (Beirut), October 4, 2001.

3. "UAE Bank Governor: No Money Laundering in UAE," *WAM* (Official press agency of the UAE), October 28, 2001.

4. "UAE Central Bank Governor on Freezing of Accounts Linked to Terrorism," *WAM*, December 26, 2001.

5. "Central Bank of Kuwait—No Banks in Kuwait Involved in 'Suspicious' Activities," *KUNA* (Official news agency of the Kuwaiti Government), November 10, 2001.

6. "Kuwait Banking Institute Official—'Money Laundering Does Not Exist in Kuwait,'" *KUNA*, May 25, 2002.

7. Hanan al-Biyali, "Egypt Free of Money-Laundering, Bill Repels Investors," *al-Ahram al-Arabi*, February 2, 2002, p. 34. (Foreign Broadcast Information Service [FBIS] translation from Arabic.)

8. "Omani Bank Official Says Oman 'Untainted' by Money Laundering," *Oman Daily Observer*, September 14, 2002.

9. Conspiracy theories abound in the Middle East. For illustrative examples, see interview with Ibrahim Ba-Laslah of Dubai Islamic Bank, *Al-Watan Al-Arabi*, November 30, 2001; and interview with Maj. Gen. Khalfan Tamim, Dubai Police Chief, *Al-Sharq al-Awsat*, October 25, 2001. Arab internet sites are even more frank and vocal about what they view to be Western conspiracies.

10. In November 2001, during a television interview, Condoleeza Rice allegedly warned that Lebanon would need to freeze Hezbollah assets and that "Lebanon's very survival depended on such compliance." Nicolas Tohme, "Hariri Plays Down Severity of Lebanese-US Conflict; Request to Freeze Hizbullah Funds a Matter of Dialogue," *Daily Star (Beirut)*, November 13, 2001.

11. Majdi Muhanna, "Cairo Editor Slams Washington's Interference in Egypt's Domestic Affairs," *al-Wafd*, January 14, 2002.

12. "Dubai Police Chief on US Ties, Terrorism and Other Issues," *Akhbar al-Khalij*, July 26, 2002.

13. Josh Martin, "Arab Banks: Tracing the Funds for Terror," *Middle East*, April 2002.

14. James M. Dorsey, "O'Neill Promises Caution in Citing Saudis—Treasury Chief Vows to Refine Intelligence That Links Charities with Terrorists," *Wall Street Journal*, March 7, 2002.

15. The exception to this was Eygpt and Lebanon. These two countries were placed on the FATF's NCCT blacklist and therefore had to demonstrate that laws were being enforced in order to be removed from the blacklist.

16. A second strategy has been to develop Islamic financial services in response to increased demand from throughout the Muslim world. Bahrain aims to become the world's premier center for Islamic banking and finance.

17. Oman and the UAE had draft laws under review prior to September 11th.

18. Interviews conducted by the author in Spring 2004.

19. Adil Sabri, "Government Prepared Anti-laundering Bill According to US Specifications," *al-Wafd*, January 4, 2002. (FBIS translation from Arabic.)

20. Abd al-Rahim Abu Shamah, "Banks Reject Money Laundering Bill," *al-Wafd*, January 15, 2002. (FBIS translation from Arabic.)

21. Adil Sabri, "Government Prepared Anti-Laundering Bill according to US Specifications," *al-Wafd*, January 4, 2002.

22. "Algerian Daily Previews Draft Bill on Money Laundering, Terrorism Financing," *L'Expression* (Algiers), December 22, 2005 (FBIS translation from French); *International Narcotics Control Strategy Report 2004, Volume II: Money Laundering and Financial Crimes* (*INCSR 2005*) (Washington, D.C.: U.S. Department of State, Bureau of International Narcotics and Law Enforcement Affairs, March 2005).

23. International Bar Association, *IBA Anti-Money Laundering Forum: The Lawyer's Guide to Legislation and Compliance*, www.anti-moneylaundering.org/.

24. "Kuwait: Financial System Stability Assessment, including Reports on the Observance of Standards and Codes on the following topics: Banking Supervision, Securities Regulation, Anti-Money Laundering and Combating the Financing of Terrorism," IMF Country Report No. 04/151 f (Washington, D.C.: IMF, May 2004), 15.

25. *INCSR 2004*.

26. *INCSR 2004*.

27. For a more detailed assessment of Saudi laws and regulations, see "Appendix D: A Technical Assessment of Certain Saudi Arabia Laws, Regulations and Institutions," from the *Update on the Global Campaign against Terrorist Financing*, Council on Foreign Relations, June 15, 2004.

28. Saudi Arabian Monetary Agency (text of law).

29. *INCSR 2004*.

30. *FATF Annual Report 2003–2004: Annex C*, Paris: Financial Action Task Force, 2004.

31. FATF has 31 member countries and two member organizations, the GCC and the EU.

32. Statements made by UAE Central Bank Governor Sultan bin Nasser Al Suwaidi and the UAE's FIU Director Abdulrahim Mohammed Al Awadi, *UAE Interact: Comprehensive News and Information on the United Arab Emirates*, September 22,

2003, http://82.195.132.90/news/default.asp?dd=22&mm=9&yy=2003&image2.x =63&image2.y=20#9435.

33. "Only 4-5% ME Banks Have Technology to Curb Laundering," *Bahrain Tribune*, October 28, 2004.

34. The deposits in these 42 frozen accounts contained approximately $5,403,405. *A Report on Initiatives and Actions Taken by Saudi Arabia to Combat Terrorist Financing and Money Laundering*, Saudi Arabian Monetary Agency, April 2004, p. 5.

35. *A Report on Initiatives and Actions Taken by Saudi Arabia*, p. 7.

36. A Royal Decree in February 2004 authorized the creation of this Commission, but it is not clear if in early 2005 it was already operational.

37. *Hawaladar*s operate *hawala* networks, informal value transfer systems, which operate on trust. Typically, these transfer systems completely circumvent the formal banking system and are often used by low-skilled expatriate workers who wish to transfer remittances back home to areas seldom serviced by major banks. If a Pakistani worker in Dubai wishes to transfer $100 to his village near the Pakistani-Afghan border, he brings the cash to the *hawaladar* in Dubai, who then contacts another *hawaladar* at the Pakistani-Afghan border. A secret code is passed on to the recipient, who presents the code to the *hawaladar* at the border and receives the cash.

38. Moyara Ruehsen, "Tracing Al-Qaeda's Money," *Middle East Insight*, January–February 2002, pp. 41–44.

39. "UAE Withdraws License of Money Exchange House," *Gulf News*, October 31, 2001.

40. According to the April 2004 report of the Saudi Arabian Monetary Agency (*A Report on Initiatives and Actions Taken by Saudi Arabia*) "Hawala systems have been made extinct. Also Hawala systems are deemed to be illegal and strict enforcement actions including financial penalties and prison terms have been taken against the violators," p. 4.

41. MENAFATF members include Algeria, Bahrain, Egypt, Jordan, Kuwait, Lebanon, Morocco, Oman, Qatar, Saudi Arabia, Syria, Tunisia, the UAE, and Yemen. Some of the countries sent their Finance Ministers to the inaugural meeting, while others were represented by their Central Bank governors. Notably absent were Libya, Turkey, Israel, Iraq, and Iran.

42. Press Release of the Inaugural Ministerial Meeting of the Middle East and North Africa Financial Action Task Force (MENAFATF) against Money Laundering and Terrorist Financing, November 30, 2004.

43. Source for heading quotation: Majdi Muhanna, "The World List Order," *Rose al-Yusuf*, January 19, 2002. (FBIS translation from Arabic.)

44. Ibid.

45. *Terrorist Financing: Report of an Independent Task Force Sponsored by the Council on Foreign Relations*, New York: Council on Foreign Relations, October 17, 2002.

46. Ibid.

47. Dana Priest and Douglas Farah, "Terror Alliance Has U.S. Worried; Hezbollah, Al Qaeda Seen Joining Forces," *Washington Post*, June 30, 2002.

48. Joseph Samaha, "Confrontation with U.S. Is Inevitable If Hizbullah Remains on List," *Daily Star (Beirut)*, November 10, 2001.

49. This view is expressed widely in the print media and on the Arab street. As a Lebanese State Prosecutor more delicately put it, "the country's enthusiasm for the anti-terror campaign has been tempered by its insistence that the international community differentiate between terrorism and legitimate resistance." Quoted in Zeina Abu Rizk, "Addoum Vows to Fight 'Hideous Acts' of Terrorism; National Prerogatives Must Come First," *Daily Star (Beirut)*, October 30, 2001.

50. *Update on the Global Campaign against Terrorist Financing*, Second Report of an Independent Task Force on Terrorist Financing, New York: Council on Foreign Relations, June 15, 2004.

51. "Arab Summit Closing Session: Ben Ali Says Outcome Reason for Optimism," *Tunisian TV Channel* 7, May 23, 2004. (FBIS Translation from Arabic)

52. Morocco has enacted an anti-terrorism bill that criminalizes terrorist financing but does not target money laundering.

CHAPTER 10

1. Mark Basile, "Going to the Source: Why Al-Qaeda's Financial Network Is Likely to Resist the Current War on Terrorist Financing," *Studies in Conflict and Terrorism* 27 (2004): 169–85.

2. Rodolfo Casadei, "Connection Europa," *Tempi Online*, 6 Anno 10, www.tempi.it.

3. Loretta Napoleoni, *Insurgent Iraq, al Zarqawi and the New Generation* (New York: Seven Stories Press, 2005).

4. James Graaff, "Terror's Tracks," *Time Europe*, April 19, 2004.

5. Jean Louis Bruguiere, "Terrorism after the War in Iraq," U.S.-France Analysis Series, The Brookings Institution, May 2003.

6. "Police 'Pounce' on Al-Qaeda Cell," *BBC News Europe*, http://news.bbc.co.uk/1/low/world/europe/3245470.stm.

7. Anthony Barnett, Jason Burke, and Zoe Smith, "Terror Cells Regroup and Now They Target Europe," *Observer*, January 11, 2004; "Tentacles of Terror: Ansar al-Islam Goes International, Causing Tremors," *Daily Star*, January 17, 2004.

8. Barnett et al., "Terror Cells Regroup and Now They Target Europe."

9. Dale Fuchs, "Spain Gives Details on Terror Cell," *International Herald Tribune*, April 15, 2004.

10. Author's interview with Nick Fielding.

11. "Al Battar Training Camp," *Northeast Intelligent Network*, March 2004, www.homelandsecurityus.com.

12. Jefferey Donovan, "U.S.: New Surveys Show Anti-Americanism Growing Stronger," *Radio Free Europe/Radio Liberty*, June 9, 2003.

13. "'Bin Laden' Offers Europe truce," *BBC World News*, http://news.bbc.co.uk/1/hi/world/middle_east/3627775.stm.

14. "Saudi Investors Pull Out of United States," *BBC News*, August 21, 2002, www.news.bbc.co.uk.

15. UN Monitoring Group, "Second Report of the Monitoring Group Established Pursuant to Resolution 1363 (2001) and Extended by Resolutions 1390 (2002) and 1455 (2003), on Sanctions against Al-Qaida, the Taliban and Individuals and Entities Associated with Them," Report S/2003/1070, December 2, 2003.

16. "Targets Inside Cities," translation of section of al Qaeda document, Site Institute, www.siteinstitute.org.

17. Neil Mackay, "Was It ETA or al Qaeda? The Confusion over What Was Behind the Madrid Bombing Obscures Intelligence Predictions of an Enhanced Terror Threat," *Sunday Herald* (Glasgow), March 14, 2004.

18. Ibid.

19. Author's interview with an Italian magistrate.

20. Loretta Napoleoni, *Terror Inc.* (London: Penguin, 2004).

21. Jacqui Walls, "Man Jailed for Raising Terrorism Funds," *The Press Association Limited*, July 10, 2003.

22. "Credit Card Fraud," *Evening Gazette* (Middlesbrough, UK), July 2, 2003.

23. Dale Fuchs, "Spain Gives Details on Terror Cell," *International Herald Tribune*, April 15, 2003.

24. "Report of the Official Account of the Bombings in London on 7th July 2005," HC 1087, Her Majesty's Stationery Office, 2006, p. 23, http://www.official-documents .co.uk/document/hc0506/hc10/1087/1087.asp.

25. Ibid. The overall cost of the operation, including overseas travel, is estimated to be less than £8,000.

26. "Tentacles of Terror: Ansar al-Islam Goes International"; Casadei, "Connection Europe."

27. Ibid.

28. Cited in Peter Brookes, "Al Qaeda's Cash," *New York Post*, December 29, 2003.

29. Douglas Farah, "Al Qaeda's Finances Ample, Say Probes. Worldwide Failure to Enforce Sanctions Cited," *Washington Post*, December 14, 2003.

30. Ibid.

31. Claes Norgren and Jamie Caruana, "Wipe Out the Treasuries of Terror," *Financial Times*, April 7, 2004.

32. UN Monitoring Group, "Second Report of the Monitoring Group."

33. Author's interview with an Italian magistrate.

34. "Measures against Terrorism—EU Response to 11th September," *European Commission Action*, http://europa.eu.int/comm/external_relations/110901/meo2_53 .htm.

35. "Terrorism: The European Union Response," *Anti-Defamation League*, June 2004, http://www.adl.org/Terror/tu/tu_0406_eu.asp.

36. "EU: ICT to Play a Crucial Role in Europe's Fight against Terrorism," *European Commission-IDABC eGovernment News*, March 29, 2004, http://ec.europa.eu/ idabc/en/document/2342/330.

37. "EU: European Commission Creates Database against Terrorism Financing," *European Commission-IDABC eGovernment News*, June 15, 2004, http://ec.europa.eu/ idabc/en/document/2628/330.

38. According to the European Union framework, a "terrorist act" is one that "may seriously damage a country or an international organization" when the objective is "(1) seriously intimidating a population, or (2) unduly compelling a Government or international organization to perform or abstain from performing any act, or (3) seriously destabilizing or destroying the fundamental political, constitutional, economic or social structures of a country or international organization." See "Terrorism: The European Union Response."

39. Tony Barber, "Italy Agrees to Extradite Terror Suspect," *Financial Times*, August 17, 2005, http://news.ft.com/cms/s/34793ad8-0f22-11da-8b31-00000e2511c8.html.

40. Deborah Summers, "Dutchman Is Europe's First Terrorism Czar; New Role as More Held Over Spain Bombs," *Herald* (Glasgow), March 26, 2004, 11.

CHAPTER II

The views and ideas expressed in this chapter are the author's own; they do not reflect the position or policy of the United States government. I would like to thank the Center for Homeland Defense and Security at the Naval Postgraduate School for support to conduct the interviews associated with this project.

1. See National Commission on Terrorist Attacks upon the United States, *The 9/ 11 Commission Report: Final Report of the National Commission on Terrorist Attacks upon the United States—Authorized Report* (New York: W. W. Norton, 2004), 116.

2. Sub-Saharan African groups on the "terrorist exclusion lists" (TEL, whose members can be denied entrance into the United States) include the Interhamwe from Rwanda, the Revolutionary United Front in Sierra Leone, and the Lord's Resistance Army in Uganda. For the list see http://www.state.gov/s/ct/rls/fs/2004/ 32678.htm, and for FTOs, see http://www.state.gov/s/ct/rls/fs/37191.htm. Both were accessed on September 11, 2006; the lists were last updated in April 2004 (TEL) and October 2005 (FTO).

3. See Anne M. Lesch, "Osama bin Laden's 'Business' in Sudan," *Current History* 101 (2002), 203–9; and Rohan Gunaratna, *Inside Al Qaeda: Global Network of Terror* (New York: Berkeley Books, 2002).

4. *The 9/11 Commission Report*, 58.

5. See, for example: E. Blanche, "Africa—Is Al-Qaeda a Target in East Africa?" *Jane's Terrorism and Security Monitor*, July 1, 2003.

6. International Crisis Group (ICG), "Somalia: Countering Terrorism in a Failed State," Africa Report No. 45 (Nairobi/Brussels, May 2002); and ICG, "Counter-

terrorism in Somalia: Losing Hearts and Minds?" *Africa Report* No. 95 (Nairobi/ Brussells, July 2005). See also Gunaratna, *Inside Al Qaeda*.

7. For an excellent analysis of the rise and implications of the Islamic Courts, see the International Crisis Group, "Can the Somali Crisis Be Contained?" *Africa Report* No. 116 (Nairobi/Brussells, August 2006). There are positive and negative aspects of the Islamic Courts, both for the Somali people and for the U.S.-led war on terror.

8. ICG, "Counter-terrorism in Somalia."

9. See Gunaratna, *Inside Al Qaeda*.

10. Gørill Husby, "Islam Gains Ground in East Africa," *Jane's Intelligence Review*, May 1, 2003. Both governments deny these claims.

11. *The 9/11 Commission Report*, 58.

12. See Gunaratna, *Inside Al Qaeda*, especially 201–21. There are no precise figures to quantify the amount of support available in open-source data.

13. For example, while in Sudan, bin Laden sent weapons and trainers to the Somali warlords battling U.S. forces in the early 1990s. *The 9/11 Commission Report*, 60. See also Husby, "Islam Gains Ground," 17.

14. Data from author's interviews with Department of State officials Tricia Bacon (Intelligence), Ruth Parent (Office of the Coordinator for Counter-Terrorism, S/CT), Stacy Williams (Bureau for International Narcotics and Law Enforcement Affairs), and Rob Stapleton (S/CT), on September 22, 2004, in Washington, D.C. See also, *The 9/11 Commission Report*.

15. Kenneth W. Dam, Deputy Secretary, U.S. Department of the Treasury, "The Role of Charities and NGO's in the Financing of Terrorist Activities," statement to the U.S. Senate Committee on Banking, Housing, and Urban Affairs, Subcommittee on International Trade and Finance, Washington, D.C., August 1, 2002.

16. Charles Goredema, "Money Laundering in East and Southern Africa: An Overview of the Threat," ISS Paper 69 (April 2003); George Kegoro, "Money Laundering Patterns in Kenya," in *Profiling Money Laundering in Eastern and Southern Africa*, Charles Goredema, ed., *ISS Monograph* 90 (December 2003).

17. Kegoro, "Money Laundering Patterns in Kenya," 141.

18. Author's interview with Phillip Carter, East Africa Bureau Chief, Department of State, Washington, D.C., September 24, 2004.

19. Paul Rogers, "Lessons from Mombasa: Al Qaeda's Long-Term Strategy," *Foreign Policy in Focus*, December 6, 2002, 3.

20. "United States Department of State, Bureau for International Narcotics and Law Enforcement Affairs, *International Narcotics Control Strategy Report (INCSR), Volume II: Money Laundering and Financial Crimes*, March 2006 (hereafter *INCSR 2006*).

21. *INCSR 2006*. Unless otherwise noted, all the information on AML and CTF regimes is derived from *INCSR* reports published in 2004, 2005, and 2006, and all of it was verified against the most recent report (2006 report) at the time of writing.

22. For more discussion, see "The Prevention and Combating of Terrorism in Africa," remarks of Ambassador Cofer Black, Coordinator for the Office of Counter Terrorism (Department of State) at the Second Intergovernmental High-Level

Meeting on the Prevention and Combating of Terrorism in Africa Algiers, Algeria, October 20, 2004, http://www.state.gov/s/ct/rls/rm/2004/37230.htm, accessed November 1, 2004.

23. The *INCSR* reported that the Central Bank of Djibouti was creating the FIU in early 2006, but as of September 2006 the website of the bank does not list an FIU. It does, however, include a link to an anti-terrorism page at its website that is still under construction. See http://www.banque-centrale.dj/index.php?option=com _content&task=view&id=52&Itemid=156&lang=EN.

24. These data are from the 2006 *INCSR* report's "money laundering country/ jurisdiction table," which monitors the extent of money laundering in each country, rather than country efforts to combat money laundering. See http://www.state.gov/ g/inl/rls/nrcrpt/.

25. Ted Dagne, "Africa and the War on Terrorism: Update," CRS Report for Congress, catalog no. EBTER213, September 24, 2004.

26. Ibid. For a similar conclusion, see J. Stephen Morrison, "Somalia and Sudan's Race to the Fore in Africa," *Washington Quarterly* 25, no.2 (Spring 2002): 191–205.

27. This idea was repeated by several U.S. government officials, speaking about all of the regional governments. The evaluation of Kenya as one of the most corrupt countries in the world can be verified by its ranking on the Corruption Perceptions Index of Transparency International, available at www.Transparency.org, accessed January 25, 2006.

28. George Kegoro, "Money Laundering Patterns in Kenya," in *Profiling Money Laundering in Eastern and Southern Africa*, 138.

29. Kegoro, "Money Laundering Patterns in Kenya," 137, 149.

30. Transparency International, "Corruption Perceptions Index 2005."

31. *INCSR* 2004.

32. Carter interview.

CHAPTER 12

1. John Gershman, "Is Southeast Asia the Second Front," *Foreign Affairs*, November/December 2002, 60–74. "Southeast Asia" is taken to mean all member countries of the Association of Southeast Asian Nations (ASEAN): Indonesia, Malaysia, the Philippines, Brunei Darussalam, Vietnam, Laos, Cambodia, Burma (Myanmar), Singapore, and Thailand (but not East Timor).

2. Peter Searle, "Ethno-Religious Conflicts: Rise or Decline? Recent Developments in Southeast Asia," *Contemporary Southeast Asia*, April 2002, 1–12; Trevor Findlay, "Turning the Corner in Southeast Asia," in Michael E. Brown, ed., *The International Dimensions of Internal Conflict* (Cambridge, MA: The MIT Press, 1996), 173–204.

3. Zachary Abuza, *Militant Islam in Southeast Asia* (Boulder, CO: Lynne Rienner, 2003); and Angel M. Rabasa, *Political Islam in Southeast Asia: Moderates, Radicals, and Terrorists*, Adelphi Paper 358 (New York: Oxford University Press, 2003).

4. Rohan Gunaratna, *Inside Al Qaeda: Global Network of Terror* (New York: Columbia University Press, 2002).

5. Brahma Chellaney, "Fighting Terrorism in Southern Asia. The Lessons of History," *International Security*, Winter 2001–02, 96; see also Niklas Swanstroem and Emma Bjornehed, "Conflict Resolution of Terrorists Conflict in Southeast Asia," *Terrorism and Political Violence*, Summer 2004, 328–49; and Sheldon Simon, "Southeast Asia: Back to the Future?" in Ashley J. Tellis and Michael Wills, eds., *Strategic Asia 2004–05: Confronting Terrorism in the Pursuit of Power* (Washington, D.C.: NBAR, 2004), 293.

6. David Wright-Neville, "Dangerous Dynamics: Activists, Militants and Terrorists in Southeast Asia," *Pacific Review*, January 2004, 30. For example, the association of Malaysia's major opposition party, Parti Islam Semalaysia (PAS), with the Kumpulan Mujahidin Malaysia (KMM), made by some scholars is mainly based on media reporting in English-language newspapers close to the United Malays National Organization (UMNO) or other Barisan Nasional coalition partners; see ibid., 35. See also David Wright-Neville, "Losing the Democratic Momentum? Southeast Asia and the War on Terror," Asia Research Center Working Paper No 110 (Perth: Murdoch University, 2004); James Cotton, "Southeast Asia after 11 September," *Terrorism and Political Violence*, Spring 2003, 148–70.

7. Patricio N. Abinales, "Southeast Asia's Last People's War: The Communist Insurgency in the Post-Marcos Philippines," in Aurel Croissant, Beate Martin, and Sascha Kneip, eds., *The Politics of Death: Political Violence in Southeast Asia* (Hamburg and Muenster, Germany: Lit Verlag, forthcoming); Rizal G. Buendia, "The Mindanao Conflict in the Philippines: Ethno-Religious War or Economic Conflict?" in Croissant, Martin, and Kneip, eds., *The Politics of Death*.

8. Michael Malley, "Class, Region, and Culture: The Sources of Social Conflict in Indonesia," in Nat J. Colletta, Teck ghee Lim, and Anita Kelles-Viitanen, eds., *Social Cohesion and Conflict Prevention in Asia* (Washington, D.C.: The World Bank, 2001), 349–82.

9. Aurel Croissant, "Unrest in South Thailand: Contours, Causes and Consequences since 2001," *Contemporary Southeast Asia*, April 2005, 21–44.

10. Kumar Ramikrishna, "Terrorism in Southeast Asia: The Ideological and Political Dimensions," *Southeast Asian Affairs*, 2004, 55.

11. Stephen Ulph, "MILF Peace Talks under Fire," *Jane's Intelligence Affairs Analyst*, October 1, 2004.

12. For more information about the various groups and their involvement in the region, see Sheldon W. Simon, "Southeast Asia and the U.S. War on Terrorism," *NBR Analysis* 13, no. 4 (June 2002); Bruce Vaughn et al., "Terrorism in Southeast Asia," *CRS Report for Congress*, updated February 7, 2005; Abuza, *Militant Islam*; Anthony Davis, "Thailand Cracks Down on Illicit Arms Trade," *Jane's Intelligence Review*, December 1, 2003.

13. Cf. Tamara Makarenko, "Tracing the Dynamics of the Illicit Arms Trade," *Jane's Intelligence Review*, September 1, 2003; David Capie, "Trading the Tools of Ter-

ror: Armed Groups and Light Weapons Proliferation in Southeast Asia," in Paul J. Smith, ed., *Terrorism and Violence in Southeast Asia. Transnational Challenges to States and Regional Stability* (Armonk, NY, and London: M. E. Sharpe, 2005), 188–211.

14. Peter Chalk, "Myanmar Leads Rise in Southeast Asian Drug Trade," *Jane's Intelligence Review*, December 1, 2004, 28–29.

15. Cf. Alfredo L. Filler, "The Abu Sayaaf Group: A Growing Menace to Civil Society," *Terrorism and Political Violence* 14, no. 4 (Winter 2002), 131–62.

16. UN Monitoring Group, "Second Report of the Analytical Support and Sanctions Monitoring Team Appointed Pursuant to Resolution 1526 (2004) Concerning Al-Qaida and the Taliban and Associated Individuals and Entities," UN Security Council, February 15, 2005. Document number: S/2005/83.

17. Graham H. Turbville Jr., "Preface: Future Trends in Low Intensity Conflict," *Low Intensity Conflict & Law Enforcement* 11, no. 2/3 (Winter 2002), 161.

18. Bureau for International Narcotics and Law Enforcement Affairs, "International Narcotics Strategy Report 2005," U.S. Department of State, March 2005.

19. Helmut Schneider, "Zur Ökonomie innerstaatlicher Konflikte. Der Regionalkonflikt im Süden der Philippine," in Michael Waibel and Peter Kreisel, eds., *The Pacific Challenge. Development Trends in the 21st Century* (Göttingen, Germany: Universitätsverlag, 2005), 130.

20. Bureau for International Narcotics and Law Enforcement Affairs, "International Narcotics Strategy Report 2005," U.S. Department of State, March 2005.

21. Peter Chalk, "Light Arms Trading in SE Asia," *Jane's Intelligence Review*, March 1, 2001.

22. UN Monitoring Group, Second Report, 23.

23. International Crisis Group, "Recycling Militants in Indonesia: Darul Islam and the Australian Embassy Bombing," Asia Report Number 92, February 22, 2005, 5.

24. For a basic explanation of *zakat*, see Mark Sidel and Iftekhar Zaman, eds., *Philanthropy and Law in South Asia, Key Themes and Key Choices*, Asia Pacific Philanthropy Consortium, http://www.asianphilanthropy.org/developments/details.html?ItemId=1852&ItemDate=2005-06-01.

25. For instance, Wolters states that in Mindanao, the number of *madrasahs* financed by Arab governments and Islamic charities increased from about 1,100 in 1981 to more than 2,000 in 1988; see Willem Wolters, "Muslim Rebel Movements in the Southern Philippines: Recruitment Area for al-Qaeda Terrorists?" *Focaal—European Journal of Anthropology*, no. 40, 2002, 157.

26. UN Monitoring Group, Second Report, 14.

27. Ibid.

28. Jo Biddle, "Bin Laden's Tentacles Stretch Round Asia," *Agence France Presse*, September 18, 2002.

29. Matthew Brzezinski, "Bust and Boom," *Washington Post*, December 30, 2001.

30. UN Monitoring Group, Second Report, 28.

31. "Agencies Acted on Their Own," *The Nation*, July 30, 2003; and Zachary

Abuza, "Funding Terrorism in Southeast Asia: The Financial Network of Al Qaeda and Jemaah Islamiyah," *Contemporary Southeast Asia*, August 2003, 169.

32. Ministry of Home Affairs, "White Paper: The Jemaah Islamiyah Arrests and the Threat of Terrorism," Cmd 2 of 2003 (Singapore: Ministry of Home Affairs, January 7, 2003), 6.

33. Brian Joyce, "Terrorist Financing in Southeast Asia," *Jane's Intelligence Review*, November 1, 2002.

34. UN Monitoring Group, Second Report, 23.

35. Ibid.

36. We borrow here from the analytical framework developed by the Targeting Terrorist Finances Project, although we deviate significantly from the TTF approach. While we employ the four dimensions developed by the TTF project, the indicators we include under each dimension differ. Also, the rating of some countries (for example, Indonesia) along each of these dimensions in this chapter differs from TTF's. For more information on the Targeting Terrorist Finance Project at Brown University's Watson Institute for International Studies, see http://www.watsoninstitute.org/project _detail.cfm?id=51. The information for this section was collected from the public domain and relies most heavily on the International Narcotics Control Strategy Report published annually by the U.S. State Department, country reports to the UN Counter-Terrorism Committee, and reports by the UN Monitoring Group established pursuant to Resolution 1267 concerning al Qaeda and the Taliban and associated individuals and entities.

37. Bala Shanmugam, Mahendhiran Nair, and R. Suganthi, "Money Laundering in Malaysia," *Journal of Money Laudering Control*, Spring 2003, 376.

38. UN Monitoring Group, Second Report, 20.

39. The Asia Pacific Group lists Cambodia as a member jurisdiction while the FATF website lists it as an observer jurisdiction. The authors have deferred to the APG listing of Cambodia as a full member.

40. Cf. Gerda Falkner, Oliver Treib, Miriam Hartlapp, and Simone Leiber, *Complying with Europe: EU Harmonisation and Soft Law in the Member States* (Cambridge: Cambridge University Press, 2005).

41. L. Errico and A. Musalan, "Offshore Banking: An Analysis of Micro- and Macro-prudential Issues," IMF Working Paper 99-05 (Washington, D.C.: IMF, 1999), 10.

42. Leonides Buencamino and Sergei Gorbunov, "Informal Money Transfer Systems," DESA Discussion Paper No. 26 (New York: UN, November 2002).

43. See Tanja Börzel and Thomas Risse, "Die Wirkung internationaler Institutionen: Von der Normanerkennung zur Normeinhaltung," in Markus Jachtenfuchs and Michele Knodt, eds., *Regieren in internationalen Organisationen* (Opladen, Germany: Leske + Budrich, 2002), 141–82; Tanja Börzel and Thomas Risse, "Conceptualizing the Domestic Impact of Europe," in K. Featherstone and C. Radaelli, eds., *The Politics of Europeanization* (Oxford: Oxford University Press, 2003), 55–78.

44. Allan Castle and Joanne Lee "Money Laundering and Corruption in the Asia

Pacific," Working Paper No. 4, International Center for Criminal Law Reform and Criminal Justice Policy, March 1999, http://www.icclr.law.ubc.ca/Publications/ Reports/Paper4.PDF#search=%22Allan%20Castle%20Money%20Laundering %20and%20Corruption%20in%20the%20Asia%20Pacific%20Working%20Paper %20No.%204%20March%201999%22. See also the Control of Corruption indicator in Daniel Kaufmann, Aart Kraay, and Massimo Mastruzzi, *Governance Matters III: Governance Indicators for 1996–2002*, The World Bank, June 30, 2003, http://www .worldbank.org/wbi/governance/pdf/govmatters3.pdf; and Transparency International, *Corruption Perception Index 2004*, http://www.transparency.org/pressreleases _archive/2004/2004.10.20.cpi.en.html.

45. "A Hard Case to Crack: Money Laundering in Asia," *Corporate Financing Week*, October 1, 2003.

46. For example, see George C. Tsebelis, "Decision Making in Political Systems: Veto Players in Presidentialism, Parliamentarism, Multicameralism and Multipartyism," *British Journal of Political Science* 25 (1995), 289–325; Tsebelis, "Veto Players and Law Production in Parliamentary Democracies: An Empirical Analysis," *American Political Science Review* 93 (1999), 591–608; Tsebelis, *Veto Players: How Political Institutions Work* (Princeton, NJ: Princeton University Press, 2002); and T. Beck, G. Clarke, A. Goff, P. Keefer, and P. Walsh, "New Tools and New Tests in Comparative Political Economy: The Database on Political Institutions," *World Bank Economic Review* 15, no. 1, 2001, 165–75.

47. After 2001, the Thai-Rak-Thai government under the leadership of Prime Minister Thaksin established near-absolute control of the parliament.

48. Zachary Abuza, "Asia Hasn't Stopped the Terror Funding," *Asian Wall Street Journal*, October 1, 2003.

The views expressed in this chapter do not represent the official position of the Department of Defense, Department of Homeland Security, or the U.S. government, but are the sole responsibility of the authors.

1. A review of the literature on terrorist networks in the TBA reveals limited substantive data after the June 2002 arrest of Assad Ahmad Barakat. More specifically, sources cited throughout the current literature are often repetitive and dated. This is, however, to be expected given the clandestine nature of these activities and of the individuals engaged in them.

2. During the 1999–2001 period, Islamic extremist groups, specifically Hezbollah and Hamas, reportedly received a total of between $50 million and $500 million from Arab residents of Foz do Iguaçu through Paraguayan financial institutions. See Rex Hudson, *Terrorist and Organized Crime Groups in the Tri-Border Area (TBA) of South America* (Washington, D.C.: Federal Research Division, Library of Congress, July 2003), 27–30.

3. LaVerle Berry, Glenn E. Curtis, John N. Gibbs, Rex A. Hudson, Tara Karacan, Nina Kollars, Ramon Miro, *Nations Hospitable to Organized Crime and Terrorism* (Washington, D.C.: Federal Research Division, Library of Congress, October 2003), 174, 192; Mark S. Steinitz, "Middle East Terrorist Activity in Latin America," *Policy Papers on the Americas* 14, Study 7 (Washington, D.C.: Center for Strategic and International Studies, July 2003), 10, 13; Rachel Ehrenfeld, *Funding Evil: How Terrorism Is Financed—and How to Stop It* (Chicago: Bonus Books, 2003), 56–57, 146–52; U.S. Department of State, *Patterns of Global Terrorism, 2003* (Washington, D.C.: U.S. Department of State, April 2004), 127 (hereafter cited as *Patterns*, with appropriate year); U.S. Department of State, "U.S. Is Concerned Tri-Border Area of South America Funds Terrorism," *International Information Programs Washington File*, December 20, 2002, http://usinfo.state.gov/regional/ar/argentina/02122002.htm; Rohan Gunaratna, *Inside Al Qaeda: Global Network of Terror* (Berkeley, CA: The Berkley Publishing Group, 2002), 219–21; Lawrence J. Martines, "Tres Fronteras (Three Borders): The Nexus of Islamic Terrorism in Latin America," *Journal of Counterterrorism & Homeland Security International* 9, no. 1 (Winter 2003); Michele Saledo, "Latin America's Fastest-Growing Faith Resents Terror Allegations from U.S.," *Sun Sentinel*, September 1, 2003, http://www.sun-sentinel.com/news/local/caribbean/sfl-901overview,0,5176531.story, accessed September 20, 2004; and Hudson, *Terrorist and Organized Crime Groups*, 9. According to *Patterns of Global Terrorism* 1996–2006, press reports of al Qaeda operatives in the TBA either have been disproved or have not been corroborated by intelligence and law enforcement officials.

4. Berry et. al., *Nations Hospitable*, 1.

5. Julio A. Cirino, Silvana L. Elizondo, and Geoffrey Wawro, "Latin America's Lawless Areas and Failed States: An Analysis of the New Threats," in *Latin American Security Challenges: A Collaborative Inquiry from North to South*, Newport Paper 21, ed. Paul D. Taylor (Newport, RI: Center for Naval Warfare Studies, Naval War College, 2004), 24.

6. Hudson, *Terrorist and Organized Crime Groups*, 12.

7. Ibid., 11.

8. Jeffrey Goldberg, "In the Party of God: Hezbollah Sets Up Operations in South America and the United States," *New Yorker*, October 28, 2002, 78.

9. Ibid., 75.

10. See LaVerle Berry, Glenn E. Curtis, Rex A. Hudson, and Nina A. Kollars, *A Global Overview of Narcotics-Funded Terrorist and Other Extremist Groups* (Washington, D.C.: Federal Research Division, Library of Congress, May 2002), 33.

11. Ibid., 34.

12. Ibid.

13. Ibid.

14. When PNP officers raided his Casa Apolo import-export trading company on October 3, 2001, Barakat was generally recognized as Hezbollah's military operations chief in the TBA, as well as its chief fund-raising officer in the Southern Cone (see Hudson, *Terrorist and Organized Crime Groups*, 71). During this raid, PNP officers

seized boxes containing financial statements detailing $250,000 in monthly transfers to the Middle East (see Ehrenfeld, *Funding Evil*, 148–49). PNP officers discovered evidence that Barakat and an associate had sent $505,200 to Hezbollah accounts in Canada, Chile, and the United States, and $524,000 to Lebanon (see Goldberg, "In the Party of God," 78).

15. Hudson, *Terrorist and Organized Crime Groups*, 26.

16. Ibid., 25–26.

17. Matthew Schroeder, *Small Arms, Terrorism, and the OAS Firearms Convention*, Federation of American Scientists, Occasional Paper no. 1, March 2004, 22.

18. Hudson, *Terrorist and Organized Crime Groups*, 31, 78.

19. Ibid., 29. See also U.S. Department of Treasury, "Treasury Designates Islamic Extremist, Two Companies Supporting Hezbollah in Tri-Border Area," June 10, 2004, from the Office of Public Affairs, http://www.ustreas.gov/press/releases/js1720.htm.

20. Hudson, *Terrorist and Organized Crime Groups*, 30.

21. Martin Brakenridge, "Analysis: The Scourge of Money Laundering," *United Press International*, Asuncion, Paraguay, June 4, 2004. See also "Paraguay: 35 Laundering Centers Reportedly Operating Illegally in Ciudad del Este," *ABC Color*, July 8, 2003.

22. Hudson, *Terrorist and Organized Crime Groups*, 27.

23. Larry Rohter, "South America Region under Watch for Signs of Terrorists," *New York Times*, December 15, 2002, 32; Jean-Charles Brisard, "Terrorism Financing: Roots and Trends of Saudi Terrorism Financing," an independent consultant's report submitted to the President of the U.N. Security Council, December 19, 2002, 12–13; and Steinitz, "Middle Eastern Terrorist Activity in Latin America," 9.

24. Goldberg, "In the Party of God," 76–77. See also U.S. Department of Treasury, "Treasury Designates Islamic Extremist."

25. Berry, *A Global Overview*, 27.

26. Goldberg, "In the Party of God," 79.

27. See Nikos Passas, *Informal Value Transfer Systems and Criminal Organizations: A Study into So-Called Underground Banking Systems*, Dutch Ministry of Justice, http://www.minjust.nl:8080/b_organ/wodc/publications/ivts.pdf, 27–29.

28. See Hudson, *Terrorist and Organized Crime Groups*, 69.

29. Ibid.

30. This section's sources regarding government-instituted legislative changes were derived primarily from the U.S. Department of State and findings from the FATF Mutual Evaluations. Consequently, the sources used in this section are considered reliable.

31. "Inter-American Convention Against Terrorism," OAS, http://www.cicte.oas.org/Docs/Treaty%20as%20approved.doc.

32. Ibid. As of February 2004, 33 of the 34 OAS member states, including Argentina, Brazil, and Paraguay, had signed this convention.

33. Cofer Black, "Building an Effective Hemispheric Counterterrorism Strategy,"

OAS-CICTE Fourth Regular Session, Montevideo, Uruguay, January 29, 2004, U.S. Department of State, http://montevideo.usembassy.gov/usaweb/paginas/18-Jan2004 -05bEN.shtml.

34. See *CICTE Mission*, http://www.cicte.oas.org/mission.htm.

35. Kevin Newmeyer, *Terrorism and Drug Trafficking: The Approach by the Organization of American States*, OAS-CICTE, February 2004, http://www.osce.org/documents/sg/2004/03/2192_en.pdf.

36. Paul Wilkinson, *Terrorism versus Democracy: The Liberal State Response* (London: Cass, 2002), 121, 195–96. Wilkinson makes a compelling argument that bilateral cooperation has been the most effective technique in combating terrorism in Europe, especially regarding border control and intelligence sharing.

37. *Patterns 2003*, 78.

38. Ibid.

39. Ibid.

40. While 9/11 changed U.S. perceptions regarding the nation's national security interests and motivated a series of aggressive military operations in support of the Global War on Terrorism, it has not had the same effect on the rest of the Western Hemisphere. See Pedro Villagra Delgado, "Hemispheric Security: A Perception from the South," (Carlisle, PA: Strategic Studies Institute, July 2003), http://www .carlisle.army.mil/ssi/pdffiles/00006.pdf.

41. See Financial Action Task Force of South America against Money Laundering (GAFISUD), "About GAFISUD," http://www.gafisud.org/home.htm.

42. Ibid.

43. Ibid.

44. For an exhaustive list of FATF members, see "FATF Members and Observers," FATF, http://www1.oecd.org/fatf/Members_en.htm, September 6, 2004.

45. "Paraguay," *FATF Annual Report 2003–2004*, http://www.oecd.org/fatf/pdf/ AR2004-Annexes_en.PDF.

46. U.S. Department of State, "Argentina," *International Narcotics Control Strategy Report, 2003*, Washington, D.C.: U.S. Department of State, March 2004. Hereafter cited as *INCSR*, with appropriate year.

47. E. Anthony Wayne, Assistant Secretary of State for Economic and Business Affairs, testimony before the Senate Committee on Banking, Housing and Urban Affairs, April 4, 2006.

48. "Brazil," *INCSR 2003*.

49. Ibid.

50. "Paraguay," *INCSR 2003*.

51. See *Patterns, 2003*, 80–81. Since Paraguay does not have any specific anti-terrorist statutes, the government of Paraguay was forced to prosecute all three alleged terrorist financiers for tax evasion and/or related illicit financial activities. Ali Nizar Dahrough obtained early release from the Ciudad del Este Penitentiary on November 2, 2005.

52. See U.S. Department of Treasury, "Treasury Designates Islamic Extremist."

53. Blanca Madani, "Hezbollah's Global Finance Network: The Triple Frontier," *Middle East Intelligence Bulletin*, January 2002, http://www.meib.org/articles/0201_l2.htm.

54. Ibid., 3.

55. Ibid.

56. The government of Brazil's insistence in this regard is well documented. See "Brasil afirma que la triple frontera está libre de actividad terrorista," *ABC Color Digital*, September 16, 2004, http://www.abc.com.py/articulos.php?fec=2004-09-16&pid=134223&sec=7. See also Madani, "Hezbollah's Global Finance Network," 4; Hudson, *Terrorism and Organized Crime Groups*, 64; and "Brazil," *INSCR 2003*.

57. Gustavo R. García, "La Fiscalía acusó a Hijazi y denunció a casas de cambio," *Ultima Hora*, February 9, 2005, Actualidad, 4–5.

58. Gustavo R. García, "Pequeño casa de empeño remesó US$ 100 milliones a Beirut y EEUU," *Ultima Hora*, February 4, 2005, Actualidad, 2–3. The original raid on Telefax occurred in March 2004.

59. See "Investigación de fiscalía sobre levado de dinero es parcial," *ABC Color*, February 7, 2005, Interior, 32; Gustavo R. García, "Seis casas de cambio del Este remesaron US $60 milliones," *Ultima Hora*, February 6, 2005, Actualidad, 2–3; and García, "Pequeño casa de empeño," 2.

60. García, "La Fiscalía acusó a Hijazi," 5.

61. See "La ilegalidad cambiaria sigue al descubierto," *Ultima Hora*, February 4, 2005, Actualidad, 3.

62. See "Casas de cambio ocultaron remesas a Superintendencia," *Ultima Hora*, February 9, 2005, Actualidad, 5.

63. See Steven Monblatt, "Terrorism and Drugs in the Americas: The OAS Response," *Americas Forum: Department of Communications and External Relations* 4, no. 2, February/March 2004.

64. Cirino et al, "Latin America's Lawless Areas and Failed States," 40–41.

65. Hudson, *Terrorist and Organized Crime Groups*, 49. See also Berry, *Nations Hospitable to Organized Crime*, 179; and Ehrenfeld, *Funding Evil*, 182. Ehrenfeld refers to this type of corruption as "government for hire."

66. Hudson, *Terrorist and Organized Crime Groups*, 61.

67. Ibid., 66. See also "Paraguay," *INSCR 2003*.

68. See Bruce Zagaris and Scott Ehlers, "Drug Trafficking & Money Laundering," *Foreign Policy in Focus* 6, no. 18 (May 2001), http://www.fpif.org/pdf/vol6/18iflaunder.pdf. According to Zagaris and Ehlers, very few money laundering cases are actually prosecuted in the United States due to this inherent difficulty.

69. *Patterns, 2003*, 79.

70. Donald M. Snow, *National Security for a New Era: Globalization and Geopolitics* (New York: Pearson Longman, 2004), 342.

71. Other South American countries in different stages of association with MERCOSUR include Chile, Bolivia, Colombia, Peru, and Venezuela. MERCOSUR is recognized as the third-largest regional trading bloc in the world.

72. Snow, *National Security for a New Era*, 342.

73. Hudson, *Terrorist and Organized Crime Groups*, 4.

74. See "Caución y medidas," *Ultima Hora*, February 10, 2005, Actualidad, 4 for detailed information regarding the alleged charges against Hijazi. Hijazi faces a maximum of 12 years in prison if found guilty on all charges.

75. See "El preso Hatem, un vil engañador," *Ultima Hora*, October 17, 2004, Sucesos, 53.

76. Ibid. See also "Hatem Barakat con prisión domiciliaria," *Ultima Hora*, October 16, 2004; and "Árabe acusado de varios delitos está con reclusion domiciliaria," *La Primicia*, October 20–26, 2004.

77. Steven Johnson, *Why the U.S. Must Re-engage in Latin America*, Heritage Foundation Policy Research and Analysis, October 9, 2004, http://www.heritage.org/Research/LatinAmerica/BG1694es.cfm.

CHAPTER 14

1. See *National Strategy for Combating Terrorism*, February 2003, http://www.whitehouse.gov/news/releases/2003/02/20030214-7.html.

2. See *The National Security Strategy of the United States of America*, September 2002, http://www.whitehouse.gov/nsc/nss.pdf.

3. See Office of Homeland Security, *National Strategy for Homeland Security*, July 2002, http://www.whitehouse.gov/homeland/book/nat_strat_hls.pdf.

4. Raphael Perl, "Terrorism and United States Foreign Policy," remarks to the German Council on Foreign Relations, Berlin, July 2, 2002, at http://www.usembassy.it/file2002_07/alia/a2070206.htm; see also Raphael Perl, "U.S. Anti-Terror Strategy," remarks to the Konrad Adenauer Foundation, Berlin, June 30, 2003, at http://usinfo.state.gov/ei/Archive/2003/Dec/31-646035.html.

5. See Raphael Perl, "U.S. Anti-Terror Strategy."

6. Martin A. Weiss, "Terrorist Financing: The 9/11 Commission Recommendation," *Congressional Research Service* (*CRS*), Report RS21902; see also, Alfred Prados and Christopher Blanchard, "Saudi Arabia: Terrorist Financing Issues," *CRS*, Report RL32499.

7. Note that many of the Commission's findings are consistent with generic findings contained in a series of pre-9/11 reports, such as the June 5, 2000, congressionally-mandated report of the bipartisan National Commission on Terrorism, "Countering the Changing Threat of International Terrorism"; see also, Raphael Perl, "National Commission on Terrorism Report: Background and Issues for Congress," *CRS*, Report RS20598.

8. See *National Strategy for Combating Terrorism*.

9. See Raphael Perl, "U.S. Anti-Terror Strategy."

10. Part of the problem is that the oil boom of the 1970s led to dramatically increased funding of Islamic religious education without concomitant oversight, often giving virtually free rein to radical Islamists.

11. Raphael Perl, "Combating Terrorism: The 9/11 Commission Recommendations and the National Strategies," testimony before the House Subcommittee on National Security, Emerging Threats, and International Relations, September 22, 2004, at http://reform.house.gov/NSETIR/News/DocumentSingle.aspx?Document ID=5481.

12. National Commission on Terrorist Attacks upon the United States, *Monograph on Terrorist Financing*, Staff Report to the Commission, 2004, 152. Hereafter referred to as *The 9/11 Staff Monograph*.

13. National Commission on Terrorist Attacks upon the United States, *Final Report of the National Commission on Terrorist Attacks upon the United States*, 382 (hereafter *The 9/11 Commission Report*).

14. See Raphael Perl, "U.S. Anti-Terror Strategy and the 9/11 Commission Report," *CRS*, Report RL32522, http://www.gpoaccess.gov/911/index.htmlm; see also *The 9/11 Commission Report*, 382.

15. *The 9/11 Staff Monograph*.

16. "Executive Summary," *The 9/11 Commission Report*, July 2004, 18–19, http://www.9.11commission.gov/report/911Report_Exec.pdf. According to the Commission, the United States should "expect less from trying to dry up terrorist money and more from following the money from intelligence, as a tool to hunt terrorists, understand their networks, and disrupt their operations."

17. *The 9/11 Commission Report*, 382. This is not to say that the amount of funding seized since 9/11 has been insignificant: roughly $200 million had been seized as of late April 2004, according to the congressional testimony of Treasury Undersecretary Samuel W. Bodman before the Senate Committee on Banking, Housing, and Urban Affairs, April 29, 2004.

18. *The 9/11 Commission Report*, 379.

19. Security Council Resolution 1373 requires member states to take measures to curb terror financing.

20. Public Law 108-458, signed into law December 12, 2004.

21. *The 9/11 Commission Report*, 382. Note that in an earlier era of state-sponsored and state-funded terrorism, making a sizable dent in the funding of terrorist groups may well have been an achievable policy objective.

22. Executive Summary, *The 9/11 Commission Report*, 18–19, at http://www.9.11 commission.gov/report/911Report_Exec.pdf.

23. Laura Sullivan, "U.S. Split on Usefulness of Tracing Money Trails to Prevent Terrorist Plots," *Seattle Times*, August 3, 2004.

24. *The 9/11 Commission Report*, 382.

25. Note, however, that funding from charity or relief organizations, though a significant source of funding for terrorist operations, is by no means the sole source. See *National Money Laundering Strategy*, July 2002, http://www.treas.gov/press/releases/docs/monlaund.pdf.

26. Wayne Parry, "U.S. Rejects Muslims' Plea for 'Approved' Charities," Associated Press dispatch, October 14, 2004.

27. Michael Kraft, "Fight against Terrorism Needs Hard Cash, Not Just Tough Talk," *Milwaukee Journal*, August 6, 2004. David Kay Johnston, "IRS Request for More Terrorism Investigators Is Denied," *New York Times*, March 31, 2004.

CHAPTER 15

The views expressed in this document do not represent the official position of the Department of Defense, Department of Homeland Security, or the U.S. government, but are the sole responsibility of the author.

1. Anne L. Clunan, Personal communication with former Clinton NSC staff member responsible for counter-terrorism, September 27, 2004.

2. Clunan, Interview with senior OFAC official, October 14, 2004. All interviews were conducted in Washington, D.C.

3. John Roth, Douglas Greenburg, Serena Wille, "Monograph on Terrorist Financing—Report to the Commission," National Commission on Terrorist Attacks upon the United States, 2004: 11 (hereafter The 9/11 Staff Monograph).

4. U.S. Department of State Bureau for International Narcotics and Law Enforcement Affairs, *International Narcotics Control Strategy Report, Part II. Money Laundering and Financial Crimes* (March 2004); hereafter *INCSR 2003*.

5. Clunan, Interviews with former NSC official for counter-terrorist financing, October 12, 2004; FinCEN official, October 12, 2004; and OFAC official, October 14, 2004.

6. Clunan, Interviews with State Department officials, September 20 and 23, 2004, and OFAC official October 14, 2004.

7. Robert D. Putnam, "Diplomacy and Domestic Politics: The Logic of Two-Level Games," *International Organization* 42, no. 3 (1988): 427–60.

8. Mancur Olson, *The Logic of Collective Action* (Cambridge, MA: Harvard University Press, 1967/1971); Robert Keohane, *After Hegemony: Cooperation and Discord in the World Political Economy* (Princeton, NJ: Princeton University Press, 1984).

9. These include the 1963 Tokyo Convention on Offenses and Certain Other Acts Committed on Board Aircraft; 1970 Hague Convention for the Unlawful Seizure of Aircraft; 1971 Montreal Convention for the Suppression of Unlawful Acts against the Safety of Civil Aviation; 1973 Convention on the Prevention and Punishment of Crimes against Internationally Protected Persons, Including Diplomatic Agents; 1979 Convention against the Taking of Hostages; 1979 Convention on the Physical Protection of Nuclear Material; 1988 Protocol for the Suppression of Unlawful Acts of Violence at Airports Serving International Civil Aviation (supplements the 1971 Montreal Convention); 1988 Rome Convention for the Suppression of Unlawful Acts against the Safety of Maritime Navigation; 1988 Protocol for the Suppression of Unlawful Acts against the Safety of Fixed Platforms Located on the Continental Shelf (supplements the Rome Convention); 1991 Convention on the Marking of Plastic Explosives for the Purpose of Detection; 1997 Convention for the Suppression of Ter-

rorist Bombings; 1999 Convention for the Suppression of the Financing of Terrorism; and 2005 International Convention for the Suppression of Acts of Nuclear Terrorism.

10. Chantal De Jonge Oudraat, "The United Nations and the Campaign against Terrorism," *Disarmament Forum* no. 1 (2004): 30–31.

11. Ilias Bantekas, "The International Law of Terrorist Financing," *American Journal of International Law* 97, no. 2 (April 2003): 316.

12. Oudraat, "UN against Terrorism," 31.

13. Bantekas, "Terrorist Financing," 316.

14. For example, the UN Convention against Transnational Organized Crime does not include terrorist acts.

15. Clunan, Interview with State Department official, September 23, 2004.

16. UN Security Council, "First Report of the Analytical Support and Sanctions Monitoring Team Appointed Pursuant to Resolution 1526 (2004) Concerning Al-Qaida and the Taliban and Associated Individuals and Entities," UN Doc. S/2004/679, 5.

17. Bantekas, "Terrorist Financing," 323–24.

18. UN Security Council, "First Report of the Analytical Support and Sanctions Monitoring Team," 5.

19. Clunan, Interview with State Department official October 13, 2004; see also Bantekas, "Terrorist Financing," 328;.

20. NCCT Initiative, FATF, at http://www1.oecd.org/fatf/NCCT_en.htm; see also *INCSR 2003*, 49–50.

21. *INCSR 2003*, 52–57.

22. The Egmont Group, "Financial Intelligence Units of the World," June 13, 2001, http://www.fatf-gafi.org/pdf/EGFIUlist2001_en.pdf, and June 14, 2006, http://www.fincen.gov/int_egmont.html; Clunan, Interview with FinCEN official, October 12, 2004.

23. *INCSR 2003*, 48.

24. Oudraat, "UN against Terrorism," 32.

25. Bantekas, "Terrorist Financing," 326.

26. Ibid.

27. The CTC is the UN's "leading body to promote collective action against international terrorism," while the UN Office on Drugs and Crime (UNODC) has been empowered as the implementing arm for the CTC. "Terrorism," UNODC, at http://unodc.org/unodc/en/terrorism.html.

28. Clunan, interview with State Department official, September 23, 2004.

29. Oudraat, "UN against Terrorism," 33.

30. Kofi Annan, "Uniting against Terrorism: Recommendations for a Global Counter-terrorism Strategy," *Report of the Secretary-General to the United Nations General Assembly*, A/60/825, April 27, 2006. See also table 2, UN Economic and Social Council, "Strengthening International Cooperation and Technical Assistance in Preventing and Combating Terrorism," *Report of the Secretary General to the Commission on Crime Prevention and Criminal Justice*, E/CN.15/2004/8, March 17, 2004, 14.

31. *The 9/11 Staff Monograph*, 45.

32. UN Security Council, "First Report of the Analytical Support and Sanctions Monitoring Team," 12; see also *The 9/11 Staff Monograph*, 45.

33. Egmont Group "Financial Intelligence Units of the World," June 13, 2001, and June 14, 2006.

34. "Twelve-Month Pilot Project of Anti-Money Laundering and Combating the Financing of Terrorism Assessments," *IMF and the World Bank Joint Report on the Review of the Pilot Project*, March 10, 2004.

35. Clunan, Interview with State Department officials, September 20 and 23 and October 13, 2004.

36. Clunan, Interview with State Department officials, October 13–14, 2004.

37. UN Economic and Social Council, "Strengthening International Cooperation and Technical Assistance in Preventing and Combating Terrorism," tables 1, 7.

38. Clunan, Interview with State Department official, September 20, 2004.

39. Clunan, Interview with FinCEN official, October 12, 2004.

40. Clunan, Interview with State Department officials, September 20 and 23, 2004.

41. Clunan, Interviews with State Department officials, September 20 and October 13, 2004.

42. Clunan, Interviews with FinCEN and State Department officials, September 20 and 23 and October 12, 2004.

43. Clunan, Interview with State Department official, September 23, 2004.

44. *INCSR 2003*; U.S. Department of State, *Patterns of Global Terrorism 2003*, Washington, D.C., April 2004; Francis T. Miko and Christian Froehlich, "Germany's Role in Fighting Terrorism: Implications for U.S. Policy," *CRS Report for Congress*, December 27, 2004; and HM Treasury, "Combating the Financing of Terrorism: A Report on UK Action," October 24, 2002; http://www.hm-treasury.gov.uk/documents/international _issues/terrorist_financing/int_terrorfinance_combatfinance.cfm.

45. "The Fight against Terrorist Financing," *Note of the Secretary General/High Representative and the Commission to the Council of the European Union*, 16089/04, December 14, 2004, http://ue.eu.int/uedocs/cmsUpload/EUplan16090.pdf; see also "EU Plan of Action on Combating Terrorism—Update," First Review by the Presidency of the European Council, 16090/04, December 14, 2004, http://ue.eu.int/uedocs/cmsUpload/16089fight_against_terrorist_financing.pdf.

46. Clunan, Interviews with State Department officials.

47. National Commission on Terrorist Attacks upon the United States, *The 9/11 Commission Report*, 98–100, 122–23, 185. The Commission points out that after the Iran-Contra scandal, the other federal bureaucracies were very skeptical about taking directives from the NSC.

48. Ibid., 100–102.

49. Ibid., 100.

50. *The 9/11 Staff Monograph*, 4–5.

51. *The 9/11 Commission Report*, 101.

52. Clunan, Interview with former Clinton national security deputy director, Washington, D.C., October 14, 2004.

53. *The 9/11 Commission Report*, 73.

54. *The 9/11 Commission Report*, 170–71; see also *The 9/11 Staff Monograph*, 34–35.

55. *The 9/11 Commission Report*, 109.

56. Ibid.

57. *The 9/11 Staff Monograph*, 40–41.

58. *The 9/11 Commission Report*, 122.

59. Executive Order 13099, Aug. 20, 1999, cited in *The 9/11 Commission Report*, 126.

60. *The 9/11 Commission Staff Monograph*, 4–6.

61. "Terrorist Financing: Current Efforts and Policy Issues for Congress," *CRS Report for Congress*, August 20, 2004, 9–10; and "Terrorist Financing: U.S. Agency Efforts and Inter-Agency Coordination," *CRS Report for Congress*, August 3, 2005, 11–12.

62. *The 9/11 Commission Report*, 100–101.

63. Bantekas, "Terrorist Financing," 328.

64. Mariano-Florentino Cuellar, "The Tenuous Relationship between the Fight against Money Laundering and the Disruption of Criminal Finance," *Stanford Public Law and Legal Theory Working Paper Series*, Research Paper No. 64 (September 2003): 337 note 88 and 338 note 90.

65. Ibid., 358.

66. Cuellar, "Tenuous Relationship," 359–60.

67. *The 9/11 Staff Monograph*, 38.

68. *The 9/11 Staff Monograph*, 38–39.

69. Cuellar, "Tenuous Relationship," 360–61.

70. *The 9/11 Staff Monograph*, 37.

71. "Executive Order 12947 Prohibiting Transactions with Terrorists Who Threaten to Disrupt the Middle East Peace Process," January 23, 1995.

72. *The 9/11 Staff Monograph*, 37–38.

73. *The 9/11 Commission Report*, 100–102; Clunan, Interview with former national security deputy director , October 14, 2004, and with former director of counter-terrorist financing at the NSC, October 12, 2004.

74. *The 9/11 Staff Monograph*, 4–6.

75. See *The 9/11 Commission Report* and *The 9/11 Staff Monograph* for further discussion of this inability.

76. *The 9/11 Commission Report*, 102–7.

77. Ibid., 106.

78. Ibid., 118–19.

79. Ibid., 107.

80. Clunan, Interview with former deputy national security advisor, October 14, 2004.

81. *The 9/11 Staff Monograph*, 41–42.

82. This unit became the Terrorism Financing Unit under the Department of Justice's Counterterrorism Section. *The 9/11 Staff Monograph*, 42.

83. *The 9/11 Staff Monograph*, 47.

84. Council on Foreign Relations, *Terrorist Financing*, Report of an Independent Task Force Sponsored by the Council on Foreign Relations, November 2002 (hereafter 2002 CFR Report), 23. This criticism was reiterated in the Independent Task Force's 2004 Update to the CFR Report, *Update on the Global Campaign against Terrorist Financing*, Report of an Independent Task Force Sponsored by the Council on Foreign Relations, June 15, 2004 (hereafter 2004 CFR Report), 31.

85. *The 9/11 Staff Monograph*, 47; see also 2002 CFR Report; and 2004 CFR Report.

86. *The 9/11 Staff Monograph*, 44; see also "Terrorist Financing: Current Efforts and Policy Issues for Congress," 27 and 37.

87. Clunan, Interviews with officials at the State Department, FinCEN, and OFAC, September 20 and 23 and October 12–14, 2004. See also "Terrorist Financing: Better Strategic Planning Needed to Coordinate U.S. Efforts to Deliver Counter-Terrorism Financing Training and Technical Assistance Abroad," *United States Government Accountability Office Report to Congressional Requesters*, October 2005, 14–19; (hereafter GAO 2005) and David M. Walker, "Terrorist Financing: Agencies Can Improve Efforts to Deliver Counter-terrorism-Financing Training and Technical Assistance Abroad," testimony before the Committee on Financial Services, Subcommittee on Oversight Investigations, U.S. House of Representatives, April 6, 2006, 1–30.

88. Clunan, Interview with State Department official, September 20, 2004.

89. Clunan, Interview with State Department officials, October 13, 2004.

90. Clunan, Interview with State Department official, October 13, 2004.

91. Clunan, Interviews with officials at FinCEN, the State Department, and OFAC, October 12–14, 2004. See also GAO 2005, 14–15.

92. Clunan, Interviews with officials at FinCEN, State Department, and OFAC, October 12–14, 2004.

93. *The 9/11 Commission Report*, chapter 3; see also *The 9/11 Staff Monograph*, 4–6.

94. *The 9/11 Staff Monograph*, 79; also Clunan, Interview with former NSC director of counter-terrorism finance, October 12, 2004, and State Department officials, September 23 and October 13, 2004.

95. Cuellar, "Tenuous Relationship," 361–62; see also 2002 CFR Report, 13, 26.

96. *The 9/11 Staff Monograph*, 99.

97. Ibid., 79.

98. Ibid., 80–81.

99. Ibid., 85–86.

100. Ibid., Illinois charities case study.

101. Clunan, Interviews with State Department officials October 13, 2004.

102. Eric Lichtblau and James Risen, "Bank Data Is Sifted by U.S. in Secret to Block Terror," *New York Times*, June 23, 2006.

103. Clunan, Interviews with OFAC, FinCEN, and State Department officials, October 12–13, 2004.

104. *The 9/11 Staff Monograph*, 37.

105. Ibid., 48–49.

106. Lichtblau and Risen, "Bank Data Is Sifted by U.S. in Secret to Block Terror."

107. Clunan, Interview with State Department and OFAC officials, October 13–14, 2004.

108. GAO 2005, 19.

109. *The 9/11 Staff Monograph*; also Clunan, all interviews.

110. Clunan, Interview with FinCEN official, October 12.

111. Clunan, Interviews with State Department and FinCEN officials, October 12–13.

112. CFR 2002; see also CFR 2004.

113. Clunan, all interviews. See also GAO 2005, 19.

114. Clunan, Interview with State Department official, September 23, 2004.

115. *The 9/11 Staff Monograph*, 46–47.

116. Clunan, Interviews with State Department officials, September 20–23 and October 13, 2004.

CHAPTER 16

1. John Horgan and Max Taylor, "Playing the 'Green Card'—Financing the Provisional IRA: Part 2," *Terrorism and Political Violence* 15, no. 2 (Summer 2003): 1–60; P. Norman, "The Terrorist Finance Unit and the Joint Action Group on Organised Crime: New Organisational Models and Investigative Strategies to Counter 'Organised Crime' in the UK," *Howard Journal of Criminal Justice* 37, no. 4 (1998), 375–92.

2. National Commission on Terrorist Attacks upon the United States, "Staff Monograph on Terrorism Financing," 2004.

3. As Richard A. Clarke, former National Coordinator for Counterterrorism on the National Security Council noted in testimony before the Senate Banking, Housing, and Urban Affairs Committee on October 22, 2003: "The questions we asked then [in 1995] of the CIA were never answered, and we asked them for six years: How much money does it cost to be Al Qaida? What's their annual operating budget? Where do they get their money? Where do they stash their money? Where do they move their money? How? . . . Those questions asked from the White House, at high levels, for five or six years were never answered, because, according to the intelligence community, it was too hard."

4. Council on Foreign Relations, *Terrorist Financing: Report of an Independent Task Force* (New York: Council on Foreign Relations, 2002), 12–14.

5. The White House, "Three Years of Progress in the War on Terror," Fact Sheet,

September 11, 2004, http://www.whitehouse.gov/news/releases/2004/09/print/20040911.html, accessed on January 24, 2006.

6. Council on Foreign Relations, *Terrorist Financing*, 12–14.

7. Botswana, Sri Lanka, the United Kingdom, and Uzbekistan were the only four parties prior to 9/11. The United States ratified the Convention on June 25, 2002.

8. The State Department's Bureau for International Narcotics and Law Enforcement Affairs tracked 203 countries and territories in its *International Narcotics Control Strategy Report 2006. Volume II: Money Laundering and Financing Crimes* (Washington, D.C.: U.S. Department of State, March 2006) (hereafter *INCSR 2006*). However, since Kosovo, Niue, and Taiwan are not eligible to subscribe to international treaties, they were excluded from the overall tally. *INCSR 2006* only provides information on parties to the treaty as of December 31, 2003. A more up-to-date list of signatories and parties to the treaty is at the United Nations Treaty Collection website, http://untreaty.un.org/ENGLISH/bible/englishinternetbible/partI/chapterXVIII/treaty12.asp, accessed on January 16, 2006.

9. "Comparative Table," *INCSR 2006*, 42–50.

10. On the costs of developing state enforcement capacity to target criminal finance, see Mario-Florentino Cuellar, "The Mismatch between State Power and State Capacity in Transnational Law Enforcement," *Stanford Public Law and Legal Theory Working Paper Series*, no. 70 (November 2003): 29–34.

11. "Comparative Table," *INCSR 2006*.

12. Thomas J. Biersteker, "Challenges Facing Multilateral Responses to Transnational Terrorist Threats: Lessons from the Counter-Terrorist Effort to Freeze Terrorist Finances," manuscript, The Watson Institute, Brown University, 2002, 4.

13. Council on Foreign Relations, *Terrorist Financing*, 16. Biersteker, "Challenges Facing Multilateral Responses to Transnational Terrorist Threats," 10.

14. See chapter 10 by Loretta Napoleoni.

15. Government Accountability Office, "Terrorist Financing: Better Strategic Planning Needed to Coordinate U.S. Efforts to Deliver Counter-Terrorism Financing Training and Technical Assistance Abroad," GAO-06-19, Washington D.C., October 2005.

16. Martin A. Weiss, "Terrorist Financing: U.S. Agency Efforts and Inter-Agency Coordination," *Congressional Research Service*, August 3, 2005, 9–10. The leadership posts were filled in November 2004, after eight months of vacancy, and as of August 2005 only a little more than half of FTATG's staffing needs had been filled by member agencies.

17. The White House, "Three Years of Progress in the War on Terror."

18. Martin A. Weiss, "Terrorist Financing."

19. See chapter 5 by Phil Williams.

20. Zachary Abuza, "Funding Terrorism in Southeast Asia: The Financial Network of Al Qaeda and Jemaah Islamiya," *NBR Analysis* 14, no. 5.

21. Though the Department of Treasury officially cites output measures that should be taken as a sign of their effectiveness in CTF, they acknowledge the difficulty

of identifying measures of effectiveness. Government Accountability Office, "Terrorist Financing," October 2005. A RAND conference of CTF experts in 2005 reached similar conclusions (personal communication with Joseph M. "Jody" Myers, former Clinton administration counter-terrorism official).

22. Government Accountability Office, "Terrorist Financing," October 2005.

Index

Abu Dhabi Declaration on Hawala, 166
Abu Sayyaf Brigade, 110
Abu Sayyaf Group (ASG), 207–9
accountability, 57–58
  rational choice, 58–60
Afghan Arabs
  bin Laden, Taliban, and, 104–6
  funding and support for, 103–4
Afghan terrorism, 94, 113–14
  Afghan Arabs, bin Laden, and, 101–4
  resistance to, from sympathetic states,
    111–13
  Taliban as harbinger of, 94–101
  Wahabbism and, 109–11
Africa, 42, 147, 187. *See also* East Africa
  rising concern for terrorism in, 187–88
Ahmed, Rabei Osman Sayed, 48
al Aqsa International Foundation, 142,
  150–51
Al Barakaat, 128
al Haramain Islamic Foundation, 121,
  122

al Manar, 139, 142
Al-Mujil, Abd Al Hamid, 120
Al-Qadi, Yasin, 116, 121–22, 125
al Qaeda, 11, 251, 300n24. *See also* East
  Africa
  budget, 32
  criminal activity and, 42, 51, 52, 86
  diamond trade and, 27–28
  financial facilitators, 117–18, 126–28.
    See also business support for al
    Qaeda; charities; *hawala*
  financial network, 57, 86, 115–17
  freezing assets of, 73–76
  funding/fund-raising for, 11, 17, 23,
    26, 51, 83
  assessing government responses,
    130–33
  organization and, 16
  groups inspired by, 18
  nature of, 32–33
  new, 126–27
  9/11 and, 30

357